Better Homes and Gardens

BIGGEST BOOK OF BREAD MACHINE RECIPES

Better Homes and Gardens® Books
Des Moines, Iowa

Better Homes and Gardens® Books
An imprint of Meredith® Books

BIGGEST BOOK OF BREAD MACHINE RECIPES
Editor: Carrie E. Holcomb
Contributing Editor: Spectrum Communication Services, Inc.
Senior Associate Design Director: John Eric Seid
Copy Chief: Terri Fredrickson
Copy and Production Editor: Victoria Forlini
Editorial Operations Manager: Karen Schirm
Managers, Book Production: Pam Kvitne, Marjorie J. Schenkelberg, Rick von Holdt
Contributing Copy Editor: Susan Fagan
Contributing Proofreaders: Maria Duryée, Gretchen Kauffman, Donna Segal
Illustrator: Daniel Pelavin
Indexer: Elizabeth Parson
Electronic Production Coordinator: Paula Forest
Editorial and Design Assistants: Karen McFadden, Mary Lee Gavin
Test Kitchen Director: Lynn Blanchard
Test Kitchen Product Supervisor: Marilyn Cornelius

Meredith® Books
Editor in Chief: Linda Raglan Cunningham
Design Director: Matt Strelecki
Executive Editor, Food and Crafts: Jennifer Dorland Darling

Publisher: James D. Blume
Executive Director, Marketing: Jeffrey Myers
Executive Director, New Business Development: Todd M. Davis
Executive Director, Sales: Ken Zagor
Director, Operations: George A. Susral
Director, Production: Douglas M. Johnston
Business Director: Jim Leonard

Vice President and General Manager: Douglas J. Guendel

Better Homes and Gardens® Magazine
Editor in Chief: Karol DeWulf Nickell
Deputy Editor, Food and Entertaining: Nancy Hopkins

Meredith Publishing Group
President, Publishing Group: Stephen M. Lacy
Vice President-Publishing Director: Bob Mate

Meredith Corporation
Chairman and Chief Executive Officer: William T. Kerr

In Memoriam: E. T. Meredith III (1933-2003)

Our Better Homes and Gardens® Test Kitchen seal on the back cover of this book assures you that every recipe in the *Biggest Book of Bread Machine Recipes* has been tested in the Better Homes and Gardens® Test Kitchen. This means that each recipe is practical and reliable, and meets our high standards of taste appeal. We guarantee your satisfaction with this book for as long as you own it.

All of us at Better Homes and Gardens® Books are dedicated to providing you with the information and ideas you need to create delicious foods. We welcome your comments and suggestions. Write to us at: Better Homes and Gardens Books, Cookbook Editorial Department, 1716 Locust St., Des Moines, IA 50309-3023.

If you would like to purchase any of our cooking, crafts, gardening, home improvement, or home decorating and design books, check wherever quality books are sold. Or visit us at: **bhgbooks.com**

TABLE OF CONTENTS

Bread Machine Baking
BASICS

Making bread just got a whole lot easier—and more enjoyable. The bread machine has created a new way to make homemade bread, one of life's little pleasures. Not only has the machine simplified the process of bread baking, it also has made this lost art accessible to those cooks who don't have much spare time.

This collection of recipes helps you make the most of your bread machine—and allows you to have fun doing it. With **more than 400 tempting recipes** to choose from, you'll enjoy limitless possibilities—classic, sourdough, whole grain, sweet, holiday, and savory breads. The tips and a thorough primer (see pages 5 to 10) guarantee success.

The recipes in this book can be made in a 1½- and/or 2-pound bread machine. Many recipes use the machine's kneading feature, which allows for **versatility** in the types of breads you can create, such as pizza, focaccia, braids, rings, and more. Read through the helpful tips, choose your recipe, and get ready for some **unforgettable homemade breads.**

Bread machines have their own unique differences. Because of these differences, it's important to learn the features of your own particular model by reading the owner's manual that comes with your machine. In the information that follows, we've gone a step further to give you everything you need to know about baking with a bread machine.

KNOW YOUR MACHINE

Brands of bread machines vary when it comes to cycles, baking times, and temperatures. Here is a listing of several common cycles and settings to compare with the ones listed in your owner's manual.

BASIC WHITE: An all-purpose setting used for most breads.

WHOLE GRAIN: This cycle provides the longer rising times necessary for heavier breads that contain whole wheat flour, rye flour, or other varieties of whole grains.

DOUGH: This cycle mixes and kneads the bread dough and usually allows it to rise once before the cycle is complete. After this point, remove the dough for shaping, rising, and baking in your conventional oven.

RAISIN: Some machines have an optional cycle that signals about 5 minutes prior to the end of the second kneading cycle. This signal indicates that raisins, dried fruits, nuts, or other similar ingredients can be added. If your machine doesn't have this option, try adding these ingredients about 15 minutes into the kneading cycle.

SWEET: The amount of sugar in a bread recipe affects its rising time and baking temperature. Some machines include this cycle for breads that have a high proportion of

sugar. Follow the manufacturer's directions for when to use this cycle. If you find that bread baked on this cycle has gummy areas, try baking the bread on the basic white cycle.

RAPID: Some machines offer a cycle that reduces the total time needed for the machine to mix, rise, and bake a loaf of bread. Follow the manufacturer's directions to determine when to use this cycle.

TIME BAKED: This feature allows ingredients to be added to the machine at one time and the processing to begin at a later time. Do not use the time-baked cycle with recipes that include fresh milk, eggs, cheese, and other perishable foods. Allowing these ingredients to stand at room temperature for long periods will cause them to spoil. (See the tip on page 13 to substitute dry milk powder for fresh milk.)

CRUST COLOR SETTING: This useful feature lets you alter the baking time to control the brownness of the crust. For most breads, the best choice is the medium setting. If you find that your machine browns breads excessively, try a light-crust setting. Recipes that are high in sugar also may benefit from a lighter setting. Keep in mind, however, that with a lighter setting the bread may be slightly gummy.

Ingredient Tips and Substitutions

✔ Most of the recipes for loaves in this book call for between 1 and 1½ teaspoons of active dry yeast or bread machine yeast. You may notice that this is less yeast than is used in many recipes supplied by bread machine manufacturers. In our testing, we found this amount of yeast makes a nicely risen loaf with an attractive shape. Adding more yeast typically produces a loaf with a very coarse and/or uneven texture. Also, it may cause the dough to rise too high, then fall or stick to the lid of your machine or run over the edges of the pan.

✔ Many recipes in this book call for bread flour rather than all-purpose flour. In making yeast breads, kneading causes gluten, a type of protein in flour, to form an elasticlike consistency. Gluten traps bubbles of carbon dioxide that form when the yeast "feeds" on sugars in the dough. Gluten holds the gas bubbles, causing the dough to rise. The more gluten, the higher a baked product rises. Bread flour is specially formulated for bread baking because it contains more gluten than all-purpose, pastry, or cake flour. This allows products made from bread flour to rise higher and form better structurally than other flours. Use bread flour for the recipes in this book unless directed otherwise.

✔ Dry milk powder can be used to replace fresh milk in recipes. (See the tip on page 13 for the correct equivalents.)

✔ Sour milk is a good substitute for buttermilk. (See the note with individual recipes to make the necessary amount of sour milk.) Dry buttermilk powder also is available.

✔ Refrigerated or thawed frozen egg product can be used in place of whole eggs. Egg whites also can be used instead of whole eggs. (See the tip on page 144 for the correct equivalents.)

✔ For best results when using margarine, follow the guidelines in the tip on page 24. In some cases, when necessary, butter is recommended by our Test Kitchen for quality assurance and is listed first.

✔ When you are using more than 2 tablespoons of either margarine or butter, cut it into small pieces to ensure that it will blend properly with the other ingredients.

Choosing a Recipe

The easiest way to ensure great results is to read a recipe completely through before you start. This helps familiarize you with the recipe steps and ensures that you have all the ingredients on hand. Most of the recipes in this book list ingredients for both 1½-and 2-pound loaves so you can select the appropriate size to fit your needs and your machine. For the most part, recipe directions apply to both sizes. Occasionally, however, there are special directions for the 2-pound recipe.

You'll find that some recipes include this note: "For the 1½-pound loaf, the bread machine pan must have a capacity of 10 cups or more. For the 2-pound loaf, the bread machine pan must have a capacity of 12 cups or more." Check your owner's manual to see if it lists your machine's pan capacity. If it doesn't, you'll need to measure the capacity of your pan. Here's how: Remove the pan from the bread machine. Keeping track of the total amount of water added to the pan, use a liquid measuring cup to fill the pan with water until it is filled to the brim. For future reference, note the pan capacity in your owner's manual.

Measuring Up

Measuring accurately is crucial when baking. Incorrect proportions of liquid to dry ingredients may cause the recipe to fail. To avoid problems, follow these suggestions:

FLOUR. Stir the flour to lighten it before measuring and use metal or plastic measuring cups designed for dry ingredients. Gently spoon the flour into the cup and level off the top with the straight edge of a knife or metal spatula. Never dip your measuring cup into the flour or shake it after filling it with flour. This results in an excess of flour, possibly causing your dough to be too dry.

LIQUID INGREDIENTS. Use a glass or clear plastic measuring cup for liquids. Place the cup on a level surface and bend down so your eye is level with the marking you wish to read. Fill the cup to the marking. Don't lift the cup off the counter to your eye—it's impossible to hold the cup steady enough for an accurate reading. When using a measuring spoon to measure a liquid, pour the liquid just to the top of the spoon without letting it spill over. Don't hold the spoon over the machine pan while measuring the liquid because the liquid could overflow from the spoon into the pan.

MARGARINE OR BUTTER. For premeasured sticks, use a sharp knife to cut off the amount needed, following the guidelines on the wrapper. (Use one ¼-pound stick for ¼ cup or half of a stick for ¼- cup.) For butter that's not in premeasured sticks, soften it and measure as directed for shortening.

SHORTENING. Using a rubber spatula, press the shortening firmly into a measuring cup designed for dry ingredients or into a measuring spoon. Level it off with the straight edge of a knife or metal spatula.

SUGAR. Press brown sugar firmly into a measuring cup designed for dry ingredients. The sugar should hold the shape of the cup when turned out. To measure granulated sugar, spoon the sugar into the measuring cup or spoon, then level it off with the straight edge of a knife or metal spatula.

Perfect Dough Consistency

Occasionally, no matter how carefully you measure, a dough may become either too wet or too dry. This often is due to the fact that some types (and brands) of flour absorb slightly more or less liquid than others. By checking the dough's consistency during the first 3 to 5 minutes of kneading, however, you can make sure the ratio of liquid to dry ingredients is perfect.

If the dough looks too dry and crumbly or forms two or more balls, add additional liquid, 1 teaspoon at a time, until one smooth ball forms. If the dough has too much moisture and does not form a ball, add additional bread flour, 1 tablespoon at a time, until a ball forms. Bread dough with the correct amount of flour and liquid will form a smooth ball.

Adding Ingredients To Your Machine

It's important to add ingredients to your machine according to the directions given in the owner's manual. Generally, manufacturers recommend adding the *liquids first, followed by the dry ingredients. The yeast goes in last.* The reason for this order is to keep the yeast separated from the liquid ingredients until the kneading cycle begins. This is the order our Test Kitchen recommends; however, it may not be the order the manufacturer recommends for your specific machine. Check your owner's manual and use the order recommended by the manufacturer of your bread machine.

Also in this book, any ingredients listed after the yeast, such as dried fruits or nuts, should be added at the raisin bread cycle, if your machine has one. If not, add them according to the manufacturer's directions or 15 minutes into the kneading cycle.

Storing Breads or Doughs

BAKED. Knowing how to store bread properly will keep it fresh for an extended period of time. Follow these tips:

✔ Remove hot bread from the machine as soon as it is done and turn it out on a wire rack to cool completely. (If the bread cools in the machine, it may become soggy.)

✔ To store at room temperature, wrap the cooled bread in foil or plastic wrap, or place it in a plastic bag. Store it in a cool, dry place up to 3 days.

✔ To freeze, place cooled bread in a freezer bag or container. Freeze up to 3 months. To serve the frozen bread, thaw it in the packaging for 1 hour. Or remove from packaging, wrap frozen bread in foil, and thaw it in a 300°F oven about 20 minutes.

UNBAKED. Tailor bread machine recipes to fit your schedule. Make the dough as directed, refrigerate or freeze it, shape, and bake it later. Here's how:

✔ To refrigerate bread dough, place it in an airtight container and refrigerate up to 24 hours. (Make sure the container is at least twice the size of the dough. The dough could rise enough to burst out of a small container.) Bring the dough to room temperature before shaping.

✔ To freeze bread dough, place it in an airtight container. Seal, label, and freeze up to 3 months. To use the dough, let it stand at room temperature about 2 hours or until thawed. Or thaw it overnight in the refrigerator. Shape and bake the bread as directed in the recipe.

Pointers from Our Test Kitchen

Here are some helpful suggestions from our Test Kitchen to help make your bread machine reliable and easy to use.

✔ Use bread flour for each of the recipes in this book unless directed otherwise. This high-protein flour is especially formulated for bread baking. (See ingredient tip, page 6.)

✔ If you store flour or specialty grains in the freezer, warm the measured amount to room temperature before using.

✔ Adding gluten flour to a bread that contains whole grain flour, especially rye flour, improves the texture of the loaf. (See gluten flour in "Ingredients Glossary," page 10.)

✔ Salt is necessary when making yeast bread because it controls the growth of yeast, which aids the rising of dough. (See the tip on page 28 to reduce the salt in breads.)

✔ Yeast is important in bread baking. When baking bread at high altitudes, it may be necessary to reduce the amount of yeast in the recipe. (See "High-Altitude Tips," page 9.)

✔ Store packages of dry yeast in a cool, dry place. Once a jar of yeast has been opened, store it tightly covered in the refrigerator. Use yeast before the expiration date stamped on the package or jar.

✔ Coat the bread pan with nonstick cooking spray before adding the ingredients. This makes for easy removal.

✔ Make cleanup easy by coating the kneading paddle of your machine with nonstick cooking spray before using.

✔ If the kneading paddle stays in the bread when you remove the hot loaf from the machine, use the handle of a wooden spoon to help remove it.

✔ Fill the machine's pan with hot soapy water immediately after removing baked bread. (Do not immerse pan in water.) Soak the kneading paddle separately if it comes out with the loaf of bread.

What Went Wrong?

Small and Heavy Loaf. *The dough may not have risen enough.*

✔ Check measurements (ratio of flour to liquid must be exact).

✔ Make sure yeast is fresh (use before

expiration date).

✔ Check dough consistency as dough kneads. You may need to add more liquid or flour (see page 7).

Gummy Texture. *Usually means bread is underbaked.*

✔ If recipe is too large for pan, heat will not penetrate to center of loaf.

✔ Make sure you're using the right setting on your machine. (The light-color setting may be too short in duration to completely bake some rich breads.)

✔ Experiment with a darker setting if you have this option.

Collapsed Loaf

✔ Recipe is too large for pan.

✔ Ratio of liquid to dry ingredients unbalanced (recheck measurements/check consistency as dough kneads).

✔ Too much yeast.

✔ Salt has been omitted.

✔ Warm, humid weather causes dough to rise too fast, then collapse before baking begins—bake during coolest part of day, use refrigerated liquids, try rapid cycle if your machine has this feature.

Mushroom-Shaped Loaf

✔ Recipe is too large for pan.

✔ Ratio of liquid to dry ingredients unbalanced (recheck measurements/check consistency as dough kneads).

✔ Warm weather—bake during coolest part of day, use refrigerated liquids, try rapid cycle if your machine has this feature.

Open, Holey Texture

✔ Ratio of liquid to dry ingredients unbalanced (recheck measurements/check consistency as dough kneads).

✔ Too much yeast.

✔ Salt has been omitted.

✔ Warm weather/high humidity.

Bumpy, Uneven Top/Very Dense Texture

✔ Flour no longer fresh—it may be dried out.

✔ Too much flour (check dough consistency while kneading—may need to add more liquid).

✔ If you live at high altitude, see "High-Altitude Tips," below.

High-Altitude Tips

If you live in an area that is more than 1,000 feet above sea level, you'll need to make some adjustments to your bread machine recipes because of the lower atmospheric pressure. First check your owner's manual for specific high-altitude directions. If no directions are given, start by reducing the yeast by ¼ teaspoon. At higher altitudes, breads will rise higher than at sea level, so they need less yeast. If your bread still rises too high, reduce the yeast by another ¼ teaspoon the next time you make the recipe.

Also, keep in mind that flour tends to be drier at high altitudes and sometimes will absorb more liquid. Watch the dough carefully as it mixes in the machine. If the dough seems too dry, add additional liquid, 1 teaspoon at a time. Keep a record of the total amount of liquid you use as a reference for the next time you make the bread.

Ingredients Glossary

ALL-PURPOSE FLOUR, a white flour, is generally a combination of soft and hard wheats, (medium-protein wheats). It works well for all types of baked products, including yeast breads, cakes, cookies, and quick breads. All-purpose flour usually is sold presifted. It is available bleached and unbleached. Either is suitable for home baking and can be used interchangeably.

BARLEY, a cereal grain, has a mild, starchy flavor and a slightly chewy texture. Pearl barley, the most popular form used for cooking, has the outer hull removed and has been polished or "pearled." It is sold in regular and quick-cooking forms. Store barley in an airtight container in a cool, dry place up to 1 year.

BREAD FLOUR, the type recommended for recipes in this book, is made from hard wheat. It has a higher gluten content than all-purpose flour. Gluten, a protein, provides structure and height to breads, making bread flour well suited for the task. Store bread flour in an airtight container in a cool, dry place up to 5 months or freeze it up to 1 year.

BULGUR, a parched, cracked wheat product, is made by soaking, cooking, and drying whole wheat kernels. Part of the bran is removed and what remains of the hard kernels is cracked into small pieces. Bulgur has a delicate, nutty flavor. Store it in an airtight container in a cool, dry place up to 6 months or freeze it up to 1 year.

CORNMEAL, a finely ground corn product, is made from dried yellow, white, or blue corn kernels. Cornmeal labeled "stone ground" is slightly coarser than regular cornmeal. Store cornmeal in an airtight container in a cool, dry place up to 6 months or freeze it up to 1 year.

GLUTEN FLOUR, sometimes called wheat gluten, is made by removing most of the starch from high-protein, hard-wheat flour. If you can't find gluten flour at your supermarket, look for it at a health food store. Store it in an airtight container in a cool, dry place up to 5 months or freeze it up to 1 year.

MILLET, a cereal grain with tiny, round, yellow kernels, tastes slightly nutty and has a chewy texture. Store millet in an airtight container in a cool, dry place up to 2 years.

OATS are the cereal grain produced by the cereal grass of the same name. Whole oats minus the hulls are called groats. Oats have a nutty flavor and a chewy texture. Store oats in an airtight container in a cool, dry place up to 6 months, or freeze up to 1 year. Two popular forms include regular and quick-cooking oats.

REGULAR ROLLED OATS are oat groats that have been steamed, then flattened by steel rollers.

QUICK-COOKING ROLLED OATS are oat groats that have been cut into small pieces—to shorten the cooking time—then flattened.

RYE FLOUR is made from finely ground rye, a cereal grain that has dark brown kernels and a distinctive robust flavor. Light rye flour is sifted and contains less bran than dark rye flour. Store rye flour in an airtight container in a cool, dry place up to 5 months or freeze it up to 1 year.

WHEAT GERM, the embryo or sprouting portion of the wheat kernel, is sold both raw and toasted. It is extremely perishable. Once opened, store in the refrigerator no more than 3 months.

WHOLE WHEAT FLOUR, unlike all-purpose and bread flour, is ground from the complete wheat berry and contains the wheat germ as well as the wheat bran. It is coarser in texture and does not rise as well as all-purpose or bread flour. Store whole wheat flour in an airtight container in a cool, dry place up to 5 months, or freeze it up to 1 year.

WILD RICE is the long, dark brown or black, nutty-flavored seed of an annual marsh grass. Wild rice is not actually a rice but a cereal grain. Store uncooked wild rice indefinitely in a cool, dry place or in the refrigerator.

CLASSIC BREADS

With its golden crust and delicate flavor, this tender classic is the bread supermarket loaves aspire to be. One taste and your family will accept no substitutes. With a bread machine, you can easily oblige.

White Bread

PREP:
10 minutes

MAKES:
1½-pound recipe (16 slices)
OR
2-pound recipe (22 slices)

1½-POUND	INGREDIENTS	2-POUND
1 cup	milk	1¼ cups
¼ cup	water*	¼ cup
4 teaspoons	margarine or butter, cut up, or olive oil	2 tablespoons
3 cups	bread flour	4 cups
4 teaspoons	sugar	2 tablespoons
¾ teaspoon	salt	1 teaspoon
1 teaspoon	active dry yeast or bread machine yeast	1¼ teaspoons

1 Select the loaf size. Add the ingredients to the machine according to the manufacturer's directions. Select the basic white bread cycle.

*Note: The Test Kitchen recommends ¼ cup water for either size recipe.

Nutrition Facts per slice: 114 cal., 2 g total fat (0 g sat. fat), 1 mg chol., 119 mg sodium, 21 g carbo., 4 g pro.

The aroma of toasted whole wheat bread is one of the best things around. Have this bread on hand for everyday eating—turkey sandwiches, grilled cheese sandwiches, or just toast.

Whole Wheat Bread

1½-POUND	INGREDIENTS	2-POUND
1 cup	milk	1⅓ cups
3 tablespoons	water	¼ cup
4 teaspoons	honey or sugar	2 tablespoons
1 tablespoon	margarine or butter	4 teaspoons
1½ cups	whole wheat flour	2 cups
1½ cups	bread flour	2 cups
¾ teaspoon	salt	1 teaspoon
1 teaspoon	active dry yeast	1¼ teaspoons
	or bread machine yeast	

PREP:
10 minutes

MAKES:
1½-pound recipe
(16 slices)
OR
2-pound recipe
(22 slices)

1 Select the loaf size. Add the ingredients to the machine according to the manufacturer's directions. If available, select the whole grain cycle, or select the basic white bread cycle.

Nutrition Facts per slice: 105 cal., 1 g total fat (0 g sat. fat), 1 mg chol., 117 mg sodium, 20 g carbo., 4 g pro.

Milk and the Time-Baked Cycle

When selecting breads to make using the time-baked cycle, look for recipes that do not contain eggs, cheese, or other perishable foods. Recipes containing milk can be used, but substitute dry milk powder and water for the fresh milk using the following equivalents.

Fresh Milk	=	Dry Milk Powder	+	Water
½ cup		2 tablespoons		½ cup
⅔ cup		2 tablespoons		⅔ cup
¾ cup		3 tablespoons		¾ cup
1 cup		¼ cup		1 cup
1¼ cups		⅓ cup		1¼ cups
1⅓ cups		⅓ cup + 1 tablespoon		1¼ cups
1½ cups		½ cup		1⅓ cups

An earthy European-style rye is easy to love but hard to make by hand, because the dough can be difficult to handle. In other words, it's the perfect recipe for a bread machine.

Rye Bread

PREP:
10 minutes

MAKES:
1½-pound recipe
(16 slices)
OR
2-pound recipe
(22 slices)

1½-POUND	INGREDIENTS	2-POUND
1 cup plus 2 tablespoons	water	1⅓ cups plus 1 tablespoon
2 tablespoons	margarine or butter, cut up; shortening; or cooking oil	3 tablespoons
2 cups	bread flour	2⅔ cups
1 cup	rye flour	1⅓ cups
2 tablespoons	gluten flour	3 tablespoons
2 tablespoons	brown sugar	3 tablespoons
1½ teaspoons	caraway seeds (optional)	2 teaspoons
¾ teaspoon	salt	1 teaspoon
1 teaspoon	active dry yeast or bread machine yeast	1¼ teaspoons

1 Select the loaf size. Add the ingredients to the machine according to the manufacturer's directions. If available, select the whole grain cycle, or select the basic white bread cycle.

Nutrition Facts per slice: 108 cal., 2 g total fat (0 g sat. fat), 0 mg chol., 118 mg sodium, 20 g carbo., 3 g pro.

Rise to the Occasion

When using the dough cycle, you often need to let the shaped dough rise before baking. For the best results, find a draft-free area where the temperature is between 80°F and 85°F.

An unheated oven works great for rising dough. Place the oven's lower rack in the lowest position; set a large pan of hot water on the rack. Cover the shaped dough loosely with a clean cloth and place it on the top rack of the oven. Close the door and let the dough rise until nearly double, using the time suggested in the recipe as a guide. Remove the dough and the water and preheat the oven for baking.

A lovely golden hue and a rich, savory flavor—it's amazing what a little egg brings to this bread recipe. Spread the slices with your favorite jam for a satisfying after-school snack.

Egg Bread

1½-POUND*	INGREDIENTS	2-POUND*
¾ cup	milk**	¾ cup
1	egg(s)	2
¼ cup	water	⅓ cup
2 tablespoons	margarine or butter, cut up**	2 tablespoons
3 cups	bread flour	4 cups
2 tablespoons	sugar	3 tablespoons
¾ teaspoon	salt	1 teaspoon
1 teaspoon	active dry yeast	1¼ teaspoons
	or bread machine yeast	

PREP:
10 minutes

MAKES:
1½-pound recipe
(20 slices)
OR
2-pound recipe
(27 slices)

1 Select the loaf size. Add the ingredients to the machine according to the manufacturer's directions. Select the basic white bread cycle.

*Note: For the 1½-pound loaf, the bread machine pan must have a capacity of 10 cups or more. For the 2-pound loaf, the bread machine pan must have a capacity of 12 cups or more.

**Note: The Test Kitchen recommends ¾ cup milk and 2 tablespoons margarine or butter for either size recipe.

Nutrition Facts per slice: 98 cal., 2 g total fat (0 g sat. fat), 11 mg chol., 102 mg sodium, 17 g carbo., 3 g pro.

Just like English muffins, this bread is best when sliced and toasted. The baking soda contributes to the traditional coarse texture.

Sesame English Muffin Bread

PREP:
15 minutes

MAKES:
1½-pound recipe
(16 slices)
OR
2-pound recipe
(22 slices)

1½-POUND	INGREDIENTS	2-POUND
1 cup	water	1⅓ cups
3 cups	bread flour	4 cups
⅓ cup	nonfat dry milk powder	½ cup
2 tablespoons	sesame seeds, toasted	3 tablespoons
2 teaspoons	sugar	1 tablespoon
¾ teaspoon	salt	1 teaspoon
⅛ teaspoon	baking soda*	⅛ teaspoon
1 teaspoon	active dry yeast	1¼ teaspoons
	or bread machine yeast	

1 Select the loaf size. Add the ingredients to the machine according to the manufacturer's directions. Select the basic white bread cycle.

*Note: The Test Kitchen recommends ⅛ teaspoon baking soda for either size recipe.

Nutrition Facts per slice: 107 cal., 1 g total fat (0 g sat. fat), 0 mg chol., 119 mg sodium, 20 g carbo., 4 g pro.

What do mashed potatoes bring to a bread? A moist, rich flavor and home-style appeal. Fortunately, you can keep your mixer covered—this recipe calls on instant mashed potatoes to streamline preparation.

Potato Bread

1½-POUND*	INGREDIENTS	2-POUND*
²/₃ cup	milk	³/₄ cup
¹/₂ cup	water	²/₃ cup
1	egg**	1
2 tablespoons	margarine or butter, cut up, or shortening	3 tablespoons
3 cups	bread flour	4 cups
¹/₂ cup	packaged instant mashed potato flakes or buds	²/₃ cup
1 tablespoon	sugar	4 teaspoons
³/₄ teaspoon	salt	1 teaspoon
1 teaspoon	active dry yeast or bread machine yeast	1¹/₄ teaspoons

PREP:
10 minutes

MAKES:
1½-pound recipe
(16 slices)
OR
2-pound recipe
(22 slices)

❶ Select the loaf size. Add the ingredients to the machine according to the manufacturer's directions. Select the basic white bread cycle.

*Note: For the 1½-pound loaf, the bread machine pan must have a capacity of 10 cups or more. For the 2-pound loaf, the bread machine pan must have a capacity of 12 cups or more.

**Note: The Test Kitchen recommends 1 egg for either size recipe.

Nutrition Facts per slice: 124 cal., 2 g total fat (1 g sat. fat), 14 mg chol., 128 mg sodium, 21 g carbo., 4 g pro.

This fragrant cheese bread has just a hint of caraway. Try it toasted, spread with Parmesan-Garlic Butter (page 263).

Cheesy Potato Bread

PREP:
30 minutes

MAKES:
1½-pound recipe
(16 slices)
OR
2-pound recipe
(22 slices)

1½-POUND	INGREDIENTS	2-POUND
³/₄ cup	water	1 cup
¹/₂ cup	chopped, peeled potato	²/₃ cup
¹/₃ cup	milk	¹/₂ cup
¹/₃ cup	shredded cheddar cheese	¹/₂ cup
2 teaspoons	margarine or butter	1 tablespoon
3 cups	bread flour	4 cups
1 tablespoon	sugar	4 teaspoons
³/₄ teaspoon	onion salt	1 teaspoon
¹/₄ teaspoon	caraway seeds, crushed	¹/₂ teaspoon
	(optional)	
1 teaspoon	active dry yeast	1¹/₄ teaspoons
	or bread machine yeast	

1 Select the loaf size. In a small saucepan combine the water and potato. Bring to boiling; reduce heat. Cover and simmer about 15 minutes or until potato is very tender. Do not drain. Mash potato in water; measure potato mixture. If necessary, add water to equal ¾ cup (or 1 cup for 2-pound) mixture; discard any excess mixture. Cool slightly.

2 Add the potato mixture and the remaining ingredients to the machine according to the manufacturer's directions, adding the cheese with milk. Select the basic white bread cycle.

Nutrition Facts per slice: 118 cal., 2 g total fat (1 g sat. fat), 3 mg chol., 101 mg sodium, 21 g carbo., 4 g pro.

For a satisfying sandwich, team this stout bread with your favorite chicken or tuna salad and a crisp lettuce leaf.

Oatmeal Bread

1½-POUND	INGREDIENTS	2-POUND
1 cup	quick-cooking or regular rolled oats	1⅓ cups
⅔ cup	milk	¾ cup
⅓ cup	water	½ cup
1 tablespoon	margarine or butter, cut up, or shortening	2 tablespoons
2½ cups	bread flour	3⅓ cups
3 tablespoons	packed brown sugar	¼ cup
¾ teaspoon	salt	1 teaspoon
1 teaspoon	active dry yeast or bread machine yeast	1¼ teaspoons

PREP:
25 minutes

MAKES:
1½-pound recipe
(16 slices)
OR
2-pound recipe
(22 slices)

1 Select the loaf size. Spread the rolled oats in a shallow baking pan. Bake in a 350°F oven for 15 to 20 minutes or until light brown, stirring occasionally. Cool slightly.

2 Add the ingredients to the machine according to the manufacturer's directions, adding the oats with flour. If available, select the whole grain cycle, or select the basic white bread cycle.

Nutrition Facts per slice: 117 cal., 2 g total fat (0 g sat. fat), 1 mg chol., 115 mg sodium, 22 g carbo., 4 g pro.

Oat Options

Not all rolled oats—the husked oat grain sliced, steamed, flattened, and dried—are created equal (although you can use them interchangeably for baking). Regular rolled oats are thicker, and add rustic texture to breads and other baked goods. Quick-cooking rolled oats are thinner, smaller flakes that create smoother doughs.

It's hearty, all right—and just as fitting with your favorite entrée at dinner as it is with morning coffee.

Buttermilk-Oatmeal Bread

1½-POUND	INGREDIENTS
1 cup	quick-cooking or regular rolled oats
1¼ cups	buttermilk or sour milk*
2 tablespoons	honey
1 tablespoon	margarine or butter
2¾ cups	bread flour
¾ teaspoon	salt
1 teaspoon	active dry yeast or bread machine yeast

1 Spread rolled oats in a shallow baking pan. Bake in a 350°F oven for 15 to 20 minutes or until light brown, stirring occasionally. Cool slightly.

2 Add the ingredients to the machine according to the manufacturer's directions, adding the oats with flour. If available, select the whole grain cycle, or select the basic white bread cycle.

*Note: To make 1¼ cups sour milk, place 3¾ teaspoons lemon juice or vinegar in a 2-cup liquid measuring cup. Add enough milk to measure 1¼ cups liquid; stir. Let stand for 5 minutes before using.

Nutrition Facts per slice: 114 cal., 2 g total fat (0 g sat. fat), 0 mg chol., 125 mg sodium, 21 g carbo., 5 g pro.

Its distinctive ladder shape gives this rustic flat country loaf an intriguing appearance. The sage and whole wheat combination will guarantee its popularity.

Fougasses

1½-POUND	INGREDIENTS	2-POUND
1 cup	water	1⅓ cups
1 tablespoon	olive oil or cooking oil	4 teaspoons
2 cups	bread flour	2⅔ cups
1 cup	whole wheat flour	1⅓ cups
1 teaspoon	sugar	1½ teaspoons
1 teaspoon	dried sage, crushed,	1½ teaspoons
	or	
1 tablespoon	snipped fresh sage	4 teaspoons
¾ teaspoon	salt	1 teaspoon
1 teaspoon	active dry yeast	1¼ teaspoons
	or bread machine yeast	
	Milk (optional)	

PREP:
25 minutes

RISE:
30 minutes

BAKE:
20 minutes

MAKES:
1½-pound recipe
(16 slices)
OR
2-pound recipe
(24 slices)

❶ Select the loaf size. Add the ingredients, except the milk, to the machine according to the manufacturer's directions. Select the dough cycle. When cycle is complete, remove dough. Punch down. Cover and let rest for 10 minutes. Grease large baking sheets; set aside.

❷ Divide the 1½-pound dough in half (divide the 2-pound dough into thirds). On a lightly floured surface, roll each portion into an 8×4-inch rectangle. Make three or four diagonal cuts, about 3 inches long, through each rectangle to within 1 inch of the edges. Stretch dough slightly to widen the slits.

❸ Place each loaf on a prepared baking sheet. Cover and let rise in a warm place about 30 minutes or until nearly double. If desired, brush with a little milk.

❹ Bake in a 375°F oven for 20 to 25 minutes or until bread is light brown and sounds hollow when lightly tapped. Remove from baking sheets; cool on wire racks.

Nutrition Facts per slice: 97 cal., 1 g total fat (0 g sat. fat), 0 mg chol., 101 mg sodium, 18 g carbo., 3 g pro.

This rich, tender loaf of Jewish origin makes an eye-catching showpiece for a meal that is a special occasion.

Challah

	PREP:	1½-POUND	INGREDIENTS
PREP: 25 minutes		³/₄ cup	milk
RISE: 35 minutes		2	eggs
		2 tablespoons	honey
BAKE: 25 minutes		2 tablespoons	cooking oil
		3¼ cups	bread flour
MAKES: 1½-pound recipe (16 slices)		³/₄ teaspoon	salt
		1 teaspoon	active dry yeast
			or bread machine yeast
		1	slightly beaten egg
		1½ teaspoons	sesame seeds, poppy seeds,
			or caraway seeds

1 Add the first 7 ingredients to the machine according to the manufacturer's directions. Select the dough cycle. When cycle is complete, remove dough. Punch down. Cover and let rest for 10 minutes. Lightly grease a baking sheet; set aside.

2 Divide the dough into thirds. On a lightly floured surface, roll each portion into an 18-inch rope. To shape, line up the ropes, 1 inch apart, on the prepared baking sheet. Starting in the middle, loosely braid by bringing the left rope under the center rope. Bring the right rope under the new center rope. Repeat to the end. On the other end, braid by bringing the outside ropes alternately over the center rope to center. Press ends together to seal; tuck under loaf. Cover and let rise in a warm place for 35 to 45 minutes or until nearly double.

3 Brush the beaten egg over top of loaf. Sprinkle with sesame seeds. Bake in a 375°F oven for 25 to 30 minutes or until bread sounds hollow when lightly tapped. If necessary, cover loosely with foil the last 10 minutes to prevent overbrowning. Remove from baking sheet; cool on a wire rack.

Nutrition Facts per slice: 132 cal., 3 g total fat (0 g sat. fat), 41 mg chol., 119 mg sodium, 21 g carbo., 5 g pro.

Take a loaf of this pleasantly tangy bread to your next family get-together or potluck. A little wheat germ gives it a slightly nutty flavor.

Buttermilk Bread

1½-POUND	INGREDIENTS	2-POUND
1 cup	buttermilk or sour milk*	1⅓ cups
¼ cup	water	⅓ cup
2 teaspoons	margarine, butter, or cooking oil	1 tablespoon
3 cups	bread flour	4 cups
2 tablespoons	toasted wheat germ	3 tablespoons
1 tablespoon	sugar	4 teaspoons
¾ teaspoon	salt	1 teaspoon
1 teaspoon	active dry yeast or bread machine yeast	1¼ teaspoons

PREP:
10 minutes

MAKES:
1½-pound recipe
(16 slices)
OR
2-pound recipe
(22 slices)

1 Select the loaf size. Add the ingredients to the machine according to the manufacturer's directions. Select the basic white bread cycle.

*Note: To make 1 cup sour milk, place 1 tablespoon lemon juice or vinegar in a 1-cup liquid measuring cup. Add enough milk to measure 1 cup liquid; stir. To make 1⅓ cups sour milk, place 4 teaspoons lemon juice or vinegar in a 2-cup liquid measuring cup. Add enough milk to measure 1⅓ cups liquid; stir. Let stand for 5 minutes before using.

Nutrition Facts per slice: 110 cal., 1 g total fat (0 g sat. fat), 1 mg chol., 122 mg sodium, 21 g carbo., 4 g pro.

Think cozy corner booth and a waitress that calls you "Hon." In the best sandwich shop tradition, this homestyle bread gets its tender crumb and rich brown crust from a big pinch of baking soda.

Soda Bread

PREP:
10 minutes

MAKES:
1½-pound recipe
(16 slices)
OR
2-pound recipe
(22 slices)

1½-POUND	INGREDIENTS	2-POUND
³/4 cup	milk	1 cup
¹/4 cup	water	¹/3 cup
4 teaspoons	margarine or butter, cut up	2 tablespoons
3 cups	bread flour	4 cups
4 teaspoons	sugar	2 tablespoons
³/4 teaspoon	salt	1 teaspoon
¹/4 teaspoon	baking soda	¹/2 teaspoon
1 teaspoon	active dry yeast	1¹/4 teaspoons
	or bread machine yeast	

1 Select the loaf size. Add the ingredients to the machine according to the manufacturer's directions. Select the basic white bread cycle.

Nutrition Facts per slice: 112 cal., 2 g total fat (0 g sat. fat), 1 mg chol., 139 mg sodium, 20 g carbo., 4 g pro.

Butter or Margarine?

The choice between butter or margarine for spreading on bread depends on your personal preference. But the decision becomes a little trickier when it comes to baking. Many bakers prefer the taste and texture that butter imparts. Others prefer margarine for health reasons.

If you choose to use margarine instead of butter, choose a stick margarine that contains at least 80 percent vegetable oil. Do not use an "extra light" spread that contains only about 40 percent vegetable oil. In a few recipes, the Test Kitchen thought that butter produced a superior bread, and in these instances butter is the first option.

Whether you choose butter or margarine, when using 2 tablespoons or more, cut it into small pieces to ensure that it mixes properly with the other ingredients.

Delicately sweet, with a hint of maple flavor and a pleasing cornmeal texture, this lovely loaf is a sure bet for some mighty special toast.

Cornmeal Bread

1½-POUND	INGREDIENTS	2-POUND
⅔ cup	milk	¾ cup
¼ cup	water	⅓ cup
2 tablespoons	pure maple syrup	3 tablespoons
	or maple-flavored syrup	
4 teaspoons	margarine or butter, cut up	2 tablespoons
¼ teaspoon	maple flavoring*	¼ teaspoon
2¼ cups	bread flour	3 cups
¾ cup	cornmeal	1 cup
¾ teaspoon	salt	1 teaspoon
1 teaspoon	active dry yeast	1¼ teaspoons
	or bread machine yeast	
¼ cup	finely chopped pecans, toasted	⅓ cup

PREP:
15 minutes

MAKES:
1½-pound recipe
(16 slices)
OR
2-pound recipe
(22 slices)

1 Select the loaf size. Add the ingredients to the machine according to the manufacturer's directions. Select the basic white bread cycle.

*Note: The Test Kitchen recommends ¼ teaspoon maple flavoring for either size recipe.

Nutrition Facts per slice: 126 cal., 3 g total fat (0 g sat. fat), 1 mg chol., 126 mg sodium, 22 g carbo., 3 g pro.

Traditionally served in colonial America as a tea bread, this loaf is said to have been named for an 18th-century English woman, Sally Lunn. She sold the coffee cake-type bread in her tea shop, located in Bath, England.

Sally Lunn

PREP:
10 minutes

MAKES:
1½-pound recipe
(16 slices)

1½-POUND*	INGREDIENTS
3	eggs
⅓ cup	evaporated milk
¼ cup	margarine or butter, cut up
3 cups	bread flour
3 tablespoons	sugar
¾ teaspoon	salt
1 teaspoon	active dry yeast
	or bread machine yeast

1 Add the ingredients to the machine according to the manufacturer's directions. Select the basic white bread cycle and, if available, the light color setting.

*Note: The bread machine pan must have a capacity of 10 cups or more.

Nutrition Facts per slice: 150 cal., 5 g total fat (2 g sat. fat), 41 mg chol., 156 mg sodium, 23 g carbo., 5 g pro.

Cheese adds gusto to this exceptional loaf. For variety, make it with equal parts cheddar cheese and Monterey Jack cheese (with or without jalapeño peppers).

Cheese Bread

1½-POUND*	INGREDIENTS	2-POUND*
⅔ cup	milk	¾ cup
1¼ cups	shredded cheddar cheese	1⅔ cups
	or Monterey Jack cheese with jalapeño peppers	
¼ cup	water	½ cup
1	egg**	1
3 cups	bread flour	4 cups
2 tablespoons	sugar	3 tablespoons
¾ teaspoon	salt	1 teaspoon
1 teaspoon	active dry yeast	1¼ teaspoons
	or bread machine yeast	

PREP:
15 minutes

MAKES:
1½-pound recipe
(16 slices)
OR
2-pound recipe
(22 slices)

1 Select the loaf size. Add the ingredients to the machine according to the manufacturer's directions, adding the cheese with the milk. Select the basic white bread cycle and, if available, the light color setting.

***Note:** For the 1½-pound loaf, the bread machine pan must have a capacity of 10 cups or more. For the 2-pound loaf, the bread machine pan must have a capacity of 12 cups or more.

****Note:** The Test Kitchen recommends 1 egg for either size recipe.

Nutrition Facts per slice: 145 cal., 4 g total fat (2 g sat. fat), 23 mg chol., 164 mg sodium, 21 g carbo., 6 g pro.

Better Breads with Bread Flour

You'll notice that most recipes in this book call for bread flour rather than all-purpose flour. That's because bread flour contains more gluten, a protein found in wheat. This protein traps bubbles of carbon dioxide that form when the yeast eats the sugars in the dough; this in turn allows the dough to rise. The more gluten in the dough, the higher the bread will rise—and the better structural form it will have. Therefore, it's important to use bread flour for recipes in this book unless directed otherwise.

No cheddar on hand? Substitute Swiss, provolone, or Havarti.

Cheddar-Sour Cream Loaf

PREP:	1½-POUND*	INGREDIENTS	2-POUND*
10 minutes	1 cup	water	1¼ cups
	½ cup	shredded cheddar cheese	1 cup
MAKES:	¼ cup	dairy sour cream	½ cup
1½-pound recipe (16 slices)	3 cups	bread flour	4 cups
OR	1 tablespoon	sugar	2 tablespoons
2-pound recipe (22 slices)	1 tablespoon	powdered buttermilk	2 tablespoons
	1 tablespoon	dry ranch salad dressing mix	2 tablespoons
	1 tablespoon	dried snipped chives	2 tablespoons
	1 teaspoon	salt	1½ teaspoons
	1 teaspoon	active dry yeast	1¼ teaspoons
		or bread machine yeast	

1 Select the loaf size. Add the ingredients to the machine according to the manufacturer's directions, adding the cheese with the water. Select the basic white bread cycle.

*Note: For the 1½-pound loaf, the bread machine pan must have a capacity of 10 cups or more. For the 2-pound loaf, the bread machine pan must have a capacity of 12 cups or more.

Nutrition Facts per slice: 120 cal., 2 g total fat (1 g sat. fat), 5 mg chol., 208 mg sodium, 20 g carbo., 4 g pro.

Remember the Salt

Salt is necessary when making yeast bread because it controls the growth of the yeast, which aids the rising of the dough. If you are on a sodium-restricted diet, you'll be glad to know that most of the recipes in this book are lower in sodium than purchased breads. If you want breads even lower in sodium, experiment by reducing the salt in a recipe a little at a time; however, do not eliminate it altogether.

Adapted from a traditional favorite of bakers in the Italian province of Umbria, this loaf gets its flavor from Pecorino Romano cheese. Look for this specific variety of Romano at Italian specialty food stores or in larger supermarkets.

Italian Cheese Bread

1½-POUND*	INGREDIENTS	2-POUND*
¾ cup	milk	1 cup
1	egg**	1
3 tablespoons	water	¼ cup
1 tablespoon	margarine or butter	4 teaspoons
3 cups	bread flour	4 cups
¾ cup	finely shredded Pecorino Romano or Romano cheese	1 cup
½ teaspoon	salt	¾ teaspoon
1 teaspoon	active dry yeast or bread machine yeast	1¼ teaspoons

PREP:
15 minutes

MAKES:
1½-pound recipe
(16 slices)
OR
2-pound recipe
(22 slices)

1 Select the loaf size. Add the ingredients to the machine according to the manufacturer's directions. Select the basic white bread cycle.

*Note: For the 1½-pound loaf, the bread machine pan must have a capacity of 10 cups or more. For the 2-pound loaf, the bread machine pan must have a capacity of 12 cups or more.

**Note: The Test Kitchen recommends 1 egg for either size recipe.

Nutrition Facts per slice: 131 cal., 3 g total fat (0 g sat. fat), 18 mg chol., 145 mg sodium, 20 g carbo., 6 g pro.

Take a walk on the wild side of bread with a loaf that gets its nutty zip and chewy texture from wild rice. Pair it with smoked turkey and cheese for a sophisticated sandwich.

Wild Rice Bread

PREP: 10 minutes	1½-POUND	INGREDIENTS	2-POUND
	1 cup	water	1¼ cups
MAKES: 1½-pound recipe (16 slices) OR 2-pound recipe (22 slices)	¾ cup	cooked wild rice, well drained and cooled*	1 cup
	4 teaspoons	margarine or butter, cut up	2 tablespoons
	2 cups	bread flour	2⅔ cups
	1 cup	whole wheat flour	1⅓ cups
	1 tablespoon	sugar	2 tablespoons
	1¼ teaspoons	instant chicken bouillon granules	1½ teaspoons
	¾ teaspoon	salt	1 teaspoon
	½ teaspoon	dried thyme, crushed	1 teaspoon
	1 teaspoon	active dry yeast or bread machine yeast	1¼ teaspoons

1 Select the loaf size. Add the ingredients to the machine according to the manufacturer's directions. If available, select the whole grain cycle, or select the basic white bread cycle.

*Note: For ¾ cup cooked wild rice, start with ¾ cup water and ¼ cup uncooked wild rice. For 1 cup cooked wild rice, start with 1 cup water and ⅓ cup uncooked wild rice. In a small saucepan bring water to boiling. Stir in wild rice; reduce heat to low. Cover and simmer about 40 minutes or just until rice is tender. Drain well; cool slightly.

Nutrition Facts per slice: 108 cal., 1 g total fat (0 g sat. fat), 0 mg chol., 180 mg sodium, 20 g carbo., 4 g pro.

This bread brings to mind the rough country breads found in France and Italy. It often is shaped into long loaves, called baguettes, which have a wonderful golden brown crust.

French Bread

1½-POUND	INGREDIENTS	2-POUND
1 cup	water	1⅓ cups
3 cups	bread flour	4 cups
¾ teaspoon	salt	1 teaspoon
1 teaspoon	active dry yeast	1½ teaspoons
	or bread machine yeast	
	Yellow cornmeal	
1	slightly beaten egg white	1
1 tablespoon	water	1 tablespoon

PREP:
25 minutes

RISE:
35 minutes

BAKE:
32 minutes

MAKES:
1½-pound recipe
(15 slices)
OR
2-pound recipe
(20 slices)

1 Select the loaf size. Add the first 4 ingredients to the machine according to the manufacturer's directions. Select the dough cycle. When cycle is complete, remove dough. Punch down. Cover and let rest for 10 minutes. Lightly grease a large baking sheet and sprinkle with cornmeal; set aside.

2 Divide the 1½-pound dough in half. On a lightly floured surface, roll each portion into a 10×8-inch rectangle. (Divide the 2-pound dough in half; roll each portion into a 15×10-inch rectangle.) Starting from a long side, roll up into a spiral; seal edge. Pinch and pull ends to taper.

3 Place loaves, seam sides down, on the prepared baking sheet. In a small bowl combine egg white and the 1 tablespoon water; brush some of the mixture over tops of loaves. Cover and let rise in a warm place for 35 to 45 minutes or until nearly double. Using a sharp knife, make three or four diagonal cuts about ¼ inch deep across the top of each loaf.

4 Bake in a 375°F oven for 20 minutes. Brush with the remaining egg white mixture. Bake for 12 to 15 minutes more or until bread sounds hollow when lightly tapped. Remove from baking sheet; cool on a wire rack.

Nutrition Facts per slice: 103 cal., 0 g total fat (0 g sat. fat), 0 mg chol., 11 mg sodium, 20 g carbo., 4 g pro.

Turn your humdrum spaghetti dinner into a feast with this homemade Italian bread. Serve with our Roasted Red Pepper Butter (page 263) and get ready for rave reviews.

Italian Bread

PREP:
10 minutes

MAKES:
1½-pound recipe
(16 slices)
OR
2-pound recipe
(22 slices)

1½-POUND*	INGREDIENTS	2-POUND*
³/₄ cup	milk	1 cup
1	egg**	1
3 tablespoons	water	¼ cup
1 tablespoon	margarine or butter	4 teaspoons
3 cups	bread flour	4 cups
½ teaspoon	salt	³/₄ teaspoon
1 teaspoon	active dry yeast	1¼ teaspoons
	or bread machine yeast	

1 Select the loaf size. Add the ingredients to the machine according to the manufacturer's directions. Select the basic white bread cycle.

*Note: For the 1½-pound loaf, the bread machine pan must have a capacity of 10 cups or more. For the 2-pound loaf, the bread machine pan must have a capacity of 12 cups or more.

**Note: The Test Kitchen recommends 1 egg for either size recipe.

Nutrition Facts per slice: 110 cal., 2 g total fat (0 g sat. fat), 14 mg chol., 85 mg sodium, 19 g carbo., 4 g pro.

This country-style bread is perfect for sopping up every last bite of tomato sauce in an Italian dish. Hint: For the most intense flavor, use freshly shredded Parmesan.

Italian Peasant Loaf

1½-POUND*	INGREDIENTS	2-POUND*
1 cup	water**	1 cup
¼ cup	cracked wheat	⅓ cup
¾ cup	milk	1 cup
1	egg**	1
1 tablespoon	olive oil	4 teaspoons
3 cups	bread flour	3¾ cups
¼ cup	finely shredded Parmesan cheese	⅓ cup
¾ teaspoon	salt**	¾ teaspoon
1¼ teaspoons	active dry yeast or bread machine yeast	1½ teaspoons

PREP:
15 minutes

MAKES:
1½-pound recipe
(16 slices)
OR
2-pound recipe
(22 slices)

❶ Select the loaf size. In a small saucepan bring the water to boiling; remove from heat. Stir in the cracked wheat. Let stand for 3 minutes; drain well.

❷ Add the drained cracked wheat and the remaining ingredients to the machine according to the manufacturer's directions. Select the basic white bread cycle.

*Note: For the 1½-pound loaf, the bread machine pan must have a capacity of 10 cups or more. For the 2-pound loaf, the bread machine pan must have a capacity of 12 cups or more.

**Note: The Test Kitchen recommends 1 cup water, 1 egg, and ¾ teaspoon salt for either size recipe.

Nutrition Facts per slice: 126 cal., 2 g total fat (1 g sat. fat), 16 mg chol., 139 mg sodium, 21 g carbo., 5 g pro.

From Bread to Bruschetta

Bruschetta ranks right up there with French toast and bread pudding as one of the favorite things to make with bread (of course, homemade bread is preferred). Rub slices of toasted or grilled crusty bread (such as Italian Peasant Loaf, French Bread, or San Francisco-Style Sourdough Bread) with the cut side of a garlic clove, then simply drizzle with olive oil and serve warm. It also tastes great topped with a sprinkling of fresh herbs.

Wow your family members by serving their favorite soup in a bowl that looks (and is) good enough to eat. The bread machine does almost all the work—but you don't have to tell anyone.

Bread Soup Bowls

	1½-POUND	INGREDIENTS	2-POUND
PREP: 30 minutes	²/₃ cup	milk	³/₄ cup
	1	egg(s)	2
BAKE: 20 minutes	3 tablespoons	margarine or butter, cut up	¼ cup
	3 cups	bread flour	4 cups
MAKES: 1½-pound recipe (4 bowls)	1 tablespoon	sugar	4 teaspoons
	³/₄ teaspoon	salt	1 teaspoon
OR	1 teaspoon	active dry yeast or bread machine yeast	1¼ teaspoons
2-pound recipe (6 bowls)	½ cup	shredded cheese (such as cheddar, Swiss, or Monterey Jack)	³/₄ cup

1 Select the recipe size. Add the first 7 ingredients to the machine according to the manufacturer's directions. Select the dough cycle. When cycle is complete, remove dough. Punch down. Cover and let rest for 10 minutes.

2 Meanwhile, generously grease the outsides of four (or six for 2-pound) 10-ounce custard cups or individual casseroles. Place, upside down, on a greased large baking sheet(s), leaving 3 to 4 inches between cups.

3 Divide the 1½-pound dough into fourths (divide the 2-pound dough into 6 portions). On a lightly floured surface, roll each portion into a 12×6-inch rectangle. Sprinkle about 2 tablespoons cheese onto half of each rectangle to within ½ inch of the edges. Moisten edges; fold each rectangle in half to form a 6-inch square. Press edges to seal.

4 Drape dough squares over greased cups, pressing lightly. *Do not let rise.* Bake in a 350°F oven for 20 to 25 minutes or until golden brown. If necessary, cover loosely with foil the last 10 minutes to prevent overbrowning. Remove bread bowls from cups; cool on wire racks.

Nutrition Facts per bowl: 559 cal., 17 g total fat (6 g sat. fat), 71 mg chol., 626 mg sodium, 80 g carbo., 19 g pro.

It's the little extras that make all the difference in this moist, soft-crusted loaf—buttermilk adds a pleasant tang; gluten brings a tender, even texture; and the pecans boast plenty of nutty flavor.

Buttermilk Wheat Bread

1½-POUND	INGREDIENTS	2-POUND
1 cup	buttermilk or sour milk*	1⅓ cups
¼ cup	water	⅓ cup
1 tablespoon	margarine, butter, or cooking oil	4 teaspoons
1½ cups	whole wheat flour	2 cups
1½ cups	bread flour	2 cups
1 tablespoon	sugar	4 teaspoons
1 tablespoon	gluten flour	4 teaspoons
¾ teaspoon	salt	1 teaspoon
1 teaspoon	active dry yeast or bread machine yeast	1¼ teaspoons
¼ cup	finely chopped pecans or walnuts, toasted	⅓ cup

PREP:
15 minutes

MAKES:
1½-pound recipe
(16 slices)
OR
2-pound recipe
(22 slices)

1 Select the loaf size. Add the ingredients to the machine according to the manufacturer's directions. If available, select the whole grain cycle, or select the basic white bread cycle.

*Note: To make 1 cup sour milk, place 1 tablespoon lemon juice or vinegar in a 1-cup liquid measuring cup. Add enough milk to measure 1 cup liquid; stir. To make 1⅓ cups sour milk, place 4 teaspoons lemon juice or vinegar in a 2-cup liquid measuring cup. Add enough milk to measure 1⅓ cups liquid; stir. Let stand for 5 minutes before using.

Nutrition Facts per slice: 114 cal., 3 g total fat (0 g sat. fat), 1 mg chol., 134 mg sodium, 20 g carbo., 4 g pro.

Shredded zucchini highlights the unique flavor of whole wheat. A little brown sugar and lemon peel add additional flavor notes. Try it toasted with Citrus Butter (page 264).

Zucchini Wheat Bread

PREP: 15 minutes	1½-POUND	INGREDIENTS	2-POUND
	1 cup	milk*	1 cup
MAKES: 1½-pound recipe (16 slices) OR 2-pound recipe (22 slices)	1 cup	coarsely shredded zucchini (lightly packed)	1½ cups
	2 tablespoons	shortening*	2 tablespoons
	2 cups	whole wheat flour	2⅔ cups
	1 cup	bread flour	1⅓ cups
	2 tablespoons	gluten flour*	2 tablespoons
	1 tablespoon	brown sugar	4 teaspoons
	1½ teaspoons	finely shredded lemon peel	2 teaspoons
	¾ teaspoon	salt	1 teaspoon
	1 teaspoon	active dry yeast or bread machine yeast	2 teaspoons

1 Select the loaf size. Add the ingredients to the machine according to the manufacturer's directions, adding the zucchini with the milk. If available, select the whole grain cycle, or select the basic white bread cycle.

*Note: The Test Kitchen recommends 1 cup milk, 2 tablespoons shortening, and 2 tablespoons gluten flour for either size recipe.

Nutrition Facts per slice: 112 cal., 2 g total fat (1 g sat. fat), 1 mg chol., 109 mg sodium, 19 g carbo., 4 g pro.

Choosing Lemons

When purchasing lemons for zesting or juicing, choose those that are smooth with evenly yellow skin. Avoid any dry, wrinkled lemons, which most likely are old. A medium-size lemon will yield about 3 tablespoons of juice and about 2 teaspoons of shredded peel.

Bring the best to your table with this perennial favorite. With just a hint of molasses, it's good served warm with hearty meals—or sliced later for sandwiches. Let it become your specialty.

Pumpernickel Bread

1½-POUND*	INGREDIENTS	2-POUND*
³/₄ cup	water	1 cup
¹/₄ cup	mild-flavored molasses	¹/₃ cup
4 teaspoons	cooking oil	2 tablespoons
2 cups	bread flour	2²/₃ cups
1 cup	rye flour	1¹/₃ cups
2 teaspoons	caraway seeds	1 tablespoon
³/₄ teaspoon	salt	1 teaspoon
1¹/₄ teaspoons	active dry yeast	1¹/₂ teaspoons
	or bread machine yeast	

PREP:
10 minutes

MAKES:
1½-pound recipe
(16 slices)
OR
2-pound recipe
(22 slices)

1 Select the loaf size. Add the ingredients to the machine according to the manufacturer's directions. If available, select the whole grain cycle, or select the basic white bread cycle.

*Note: For the 1½-pound loaf, the bread machine pan must have a capacity of 10 cups or more. For the 2-pound loaf, the bread machine pan must have a capacity of 12 cups or more.

Nutrition Facts per slice: 109 cal., 2 g total fat (0 g sat. fat), 0 mg chol., 102 mg sodium, 21 g carbo., 3 g pro.

A flavor trinity of coffee, molasses, and cocoa powder creates an exotic taste blend. For a real treat, wrap this bread around grilled sausage links.

Russian Rye Bread

	1½-POUND	INGREDIENTS	2-POUND
PREP: 10 minutes	³/₄ cup	water	1 cup
	¼ cup	strong coffee	¹/₃ cup
	2 tablespoons	mild-flavored molasses	3 tablespoons
MAKES: 1½-pound recipe (16 slices) OR 2-pound recipe (22 slices)	1 tablespoon	margarine or butter, cut up	2 tablespoons
	2 cups	bread flour	2²/₃ cups
	1 cup	rye flour	1¹/₃ cups
	2 tablespoons	unsweetened cocoa powder	3 tablespoons
	1 teaspoon	gluten flour	1¹/₂ teaspoons
	³/₄ teaspoon	salt	1 teaspoon
	³/₄ teaspoon	caraway seeds	1 teaspoon
	¼ teaspoon	fennel seeds, crushed	¹/₂ teaspoon
	1¹/₄ teaspoons	active dry yeast	1¹/₂ teaspoons
		or bread machine yeast	

1 Select the loaf size. Add the ingredients to the machine according to the manufacturer's directions. If available, select the whole grain cycle, or select the basic white bread cycle.

Nutrition Facts per slice: 102 cal., 1 g total fat (0 g sat. fat), 0 mg chol., 110 mg sodium, 20 g carbo., 3 g pro.

Measuring Molasses

Measuring and pouring molasses (or honey or corn syrup) can prove a sticky problem. Smooth the way by first coating the measuring cup or measuring spoon with nonstick cooking spray or brushing it with an unflavored oil. The molasses will slide right out.

Buckwheat is actually an herb, not a grain or cereal. Therefore, it does not contain gluten—
necessary in making breads rise—which means it must be used with other flours in baking.

Buckwheat Bread

1½-POUND	INGREDIENTS	2-POUND
1 cup	water	1¼ cups
1 tablespoon	shortening	2 tablespoons
2 cups	bread flour	2⅔ cups
1 cup	buckwheat flour	1½ cups
2 tablespoons	gluten flour*	2 tablespoons
2 tablespoons	brown sugar*	2 tablespoons
¾ teaspoon	salt	1 teaspoon
1¼ teaspoons	active dry yeast	1½ teaspoons
	or bread machine yeast	

PREP:
10 minutes

MAKES:
1½-pound recipe
(16 slices)
OR
2-pound recipe
(22 slices)

1 Select the loaf size. Add the ingredients to the machine according to the manufacturer's directions. If available, select the whole grain cycle, or select the basic white bread cycle.

*Note: The Test Kitchen recommends 2 tablespoons gluten flour and 2 tablespoons brown sugar for either size recipe.

Nutrition Facts per slice: 104 cal., 1 g total fat (0 g sat. fat), 0 mg chol., 101 mg sodium, 20 g carbo., 4 g pro.

Buckwheat Know-How

Despite its name, buckwheat is not kin to wheat, although it is ground and used as a flour like wheat. Fans love its earthy, nutty flavor. Keep this specialty flour in the refrigerator or freezer up to three months. Bring to room temperature before using, or it will slow yeast activity.

Black walnuts, native to America, are particularly tasty in baked goods. This tender loaf, abundant with nutty nuggets, showcases them perfectly.

Black Walnut Bread

	1½-POUND*	INGREDIENTS	2-POUND*
PREP: 15 minutes	⅔ cup	milk	¾ cup
	1	egg**	1
MAKES: 1½-pound recipe (16 slices)	3 tablespoons	water	¼ cup
	2 tablespoons	walnut oil or cooking oil	3 tablespoons
OR	3 cups	bread flour	4 cups
2-pound recipe (22 slices)	2 tablespoons	sugar	3 tablespoons
	¾ teaspoon	salt	1 teaspoon
	1 teaspoon	active dry yeast or bread machine yeast	1¼ teaspoons
	⅔ cup	chopped black walnuts or English walnuts	¾ cup

1 Select the loaf size. Add the ingredients to the machine according to the manufacturer's directions. Select the basic white bread cycle.

*Note: For the 1½-pound loaf, the bread machine pan must have a capacity of 10 cups or more. For the 2-pound loaf, the bread machine pan must have a capacity of 12 cups or more.

**Note: The Test Kitchen recommends 1 egg for either size recipe.

Nutrition Facts per slice: 156 cal., 6 g total fat (1 g sat. fat), 14 mg chol., 110 mg sodium, 21 g carbo., 5 g pro.

Opt for Walnut Oil

In French villages, fresh walnuts are cold-pressed following time-honored methods to extract their aromatic oils—a traditional culinary specialty. Just a splash of this nutty elixir elevates a simple salad dressing into something special, or intensifies the flavor of a nut bread. Store this delicate oil away from light and heat up to three months.

German bakers use caraway seeds to add a distinctive flavor to both white and whole grain breads. Serve slices of this loaf with your favorite soup.

German Caraway Seed Loaf

1½-POUND*	INGREDIENTS	2-POUND*
⅓ cup	milk	½ cup
⅓ cup	water	½ cup
¼ cup	margarine or butter, cut up	⅓ cup
1	egg**	1
3 cups	bread flour	4 cups
2 teaspoons	caraway seeds	1 tablespoon
1½ teaspoons	sugar	2 teaspoons
¾ teaspoon	salt	1 teaspoon
1 teaspoon	active dry yeast	1¼ teaspoons
	or bread machine yeast	

PREP:
10 minutes

MAKES:
1½-pound recipe
(16 slices)
OR
2-pound recipe
(22 slices)

1 Select the loaf size. Add the ingredients to the machine according to the manufacturer's directions. Select the basic white bread cycle.

*Note: For the 1½-pound loaf, the bread machine pan must have a capacity of 10 cups or more. For the 2-pound loaf, the bread machine pan must have a capacity of 12 cups or more.

**Note: The Test Kitchen recommends 1 egg for either size recipe.

Nutrition Facts per slice: 129 cal., 4 g total fat (1 g sat. fat), 14 mg chol., 141 mg sodium, 20 g carbo., 4 g pro.

More than a little bit nutty, this delectable bread is one of the best things to ever happen to a walnut. Try it in your favorite bread pudding recipe for some extra razzle-dazzle.

Honeyed Walnut Bread

PREP:
15 minutes

MAKES:
1½-pound recipe
(20 slices)
OR
2-pound recipe
(27 slices)

1½-POUND	INGREDIENTS	2-POUND
1 cup	water	1⅓ cups
¼ cup	honey	5 tablespoons
2 tablespoons	walnut oil or cooking oil	3 tablespoons
3 cups	bread flour	4 cups
¼ cup	nonfat dry milk powder	⅓ cup
¾ teaspoon	salt	1 teaspoon
1 teaspoon	active dry yeast	1¼ teaspoons
	or bread machine yeast	
¾ cup	coarsely chopped walnuts,	1 cup
	toasted	

1 Select the loaf size. Add the ingredients to the machine according to the manufacturer's directions. Select the basic white bread cycle.

Nutrition Facts per slice: 132 cal., 5 g total fat (0 g sat. fat), 0 mg chol., 86 mg sodium, 20 g carbo., 3 g pro.

Honey Hint

When a jar of honey gets as thick as sludge and won't pour, don't throw it out—microwave it. Using 100-percent power (high), microwave the honey (metal cap off, if it's a jar) until it softens, for 5 to 20 seconds depending on the amount.

A hint of spice and a sprinkling of raisins make this traditional bread fragrant and flavorful.

Cinnamon-Raisin Bread

1½-POUND	INGREDIENTS
1 cup plus	milk
2 tablespoons	
1 tablespoon	margarine or butter
3 cups	bread flour
1 tablespoon	brown sugar
1½ teaspoons	ground cinnamon
¾ teaspoon	salt
1 teaspoon	active dry yeast
	or bread machine yeast
¾ cup	dark raisins

PREP:
10 minutes

MAKES:
1½-pound recipe
(16 slices)

1 Add the ingredients to the machine according to the manufacturer's directions. Select the basic white bread cycle.

Nutrition Facts per slice: 135 cal., 2 g total fat (0 g sat. fat), 2 mg chol., 120 mg sodium, 27 g carbo., 5 g pro.

So delicious, so easy, and so good describes this spirited bread. Subtle overtones of rum complement the plump, moist raisins in the loaf.

Raisin-Rum Loaf

PREP:
10 minutes

MAKES:
1½-pound recipe
(16 slices)
OR
2-pound recipe
(22 slices)

1½-POUND*	INGREDIENTS	2-POUND*
½ cup	dairy sour cream	⅔ cup
⅓ cup	water	½ cup
1	egg**	1
3 tablespoons	dark or light rum	¼ cup
2 teaspoons	margarine or butter	1 tablespoon
1 teaspoon	vanilla	1½ teaspoons
3 cups	bread flour	4 cups
3 tablespoons	sugar	¼ cup
¾ teaspoon	salt	1 teaspoon
1 teaspoon	active dry yeast	1¼ teaspoons
	or bread machine yeast	
½ cup	dark raisins	⅔ cup

❶ Select the loaf size. Add the ingredients to the machine according to the manufacturer's directions. Select the basic white bread cycle.

*Note: For the 1½-pound loaf, the bread machine pan must have a capacity of 10 cups or more. For the 2-pound loaf, the bread machine pan must have a capacity of 12 cups or more.

**Note: The Test Kitchen recommends 1 egg for either size recipe.

Nutrition Facts per slice: 147 cal., 3 g total fat (1 g sat. fat), 17 mg chol., 114 mg sodium, 25 g carbo., 4 g pro.

Raisin Advice

When raisins are called for in bread machine-baked recipes, the Test Kitchen recommends using dark raisins rather than golden raisins. Golden raisins are generally treated with a sulphur substance, which reacts with the yeast in the bread dough. This reaction results in breads that will not rise properly.

Sweetness and spice—and everything nice! A touch of honey and a dash of cinnamon make this loaf a favorite anytime.

Honey-Spice Loaf

1½-POUND	INGREDIENTS	2-POUND
¾ cup	milk	1 cup
3 tablespoons	honey	¼ cup
2 tablespoons	cooking oil	3 tablespoons
4 teaspoons	water	2 tablespoons
3 cups	bread flour	4 cups
2 teaspoons	gluten flour	1 tablespoon
¾ teaspoon	salt	1 teaspoon
¾ teaspoon	ground cinnamon	1 teaspoon
⅛ teaspoon	ground cloves	¼ teaspoon
1¼ teaspoons	active dry yeast	1½ teaspoons
	or bread machine yeast	

PREP:
10 minutes

MAKES:
1½-pound recipe
(16 slices)
OR
2-pound recipe
(22 slices)

1 Select the loaf size. Add the ingredients to the machine according to the manufacturer's directions. Select the basic white bread cycle.

Nutrition Facts per slice: 128 cal., 2 g total fat (0 g sat. fat), 1 mg chol., 116 mg sodium, 23 g carbo., 4 g pro.

Win warm accolades by baking all the favorite flavors of pumpkin pie into bread. It's great served on its own or tasty with a quick spread of Cream Cheese Butter (page 264).

Pumpkin-Pecan Bread

PREP:
15 minutes

MAKES:
1½-pound recipe
(16 slices)
OR
2-pound recipe
(22 slices)

1½-POUND*	INGREDIENTS	2-POUND*
½ cup	milk	⅔ cup
½ cup	canned pumpkin	⅔ cup
1	egg**	1
2 tablespoons	margarine or butter, cut up	3 tablespoons
3 cups	bread flour	4 cups
3 tablespoons	packed brown sugar	¼ cup
¾ teaspoon	salt	1 teaspoon
¼ teaspoon	ground nutmeg	½ teaspoon
¼ teaspoon	ground ginger**	¼ teaspoon
⅛ teaspoon	ground cloves	¼ teaspoon
1 teaspoon	active dry yeast	1¼ teaspoons
	or bread machine yeast	
¾ cup	coarsely chopped pecans	1 cup

1 Select the loaf size. Add the ingredients to the machine according to the manufacturer's directions. Select the basic white bread cycle.

*Note: For the 1½-pound loaf, the bread machine pan must have a capacity of 10 cups or more. For the 2-pound loaf, the bread machine pan must have a capacity of 12 cups or more.

**Note: The Test Kitchen recommends 1 egg and ¼ teaspoon ground ginger for either size recipe.

Nutrition Facts per slice: 159 cal., 6 g total fat (1 g sat. fat), 14 mg chol., 126 mg sodium, 23 g carbo., 4 g pro.

A popular Scandinavian spice, cardamom gives this rich bread a wonderful fragrance and a spicy-sweet flavor.

Finnish Cardamom Loaf

1½-POUND*	INGREDIENTS	2-POUND*
³/₄ cup	evaporated milk	1 cup
¹/₄ cup	water**	¹/₄ cup
1	egg**	1
2 tablespoons	margarine or butter, cut up	3 tablespoons
3 cups	bread flour	4 cups
¹/₃ cup	sugar	¹/₂ cup
³/₄ teaspoon	salt	1 teaspoon
³/₄ teaspoon	ground cardamom	1 teaspoon
1 teaspoon	active dry yeast	1¹/₄ teaspoons
	or bread machine yeast	

PREP:
10 minutes

MAKES:
1½-pound recipe
(20 slices)
OR
2-pound recipe
(27 slices)

1 Select the loaf size. Add the ingredients to the machine according to the manufacturer's directions. Select the basic white bread cycle and, if available, the light color setting.

*Note: For the 1½-pound loaf, the bread machine pan must have a capacity of 10 cups or more. For the 2-pound loaf, the bread machine pan must have a capacity of 12 cups or more.

**Note: The Test Kitchen recommends ¼ cup water and 1 egg for either size recipe.

Nutrition Facts per slice: 115 cal., 2 g total fat (1 g sat. fat), 13 mg chol., 107 mg sodium, 19 g carbo., 4 g pro.

This extra-moist autumnal bread tastes great without any adornments. But if you want to turn it into a kid's favorite, serve it toasted and spread with Nut 'n' Honey Butter (page 264).

Apple Bread

	1½-POUND	I N G R E D I E N T S	2-POUND
PREP: 10 minutes	³/₄ cup	apple juice	1 cup
	¹/₃ cup	applesauce	¹/₂ cup
MAKES:	1 tablespoon	honey	4 teaspoons
1½-pound recipe (16 slices)	1 tablespoon	margarine or butter*	1 tablespoon
OR	2 cups	bread flour	2¹/₂ cups
2-pound recipe (22 slices)	1 cup	whole wheat flour	1¹/₂ cups
	1¹/₂ teaspoons	ground cinnamon	2 teaspoons
	³/₄ teaspoon	salt	1 teaspoon
	1 teaspoon	active dry yeast	2 teaspoons
		or bread machine yeast	

1 Select the loaf size. Add the ingredients to the machine according to the manufacturer's directions. If available, select the whole grain cycle, or select the basic white bread cycle.

*Note: The Test Kitchen recommends 1 tablespoon margarine or butter for either size recipe.

Nutrition Facts per slice: 109 cal., 1 g total fat (0 g sat. fat), 0 mg chol., 110 mg sodium, 21 g carbo., 3 g pro.

Make this yeast bread when your bananas look their sorriest—very dark, brown-speckled skin. That's when they're at their ripe-and-ready best.

Banana-Walnut Bread

1½-POUND*	I N G R E D I E N T S	2-POUND*
⅓ cup	milk	½ cup
½ cup	mashed ripe banana	⅔ cup
1	egg**	1
2 tablespoons	margarine or butter, cut up**	2 tablespoons
3 cups	bread flour	4 cups
3 tablespoons	sugar	¼ cup
¾ teaspoon	salt	1 teaspoon
¼ teaspoon	ground cinnamon** (optional)	¼ teaspoon
1 teaspoon	active dry yeast	1¼ teaspoons
	or bread machine yeast	
¾ cup	chopped walnuts	1 cup
	or pecans, toasted	

PREP:
15 minutes

MAKES:
1½-pound recipe
(16 slices)
OR
2-pound recipe
(22 slices)

1 Select the loaf size. Add the ingredients to the machine according to the manufacturer's directions, adding the banana with the milk. Select the basic white bread cycle.

*Note: For the 1½-pound loaf, the bread machine pan must have a capacity of 10 cups or more. For the 2-pound loaf, the bread machine pan must have a capacity of 12 cups or more.

**Note: The Test Kitchen recommends 1 egg, 2 tablespoons margarine or butter, and ¼ teaspoon cinnamon for either size recipe.

Nutrition Facts per slice: 167 cal., 6 g total fat (1 g sat. fat), 14 mg chol., 124 mg sodium, 25 g carbo., 5 g pro.

This delicate citrus bread gets its subtle tang and moistness from sour cream.

Lemon-Pecan Bread

PREP:
15 minutes

MAKES:
1½-pound recipe
(16 slices)

1½-POUND*	INGREDIENTS
¾ cup	milk
⅓ cup	dairy sour cream
1	egg
1 tablespoon	margarine or butter
3½ cups	bread flour
3 tablespoons	sugar
¾ teaspoon	salt
¾ teaspoon	finely shredded lemon peel
1 teaspoon	active dry yeast
	or bread machine yeast
¾ cup	chopped pecans, toasted

1 Add the ingredients to the machine according to the manufacturer's directions. Select the basic white bread cycle and, if available, the light color setting.

*Note: The bread machine pan must have a capacity of 10 cups or more.

Nutrition Facts per slice: 260 cal., 6 g total fat (2 g sat. fat), 21 mg chol., 129 mg sodium, 47 g carbo., 6 g pro.

The aroma of cinnamon bread is enough to wake even the sleepiest of sleepyheads. Discover the delights of this comfort food for breakfast, or anytime you're in need of some TLC.

Cinnamon Swirl Bread

1½-POUND	INGREDIENTS	2-POUND
¾ cup	milk	1 cup
1	egg(s)	2
3 tablespoons	margarine or butter, cut up	¼ cup
3 cups	bread flour	4 cups
3 tablespoons	granulated sugar	¼ cup
¾ teaspoon	salt	1 teaspoon
1¼ teaspoons	active dry yeast	1½ teaspoons
	or bread machine yeast	
⅓ cup	chopped walnuts	½ cup
	or pecans, toasted	
⅓ cup	packed brown sugar	½ cup
1½ teaspoons	ground cinnamon	2 teaspoons
1 tablespoon	margarine or butter, softened	2 tablespoons
	Sifted powdered sugar	

PREP:
25 minutes

RISE:
30 minutes

BAKE:
30 minutes

MAKES:
1½-pound recipe
(16 slices)
OR
2-pound recipe
(24 slices)

1 Select the recipe size. Add the first 7 ingredients to the machine according to the manufacturer's directions. Select the dough cycle. When cycle is complete, remove dough. Punch down. Cover and let rest for 10 minutes.

2 Meanwhile, for filling, in a small bowl stir together the walnuts, brown sugar, and cinnamon; set aside.

3 *For the 1½-pound recipe:* Grease a 9×5×3-inch loaf pan; set aside. On a lightly floured surface, roll the dough into a 14×9-inch rectangle. Spread with the softened margarine and sprinkle with filling. Starting from both short sides, roll up each side into a spiral toward the center. Place, rolled side up, in the prepared loaf pan. Cover and let rise in a warm place about 30 minutes or until nearly double.

4 Bake in a 350°F oven about 30 minutes or until bread sounds hollow when lightly tapped. If necessary, cover loosely with foil the last 10 minutes to prevent overbrowning. Remove from pan; cool on a wire rack. Before serving, sprinkle with powdered sugar.

For the 2-pound recipe: Prepare as above, except divide the dough, softened margarine, and filling in half. Form two loaves; place in two greased 9×5×3- or 8×4×2-inch loaf pans.

Nutrition Facts per slice: 171 cal., 5 g total fat (1 g sat. fat), 14 mg chol., 145 mg sodium, 26 g carbo., 4 g pro.

For a striking loaf, arrange the balls of dough into loose rows, occasionally making the rows two balls high. Decorate the cluster with dough shaped as leaves.

Grape Cluster Bread

PREP:	1½-POUND	INGREDIENTS	2-POUND
30 minutes	⅔ cup	milk	¾ cup
RISE:	1	egg(s)	2
30 minutes	¼ cup	butter or margarine, cut up	⅓ cup
BAKE:	2 tablespoons	water	3 tablespoons
20 minutes	3 cups	bread flour	4 cups
	2 tablespoons	sugar	3 tablespoons
MAKES:	¾ teaspoon	salt	1 teaspoon
1½-pound recipe (15 servings)	1 teaspoon	active dry yeast	1¼ teaspoons
OR		or bread machine yeast	
2-pound recipe (20 servings)	1	egg yolk	1
	1 teaspoon	water	1 teaspoon
	½ teaspoon	poppy seeds	1 teaspoon

❶ Select the recipe size. Add the first 8 ingredients to the machine according to the manufacturer's directions. Select the dough cycle. When cycle is complete, remove dough. Punch down. Cover and let rest for 10 minutes.

❷ *For the 1½-pound recipe:* Grease a baking sheet; set aside. Remove one-fourth of the dough; cover and set aside. Divide the remaining dough into 30 portions. Using lightly floured hands, shape each portion into a smooth ball. Arrange on the prepared baking sheet in the shape of a bunch of grapes. In a small bowl combine egg yolk and the 1 teaspoon water; brush some of the mixture over top of loaf. Sprinkle with poppy seeds.

❸ On a lightly floured surface, roll the reserved dough into an 8×4-inch rectangle; cut in half crosswise. Cut each square in half diagonally to form grape leaves. If desired, score leaves to resemble leaf veins. Place leaves on top of the widest end of bunch of grapes. Brush the leaves with the remaining egg yolk mixture. Cover and let rise in a warm place for 30 to 40 minutes or until nearly double.

❹ Bake in a 375°F oven for 20 to 25 minutes or until bread sounds hollow when lightly tapped. If necessary, cover loosely with foil the last 5 to 10 minutes to prevent overbrowning. Remove from baking sheet; cool on a wire rack.

For the 2-pound recipe: Prepare as above, except divide the dough in half. Set aside one-fourth of each half of dough. Shape each remaining half into 20 balls. Form 2 bunches of grapes on 2 greased baking sheets. Continue as above, baking in a 375°F oven for 15 to 20 minutes.

Nutrition Facts per serving: 149 cal., 5 g total fat (1 g sat. fat), 33 mg chol., 145 mg sodium, 22 g carbo., 4 g pro.

SAVORY LOAVES

Almonds and curry often complement each other in Indian cooking, and they marry well in this light and tender loaf too.

Smoked Almond-Curry Bread

PREP: 15 minutes	1½-POUND*	INGREDIENTS	2-POUND*
	1 tablespoon	margarine or butter	2 tablespoons
	1½ teaspoons	curry powder	2 teaspoons
MAKES: 1½-pound recipe (16 slices) OR 2-pound recipe (22 slices)	³/4 cup	milk	1 cup
	1	egg(s)	2
	3 tablespoons	water**	3 tablespoons
	3 cups	bread flour	4 cups
	1 tablespoon	brown sugar	2 tablespoons
	½ teaspoon	salt	³/4 teaspoon
	1¼ teaspoons	active dry yeast or bread machine yeast	1½ teaspoons
	⅓ cup	smoked almonds, chopped	½ cup
	¼ cup	dried currants	⅓ cup

1 Select the loaf size. In a small saucepan heat the margarine until melted; add the curry powder. Cook and stir over low heat for 1 minute. Cool slightly.

2 Add the curry mixture and the remaining ingredients to the machine according to the manufacturer's directions. Select the basic white bread cycle.

*Note: For the 1½-pound loaf, the bread machine pan must have a capacity of 10 cups or more. For the 2-pound loaf, the bread machine pan must have a capacity of 12 cups or more.

**Note: The Test Kitchen recommends 3 tablespoons water for either size recipe.

Nutrition Facts per slice: 137 cal., 3 g total fat (1 g sat. fat), 14 mg chol., 111 mg sodium, 23 g carbo., 5 g pro.

Serve the flavors of Thanksgiving in a sandwich. Top this bread with sliced roasted turkey and a spoonful of cranberry-orange relish for a taste of the holiday without all the fuss.

Sage and Onion Bread

1½-POUND	INGREDIENTS	2-POUND
⅓ cup	finely chopped onion	½ cup
4 teaspoons	margarine or butter	2 tablespoons
1 cup	milk	1¼ cups
3 tablespoons	water*	3 tablespoons
3 cups	bread flour	4 cups
2 teaspoons	sugar	1 tablespoon
2 teaspoons	dried sage, crushed,	1 tablespoon
	or	
2 tablespoons	snipped fresh sage	3 tablespoons
¾ teaspoon	salt	1 teaspoon
1 teaspoon	active dry yeast	1¼ teaspoons
	or bread machine yeast	

PREP:
15 minutes

MAKES:
1½-pound recipe
(16 slices)
OR
2-pound recipe
(22 slices)

1 Select the loaf size. In a small saucepan cook the onion in hot margarine until tender, stirring occasionally. Cool slightly.

2 Add the onion mixture and the remaining ingredients to the machine according to the manufacturer's directions. Select the basic white bread cycle.

*Note: The Test Kitchen recommends 3 tablespoons water for either size recipe.

Nutrition Facts per slice: 113 cal., 2 g total fat (0 g sat. fat), 1 mg chol., 119 mg sodium, 20 g carbo., 4 g pro.

Dried Herb Pointers

Dried herbs have rightly earned their place as a convenient staple. When using them, keep these tips in mind: Always crush dried herbs before using to release their aromatic oils. The easiest way to do this is to rub the leaves between your fingers. Replace unused dried herbs every six months as their flavor fades with time.

A simple blend of mustard, honey, and thyme accents this delightful dinner bread. Serve it with roasted or broiled chicken.

Honey-Dijon Bread

	1½-POUND	INGREDIENTS	2-POUND
PREP: 10 minutes	1 cup	water	1¼ cups
	2 tablespoons	honey	3 tablespoons
MAKES: 1½-pound recipe (12 slices)	2 tablespoons	Dijon-style mustard	3 tablespoons
	1 tablespoon	olive oil or cooking oil	4 teaspoons
OR	3 cups	bread flour	4 cups
2-pound recipe (16 slices)	¾ teaspoon	salt	1 teaspoon
	½ teaspoon	dry mustard	¾ teaspoon
	½ teaspoon	dried thyme, crushed	¾ teaspoon
	1¼ teaspoons	active dry yeast or bread machine yeast	1½ teaspoons

1 Select the loaf size. Add the ingredients to the machine according to the manufacturer's directions. Select the basic white bread cycle.

Nutrition Facts per slice: 150 cal., 2 g total fat (0 g sat. fat), 0 mg chol., 161 mg sodium, 28 g carbo., 4 g pro.

Three types of mustard (dried, prepared, and seeds) may sound like a lot, but we found the combo just right to bring a lively and distinct—but not overpowering—flavor to this loaf.

Triple Mustard Loaf

1½-POUND	INGREDIENTS	2-POUND
¾ cup	milk	1 cup
¼ cup	water	⅓ cup
2 tablespoons	Dijon-style mustard	3 tablespoons
	or honey mustard	
4 teaspoons	margarine or butter, cut up	2 tablespoons
3 cups	bread flour	4 cups
1 tablespoon	mustard seeds, coarsely	4 teaspoons
	crushed	
1½ teaspoons	dry mustard	2 teaspoons
¾ teaspoon	salt	1 teaspoon
1 teaspoon	active dry yeast	1¼ teaspoons
	or bread machine yeast	

PREP:
10 minutes

MAKES:
1½-pound recipe
(16 slices)
OR
2-pound recipe
(22 slices)

1 Select the loaf size. Add the ingredients to the machine according to the manufacturer's directions. Select the basic white bread cycle.

Nutrition Facts per slice: 114 cal., 2 g total fat (0 g sat. fat), 1 mg chol., 137 mg sodium, 20 g carbo., 4 g pro.

If you like the taste of pizza, you'll love this variation on the theme. Subtly spiced with oregano, onion, and dried tomatoes, it's a perfect accompaniment to minestrone.

Dried Tomato Bread

PREP:
15 minutes

MAKES:
1½-pound recipe
(16 slices)
OR
2-pound recipe
(22 slices)

1½-POUND	INGREDIENTS	2-POUND
½ cup	finely chopped onion	⅔ cup
4 teaspoons	olive oil or cooking oil	2 tablespoons
¾ cup plus 2 tablespoons	water	1¼ cups
2 tablespoons	snipped dried tomatoes (not oil-packed)	3 tablespoons
3 cups	bread flour	4 cups
1 tablespoon	sugar	4 teaspoons
1 teaspoon	dried oregano, crushed, or	1¼ teaspoons
1 tablespoon	snipped fresh oregano	4 teaspoons
¾ teaspoon	salt	1 teaspoon
1 teaspoon	active dry yeast or bread machine yeast	1¼ teaspoons

1 Select the loaf size. In a small saucepan cook the onion in hot oil until tender, stirring occasionally. Cool slightly.

2 Add the ingredients to the machine according to the manufacturer's directions, adding the onion mixture and the dried tomatoes with the water. Select the basic white bread cycle.

Nutrition Facts per slice: 109 cal., 2 g total fat (0 g sat. fat), 0 mg chol., 110 mg sodium, 20 g carbo., 3 g pro.

For a perfect B.L.T., start with this bread that has bacon and tomato baked into it.

Bacon and Tomato Bread

1½-POUND*	INGREDIENTS	2-POUND*
1 cup	water	1⅓ cups
¼ cup	drained and snipped, oil-packed dried tomatoes	⅓ cup
1 tablespoon	olive oil or cooking oil	4 teaspoons
3 cups	bread flour	4 cups
¼ cup	cooked bacon pieces	⅓ cup
1 tablespoon	sugar	4 teaspoons
¾ teaspoon	salt	1 teaspoon
¾ teaspoon	dried basil, crushed	1 teaspoon
1 teaspoon	active dry yeast or bread machine yeast**	1 teaspoon

PREP:
10 minutes

MAKES:
1½-pound recipe
(20 slices)
OR
2-pound recipe
(27 slices)

① Select the loaf size. Add the ingredients to the machine according to the manufacturer's directions. Select the basic white bread cycle.

*Note: For the 1½-pound loaf, the bread machine pan must have a capacity of 10 cups or more. For the 2-pound loaf, the bread machine pan must have a capacity of 12 cups or more.

**Note: The Test Kitchen recommends 1 teaspoon yeast for either size recipe.

Nutrition Facts per slice: 92 cal., 2 g total fat (0 g sat. fat), 1 mg chol., 99 mg sodium, 16 g carbo., 3 g pro.

The appealing flavor of an herb bread—plus a distinct hit of pepper—make this aromatic loaf a natural to serve with your favorite Italian soup or salad.

Rosemary Bread

PREP:
10 minutes

MAKES:
1½-pound recipe
(16 slices)

1½-POUND	INGREDIENTS
1¼ cups	milk
4 teaspoons	olive oil
Dash	bottled hot pepper sauce
3 cups	bread flour
3 tablespoons	cornmeal
1 tablespoon	sugar
1½ teaspoons	snipped fresh rosemary
	or
¾ teaspoon	dried rosemary, crushed
¾ teaspoon	salt
½ teaspoon	coarsely ground black pepper
1 teaspoon	active dry yeast
	or bread machine yeast

1 Add the ingredients to the machine according to the manufacturer's directions. Select the basic white bread cycle.

Nutrition Facts per slice: 123 cal., 2 g total fat (0 g sat. fat), 2 mg chol., 110 mg sodium, 21 g carbo., 5 g pro.

Look for jars of roasted garlic in the produce section with regular minced garlic.

Garlic-Herb Bread

1½-POUND	INGREDIENTS	2-POUND
1 cup	water	1⅓ cups
2 teaspoons	olive oil or cooking oil	1 tablespoon
3 cups	bread flour	4 cups
⅓ cup	grated Parmesan cheese	½ cup
2 teaspoons	sugar	1 tablespoon
¾ teaspoon	salt	1 teaspoon
1 teaspoon	active dry yeast	1¼ teaspoons
	or bread machine yeast	
1½ teaspoons	bottled minced roasted garlic	2 teaspoons
2 tablespoons	margarine or butter	3 tablespoons
⅔ cup	snipped fresh parsley	1 cup
½ cup	snipped fresh chives	¾ cup

PREP:
30 minutes

RISE:
35 minutes

BAKE:
25 minutes

MAKES:
1½-pound recipe
(20 slices)
OR
2-pound recipe
(24 slices)

1 Select the recipe size. Add the first 7 ingredients to the machine according to the manufacturer's directions. Select the dough cycle. When cycle is complete, remove dough. Punch down. Cover and let rest for 10 minutes.

2 Meanwhile, for filling, in a small saucepan cook the roasted garlic in hot margarine for 30 seconds. Remove from heat. Stir in the parsley and chives.

3 *For the 1½-pound recipe:* Lightly grease a large baking sheet; set aside. Divide the dough in half. On a lightly floured surface, roll each portion into a 16×10-inch rectangle. Spread with the filling. Starting from a long side, loosely roll up into a spiral; seal edge. Place loaves, seam sides down, on the prepared baking sheet, tucking ends under loaves.

4 Cover and let rise in a warm place for 35 to 45 minutes or until nearly double. Bake in a 350°F oven for 25 to 30 minutes or until bread sounds hollow when lightly tapped. Remove from baking sheet; cool on a wire rack.

For the 2-pound recipe: Prepare as above, except divide the dough and filling into thirds. Roll each portion into a 12×10-inch rectangle. Continue as above, using 2 greased large baking sheets.

Nutrition Facts per slice: 100 cal., 2 g total fat (1 g sat. fat), 1 mg chol., 126 mg sodium, 16 g carbo., 3 g pro.

If you grow your own herbs, take advantage of their fresh flavor by substituting three times the amount of fresh herb for the dried form in this onion loaf.

Herbed Green Onion Bread

	1½-POUND*	INGREDIENTS	2-POUND*
PREP: 15 minutes	½ cup	thinly sliced green onions	¾ cup
	½ teaspoon	dried basil, crushed	¾ teaspoon
MAKES: 1½-pound recipe (16 slices)	½ teaspoon	dried thyme, crushed	¾ teaspoon
	¼ teaspoon	dried rosemary, crushed**	¼ teaspoon
OR 2-pound recipe (22 slices)	2 tablespoons	margarine or butter	3 tablespoons
	1 cup	milk	1⅓ cups
	1	egg**	1
	3 cups	bread flour	4 cups
	2 tablespoons	sugar	3 tablespoons
	¾ teaspoon	salt	1 teaspoon
	1 teaspoon	active dry yeast	1¼ teaspoons
		or bread machine yeast	

① Select the loaf size. In a small saucepan cook the green onions, basil, thyme, and rosemary in hot margarine until green onions are tender, stirring occasionally. Cool slightly.

② Add the green onion mixture and the remaining ingredients to the machine according to the manufacturer's directions. Select the basic white bread cycle.

*Note: For the 1½-pound loaf, the bread machine pan must have a capacity of 10 cups or more. For the 2-pound loaf, the bread machine pan must have a capacity of 12 cups or more.

**Note: The Test Kitchen recommends ¼ teaspoon dried rosemary and 1 egg for either size recipe.

Nutrition Facts per slice: 125 cal., 2 g total fat (1 g sat. fat), 14 mg chol., 129 mg sodium, 21 g carbo., 4 g pro.

This bread's flavor brings stuffing to mind. So why not try cutting the cooled bread into cubes, drying it, and using it as bread stuffing for poultry or meat. Of course it's great in sandwiches.

Sage-Cornmeal Loaf

1½-POUND	INGREDIENTS	2-POUND
⅓ cup	chopped onion	½ cup
4 teaspoons	margarine or butter	2 tablespoons
¾ cup	milk	1 cup
¼ cup	water	⅓ cup
2½ cups	bread flour	3½ cups
½ cup	cornmeal	⅔ cup
1 tablespoon	ground sage	4 teaspoons
	or poultry seasoning	
¾ teaspoon	salt	1 teaspoon
½ teaspoon	sugar	¾ teaspoon
1 teaspoon	active dry yeast	1¼ teaspoons
	or bread machine yeast	

PREP:
15 minutes

MAKES:
1½-pound recipe
(16 slices)
OR
2-pound recipe
(22 slices)

1 Select the loaf size. In a small saucepan cook the onion in hot margarine until tender, stirring occasionally. Cool slightly.

2 Add the onion mixture and the remaining ingredients to the machine according to the manufacturer's directions. Select the basic white bread cycle.

Nutrition Facts per slice: 111 cal., 2 g total fat (0 g sat. fat), 1 mg chol., 118 mg sodium, 20 g carbo., 3 g pro.

Toasted cumin seeds combined with black pepper make your taste buds zing when you nibble a slice of this fiery loaf.

Cumin and Pepper Bread

	1½-POUND	INGREDIENTS	2-POUND
PREP: 15 minutes	³/₄ cup	water	1 cup
	¹/₂ cup	dairy sour cream	²/₃ cup
MAKES: 1½-pound recipe (16 slices) OR 2-pound recipe (22 slices)	2³/₄ cups	bread flour	3²/₃ cups
	¹/₄ cup	toasted wheat germ	¹/₃ cup
	2 teaspoons	gluten flour	1 tablespoon
	1½ teaspoons	dried minced onion	2 teaspoons
	1 teaspoon	sugar	1½ teaspoons
	1 teaspoon	cumin seeds, toasted*	1½ teaspoons
	³/₄ teaspoon	salt	1 teaspoon
	¹/₂ teaspoon	coarsely ground black pepper	³/₄ teaspoon
	1 teaspoon	active dry yeast	1¹/₄ teaspoons
		or bread machine yeast	

1 Select the loaf size. Add the ingredients to the machine according to the manufacturer's directions. Select the basic white bread cycle.

*Note: To toast the cumin seeds, spread in a single layer in a shallow baking pan. Bake in a 350°F oven for 5 to 10 minutes or until light golden brown, watching carefully and stirring once or twice so the seeds do not burn.

Nutrition Facts per slice: 109 cal., 2 g total fat (1 g sat. fat), 3 mg chol., 113 mg sodium, 19 g carbo., 4 g pro.

Satisfy culinary wanderlust without leaving home. A blend of Indian spices, known as curry, is added to this whole grain bread. Peanuts, a traditional ingredient of curries, also are added.

Curried Wheat Loaf

1¹/₂-POUND*	I N G R E D I E N T S	2-POUND*
³/₄ cup	milk	1 cup
1	egg(s)	2
3 tablespoons	water	¹/₄ cup
1 tablespoon	margarine or butter, cut up	2 tablespoons
2¹/₂ cups	bread flour	3¹/₃ cups
³/₄ cup	whole wheat flour	1 cup
1 tablespoon	brown sugar	2 tablespoons
1 teaspoon	curry powder	1¹/₄ teaspoons
³/₄ teaspoon	salt	1 teaspoon
1¹/₄ teaspoons	active dry yeast	1¹/₂ teaspoons
	or bread machine yeast	
¹/₄ cup	chopped peanuts	¹/₃ cup

PREP:
15 minutes

MAKES:
1¹/₂-pound recipe
(16 slices)
OR
2-pound recipe
(22 slices)

1 Select the loaf size. Add the ingredients to the machine according to the manufacturer's directions. If available, select the whole grain cycle, or select the basic white bread cycle.

*Note: For the 1¹/₂-pound loaf, the bread machine pan must have a capacity of 10 cups or more. For the 2-pound loaf, the bread machine pan must have a capacity of 12 cups or more.

Nutrition Facts per slice: 130 cal., 3 g total fat (1 g sat. fat), 14 mg chol., 138 mg sodium, 22 g carbo., 5 g pro.

Peanut Choices

Salty peanuts or salt-free? On this contentious culinary issue, fans line up on both sides of the salt shaker. In most recipes, including those for baking, it's a taste toss-up that makes no difference to success. Unless a certain kind is specified, choose the one you prefer.

Tap into the tapenade craze—our lively mix of olives, sweet peppers, and thyme adds Mediterranean appeal to this nicely tuggy bread. If you use a purchased tapenade, opt for a chopped variety—the paste-type tapenade can cast a grayish hue on the loaf.

Tapenade Loaf

PREP:	1½-POUND	INGREDIENTS	2-POUND
25 minutes	1 cup	water	1¼ cups
	⅓ cup	Homemade Tapenade	½ cup
MAKES:		or purchased tapenade	
1½-pound recipe (16 slices)	2 teaspoons	honey	1 tablespoon
OR	2 teaspoons	olive oil	1 tablespoon
2-pound recipe (22 slices)	3 cups	bread flour	4 cups
	2 tablespoons	toasted wheat germ	3 tablespoons
	1½ teaspoons	snipped fresh thyme	2 teaspoons
		or	
	½ teaspoon	dried thyme, crushed	¾ teaspoon
	½ teaspoon	salt	¾ teaspoon
	1 teaspoon	active dry yeast	1¼ teaspoons
		or bread machine yeast	

1 Select the loaf size. Add the ingredients to the machine according to the manufacturer's directions. Select the basic white bread cycle.

Homemade Tapenade: In a food processor bowl combine ⅓ cup drained, bottled roasted red sweet peppers, ¼ cup pitted ripe olives, ¼ cup pitted kalamata olives, ¼ cup pitted green olives, 2 teaspoons olive oil, and ½ teaspoon snipped fresh thyme or ¼ teaspoon dried thyme, crushed. Cover and process with several on-off turns until coarsely chopped. (Or coarsely chop roasted peppers and olives by hand. Stir in oil and thyme.) Makes about 1 cup.

Nutrition Facts per slice: 109 cal., 2 g total fat (0 g sat. fat), 0 mg chol., 105 mg sodium, 20 g carbo., 3 g pro.

Green olives, ripe olives, and olive oil make this fabulous bread a triple treat. Serve it with broiled pork chops or roast turkey breast.

Olive Bread

1½-POUND	INGREDIENTS	2-POUND
1 cup	water	1¼ cups
¼ cup	chopped pimiento-stuffed green olives	⅓ cup
3 tablespoons	chopped pitted ripe olives	¼ cup
2 teaspoons	olive oil or cooking oil	1 tablespoon
3 cups	bread flour	4 cups
2 teaspoons	sugar	1 tablespoon
1 teaspoon	dried Italian seasoning, crushed	1½ teaspoons
¾ teaspoon	salt	1 teaspoon
1 teaspoon	active dry yeast or bread machine yeast	1¼ teaspoons

PREP:
15 minutes

MAKES:
1½-pound recipe
(16 slices)
OR
2-pound recipe
(22 slices)

1 Select the loaf size. Add the ingredients to the machine according to the manufacturer's directions. Select the basic white bread cycle.

Nutrition Facts per slice: 105 cal., 2 g total fat (0 g sat. fat), 0 mg chol., 148 mg sodium, 19 g carbo., 3 g pro.

For a change-of-pace garlic bread, cut slices of this lively loaf in half diagonally to form triangles and spread them with butter. Sprinkle the triangles with Parmesan cheese and broil until golden.

Garlic and Dried Tomato Bread

PREP:
15 minutes

MAKES:
1½-pound recipe
(16 slices)
OR
2-pound recipe
(22 slices)

1½-POUND*	INGREDIENTS	2-POUND*
1 cup	water	1⅓ cups
¼ cup	snipped dried tomatoes	⅓ cup
	(not oil-packed)	
3 tablespoons	finely chopped onion	¼ cup
2 teaspoons	olive oil or cooking oil	1 tablespoon
3 large cloves	garlic, minced	4 large cloves
2⅓ cups	bread flour	3 cups
⅔ cup	whole wheat flour	1 cup
2 teaspoons	sugar	1 tablespoon
¾ teaspoon	salt	1 teaspoon
¾ teaspoon	dried rosemary, crushed	1 teaspoon
1 teaspoon	active dry yeast	1¼ teaspoons
	or bread machine yeast	

1 Select the loaf size. Add the ingredients to the machine according to the manufacturer's directions, adding the dried tomatoes with the water. If available, select the whole grain cycle, or select the basic white bread cycle.

*Note: For the 1½-pound loaf, the bread machine pan must have a capacity of 10 cups or more. For the 2-pound loaf, the breach machine pan must have a capacity of 12 cups or more.

Nutrition Facts per slice: 101 cal., 1 g total fat (0 g sat. fat), 0 mg chol., 119 mg sodium, 20 g carbo., 3 g pro.

Test for Freshness

Is there a way to tell if a dried herb is still fresh? Yes. If you've had an herb on the shelf awhile, you can check it by crushing a small amount of the herb in the palm of your hand. It should still be aromatic. If the aroma is weak, it's time to buy a new jar. Faded or straw-colored herbs should also be discarded.

Just a couple of basic ingredients transform an ordinary loaf of bread into something noteworthy. Here, onion powder and celery seeds are the notable flavor stars.

Celery Seed Bread

1½-POUND*	INGREDIENTS	2-POUND*
1 cup	milk	1¼ cups
¼ cup	water**	¼ cup
2 teaspoons	shortening or cooking oil	1 tablespoon
3 cups	bread flour	4 cups
1 tablespoon	sugar	4 teaspoons
¾ teaspoon	salt	1 teaspoon
¾ teaspoon	onion powder	1 teaspoon
½ teaspoon	celery seeds	¾ teaspoon
1 teaspoon	active dry yeast	1¼ teaspoons
	or bread machine yeast	

PREP:
10 minutes

MAKES:
1½-pound recipe
(16 slices)
OR
2-pound recipe
(22 slices)

1 Select the loaf size. Add the ingredients to the machine according to the manufacturer's directions. Select the basic white bread cycle.

*Note: For the 1½-pound loaf, the bread machine pan must have a capacity of 10 cups or more. For the 2-pound loaf, the bread machine pan must have a capacity of 12 cups or more.

**Note: The Test Kitchen recommends ¼ cup water for either size recipe.

Nutrition Facts per slice: 109 cal., 1 g total fat (0 g sat. fat), 1 mg chol., 108 mg sodium, 20 g carbo., 4 g pro.

With its duo of distinctive flavors, this bread makes a great choice when you're serving something simple. In summer, try it with slices of cold roast beef and a marinated vegetable salad; in winter, pair it with a steaming bowl of soup.

Cheddar-Chive Bread

PREP: 15 minutes	1½-POUND*	INGREDIENTS	2-POUND*
	½ cup	milk	⅔ cup
MAKES:	1¼ cups	shredded sharp cheddar cheese	1⅔ cups
1½-pound recipe (16 slices)	¼ cup	water**	¼ cup
OR	1	egg**	1
2-pound recipe (22 slices)	2 tablespoons	margarine or butter, cut up	3 tablespoons
	3 cups	bread flour	4 cups
	2 tablespoons	snipped fresh chives	3 tablespoons
		or	
	1 tablespoon	dried snipped chives	4 teaspoons
	1 teaspoon	sugar	1¼ teaspoons
	¾ teaspoon	salt	1 teaspoon
	1 teaspoon	active dry yeast	1¼ teaspoons
		or bread machine yeast	

1 Select the loaf size. Add the ingredients to the machine according to the manufacturer's directions, adding the cheese with the milk. Select the basic white bread cycle. (Dough may appear a little dry at first, but will become moister as the cheese melts and is incorporated into the dough.)

*Note: For the 1½-pound loaf, the bread machine pan must have a capacity of 10 cups or more. For the 2-pound loaf, the bread machine pan must have a capacity of 12 cups or more.

**Note: The Test Kitchen recommends ¼ cup water and 1 egg for either size recipe.

Nutrition Facts per slice: 151 cal., 5 g total fat (2 g sat. fat), 23 mg chol., 189 mg sodium, 20 g carbo., 6 g pro.

The sassy flavor of smoked cheddar makes this rich, moist bread extraordinary. For a golden loaf, it's best to use light-colored rather than dark beer.

Smoked Cheddar Loaf

1½-POUND*	INGREDIENTS	2-POUND*
¾ cup	mild-flavored beer	1 cup
1¼ cups	shredded smoked cheddar cheese	1⅔ cups
1	egg**	1
3 cups	bread flour	4 cups
1 tablespoon	sugar	4 teaspoons
¾ teaspoon	salt	1 teaspoon
1 teaspoon	active dry yeast	1¼ teaspoons
	or bread machine yeast	

PREP:
15 minutes

MAKES:
1½-pound recipe
(16 slices)
OR
2-pound recipe
(22 slices)

1 Select the loaf size. Add the ingredients to the machine according to the manufacturer's directions, adding the cheese with the beer. Select the basic white bread cycle.

*Note: For the 1½-pound loaf, the bread machine pan must have a capacity of 10 cups or more. For the 2-pound loaf, the bread machine pan must have a capacity of 12 cups or more.

**Note: The Test Kitchen recommends 1 egg for either size recipe.

Nutrition Facts per slice: 141 cal., 4 g total fat (2 g sat. fat), 23 mg chol., 160 mg sodium, 20 g carbo., 6 g pro.

Cooking with Beer

Although flat beer is dismal to drink, it's better for cooking because it's easier to measure free of fizz. Let an open beer stand until it loses its carbonation, then pour just what you need. No more waiting for the foamy head to subside to check the real volume.

Your mouth will water when you slice into this freshly baked loaf and detect the aromatic blend of onion, Swiss cheese, and caraway seeds. Spread with a little butter and enjoy!

Swiss-Onion Bread

	1½-POUND*	INGREDIENTS	2-POUND*
PREP: 15 minutes	¼ cup	chopped onion	⅓ cup
	1 tablespoon	margarine or butter	4 teaspoons
MAKES: 1½-pound recipe (16 slices) OR 2-pound recipe (22 slices)	½ cup	milk	⅔ cup
	1 cup	shredded Swiss cheese	1⅓ cups
	¼ cup	water	⅓ cup
	1	egg**	1
	2¼ cups	bread flour	2¾ cups
	¾ cup	whole wheat flour	1¼ cups
	¾ teaspoon	caraway seeds	1 teaspoon
	½ teaspoon	salt	¾ teaspoon
	1 teaspoon	active dry yeast or bread machine yeast	1¼ teaspoons

1 Select the loaf size. In a small saucepan cook the onion in hot margarine until tender, stirring occasionally. Cool slightly.

2 Add the ingredients to the machine according to the manufacturer's directions, adding the onion mixture and the cheese with the milk. If available, select the whole grain cycle, or select the basic white bread cycle.

*Note: For the 1½-pound loaf, the bread machine pan must have a capacity of 10 cups or more. For the 2-pound loaf, the bread machine pan must have a capacity of 12 cups or more.

**Note: The Test Kitchen recommends 1 egg for either size recipe.

Nutrition Facts per slice: 132 cal., 4 g total fat (2 g sat. fat), 20 mg chol., 102 mg sodium, 19 g carbo., 6 g pro.

To make extra-cheesy Reuben sandwiches, use this Swiss-cheese-laced bread instead of rye or pumpernickel. If you carry your lunch, save a slice to pack with vegetable soup.

Caraway-Cheese Loaf

1½-POUND*	INGREDIENTS	2-POUND*
¾ cup	shredded Swiss cheese	1 cup
3 tablespoons	bread flour	⅓ cup
1¼ cups	dark beer	1⅔ cups
1	egg**	1
3 cups	bread flour	4 cups
1 tablespoon	sugar	4 teaspoons
1 teaspoon	caraway seeds, crushed	1¼ teaspoons
¾ teaspoon	salt	1 teaspoon
1 teaspoon	active dry yeast	1¼ teaspoons
	or bread machine yeast	

PREP:
15 minutes

MAKES:
1½-pound recipe
(16 slices)
OR
2-pound recipe
(22 slices)

1 Select the loaf size. In a small bowl toss together the cheese and the 3 tablespoons or ⅓ cup bread flour.

2 Add the cheese mixture and the remaining ingredients to the machine according to the manufacturer's directions. Select the basic white bread cycle.

*Note: For the 1½-pound loaf, the bread machine pan must have a capacity of 10 cups or more. For the 2-pound loaf, the bread machine pan must have a capacity of 12 cups or more.

**Note: The Test Kitchen recommends 1 egg for either size recipe.

Nutrition Facts per slice: 135 cal., 2 g total fat (1 g sat. fat), 18 mg chol., 119 mg sodium, 22 g carbo., 5 g pro.

Treat yourself to a slice of this cheesy herb bread—it's like taking a mini vacation to Italy.

Oregano and Mozzarella Cheese Bread

PREP:	1½-POUND*	INGREDIENTS
15 minutes	1 cup	milk
	½ cup	shredded mozzarella cheese
MAKES:	1	egg
1½-pound recipe	2¼ cups	bread flour
(16 slices)	¾ cup	whole wheat flour
	4 teaspoons	sugar
	4 teaspoons	snipped fresh oregano
		or
	1½ teaspoons	dried oregano, crushed
	¾ teaspoon	salt
	1 teaspoon	active dry yeast
		or bread machine yeast

1 Add the ingredients to the machine according to the manufacturer's directions, adding the cheese with the milk. If available, select the whole grain cycle, or select the basic white bread cycle.

*Note: The bread machine pan must have a capacity of 10 cups or more.

Nutrition Facts per slice: 129 cal., 3 g total fat (2 g sat. fat), 26 mg chol., 152 mg sodium, 21 g carbo., 6 g pro.

Chiles lend a provocative and spicy flavor that embraces the sharp cheddar cheese—a perfect combination for tomato soup. For extra zing, choose well-aged cheddar cheese.

Chile-Cheese Bread

1½-POUND	INGREDIENTS	2-POUND
½ cup	milk	⅔ cup
1 cup	shredded sharp cheddar cheese	1⅓ cups
½ of a 4½-ounce can	diced green chile peppers, drained	1 (4½-ounce) can
¼ cup	water	⅓ cup
2 teaspoons	margarine or butter	1 tablespoon
3 cups	bread flour	4 cups
1½ teaspoons	sugar	2 teaspoons
¾ teaspoon	chili powder	1 teaspoon
½ teaspoon	salt	¾ teaspoon
1 teaspoon	active dry yeast or bread machine yeast	1¼ teaspoons

PREP:
15 minutes

MAKES:
1½-pound recipe
(16 slices)
OR
2-pound recipe
(22 slices)

1 Select the loaf size. Add the ingredients to the machine according to the manufacturer's directions, adding the cheese with the milk. Select the basic white bread cycle.

Nutrition Facts per slice: 133 cal., 3 g total fat (2 g sat. fat), 8 mg chol., 132 mg sodium, 20 g carbo., 5 g pro.

Are All Chili Powders the Same?

The blend of ground dried red chiles and other spices sold as chili powder came to be, some say, as a preparation shortcut for the famous Texas bowl of red. These blends vary in flavor (and heat) from label to label, so experiment with different brands.

Italian seasoning infuses this bread with mild herb flavor, while pine nuts contribute delightful crunchy texture. It's the perfect partner for lasagna or ravioli.

Parmesan-Pine Nut Bread

PREP:
10 minutes

MAKES:
1½-pound recipe
(18 slices)
OR
2-pound recipe
(24 slices)

1½-POUND*	INGREDIENTS	2-POUND*
1 cup	milk	1⅓ cups
1	egg**	1
1 tablespoon	olive oil or cooking oil	4 teaspoons
3 cups	bread flour	4 cups
⅓ cup	grated Parmesan or Asiago cheese	½ cup
1 teaspoon	dried Italian seasoning, crushed	1½ teaspoons
½ teaspoon	salt	¾ teaspoon
¼ teaspoon	sugar	½ teaspoon
1 teaspoon	active dry yeast or bread machine yeast	1¼ teaspoons
⅓ cup	pine nuts	½ cup

1 Select the loaf size. Add the ingredients to the machine according to the manufacturer's directions. Select the basic white bread cycle.

*Note: For the 1½-pound loaf, the bread machine pan must have a capacity of 10 cups or more. For the 2-pound loaf, the bread machine pan must have a capacity of 12 cups or more.

**Note: The Test Kitchen recommends 1 egg for either size recipe.

Nutrition Facts per slice: 125 cal., 4 g total fat (1 g sat. fat), 14 mg chol., 104 mg sodium, 18 g carbo., 5 g pro.

Pine Nut Tidbits

Italians call the rich and buttery pine nut—which comes from pine trees—pignoli. They enjoy these tiny treasures in everything from pesto sauce to cookies to stuffings. Flavors like cheese, herbs, and spices marry well with their nutty, creamy personality. Keep pine nuts fresh by refrigerating them up to two weeks, or freezing up to three months.

The combination of feta cheese and dill provides a melding of flavors so rich this bread is a meal in itself. Team with wine, assorted cheeses, and your favorite dining companion.

Feta-Dill Bread

1½-POUND*	INGREDIENTS	2-POUND*
1 cup	water	1¼ cups
²/₃ cup	crumbled feta cheese	³/₄ cup
1	egg**	1
1 tablespoon	margarine or butter	4 teaspoons
3 cups	bread flour	4 cups
¹/₃ cup	packaged instant mashed potato flakes or buds	¹/₂ cup
¹/₄ cup	nonfat dry milk powder	¹/₃ cup
1 tablespoon	sugar	4 teaspoons
1 teaspoon	dried dill	1¼ teaspoons
	or	
1 tablespoon	snipped fresh dill	4 teaspoons
³/₄ teaspoon	salt	1 teaspoon
1 teaspoon	active dry yeast or bread machine yeast	1¼ teaspoons

PREP:
15 minutes

MAKES:
1½-pound recipe
(16 slices)
OR
2-pound recipe
(22 slices)

1 Select the loaf size. Add the ingredients to the machine according to the manufacturer's directions, adding the cheese with the water. Select the basic white bread cycle.

*Note: For the 1½-pound loaf, the bread machine pan must have a capacity of 10 cups or more. For the 2-pound loaf, the bread machine pan must have a capacity of 12 cups or more.

**Note: The Test Kitchen recommends 1 egg for either size recipe.

Nutrition Facts per slice: 127 cal., 2 g total fat (1 g sat. fat), 17 mg chol., 170 mg sodium, 21 g carbo., 5 g pro.

Fans of Greek salad will find much to like here. The key flavors—piquant kalamata olives, tangy feta cheese, and a touch of rosemary—infuse moist, high-rising country loaves.

Greek Bread

PREP:
15 minutes

MAKES:
1½-pound recipe
(18 slices)
OR
2-pound recipe
(24 slices)

1½-POUND*	INGREDIENTS	2-POUND*
1 cup	milk	1¼ cups
½ cup	crumbled feta cheese	¾ cup
⅓ cup	chopped, pitted kalamata olives	½ cup
2 tablespoons	water	3 tablespoons
2 teaspoons	shortening or cooking oil	1 tablespoon
3 cups	bread flour	4 cups
1 tablespoon	sugar	4 teaspoons
1 teaspoon	dried rosemary, crushed,	1¼ teaspoons
	or	
1 tablespoon	snipped fresh rosemary	4 teaspoons
½ teaspoon	salt	¾ teaspoon
1 teaspoon	active dry yeast	1¼ teaspoons
	or bread machine yeast	

1 Select the loaf size. Add the ingredients to the machine according to the manufacturer's directions, adding the cheese with the milk. Select the basic white bread cycle.

*Note: For the 1½-pound loaf, the bread machine pan must have a capacity of 10 cups or more. For the 2-pound loaf, the bread machine pan must have a capacity of 12 cups or more.

Nutrition Facts per slice: 110 cal., 2 g total fat (1 g sat. fat), 4 mg chol., 118 mg sodium, 18 g carbo., 4 g pro.

Storing Feta Cheese

If you've bought more feta—a soft, white, brine-cured, crumbly goat- or sheep-milk cheese—than you can use right away, freeze it. You'll have it conveniently at hand for another loaf, or a great Greek salad. Thaw in the refrigerator before using.

Enhance the flavor of a loaf of bread with fennel and hazelnuts. Ricotta cheese produces the light, airy texture in this much-loved loaf. It's so good, you may want to eat it straight from the bread machine.

Fennel-Cheese Bread

1½-POUND*	INGREDIENTS	2-POUND*
³/₄ cup	part-skim ricotta cheese	1 cup
²/₃ cup	milk	³/₄ cup
1	egg(s)	2
2 tablespoons	margarine or butter, cut up	3 tablespoons
3 cups	bread flour	4 cups
2 tablespoons	brown sugar	3 tablespoons
1½ teaspoons	fennel seeds, crushed	2 teaspoons
³/₄ teaspoon	salt	1 teaspoon
1 teaspoon	active dry yeast	1¼ teaspoons
	or bread machine yeast	
¹/₃ cup	finely chopped hazelnuts	¹/₂ cup
	(filberts), toasted	

PREP:
15 minutes

MAKES:
1½-pound recipe
(16 slices)
OR
2-pound recipe
(22 slices)

1 Select the loaf size. Add the ingredients to the machine according to the manufacturer's directions. Select the basic white bread cycle.

*Note: For the 1½-pound loaf, the bread machine pan must have a capacity of 10 cups or more. For the 2-pound loaf, the bread machine pan must have a capacity of 12 cups or more.

Nutrition Facts per slice: 153 cal., 5 g total fat (1 g sat. fat), 18 mg chol., 141 mg sodium, 22 g carbo., 6 g pro.

This moist bread is a blue cheese lover's delight. Serve it with a chef's salad or creamy potato soup. For convenience, the recipe calls for instant potatoes.

Blue Cheese-Potato Bread

PREP:
15 minutes

MAKES:
1½-pound recipe
(20 slices)
OR
2-pound recipe
(27 slices)

1½-POUND*	INGREDIENTS	2-POUND*
1¼ cups	water	1½ cups
½ cup	crumbled blue cheese	⅔ cup
1	egg**	1
1 tablespoon	margarine or butter	4 teaspoons
3 cups	bread flour	4 cups
⅓ cup	packaged instant mashed potato flakes or buds	½ cup
¼ cup	nonfat dry milk powder	⅓ cup
1 tablespoon	sugar	4 teaspoons
¾ teaspoon	salt	1 teaspoon
½ teaspoon	onion powder	¾ teaspoon
1 teaspoon	active dry yeast or bread machine yeast**	1 teaspoon

❶ Select the loaf size. Add the ingredients to the machine according to the manufacturer's directions, adding the cheese with the water. Select the basic white bread cycle.

*Note: For the 1½-pound loaf, the bread machine pan must have a capacity of 10 cups or more. For the 2-pound loaf, the bread machine pan must have a capacity of 12 cups or more.

**Note: The Test Kitchen recommends 1 egg and 1 teaspoon yeast for either size recipe.

Nutrition Facts per slice: 102 cal., 2 g total fat (1 g sat. fat), 13 mg chol., 136 mg sodium, 17 g carbo., 4 g pro.

Dunking wedges of this spiced-up corn bread into bowls of piping-hot chili will really take the edge off cold winter nights.

Southern Cheese Bread

1½-POUND	INGREDIENTS
½ cup	milk
1 cup	shredded cheddar cheese
½ cup	bottled salsa
2 tablespoons	butter or margarine, melted
2¼ cups	all-purpose flour
¾ cup	cornmeal
2 tablespoons	sugar
¼ teaspoon	salt
2¼ teaspoons	active dry yeast
	or bread machine yeast

PREP:
20 minutes

RISE:
30 minutes

BAKE:
25 minutes

MAKES:
1½-pound recipe
(8 servings)

1 Add the ingredients to the machine according to the manufacturer's directions, adding the cheese with the milk. Select the dough cycle. When cycle is complete, remove dough. Punch down. Cover and let rest for 10 minutes.

2 Grease a large baking sheet. On the prepared baking sheet, press the dough into an 8-inch circle. Cut into 8 wedges. Cover and let rise in a warm place about 30 minutes or until nearly double.

3 Bake in a 350°F oven about 25 minutes or until bottom of bread is golden brown. If necessary, cover loosely with foil the last 5 minutes to prevent overbrowning. Remove from baking sheet; cool slightly on a wire rack. Serve warm.

Nutrition Facts per serving: 284 cal., 9 g total fat (5 g sat. fat), 24 mg chol., 304 mg sodium, 42 g carbo., 9 g pro.

Boldly flavored Parmesan cheese and full-flavored herbs provide an easy update to this all-American classic.

Parmesan Corn Bread

PREP:
10 minutes

MAKES:
1½-pound recipe
(16 slices)
OR
2-pound recipe
(22 slices)

1½-POUND	INGREDIENTS	2-POUND
1 cup	water	1⅓ cups
2 teaspoons	olive oil or cooking oil	1 tablespoon
2¾ cups	bread flour	3⅔ cups
½ cup	cornmeal	⅔ cup
¼ cup	grated Parmesan cheese	⅓ cup
2 teaspoons	sugar	1 tablespoon
¾ teaspoon	salt	1 teaspoon
¾ teaspoon	dried basil, crushed,	1 teaspoon
	or	
2 teaspoons	snipped fresh basil	1 tablespoon
1 teaspoon	active dry yeast	1¼ teaspoons
	or bread machine yeast	

1 Select the loaf size. Add the ingredients to the machine according to the manufacturer's directions. Select the basic white bread cycle.

Nutrition Facts per slice: 114 cal., 2 g total fat (0 g sat. fat), 1 mg chol., 131 mg sodium, 21 g carbo., 4 g pro.

Cornmeal gives this whole wheat bread a crunchy, pleasantly dense texture and a golden crust—well suited for a club sandwich.

Whole Wheat-Cornmeal Bread

1½-POUND	INGREDIENTS	2-POUND
1 cup	milk	1¼ cups
¼ cup	water	⅓ cup
1 tablespoon	shortening or cooking oil	2 tablespoons
2 cups	bread flour	2⅔ cups
¾ cup	whole wheat flour	1 cup
½ cup	cornmeal	⅔ cup
1 tablespoon	gluten flour	4 teaspoons
1 tablespoon	sugar	4 teaspoons
1½ teaspoons	dried basil or thyme, crushed,	2 teaspoons
	or	
1 tablespoon	snipped fresh basil or thyme	4 teaspoons
¾ teaspoon	salt	1 teaspoon
1¼ teaspoons	active dry yeast	1½ teaspoons
	or bread machine yeast	

PREP:
10 minutes

MAKES:
1½-pound recipe
(16 slices)
OR
2-pound recipe
(22 slices)

1 Select the loaf size. Add the ingredients to the machine according to the manufacturer's directions. If available, select the whole grain cycle, or select the basic white bread cycle.

Nutrition Facts per slice: 118 cal., 2 g total fat (0 g sat. fat), 1 mg chol., 109 mg sodium, 22 g carbo., 4 g pro.

Every bite of this cheesy, Italian-seasoned bread is worth savoring!

Pesto Bread

PREP:
10 minutes

MAKES:
1½-pound recipe
(16 slices)

1½-POUND	INGREDIENTS
1 cup	buttermilk or sour milk*
⅓ cup	dry white wine
3 tablespoons	purchased pesto
2 cloves	garlic, minced
3⅓ cups	bread flour
3 tablespoons	grated Parmesan cheese
1 tablespoon	sugar
¾ teaspoon	salt
1 teaspoon	active dry yeast
	or bread machine yeast

1 Add the ingredients to the machine according to the manufacturer's directions. Select the basic white bread cycle.

*Note: To make 1 cup sour milk, place 1 tablespoon lemon juice or vinegar in a 1-cup liquid measuring cup. Add enough milk to measure 1 cup liquid; stir. Let stand for 5 minutes before using.

Nutrition Facts per slice: 128 cal., 2 g total fat (0 g sat. fat), 2 mg chol., 140 mg sodium, 24 g carbo., 5 g pro.

Experience a lively taste of Italian "street" life. You create this savory flatbread by snipping off pieces of dough and letting them fall randomly into the pan. The result? Cobblestone bread.

Quick Cobblestone Bread

1½-POUND	INGREDIENTS	2-POUND
1 cup	water	1⅓ cups
2 tablespoons	margarine or butter, cut up	3 tablespoons
3 cups	bread flour	4 cups
⅓ cup	grated Parmesan cheese	½ cup
1 tablespoon	sugar	4 teaspoons
½ teaspoon	salt	¾ teaspoon
½ teaspoon	dried Italian seasoning, crushed	¾ teaspoon
1¼ teaspoons	active dry yeast or bread machine yeast	1½ teaspoons
	Nonstick cooking spray	
2 tablespoons	margarine or butter, melted	3 tablespoons
½ teaspoon	dried Italian seasoning, crushed	¾ teaspoon
¼ teaspoon	garlic salt*	¼ teaspoon

PREP:
20 minutes

RISE:
25 minutes

BAKE:
30 minutes

MAKES:
1½-pound recipe
(12 servings)
OR
2-pound recipe
(16 servings)

1 Select the recipe size. Add the first 8 ingredients to the machine according to the manufacturer's directions. Select the dough cycle. When cycle is complete, remove dough. Punch down. Cover and let rest for 10 minutes.

2 *For the 1½-pound recipe:* Generously grease an 11×7×1½-inch baking pan. Using kitchen scissors coated with cooking spray, snip the dough directly into the prepared baking pan. Cut into ¾- to 1-inch irregular pieces, covering pan evenly in 1 or 2 layers. Cover and let rise in a warm place about 25 minutes or until nearly double.

3 Meanwhile, in a small bowl stir together the melted margarine, ½ or ¾ teaspoon Italian seasoning, and garlic salt. Drizzle over dough. Bake in a 350°F oven about 30 minutes or until golden brown. Cool slightly in pan on a wire rack. Serve warm.

For the 2-pound recipe: Prepare as above, except use a well-greased 13×9×2-inch baking pan.

*Note: The Test Kitchen recommends ¼ teaspoon garlic salt for either size recipe.

Nutrition Facts per serving: 176 cal., 5 g total fat (1 g sat. fat), 2 mg chol., 229 mg sodium, 26 g carbo., 5 g pro.

Kids will be intrigued by this bread's fun shape and delighted with its pizzalike flavor.

Pinwheel Bread

PREP:	1½-POUND	INGREDIENTS	2-POUND
30 minutes	¾ cup	milk	1 cup
RISE:	1	egg*	1
30 minutes	3 tablespoons	margarine or butter, cut up	¼ cup
BAKE:	2 tablespoons	water	3 tablespoons
20 minutes	3 cups	bread flour	4 cups
MAKES:	1 tablespoon	sugar	4 teaspoons
1½-pound recipe	¾ teaspoon	salt	1 teaspoon
(8 servings)	1 teaspoon	active dry yeast	1¼ teaspoons
OR		or bread machine yeast	
2-pound recipe	2 tablespoons	grated Parmesan cheese	3 tablespoons
(16 servings)	½ teaspoon	dried Italian seasoning,	¾ teaspoon
		crushed	
	2 tablespoons	sesame seeds	3 tablespoons
	1	slightly beaten egg	1
	1 tablespoon	water	1 tablespoon

1 Select the recipe size. Add the first 8 ingredients to the machine according to the manufacturer's directions. Select the dough cycle. When cycle is complete, remove dough. Punch down. Cover and let rest for 10 minutes. Meanwhile, on a sheet of waxed paper, combine the Parmesan cheese and Italian seasoning. Place the sesame seeds on another sheet of waxed paper. Generously grease a large baking sheet; set aside.

2 *For the 1½-pound recipe:* Divide the dough into 8 portions. On a lightly floured surface, roll each portion into a 10-inch rope. In a small bowl combine the beaten egg and the 1 tablespoon water; brush over the ropes. Roll half of the ropes in the cheese mixture and half in the sesame seeds.

3 On the prepared baking sheet, arrange ropes to form a spoke shape, alternating cheese- and sesame-coated ropes. Press the ends in the center together to seal. Curve each rope into a half-circle to form a pinwheel shape, allowing each rope to touch the next one. Cover and let rise in a warm place about 30 minutes or until nearly double. Bake in a 350°F oven about 20 minutes or until golden brown. Remove from baking sheet; cool on a wire rack.

For the 2-pound recipe: Prepare as above, except divide the dough into 16 portions; roll each portion into an 8-inch rope. Form 2 pinwheels on 2 well-greased large baking sheets. Continue as above.

*Note: The Test Kitchen recommends 1 egg for either size recipe.

Nutrition Facts per serving: 281 cal., 8 g total fat (2 g sat. fat), 56 mg chol., 308 mg sodium, 41 g carbo., 10 g pro.

Make a tasty Tex-Mex sandwich with cream cheese, chicken, and roasted peppers.

Salsa Bread

1½-POUND	INGREDIENTS	2-POUND
1 cup	bottled chunky salsa	1¼ cups
⅓ cup	water*	⅓ cup
1 tablespoon	cooking oil	2 tablespoons
3 cups	bread flour	4 cups
1 tablespoon	sugar	2 tablespoons
½ teaspoon	ground cumin	¾ teaspoon
½ teaspoon	chili powder	¾ teaspoon
¼ teaspoon	ground red pepper*	¼ teaspoon
1¼ teaspoons	active dry yeast	1¼ teaspoons
	or bread machine yeast*	

PREP:
10 minutes

MAKES:
1½-pound recipe
(12 slices)
OR
2-pound recipe
(16 slices)

1 Select the loaf size. Add the ingredients to the machine according to the manufacturer's directions. Select the basic white bread cycle. (Dough may appear dry until the salsa is kneaded in. Do not add additional water.)

*Note: The Test Kitchen recommends ⅓ cup water, ¼ teaspoon ground red pepper, and 1¼ teaspoons yeast for either size recipe.

Nutrition Facts per slice: 143 cal., 2 g total fat (0 g sat. fat), 0 mg chol., 49 mg sodium, 27 g carbo., 4 g pro.

Like flecks of colorful jewels, vegetables add nutrition and visual impact to this healthful bread. Thyme is the suggested herb, but substitute your favorite, such as basil or oregano, if you prefer.

Confetti Bread

PREP:
15 minutes

MAKES:
1½-pound recipe
(16 slices)
OR
2-pound recipe
(22 slices)

1½-POUND	INGREDIENTS	2-POUND
¾ cup	water	1 cup
½ cup	shredded carrot	⅔ cup
⅓ cup	shredded zucchini	½ cup
¼ cup	finely chopped red sweet pepper	⅓ cup
¼ cup	sliced green onions	⅓ cup
1 tablespoon	margarine or butter	4 teaspoons
3 cups	bread flour	4 cups
1 teaspoon	sugar	1½ teaspoons
¾ teaspoon	salt	1 teaspoon
½ teaspoon	dried thyme, crushed, or	¾ teaspoon
1½ teaspoons	snipped fresh thyme	2 teaspoons
1 teaspoon	active dry yeast or bread machine yeast	1¼ teaspoons

1 Select the loaf size. Add the ingredients to the machine according to the manufacturer's directions. Select the basic white bread cycle. (Dough may appear stiff until the vegetables have released some of their liquid during the kneading cycle. Watch closely; it may be necessary to add 1 to 3 tablespoons additional bread flour.)

Nutrition Facts per slice: 103 cal., 1 g total fat (0 g sat. fat), 0 mg chol., 111 mg sodium, 20 g carbo., 3 g pro.

Heading to the local farmer's market or produce stand? Pick up some mushrooms and leeks for this veggie-flecked wheat bread.

Mushroom-Leek Bread

1½-POUND	INGREDIENTS
1½ cups	chopped fresh mushrooms
½ cup	thinly sliced leek
¾ teaspoon	dried rosemary, crushed
3 tablespoons	margarine or butter
1 cup plus 2 tablespoons	milk
2 cups	whole wheat flour
1 cup	bread flour
2 tablespoons	gluten flour
1 tablespoon	brown sugar
¾ teaspoon	salt
1 teaspoon	active dry yeast or bread machine yeast

PREP:
15 minutes

MAKES:
1½-pound recipe
(16 slices)

1 In a large skillet cook the mushrooms, leek, and rosemary in hot margarine over medium-high heat for 4 to 5 minutes or until tender and most of the liquid is evaporated, stirring occasionally. Cool slightly.

2 Add the mushroom mixture and the remaining ingredients to the machine according to the manufacturer's directions. If available, select the whole grain cycle, or select the basic white bread cycle.

Nutrition Facts per slice: 117 cal., 3 g total fat (0 g sat. fat), 2 mg chol., 137 mg sodium, 20 g carbo., 5 g pro.

What? Baby food in a bread recipe? Yes—the squash brings sweetness and a harvestlike gold color to this veggie-speckled bread. And you don't have to hassle with cooking and mashing the gourd yourself.

Autumn Harvest Loaf

	1½-POUND	INGREDIENTS	2-POUND
PREP: 15 minutes	1 (6-ounce) jar	squash baby food*	1 (6-ounce) jar
	⅓ cup	water	½ cup
MAKES: 1½-pound recipe (16 slices)	⅓ cup	coarsely shredded carrot	½ cup
	2 tablespoons	finely chopped onion	3 tablespoons
OR	1 tablespoon	margarine or butter	4 teaspoons
2-pound recipe (22 slices)	1½ cups	whole wheat flour	2 cups
	1½ cups	bread flour	2 cups
	1 tablespoon	gluten flour	4 teaspoons
	1 teaspoon	sugar	1½ teaspoons
	1 teaspoon	dried sage, crushed	1½ teaspoons
	¾ teaspoon	salt	1 teaspoon
	1 teaspoon	active dry yeast or bread machine yeast	1¼ teaspoons

❶ Select the loaf size. Add the ingredients to the machine according to the manufacturer's directions. If available, select the whole grain cycle, or select the basic white bread cycle.

*Note: The Test Kitchen recommends one 6-ounce jar squash baby food for either size recipe.

Nutrition Facts per slice: 99 cal., 1 g total fat (0 g sat. fat), 0 mg chol., 120 mg sodium, 19 g carbo., 3 g pro.

Bursting with flavor from two cheeses and three kinds of herbs, this bread is terrific warm from the machine or cooled to room temperature.

Garden Herb-Cheese Bread

1½-POUND	INGREDIENTS
1¼ cups	milk
⅓ cup	shredded sharp cheddar cheese
3 cups	bread flour
⅓ cup	grated Parmesan cheese
1 tablespoon	sugar
1 teaspoon	onion salt
¾ teaspoon	dried dill
¾ teaspoon	snipped fresh basil
	or
½ teaspoon	dried basil, crushed
½ teaspoon	snipped fresh rosemary
	or
¼ teaspoon	dried rosemary, crushed
1 teaspoon	active dry yeast
	or bread machine yeast

PREP:
15 minutes

MAKES:
1½-pound recipe
(16 slices)

① Add the ingredients to the machine according to the manufacturer's directions, adding the cheddar cheese with the milk. Select the basic white bread cycle.

Nutrition Facts per slice: 128 cal., 2 g total fat (2 g sat. fat), 9 mg chol., 288 mg sodium, 21 g carbo., 6 g pro.

The traditional flavors of a Scandinavian smorgasbord—cucumber, dill, and sour cream—reprise in a bread that requires only silken slices of smoked salmon or gravlax.

Cucumber-Dill Bread

PREP:
15 minutes

MAKES:
1½-pound recipe
(18 slices)
OR
2-pound recipe
(24 slices)

1½-POUND	INGREDIENTS	2-POUND
¾ cup	coarsely shredded, seeded cucumber	1 cup
½ cup	water	⅔ cup
⅓ cup	dairy sour cream	½ cup
3 cups	bread flour	4 cups
2 teaspoons	sugar	1 tablespoon
¾ teaspoon	salt	1 teaspoon
½ teaspoon	dried dill	¾ teaspoon
	or	
1½ teaspoons	snipped fresh dill	2 teaspoons
1 teaspoon	active dry yeast	1 teaspoon
	or bread machine yeast*	

1 Select the loaf size. Drain the cucumber, pressing out excess liquid. Add the ingredients to the machine according to the manufacturer's directions. Select the basic white bread cycle.

*Note: The Test Kitchen recommends 1 teaspoon yeast for either size recipe.

Nutrition Facts per slice: 95 cal., 1 g total fat (1 g sat. fat), 2 mg chol., 92 mg sodium, 17 g carbo., 3 g pro.

Although you can make this bread any time of year, it's especially great in summer, when the vegetables are at their seasonal best.

Garden Patch Bread

1½-POUND	INGREDIENTS	2-POUND
½ cup	water	⅔ cup
½ cup	coarsely shredded carrot	⅔ cup
⅓ cup	tomato juice	½ cup
2 tablespoons	coarsely chopped green sweet pepper	3 tablespoons
2 tablespoons	sliced green onion	3 tablespoons
1 tablespoon	margarine, butter, or cooking oil	4 teaspoons
3 cups	bread flour	4 cups
1 teaspoon	sugar	1½ teaspoons
¾ teaspoon	salt	1 teaspoon
¼ teaspoon	dried basil, crushed	½ teaspoon
1 teaspoon	active dry yeast or bread machine yeast*	1 teaspoon

PREP:
15 minutes

MAKES:
1½-pound recipe
(20 slices)
OR
2-pound recipe
(27 slices)

1 Select the loaf size. Add the ingredients to the machine according to the manufacturer's directions. Select the basic white bread cycle.

*Note: The Test Kitchen recommends 1 teaspoon yeast for either size recipe.

Nutrition Facts per slice: 83 cal., 1 g total fat (0 g sat. fat), 0 mg chol., 102 mg sodium, 16 g carbo., 3 g pro.

Broccoli lends flecks of green color and a hint of vegetable flavor to this cream-of-the-crop loaf while Parmesan cheese adds a zesty tang.

Broccoli-Cheese Bread

PREP:
15 minutes

MAKES:
1½-pound recipe
(16 slices)

1½-POUND*	INGREDIENTS
¾ cup	fresh or frozen chopped broccoli
¼ cup	finely chopped onion
4 teaspoons	margarine or butter
1 cup	milk
1	egg
3 cups	bread flour
⅓ cup	grated Parmesan cheese
¾ teaspoon	salt
1 teaspoon	active dry yeast or bread machine yeast

1 If using frozen broccoli, thaw and drain well. In a medium skillet cook the broccoli and onion in hot margarine until tender, stirring occasionally. Cool slightly.

2 Add the broccoli mixture and the remaining ingredients to the machine according to the manufacturer's directions. Select the basic white bread cycle.

*Note: The bread machine pan must have a capacity of 10 cups or more.

Nutrition Facts per slice: 120 cal., 3 g total fat (0 g sat. fat), 21 mg chol., 128 mg sodium, 20 g carbo., 5 g pro.

Cornmeal and corn color this loaf golden; yogurt lends a delightful sourdoughlike tang.

Yogurt Corn Bread

1½-POUND	INGREDIENTS	2-POUND
³/₄ cup	plain low-fat yogurt	1 cup
³/₄ cup	drained, canned whole kernel corn	1 cup
¹/₃ cup	water	¹/₂ cup
1 tablespoon	margarine or butter	4 teaspoons
2¹/₂ cups	bread flour	3¹/₃ cups
³/₄ cup	cornmeal	1 cup
2 teaspoons	sugar	1 tablespoon
1 teaspoon	onion powder	1¹/₂ teaspoons
³/₄ teaspoon	salt	1 teaspoon
1 teaspoon	active dry yeast or bread machine yeast	1¹/₄ teaspoons

PREP:
10 minutes

MAKES:
1½-pound recipe
(20 slices)
OR
2-pound recipe
(27 slices)

1 Select the loaf size. Add the ingredients to the machine according to the manufacturer's directions. If available, select the whole grain cycle, or select the basic white bread cycle.

Nutrition Facts per slice: 99 cal., 1 g total fat (0 g sat. fat), 1 mg chol., 113 mg sodium, 19 g carbo., 3 g pro.

Cornmeal Choices

Cornmeal—ground from dried corn kernels—is as regional as an accent. Southern cooks prefer white cornmeal for their famous breads and batters, while in Southwest kitchens blue cornmeal ground from New Mexico's blue corn is favored. Most elsewhere, yellow cornmeal is preferred, but all colors are interchangeable. Store cornmeal tightly covered up to one year in a cool, dry place.

Don't be surprised by the surprise ingredient in this bread. A jar of baby food lends convenience and flavor to this sweet potato loaf. Try deli meats tucked between a couple of slices.

Sweet Potato-Onion Bread

PREP:
15 minutes

MAKES:
1½-pound recipe
(16 slices)
OR
2-pound recipe
(22 slices)

1½-POUND	INGREDIENTS	2-POUND
1 (6-ounce) jar	sweet potato baby food*	1 (6-ounce) jar
⅓ cup	water	½ cup
⅓ cup	sliced green onions	½ cup
1 tablespoon	margarine or butter	4 teaspoons
3 cups	bread flour	4 cups
1 teaspoon	sugar	1¼ teaspoons
1 teaspoon	dried thyme, crushed,	1¼ teaspoons
	or	
1 tablespoon	snipped fresh thyme	4 teaspoons
¾ teaspoon	salt	1 teaspoon
1 teaspoon	active dry yeast	1¼ teaspoons
	or bread machine yeast	

1 Select the loaf size. Add the ingredients to the machine according to the manufacturer's directions. Select the basic white bread cycle.

Note: The Test Kitchen recommends one 6-ounce jar sweet potato baby food for either size recipe.

Nutrition Facts per slice: 107 cal., 1 g total fat (0 g sat. fat), 0 mg chol., 111 mg sodium, 20 g carbo., 3 g pro.

Imbued throughout with autumnal flavors, this warming loaf would be perfect for passing at Thanksgiving or at any meal featuring the hearty foods of the harvest.

Maple-Sweet Potato Bread

1½-POUND	INGREDIENTS	2-POUND
²/₃ cup	water	³/₄ cup
²/₃ cup	drained and mashed, canned sweet potatoes	³/₄ cup
1 tablespoon	pure maple syrup or maple-flavored syrup	4 teaspoons
1 tablespoon	margarine or butter	4 teaspoons
¼ teaspoon	maple flavoring*	¼ teaspoon
3 cups	bread flour	4 cups
³/₄ teaspoon	salt	1 teaspoon
½ teaspoon	apple pie spice	³/₄ teaspoon
1 teaspoon	active dry yeast or bread machine yeast	1¼ teaspoons
¼ cup	chopped pecans, toasted	¹/₃ cup

PREP:
15 minutes

MAKES:
1½-pound recipe
(16 slices)
OR
2-pound recipe
(22 slices)

1 Select the loaf size. Add the ingredients to the machine according to the manufacturer's directions. Select the basic white bread cycle.

*Note: The Test Kitchen recommends ¼ teaspoon maple flavoring for either size recipe.

Nutrition Facts per slice: 126 cal., 2 g total fat (0 g sat. fat), 0 mg chol., 126 mg sodium, 22 g carbo., 4 g pro.

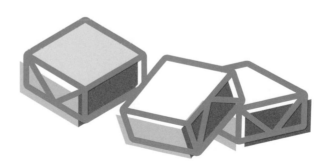

Go beyond the basics by spreading thick slices of this colorful veggie bread with Cheese Bread Spread (page 266) and toasting to golden perfection.

Carrot-Herb Bread

PREP:
15 minutes

MAKES:
1½-pound recipe
(16 slices)

1½-POUND	INGREDIENTS
1 cup	milk
1 cup	finely shredded carrots
2 tablespoons	honey
1 tablespoon	margarine or butter
2 cups	whole wheat flour
1 cup	bread flour
2 teaspoons	poppy seeds (optional)
³/₄ teaspoon	salt
³/₄ teaspoon	dried dill
³/₄ teaspoon	dried thyme, crushed
³/₄ teaspoon	dried parsley flakes
1 teaspoon	active dry yeast
	or bread machine yeast

① Add the ingredients to the machine according to manufacturer's directions, adding carrots with milk. If available, select the whole grain cycle, or select the basic white bread cycle.

Nutrition Facts per slice: 108 cal., 2 g total fat (0 g sat. fat), 2 mg chol., 119 mg sodium, 21 g carbo., 5 g pro.

Three simple ingredients—Parmesan cheese, pepperoni, and fennel seeds—turn ordinary bread into pizza! For a lunch with pizzazz, try it in your next grilled cheese sandwich.

Pepperoni Pizza Loaf

1½-POUND*	INGREDIENTS	2-POUND*
³/₄ cup	water	1 cup
¹/₂ cup	finely chopped pepperoni	³/₄ cup
¹/₄ cup	chopped green sweet pepper	¹/₃ cup
2 tablespoons	olive oil or cooking oil	3 tablespoons
1 tablespoon	tomato paste	2 tablespoons
3 cups	bread flour	4 cups
¹/₄ cup	grated Parmesan cheese	¹/₃ cup
2 teaspoons	sugar	1 tablespoon
1 teaspoon	fennel seeds, crushed	1½ teaspoons
¹/₂ teaspoon	salt	³/₄ teaspoon
1 teaspoon	active dry yeast	1¹/₄ teaspoons
	or bread machine yeast	

PREP:
15 minutes

MAKES:
1½-pound recipe
(16 slices)
OR
2-pound recipe
(22 slices)

1 Select the loaf size. Add the ingredients to the machine according to the manufacturer's directions. Select the basic white bread cycle. Store any leftover bread in the refrigerator.

*Note: For the 1½-pound loaf, the bread machine pan must have a capacity of 10 cups or more. For the 2-pound loaf, the bread machine pan must have a capacity of 12 cups or more.

Nutrition Facts per slice: 142 cal., 5 g total fat (1 g sat. fat), 7 mg chol., 188 mg sodium, 20 g carbo., 5 g pro.

Tomato Paste in a Tube

Stuck time after time with leftover canned tomato paste that goes to waste? Tomato paste in a screw-cap tube lets you squirt out a tablespoon or two—perfect for many recipes—and safely store the rest for next time. A tube of tomato paste keeps in the refrigerator for a couple of months.

Cilantro and refried beans fill this loaf with authentic Southwestern flavor. The result is a savory, protein-rich bread that pairs nicely with Mexican-style entrées.

Burrito Bread

PREP:
15 minutes

MAKES:
1½-pound recipe
(16 slices)
OR
2-pound recipe
(22 slices)

1½-POUND	INGREDIENTS	2-POUND
⅓ cup	chopped onion	½ cup
1 tablespoon	cooking oil	4 teaspoons
½ cup	milk	⅔ cup
⅓ cup	water	½ cup
⅓ cup	refried beans	½ cup
¼ cup	shredded cheddar cheese	⅓ cup
3 cups	bread flour	4 cups
2 tablespoons	snipped fresh cilantro	3 tablespoons
1 tablespoon	sugar	4 teaspoons
2 teaspoons	chili powder	1 tablespoon
½ teaspoon	salt	¾ teaspoon
1 teaspoon	active dry yeast	1¼ teaspoons
	or bread machine yeast	

❶ Select the loaf size. In a small saucepan cook the onion in hot oil until tender, stirring occasionally. Cool slightly.

❷ Add the onion mixture and the remaining ingredients to the machine according to the manufacturer's directions. Select the basic white bread cycle.

Nutrition Facts per slice: 123 cal., 2 g total fat (1 g sat. fat), 2 mg chol., 108 mg sodium, 21 g carbo., 4 g pro.

Studded throughout with flavors of Italy, this bread would be the perfect complement to a simple appetizer tray of marinated olives, roasted red peppers, and a big wedge of Parmigiano-Reggiano cheese.

Salami-Basil Bread

1½-POUND	INGREDIENTS	2-POUND
¾ cup	water	1 cup
1 cup	chopped salami	1⅓ cups
4 teaspoons	olive oil	2 tablespoons
1 tablespoon	tomato paste	2 tablespoons
3 cups	bread flour	4 cups
2 teaspoons	sugar	1 tablespoon
1 teaspoon	dried basil, crushed	1¾ teaspoons
¾ teaspoon	salt*	¾ teaspoon
1 teaspoon	active dry yeast	1¾ teaspoons
	or bread machine yeast	

PREP:
15 minutes

MAKES:
1½-pound recipe
(16 slices)
OR
2-pound recipe
(22 slices)

1 Select the loaf size. Add the ingredients to the machine according to the manufacturer's directions, adding the salami with the water. Select the basic white bread cycle. Store any leftover bread in the refrigerator.

*Note: The Test Kitchen recommends ¾ teaspoon salt for either size recipe.

Nutrition Facts per slice: 133 cal., 4 g total fat (1 g sat. fat), 7 mg chol., 203 mg sodium, 19 g carbo., 5 g pro.

Yeast Matters

Without yeast, breads would fall flat! Yeast produces a carbon dioxide gas that makes the dough rise. Here are a few facts about yeast and the rising process:
• Either active dry yeast or bread machine yeast can be used in the recipes in this book. However, we do not recommend using fast-rising yeast. This ingredient simply won't last through the bread machine process.
• Our recipes may call for less yeast than is used in many recipes supplied by bread machine manufacturers. In testing, we found our amounts made a nicely risen loaf with an attractive shape. Adding more yeast typically produces a loaf with a very coarse, uneven texture and may cause the dough to rise too high and then fall, or to stick to the lid of your machine.
• Store packages of yeast in a cool, dry place. Keep open jars of yeast tightly covered in the refrigerator. Check the expiration date on the package or jar label before using.

Dried tomatoes are now a bumper crop in supermarkets year-round. So even on winter's darkest days, you can make this appealing ring of tomatoey rolls, created to sop up a thick spaghetti sauce.

Dried Tomato Focaccia Ring

PREP: 35 minutes	1½-POUND	INGREDIENTS	2-POUND
	4	dried tomatoes (not oil-packed)	6
		Boiling water	
RISE: 30 minutes	¾ cup	water	1 cup
	¼ cup	olive oil or cooking oil	⅓ cup
BAKE: 20 minutes	3 cups	bread flour	4 cups
	1 teaspoon	sugar	1½ teaspoons
MAKES:	¾ teaspoon	salt	1 teaspoon
1½-pound recipe (12 servings)	¾ teaspoon	dried rosemary, crushed,	1 teaspoon
OR		or	
2-pound recipe (16 servings)	2 teaspoons	snipped fresh rosemary	1 tablespoon
	1 teaspoon	active dry yeast	1¼ teaspoons
		or bread machine yeast	
	1	slightly beaten egg white	1
	2 tablespoons	grated Parmesan cheese	3 tablespoons
		Spaghetti sauce, warmed	
		(optional)	

1 Select the recipe size. Place the dried tomatoes in a small bowl; add enough boiling water to cover. Let stand for 10 minutes. Drain well; pat dry with paper towels. Snip tomatoes.

2 Add the tomatoes and the next 7 ingredients to the machine according to the manufacturer's directions. Select the dough cycle. When cycle is complete, remove dough. Punch down. Cover and let rest for 10 minutes.

3 Meanwhile, grease the outside of a 6-ounce custard cup. Place custard cup, upside down, on a greased baking sheet.

4 Divide the 1½-pound dough into 24 portions (divide the 2-pound dough into 32 portions). Using lightly floured hands, shape each portion into a smooth ball. Place the balls of dough, about ½ inch apart, in rings around the custard cup. Brush dough with egg white; sprinkle with Parmesan cheese. Cover and let rise in a warm place for 30 to 45 minutes or until nearly double.

5 Bake in a 375°F oven for 20 to 25 minutes or until golden brown. Cool on baking sheet for 10 minutes; remove cup. Remove bread from baking sheet; cool slightly on a wire rack. Serve warm. If desired, serve with spaghetti sauce.

Nutrition Facts per serving: 174 cal., 5 g total fat (1 g sat. fat), 1 mg chol., 159 mg sodium, 26 g carbo., 5 g pro.

These sausage- and egg-filled mini loaves make wonderful brunch features because you can assemble them the night before and bake them in the morning.

Brunch Braids

1¹/₂-POUND	I N G R E D I E N T S	2-POUND
¹/₂ cup	milk	²/₃ cup
¹/₄ cup	water	¹/₃ cup
1	egg*	1
2 tablespoons	margarine or butter, cut up	3 tablespoons
3 cups	bread flour	4 cups
3 tablespoons	sugar	¹/₄ cup
³/₄ teaspoon	salt	1 teaspoon
1¹/₄ teaspoons	active dry yeast	1¹/₂ teaspoons
	or bread machine yeast	
6 ounces	spicy bulk pork sausage	8 ounces
6	eggs	8
3 tablespoons	milk	¹/₄ cup
¹/₄ teaspoon	salt*	¹/₄ teaspoon
¹/₈ teaspoon	black pepper*	¹/₈ teaspoon

PREP:
30 minutes

RISE:
15 minutes

BAKE:
15 minutes

MAKES:
1¹/₂-pound recipe
(6 servings)
OR
2-pound recipe
(8 servings)

1 Select the recipe size. Add the first 8 ingredients to the machine according to the manufacturer's directions. Select the dough cycle. When cycle is complete, remove dough. Punch down. Cover and let rest for 10 minutes. Grease baking sheets; set aside.

2 Meanwhile, for filling, in a large skillet cook sausage until done; drain off fat. Beat together the 6 or 8 eggs, 3 tablespoons or ¹/₄ cup milk, ¹/₄ teaspoon salt, and pepper; add to skillet. Cook over medium heat, without stirring, until mixture begins to set on bottom and around edges. Lift and fold partially cooked eggs so the uncooked portion flows underneath. Continue cooking until eggs are cooked through, but are still glossy and moist. Remove.

3 *For the 1¹/₂-pound recipe:* On a lightly floured surface, roll the dough into an 18×16-inch rectangle. Cut into six 8×6-inch rectangles. Transfer to the prepared baking sheets. Spoon about ¹/₃ cup filling down the center of each rectangle. On the long sides, make 2-inch cuts from the edges toward the center at 1-inch intervals. Alternately fold opposite strips of dough, at an angle, across filling. Lightly press ends in center together to seal. Cover and let rise in a warm place about 15 minutes or until nearly double. Bake in a 350°F oven about 15 minutes or until golden brown. Remove from baking sheets; cool slightly on wire racks. Serve warm.

For the 2-pound recipe: Prepare and shape as above, except roll the dough into a 24×16-inch rectangle; cut into eight 8×6-inch rectangles.

*Note: The Test Kitchen recommends 1 egg for either size dough and ¹/₄ teaspoon salt and ¹/₈ teaspoon black pepper for either size filling.

Nutrition Facts per serving: 458 cal., 15 g total fat (4 g sat. fat), 262 mg chol., 659 mg sodium, 59 g carbo., 19 g pro.

Love smoked Gouda? Love fennel? See how they taste together in a bread! With your bread machine and this master recipe, you can easily invent your own one-of-a-kind recipe using some of your favorite savory flavors. Just follow these guidelines for the procedures and proportions.

Basic Savory Bread

1½-POUND	INGREDIENTS
1 cup	milk
3 tablespoons	water
1 tablespoon	margarine, butter, shortening, or cooking oil
3 cups	bread flour
	or
	2 cups bread flour plus 1 cup whole wheat flour
4 teaspoons	sugar or honey
¾ teaspoon	salt
1 teaspoon	active dry yeast
	or bread machine yeast

1 Select one or more of the Seasoning Options. Add the ingredients to the machine according to the manufacturer's directions. Select the basic white bread cycle, or if using whole wheat flour, select the whole grain cycle, if available.

Seasoning Options:
• ¾ teaspoon dried basil, thyme, or sage, crushed; or 1 tablespoon snipped fresh basil, thyme, or sage
• 2 tablespoons snipped dried tomatoes (not oil-packed) or dried cranberries, currants, or dark raisins *(Note:* Do not use dried apricots or other dried fruit treated with sulfur.)
• 1 teaspoon anise, cumin, dill, fennel, or caraway seeds, toasted
• ⅔ cup mashed, cooked sweet potato or winter squash, or canned pumpkin. *Note:* Omit milk and increase water to ⅔ cup
• 1 cup shredded Swiss, smoked cheddar, smoked Gouda, or Monterey Jack cheese with jalapeño peppers *(Note:* Reduce milk to ⅔ cup and add 1 egg.)
• ¼ cup chopped pecans, walnuts, macadamia nuts, or almonds

SOURDOUGH FAVORITES

A pleasantly pungent mixture of flour, liquid, yeast, and sugar ferments to create what's called starter. A portion is used to leaven bread, lending a "sour" flavor, and then replenished for future use.

Sourdough Starter

	AMOUNT	I N G R E D I E N T S
PREP: 10 minutes	1¹/₂ teaspoons	active dry yeast
		or bread machine yeast
STAND: 5 days	³/₄ cup	warm water (105°F to 115°F)
	3 cups	warm water (105°F to 115°F)
MAKES: 4 cups	3 cups	all-purpose flour
	4 teaspoons	granulated sugar
		or brown sugar

1 *To make the starter:* In a large mixing bowl dissolve the yeast in the ³/₄ cup warm water. Add the 3 cups warm water; stir in flour and sugar. Beat with an electric mixer on medium speed just until smooth.

2 Cover with 100-percent-cotton cheesecloth. Let stand at room temperature (70°F to 80°F) for 5 to 10 days or until mixture has a sour, fermented aroma, stirring two or three times every day. (The fermentation time depends upon the room temperature. A warmer room speeds the fermentation process.) When the mixture has fermented, transfer to a 2-quart or larger plastic container with a tight-fitting lid. Refrigerate the starter until needed.

3 *To use the starter:* Remove the starter from the refrigerator and stir thoroughly. Measure the amount needed and bring it to room temperature before using. (The cold starter should be the consistency of buttermilk or thin pancake batter. If necessary, add water to thin the starter after it is stirred and before it is measured.)

4 For each cup of starter used, replenish remaining starter by stirring in ³/₄ cup all-purpose flour, ³/₄ cup water, and 1 teaspoon granulated sugar or brown sugar. Cover and let mixture stand at room temperature at least 1 day or until bubbly. Refrigerate starter for later use.

5 If you have not used the starter within 10 days, stir in 1 teaspoon granulated sugar or brown sugar. Repeat every 10 days unless starter is replenished.

Like a seed, sourdough starter needs time to grow. This version uses rye flour, giving it a different flavor than the plain starter (opposite). Use it in Pumpernickel Sourdough Bread (page 127).

Rye Sourdough Starter

AMOUNT	INGREDIENTS
2¼ teaspoons	active dry yeast
	or bread machine yeast
½ cup	warm water (105°F to 115°F)
2 cups	warm water (105°F to 115°F)
2 cups	rye flour
1 tablespoon	sugar or honey

PREP:
10 minutes

STAND:
5 days

MAKES:
2½ cups

1 *To make the starter:* In a medium mixing bowl dissolve the yeast in the ½ cup warm water. Add the 2 cups warm water; stir in rye flour and sugar. Beat with an electric mixer on medium speed just until smooth.

2 Cover with 100-percent-cotton cheesecloth. Let stand at room temperature (70°F to 80°F) for 5 to 10 days or until mixture has a sour, fermented aroma, stirring two or three times every day. (The fermentation time depends upon the room temperature. A warmer room speeds the fermentation process.) When the mixture has fermented, transfer to a jar and cover with 100-percent-cotton cheesecloth (do not cover tightly or use a metal lid). Refrigerate the starter until needed.

3 *To use the starter:* Remove the starter from the refrigerator and stir thoroughly. Measure the amount needed and bring it to room temperature before using. (The cold starter should be the consistency of buttermilk or thin pancake batter. If necessary, add water to thin the starter after it is stirred and before it is measured.)

4 For each cup of starter used, replenish the remaining starter by stirring in 1 cup water, ¾ cup rye flour, and 1 teaspoon sugar or honey. Cover and let mixture stand at room temperature at least 1 day or until bubbly. Refrigerate starter for later use.

5 If you have not used the starter within 10 days, stir in 1 teaspoon sugar or honey. Repeat every 10 days unless starter is replenished.

San Francisco's reputation for making superior sourdough harkens back to days of the California gold rush, when the city's bakers staked their reputation on their exceptional versions. A batch of this bread will give you bragging rights too.

San Francisco-Style Sourdough Bread

	1½-POUND	INGREDIENTS
PREP: 20 minutes	1¼ cups	Sourdough Starter (page 106)
	2 tablespoons	milk
RISE: 30 minutes	3 cups	bread flour
	1 tablespoon	sugar
BAKE: 20 minutes	¾ teaspoon	salt
	1 teaspoon	active dry yeast
MAKES: 1½-pound recipe (20 slices)		or bread machine yeast
		Yellow cornmeal

1 Add the ingredients, except the cornmeal, to the machine according to the manufacturer's directions. Select the dough cycle. When cycle is complete, remove dough. Punch down. Cover and let rest for 10 minutes. Lightly grease a baking sheet and sprinkle with cornmeal; set baking sheet aside.

2 On a lightly floured surface, shape the dough into a ball. Place on the prepared baking sheet. Flatten slightly to an 8-inch round loaf.

3 Using a sharp knife, make several cuts about ¼ inch deep across top of loaf. Cover and let rise in a warm place for 30 to 45 minutes or until nearly double. Lightly brush top with water.

4 Bake in a 400°F oven for 20 to 30 minutes or until bread sounds hollow when lightly tapped. Remove from baking sheet; cool on a wire rack.

Nutrition Facts per slice: 102 cal., 0 g total fat (0 g sat. fat), 0 mg chol., 82 mg sodium, 21 g carbo., 3 g pro.

Classic French bread is reinvented using tangy sourdough flavor. Brush the unbaked loaf with a mixture of egg white and water for a beautiful, shiny golden finish.

Sourdough French Bread

1½-POUND	INGREDIENTS	2-POUND
1¼ cups	Sourdough Starter (page 106)	1¾ cups
2 tablespoons	water	¼ cup
3 cups	bread flour	4 cups
¾ teaspoon	salt	1 teaspoon
1 teaspoon	active dry yeast	1¼ teaspoons
	or bread machine yeast	
	Yellow cornmeal	
1	slightly beaten egg white	1
1 tablespoon	water	1 tablespoon

PREP:
25 minutes

RISE:
35 minutes

BAKE:
35 minutes

MAKES:
1½-pound recipe
(16 slices)
OR
2-pound recipe
(22 slices)

1 Select the loaf size. Add the first 5 ingredients to the machine according to the manufacturer's directions. Select the dough cycle. When cycle is complete, remove dough. Punch down. Cover and let rest for 10 minutes. Lightly grease a baking sheet and sprinkle with cornmeal; set aside.

2 On a lightly floured surface, roll the 1½-pound dough into a 12×8-inch rectangle (roll the 2-pound dough into a 15×10-inch rectangle). Starting from a long side, roll up into a spiral; seal edge. Pinch and pull ends to taper. Place loaf, seam side down, on the prepared baking sheet. In a small bowl combine egg white and the 1 tablespoon water; brush some of the mixture over top of loaf.

3 Cover and let rise in a warm place for 35 to 45 minutes or until nearly double. Using a sharp knife, make 3 to 5 diagonal cuts about ¼ inch deep across top of loaf.

4 Bake in a 375°F oven for 20 minutes. Brush with the remaining egg white mixture. Bake for 15 to 20 minutes more or until bread sounds hollow when lightly tapped. Remove from baking sheet; cool on a wire rack.

Nutrition Facts per slice: 125 cal., 1 g total fat (0 g sat. fat), 0 mg chol., 105 mg sodium, 25 g carbo., 4 g pro.

With whole wheat flour and wheat germ added for good measure, this bread will fit the bill for those who only turn to hearty, textural loaves for their daily bread.

Sourdough Wheat Bread

PREP:	1½-POUND*	INGREDIENTS	2-POUND*
10 minutes	1¼ cups	Sourdough Starter (page 106)	1½ cups
	¼ cup	milk or water	⅔ cup
MAKES:	1 tablespoon	cooking oil	2 tablespoons
1½-pound recipe (16 slices)	2 cups	whole wheat flour	2⅓ cups
OR	1 cup	bread flour	1⅓ cups
2-pound recipe (22 slices)	¼ cup	toasted wheat germ	⅓ cup
	2 tablespoons	gluten flour**	2 tablespoons
	1 tablespoon	brown sugar	4 teaspoons
	¾ teaspoon	salt	1 teaspoon
	1 teaspoon	active dry yeast	1½ teaspoons
		or bread machine yeast	

1 Select the loaf size. Add the ingredients to the machine according to the manufacturer's directions. If available, select the whole grain cycle, or select the basic white bread cycle.

*Note: For the 1½-pound loaf, the bread machine pan must have a capacity of 10 cups or more. For the 2-pound loaf, the bread machine pan must have a capacity of 12 cups or more.

**Note: The Test Kitchen recommends 2 tablespoons gluten flour for either size recipe.

Nutrition Facts per slice: 134 cal., 2 g total fat (0 g sat. fat), 0 mg chol., 104 mg sodium, 25 g carbo., 5 g pro.

This distinctive sourdough bread captures two of the flavors of classic Italian cuisine—roasted garlic and rosemary.

Rustic Italian Bread

1½-POUND	INGREDIENTS	2-POUND
1 teaspoon	active dry yeast	1¼ teaspoons
	or bread machine yeast	
⅓ cup	warm water (105°F to 115°F)	½ cup
¾ cup	bread flour	1 cup
¼ cup	milk	⅓ cup
1 teaspoon	sugar	1½ teaspoons
⅓ cup	water	½ cup
4 teaspoons	olive oil	2 tablespoons
1 teaspoon	bottled minced roasted garlic	1½ teaspoons
2¼ cups	bread flour	3½ cups
¾ teaspoon	salt	1 teaspoon
¾ teaspoon	dried rosemary, crushed	1 teaspoon
	Yellow cornmeal	
1½ teaspoons	bread flour	2 teaspoons

PREP: 25 minutes

STAND: 24 hours

RISE: 30 minutes

BAKE: 25 minutes

MAKES: 1½-pound recipe (16 slices) OR 2-pound recipe (22 slices)

1 *To make the starter:* Select the recipe size. In a medium bowl dissolve the yeast in the ⅓ or ½ cup warm water. Stir in the ¾ or 1 cup bread flour, milk, and sugar. Beat with a wire whisk or rotary beater just until smooth. Cover with plastic wrap. Let stand at room temperature (70°F to 80°F) about 24 hours or until mixture has a slightly fermented aroma, stirring two or three times. (Or refrigerate up to 4 days.)

2 *To finish the bread:* Add the starter and the next 6 ingredients to the machine according to the manufacturer's directions. Select the dough cycle. When cycle is complete, remove dough. Punch down. Cover and let rest for 10 minutes. Lightly grease a baking sheet and sprinkle with cornmeal; set aside.

3 *For the 1½-pound recipe:* On a lightly floured surface, shape the dough into a ball. Place on the prepared baking sheet. Flatten slightly to an 8-inch round loaf. Lightly rub top with the 1½ teaspoons bread flour. Using a sharp knife, make several cuts about ¼ inch deep across top of loaf. Cover and let rise in a warm place for 30 to 35 minutes or until nearly double.

4 Bake in a 400°F oven about 25 minutes or until bread sounds hollow when lightly tapped. Remove from baking sheet; cool on a wire rack.

For the 2-pound recipe: Prepare as above, except divide dough in half. Shape each portion into a 6-inch round loaf. Continue as above, rubbing tops with the 2 teaspoons bread flour.

Nutrition Facts per slice: 109 cal., 2 g total fat (0 g sat. fat), 0 mg chol., 103 mg sodium, 20 g carbo., 3 g pro.

A toasted oat flavor and tuggy texture are the hallmarks of this tangy sourdough loaf.

Oatmeal Sourdough Bread

PREP:
25 minutes

MAKES:
1½-pound recipe
(16 slices)

1½-POUND*	INGREDIENTS
⅓ cup	regular or quick-cooking rolled oats
¾ cup	Sourdough Starter (page 106)
¾ cup	milk
4 teaspoons	margarine or butter
3 cups	bread flour
1 tablespoon	sugar
¾ teaspoon	salt
1 teaspoon	active dry yeast or bread machine yeast

1 Spread the rolled oats in a shallow baking pan. Bake in a 350°F oven for 15 to 20 minutes or until light brown, stirring occasionally. Cool slightly.

2 Add the ingredients to the machine according to the manufacturer's directions, adding the oats with the flour. Select the basic white bread cycle.

*Note: The bread machine pan must have a capacity of 10 cups or more.

Nutrition Facts per slice: 140 cal., 2 g total fat (0 g sat. fat), 2 mg chol., 119 mg sodium, 26 g carbo., 5 g pro.

The sharp flavors of robust sourdough bread blend well with the aromatic flavors of three members of the onion family—leeks, onions, and shallots.

Triple Onion Sourdough Bread

1½-POUND*	INGREDIENTS	2-POUND*
⅓ cup	sliced leek or green onions	½ cup
¼ cup	chopped onion	⅓ cup
1 tablespoon	chopped shallot	2 tablespoons
2 tablespoons	olive oil or cooking oil	3 tablespoons
1¼ cups	Sourdough Starter (page 106)	1½ cups
¼ cup	water	⅓ cup
3 cups	bread flour	4 cups
¾ teaspoon	salt	1 teaspoon
½ teaspoon	sugar	¾ teaspoon
1 teaspoon	active dry yeast	1¼ teaspoons
	or bread machine yeast	

PREP:
20 minutes

MAKES:
1½-pound recipe
(18 slices)
OR
2-pound recipe
(24 slices)

1 Select the loaf size. In a small saucepan cook the leek, onion, and shallot in hot oil until tender, stirring occasionally. Cool slightly.

2 Add the leek mixture and the remaining ingredients to the machine according to the manufacturer's directions. Select the basic white bread cycle.

*Note: For the 1½-pound loaf, the bread machine pan must have a capacity of 10 cups or more. For the 2-pound loaf, the bread machine pan must have a capacity of 12 cups or more.

Nutrition Facts per slice: 125 cal., 2 g total fat (0 g sat. fat), 0 mg chol., 91 mg sodium, 23 g carbo., 4 g pro.

Dill, onion, and garlic meld deliciously with the tang of the sourdough starter in this unbeatable loaf.

Dill and Onion Sourdough Bread

PREP:
20 minutes

MAKES:
1½-pound recipe
(16 slices)

1½-POUND*	INGREDIENTS
1 cup	chopped onion
1 clove	garlic, minced
2 tablespoons	olive oil or cooking oil
1¼ cups	Sourdough Starter (page 106)
2 tablespoons	milk or water
3 cups	bread flour
1 tablespoon	sugar
¾ teaspoon	salt
¾ teaspoon	dried dill
1 teaspoon	active dry yeast
	or bread machine yeast

1 In a medium skillet cook the onion and garlic in hot oil until onion is tender, stirring occasionally. Cool slightly.

2 Add the onion mixture and the remaining ingredients to the machine according to the manufacturer's directions. Select the basic white bread cycle.

*Note: The bread machine pan must have a capacity of 10 cups or more.

Nutrition Facts per slice: 141 cal., 2 g total fat (0 g sat. fat), 0 mg chol., 105 mg sodium, 27 g carbo., 5 g pro.

> **Minimizing Teary Eyes**
>
> It's the volatile oils released when you cut an onion—whether it's a leek, green onion, yellow onion, or shallot—that make you teary. You can minimize this unpleasant effect by using a sharp knife (always a good idea). A dull knife mashes more than it cuts, sending irritating vapors into the air and into your eyes, while a sharp knife makes quick, clean cuts.

This recipe fulfills all the requirements of a great bread—it's flavorful, high-rising, and golden. Tarragon gives it a Gallic connection, as the long-leaf herb is a favorite in French cooking.

Tarragon Sourdough Bread

1½-POUND*	INGREDIENTS	2-POUND*
¾ cup	Sourdough Starter (page 106)	1 cup
¾ cup	cream-style cottage cheese	1 cup
1	egg**	1
2 tablespoons	water	3 tablespoons
2 tablespoons	margarine or butter, cut up	3 tablespoons
3 cups	bread flour	4 cups
2 teaspoons	sugar	1 tablespoon
1¼ teaspoons	dried tarragon, crushed,	1½ teaspoons
	or	
4 teaspoons	snipped fresh tarragon	2 tablespoons
¾ teaspoon	salt	1 teaspoon
1 teaspoon	active dry yeast	1¼ teaspoons
	or bread machine yeast	

PREP:
10 minutes

MAKES:
1½-pound recipe
(18 slices)
OR
2-pound recipe
(24 slices)

1 Select the loaf size. Add the ingredients to the machine according to the manufacturer's directions. Select the basic white bread cycle.

*Note: For the 1½-pound loaf, the bread machine pan must have a capacity of 10 cups or more. For the 2-pound loaf, the bread machine pan must have a capacity of 12 cups or more.

**Note: The Test Kitchen recommends 1 egg for either size recipe.

Nutrition Facts per slice: 125 cal., 2 g total fat (1 g sat. fat), 13 mg chol., 144 mg sodium, 21 g carbo., 5 g pro.

One bite and you'll be hooked on this delicious combination of tangy sourdough and honey. It's a great basic bread for any use.

Cornmeal Sourdough Loaf

PREP:
10 minutes

MAKES:
1½-pound recipe
(16 slices)
OR
2-pound recipe
(22 slices)

1½-POUND*	INGREDIENTS	2-POUND*
1¼ cups	Sourdough Starter (page 106)	1⅔ cups
½ cup	milk	⅔ cup
2 tablespoons	honey	3 tablespoons
2 tablespoons	margarine or butter, cut up	3 tablespoons
2½ cups	bread flour	3⅓ cups
½ cup	cracked wheat	⅔ cup
½ cup	cornmeal	⅔ cup
2 tablespoons	gluten flour**	2 tablespoons
¾ teaspoon	salt	1 teaspoon
1¼ teaspoons	active dry yeast	1½ teaspoons
	or bread machine yeast	

1 Select the loaf size. Add the ingredients to the machine according to the manufacturer's directions. If available, select the whole grain cycle, or select the basic white bread cycle.

*Note: For the 1½-pound loaf, the bread machine pan must have a capacity of 10 cups or more. For the 2-pound loaf, the bread machine pan must have a capacity of 12 cups or more.

**Note: The Test Kitchen recommends 2 tablespoons gluten flour for either size recipe.

Nutrition Facts per slice: 161 cal., 2 g total fat (0 g sat. fat), 1 mg chol., 122 mg sodium, 30 g carbo., 5 g pro.

This cheese-laced sourdough has an unmistakable garlic flavor and is guaranteed to become a family favorite. It's good on its own or with our Pesto-Cream Cheese Spread (page 265).

Garlic Sourdough Bread

1$^1/_2$-POUND*	INGREDIENTS	2-POUND*
1$^1/_4$ cups	Sourdough Starter (page 106)	1$^1/_2$ cups
2 tablespoons	milk	$^1/_2$ cup
1 tablespoon	cooking oil	2 tablespoons
1 tablespoon	honey**	1 tablespoon
2 cloves	garlic, minced	3 cloves
3 cups	bread flour	4 cups
$^1/_2$ cup	grated Parmesan cheese	$^2/_3$ cup
$^3/_4$ teaspoon	salt	1 teaspoon
1 teaspoon	active dry yeast	1$^1/_2$ teaspoons
	or bread machine yeast	

PREP:
10 minutes

MAKES:
1$^1/_2$-pound recipe
(20 slices)
OR
2-pound recipe
(27 slices)

1 Select the loaf size. Add the ingredients to the machine according to the manufacturer's directions. Select the basic white bread cycle.

*Note: For the 1$^1/_2$-pound loaf, the bread machine pan must have a capacity of 10 cups or more. For the 2-pound loaf, the bread machine pan must have a capacity of 12 cups or more.

**Note: The Test Kitchen recommends 1 tablespoon honey for either size recipe.

Nutrition Facts per slice: 119 cal., 2 g total fat (1 g sat. fat), 2 mg chol., 128 mg sodium, 21 g carbo., 4 g pro.

Mincing Garlic

Most recipes call for minced garlic cloves—the tear-shape segments that form a bulb of garlic. A stainless-steel garlic press will do the job, or you can mince cloves with a knife. Smash the clove lightly with the flat side of the knife to loosen the papery skin. Peel, then chop or mince as needed.

This tangy, tomato-studded bread, seasoned with fragrant tarragon, partners perfectly with a warming bowl of beefy vegetable soup.

Sourdough Bread with Dried Tomatoes

PREP:
10 minutes

MAKES:
1½-pound recipe
(16 slices)

1½-POUND*	INGREDIENTS
1¼ cups	Sourdough Starter (page 106)
⅓ cup	drained and snipped, oil-packed dried tomatoes
2 tablespoons	milk or water
1 tablespoon	cooking oil
3 cups	bread flour
1 tablespoon	sugar
¾ teaspoon	salt
¾ teaspoon	dried tarragon, crushed
1 teaspoon	active dry yeast or bread machine yeast

1 Add the ingredients to the machine according to the manufacturer's directions. Select the basic white bread cycle.

*Note: The bread machine pan must have a capacity of 10 cups or more.

Nutrition Facts per slice: 141 cal., 2 g total fat (0 g sat. fat), 0 mg chol., 111 mg sodium, 26 g carbo., 5 g pro.

The blend of olive oil, pimiento-stuffed green olives, and oregano produces a memorable bread. Even a bologna sandwich will take on a fresh personality with this loaf.

Olive Sourdough Bread

1½-POUND*	INGREDIENTS	2-POUND*
1¼ cups	Sourdough Starter (page 106)	1¾ cups
½ cup	chopped pimiento-stuffed green olives	⅔ cup
¼ cup	water	⅓ cup
1 tablespoon	olive oil	2 tablespoons
3 cups	bread flour	4 cups
1 tablespoon	sugar	4 teaspoons
¾ teaspoon	salt	1 teaspoon
¾ teaspoon	dried oregano, crushed, or	1 teaspoon
2 teaspoons	snipped fresh oregano	1 tablespoon
1 teaspoon	active dry yeast or bread machine yeast	1¼ teaspoons

PREP:
15 minutes

MAKES:
1½-pound recipe
(16 slices)
OR
2-pound recipe
(22 slices)

1 Select the loaf size. Add the ingredients to the machine according to the manufacturer's directions. Select the basic white bread cycle.

*Note: For the 1½-pound loaf, the bread machine pan must have a capacity of 10 cups or more. For the 2-pound loaf, the bread machine pan must have a capacity of 12 cups or more.

Nutrition Facts per slice: 138 cal., 2 g total fat (0 g sat. fat), 0 mg chol., 212 mg sodium, 26 g carbo., 4 g pro.

This light, even-textured loaf boasts a delightfully bold flavor that will complement a variety of foods. For example, dry and cube slices to jump-start your favorite bread stuffing.

Beer Sourdough Bread

PREP:
15 minutes

STAND:
12 hours

MAKES:
1½-pound recipe (24 slices)
OR
2-pound recipe (32 slices)

1½-POUND*	INGREDIENTS	2-POUND*
1 teaspoon	active dry yeast	1 teaspoon
	or bread machine yeast**	
¾ cup	beer	1 cup
1 cup	bread flour	1⅓ cups
4 teaspoons	brown sugar	2 tablespoons
⅓ cup	milk	½ cup
1	egg**	1
4 teaspoons	olive oil or cooking oil	2 tablespoons
2 cups	bread flour	2⅔ cups
¾ teaspoon	salt	1 teaspoon
1 teaspoon	active dry yeast	1¼ teaspoons
	or bread machine yeast	

❶ *To make the starter:* Select the loaf size. In a medium bowl dissolve 1 teaspoon yeast in the beer. Stir in the 1 or 1 ⅓ cups bread flour and brown sugar. Beat with a wire whisk or rotary beater just until smooth. Cover with plastic wrap. Let stand at room temperature (70°F to 80°F) for 12 to 24 hours or until mixture has a slightly fermented aroma, stirring two or three times.

❷ *To finish the bread:* Add the starter and the remaining ingredients to the machine according to the manufacturer's directions. Select the basic white bread cycle.

*Note: For the 1½-pound loaf, the bread machine pan must have a capacity of 10 cups or more. For the 2-pound loaf, the bread machine pan must have a capacity of 12 cups or more.

**Note: The Test Kitchen recommends 1 teaspoon yeast for either size starter and 1 egg for either size dough.

Nutrition Facts per slice: 80 cal., 1 g total fat (0 g sat. fat), 9 mg chol., 72 mg sodium, 14 g carbo., 3 g pro.

The sharp flavors of cracked black pepper and Parmesan cheese complement this loaf's tangy sourdough taste.

Pepper-Parmesan Sourdough Bread

1½-POUND*	INGREDIENTS	2-POUND*
1 cup	Sourdough Starter (page 106)	1⅓ cups
½ cup	water	⅔ cup
1 tablespoon	margarine or butter	4 teaspoons
2½ cups	bread flour	3⅓ cups
½ cup	whole wheat flour	⅔ cup
⅓ cup	grated Parmesan cheese	½ cup
¾ teaspoon	salt	1 teaspoon
¾ teaspoon	cracked black pepper	1 teaspoon
1 teaspoon	active dry yeast	1 teaspoon
	or bread machine yeast**	

PREP:
10 minutes

MAKES:
1½-pound recipe
(20 slices)
OR
2-pound recipe
(27 slices)

1 Select the loaf size. Add the ingredients to the machine according to the manufacturer's directions. If available, select the whole grain cycle, or select the basic white bread cycle.

*Note: For the 1½-pound loaf, the bread machine pan must have a capacity of 10 cups or more. For the 2-pound loaf, the bread machine pan must have a capacity of 12 cups or more.

**Note: The Test Kitchen recommends 1 teaspoon yeast for either size recipe.

Nutrition Facts per slice: 104 cal., 1 g total fat (0 g sat. fat), 1 mg chol., 119 mg sodium, 19 g carbo., 4 g pro.

If the Gold Rush '49ers—famous for sourdough bread—had stopped in Texas first, they may never have moved farther west. This slightly spicy cheese bread is as good as gold (well, almost).

Tex-Mex Sourdough Bread

PREP:	1½-POUND*	INGREDIENTS	2-POUND*
15 minutes	¾ cup	Sourdough Starter (page 106)	1 cup
	1 cup	shredded Monterey Jack cheese	1⅓ cups
MAKES:		with jalapeño peppers	
1½-pound recipe (16 slices)	⅓ cup	water	½ cup
OR	2 tablespoons	drained and chopped,	3 tablespoons
2-pound recipe (22 slices)		bottled roasted red sweet peppers	
	1 tablespoon	margarine or butter	4 teaspoons
	2⅔ cups	bread flour	3½ cups
	⅓ cup	cornmeal	½ cup
	2 teaspoons	sugar	1 tablespoon
	½ teaspoon	salt	¾ teaspoon
	½ teaspoon	chili powder	¾ teaspoon
	1 teaspoon	active dry yeast	1¼ teaspoons
		or bread machine yeast	

1 Select the loaf size. Add the ingredients to the machine according to the manufacturer's directions, adding the cheese with the starter. Select the basic white bread cycle.

*Note: For the 1½-pound loaf, the bread machine pan must have a capacity of 10 cups or more. For the 2-pound loaf, the bread machine pan must have a capacity of 12 cups or more.

Nutrition Facts per slice: 146 cal., 3 g total fat (2 g sat. fat), 6 mg chol., 115 mg sodium, 23 g carbo., 5 g pro.

Cheese History

There really was a Monterey Jack—David Jacks, a 19th-century cheesemaker who lived in Monterey, along California's central coast. His mild cheese took inspiration from similar ones made by the local missionary fathers. Today Jack cheese is sold plain and in flavors such as pepper Jack, with jalapeño peppers; dill; and garlic.

Colorful yellow corn and green broccoli brighten this savory sourdough loaf. Enjoy slices with Herbed Feta Spread (page 265) and fresh garden salads.

Broccoli-Corn Sourdough Bread

1½-POUND*	INGREDIENTS	2-POUND*
½ cup	finely chopped broccoli**	½ cup
⅓ cup	frozen whole kernel corn**	⅓ cup
2 tablespoons	finely chopped onion**	2 tablespoons
2 tablespoons	cooking oil**	2 tablespoons
1 cup	Sourdough Starter (page 106)	1⅓ cups
¼ cup	water	⅓ cup
3 cups	bread flour	4 cups
1 tablespoon	sugar	4 teaspoons
¾ teaspoon	salt	1 teaspoon
¼ teaspoon	ground sage	½ teaspoon
1 teaspoon	active dry yeast	1 teaspoon
	or bread machine yeast**	

PREP:
15 minutes

MAKES:
1½-pound recipe
(18 slices)
OR
2-pound recipe
(24 slices)

1 Select the loaf size. In a small saucepan cook the broccoli, corn, and onion in hot oil for 2 to 3 minutes or until tender, stirring occasionally. Cool slightly.

2 Add the vegetable mixture and the remaining ingredients to the machine according to the manufacturer's directions. Select the basic white bread cycle.

*Note: For the 1½-pound loaf, the bread machine pan must have a capacity of 10 cups or more. For the 2-pound loaf, the bread machine pan must have a capacity of 12 cups or more.

**Note: The Test Kitchen recommends ½ cup broccoli, ⅓ cup corn, 2 tablespoons onion, 2 tablespoons oil, and 1 teaspoon yeast for either size recipe.

Nutrition Facts per slice: 123 cal., 2 g total fat (0 g sat. fat), 0 mg chol., 91 mg sodium, 22 g carbo., 4 g pro.

Pesto and Parmesan provide the perfect pairing of flavors to enhance this sourdough bread. Serve it with a full-bodied Merlot to experience a taste of life's simple pleasures.

Pesto Sourdough Loaf

PREP:
10 minutes

MAKES:
1½-pound recipe
(16 slices)
OR
2-pound recipe
(22 slices)

1½-POUND*	INGREDIENTS	2-POUND*
1 cup	Sourdough Starter (page 106)	1⅓ cups
¼ cup	water	⅓ cup
3 tablespoons	purchased pesto	¼ cup
3 cups	bread flour	4 cups
¼ cup	grated Parmesan cheese	⅓ cup
¾ teaspoon	salt	1 teaspoon
⅛ teaspoon	cracked black pepper	¼ teaspoon
1 teaspoon	active dry yeast	1¼ teaspoons
	or bread machine yeast	

1 Select the loaf size. Add the ingredients to the machine according to the manufacturer's directions. Select the basic white bread cycle.

*Note: For the 1½-pound loaf, the bread machine pan must have a capacity of 10 cups or more. For the 2-pound loaf, the bread machine pan must have a capacity of 12 cups or more.

Nutrition Facts per slice: 144 cal., 3 g total fat (0 g sat. fat), 2 mg chol., 152 mg sodium, 24 g carbo., 5 g pro.

Tart and tangy, this beloved bread is flavored with a hint of onion. Millet, a protein-rich cereal grass found in health-food stores, adds nutrition and crunch to every slice.

Millet and Onion Sourdough Bread

1½-POUND*	INGREDIENTS	2-POUND*
1 cup	chopped onion	1¼ cups
1 clove	garlic, minced**	1 clove
2 tablespoons	olive oil or cooking oil**	2 tablespoons
1¼ cups	Sourdough Starter (page 106)	1½ cups
¼ cup	milk or water	½ cup
3 cups	bread flour	4 cups
¼ cup	millet	⅓ cup
1 tablespoon	sugar	4 teaspoons
¾ teaspoon	salt	1 teaspoon
1 teaspoon	active dry yeast	1 teaspoon
	or bread machine yeast**	

PREP:
15 minutes

MAKES:
1½-pound recipe
(20 slices)
OR
2-pound recipe
(27 slices)

1 Select the loaf size. In a small saucepan cook the onion and garlic in hot oil until onion is tender, stirring occasionally. Cool slightly.

2 Add the onion mixture and the remaining ingredients to the machine according to the manufacturer's directions. Select the basic white bread cycle.

***Note:** For the 1½-pound loaf, the bread machine pan must have a capacity of 10 cups or more. For the 2-pound loaf, the bread machine pan must have a capacity of 12 cups or more.

****Note:** The Test Kitchen recommends 1 clove garlic, 2 tablespoons oil, and 1 teaspoon yeast for either size recipe.

Nutrition Facts per slice: 125 cal., 2 g total fat (0 g sat. fat), 0 mg chol., 82 mg sodium, 23 g carbo., 4 g pro.

Is Millet Just for the Birds?

If you think millet is for the birds because it's used in birdseed, consider that other cultures prize it for its hardiness as a crop and its heartiness as a food. Particularly in India, but also in China and Africa, millet is used for breads, cereals, and side dishes. Look for these tiny yellow kernels in health food markets. Store millet in an airtight container in a cool spot up to two years.

This chewy sandwich bread boasts cornmeal and three kinds of flour, but it's the fennel seed's hint of licorice flavor that makes the bread unique.

Multigrain Sourdough Bread

PREP:
10 minutes

MAKES:
1½-pound recipe
(16 slices)
OR
2-pound recipe
(22 slices)

1½-POUND*	INGREDIENTS	2-POUND*
1¼ cups	Sourdough Starter (page 106)	1½ cups
¼ cup	milk	½ cup
1 tablespoon	honey	2 tablespoons
1 tablespoon	margarine or butter, cut up; shortening; or cooking oil	2 tablespoons
1¼ cups	whole wheat flour	1²⁄₃ cups
1 cup	bread flour	1¹⁄₃ cups
½ cup	rye flour	²⁄₃ cup
¼ cup	cornmeal	¹⁄₃ cup
2 tablespoons	gluten flour*	2 tablespoons
1 teaspoon	fennel seeds	1½ teaspoons
³⁄₄ teaspoon	salt	1 teaspoon
1 teaspoon	active dry yeast or bread machine yeast	1¼ teaspoons

1 Select the loaf size. Add the ingredients to the machine according to the manufacturer's directions. If available, select the whole grain cycle, or select the basic white bread cycle.

*Note: For the 1½-pound loaf, the bread machine pan must have a capacity of 10 cups or more. For the 2-pound loaf, the bread machine pan must have a capacity of 12 cups or more.

**Note: The Test Kitchen recommends 2 tablespoons gluten flour for either size loaf.

Nutrition Facts per slice: 128 cal., 1 g total fat (0 g sat. fat), 0 mg chol., 112 mg sodium, 25 g carbo., 4 g pro.

Coffee, molasses, and cocoa contribute the dark color to this German-style bread. Sliced and topped with smoked ham and baby Swiss, it becomes an exceptional sandwich.

Pumpernickel Sourdough Bread

1½-POUND*	INGREDIENTS	2-POUND*
³/₄ teaspoon	instant coffee crystals	1 teaspoon
¼ cup	water	¹/₃ cup
1 cup	Rye Sourdough Starter	1¹/₃ cups
	(page 107)	
3 tablespoons	mild-flavored molasses	¼ cup
1 tablespoon	cooking oil	4 teaspoons
1³/₄ cups	bread flour	2¹/₃ cups
³/₄ cup	rye flour	1 cup
¹/₂ cup	whole wheat flour	²/₃ cup
4 teaspoons	gluten flour	2 tablespoons
4 teaspoons	unsweetened cocoa powder	2 tablespoons
1¹/₂ teaspoons	caraway seeds or fennel seeds	2 teaspoons
³/₄ teaspoon	salt	1 teaspoon
1 teaspoon	active dry yeast	1¹/₄ teaspoons
	or bread machine yeast	

PREP:
10 minutes

MAKES:
1½-pound recipe
(16 slices)
OR
2-pound recipe
(22 slices)

① Select the loaf size. In a small bowl dissolve the coffee crystals in the water. Add the coffee mixture and the remaining ingredients to the machine according to the manufacturer's directions. If available, select the whole grain cycle, or select the basic white bread cycle.

*Note: For the 1½-pound loaf, the bread machine pan must have a capacity of 10 cups or more. For the 2-pound loaf, the bread machine pan must have a capacity of 12 cups or more.

Nutrition Facts per slice: 122 cal., 1 g total fat (0 g sat. fat), 0 mg chol., 102 mg sodium, 24 g carbo., 4 g pro.

Selecting the Right Cocoa Powder

Cocoa powder, along with coffee and rye flour, gives this bread its traditional dark color. Use pure unsweetened cocoa powder. Instant cocoa mix or presweetened cocoa powder—drink mixes made of ground cocoa plus sugar and other flavorings—will give different results.

Pungent caraway seeds speckle this classic, bold Eastern European rye bread. It has a more intense flavor and character than light rye loaves purchased from the deli.

Caraway-Rye Sourdough Bread

PREP:
15 minutes

STAND:
3 days

MAKES:
1½-pound recipe
(18 slices)
OR
2-pound recipe
(24 slices)

1½-POUND*	INGREDIENTS	2-POUND*
¾ teaspoon	active dry yeast	1 teaspoon
	or bread machine yeast	
1 cup	warm water (105°F to 115°F)	1¼ cups
½ cup	rye flour	⅔ cup
1	egg**	1
2 tablespoons	mild-flavored molasses**	2 tablespoons
1 tablespoon	olive oil or cooking oil	4 teaspoons
2¼ cups	bread flour	3 cups
¾ cup	rye flour	1 cup
4 teaspoons	gluten flour	2 tablespoons
1 tablespoon	caraway seeds	4 teaspoons
¾ teaspoon	salt	1 teaspoon
1 teaspoon	active dry yeast	1¼ teaspoons
	or bread machine yeast	

1 *To make the starter:* Select the loaf size. In a medium bowl dissolve the ¾ or 1 teaspoon yeast in the warm water. Stir in the ½ or ⅔ cup rye flour just until smooth. Cover with plastic wrap. Let stand at room temperature (70°F to 80°F) about 3 days or until mixture has a slightly fermented aroma, stirring two or three times every day.

2 *To finish the bread:* Add the starter and the remaining ingredients to the machine according to the manufacturer's directions. If available, select the whole grain cycle, or select the basic white bread cycle.

*Note: For the 1½-pound loaf, the bread machine pan must have a capacity of 10 cups or more. For the 2-pound loaf, the bread machine pan must have a capacity of 12 cups or more.

**Note: The Test Kitchen recommends 1 egg and 2 tablespoons molasses for either size recipe.

Nutrition Facts per slice: 108 cal., 2 g total fat (0 g sat. fat), 12 mg chol., 94 mg sodium, 20 g carbo., 4 g pro.

With a nod to peasant influences, this rustic country loaf is good with smoked cheese and meats. The starter contains beer (if you choose), creating a real zippy bread.

Finnish Sourdough Rye Bread

1½-POUND*	INGREDIENTS	2-POUND*
1 cup	beer	1⅓ cups
½ cup	rye flour	⅔ cup
2 teaspoons	shortening or cooking oil	1 tablespoon
2 cups	bread flour	2⅔ cups
½ cup	rye flour	⅔ cup
1 tablespoon	gluten flour	2 tablespoons
2 teaspoons	brown sugar	1 tablespoon
¾ teaspoon	salt	1 teaspoon
1 teaspoon	active dry yeast	1¼ teaspoons
	or bread machine yeast	

PREP:
15 minutes

STAND:
2 days

MAKES:
1½-pound recipe
(16 slices)
OR
2-pound recipe
(22 slices)

1 *To make the starter:* Select the loaf size. In a medium bowl stir the beer into the ½ or ⅔ cup rye flour just until smooth. Cover with plastic wrap. Let stand at room temperature (70°F to 80°F) about 2 days or until mixture bubbles and has a slightly fermented aroma, stirring two or three times every day.

2 *To finish the bread:* Add the starter and the remaining ingredients to the machine according to the manufacturer's directions. If available, select the whole grain cycle, or select the basic white bread cycle.

*Note: For the 1½-pound loaf, the bread machine pan must have a capacity of 10 cups or more. For the 2-pound loaf, the bread machine pan must have a capacity of 12 cups or more.

Nutrition Facts per slice: 98 cal., 1 g total fat (0 g sat. fat), 0 mg chol., 101 mg sodium, 19 g carbo., 3 g pro.

Slather toasted, thick slices with jam in the morning or spread with Apricot Butter (page 264) before bedtime.

Raisin Sourdough Bread

1½-POUND*	INGREDIENTS
1¼ cups	Sourdough Starter (page 106)
2 tablespoons	milk or water
1 tablespoon	margarine or butter
3 cups	bread flour
2 tablespoons	brown sugar
1 teaspoon	ground cinnamon
¾ teaspoon	salt
¼ teaspoon	ground nutmeg
1 teaspoon	active dry yeast
	or bread machine yeast
¾ cup	dark raisins
	Margarine or butter, melted
½ teaspoon	granulated sugar
⅛ teaspoon	ground cinnamon

1 Add the first 10 ingredients to the machine according to the manufacturer's directions. Select the basic white bread cycle.

2 Brush the top of the warm loaf with melted margarine. In a small bowl stir together granulated sugar and the ⅛ teaspoon cinnamon; sprinkle over loaf.

*Note: The bread machine pan must have a capacity of 10 cups or more.

Nutrition Facts per slice: 162 cal., 2 g total fat (0 g sat. fat), 0 mg chol., 122 mg sodium, 32 g carbo., 5 g pro.

The combination of maple syrup and toasted walnuts provides a perfect balance to the sourdough base of this prizewinning recipe. It's good enough to eat au naturel or ideal for a very classy French toast.

Maple-Walnut Sourdough Bread

1½-POUND*	INGREDIENTS	2-POUND*
1 cup	Sourdough Starter (page 106)	1⅓ cups
1	egg**	1
3 tablespoons	water	¼ cup
2 tablespoons	maple-flavored syrup	3 tablespoons
1 tablespoon	margarine or butter, cut up	2 tablespoons
¼ teaspoon	maple flavoring	½ teaspoon
3 cups	bread flour	4 cups
¾ teaspoon	salt	1 teaspoon
¾ teaspoon	ground cinnamon	1 teaspoon
1 teaspoon	active dry yeast or bread machine yeast	1¼ teaspoons
½ cup	chopped walnuts, toasted	⅔ cup
½ cup	dark raisins	⅔ cup

PREP:
15 minutes

MAKES:
1½-pound recipe
(16 slices)
OR
2-pound recipe
(22 slices)

1 Select the loaf size. Add the ingredients to the machine according to the manufacturer's directions. Select the basic white bread cycle.

*Note: For the 1½-pound loaf, the bread machine pan must have a capacity of 10 cups or more. For the 2-pound loaf, the bread machine pan must have a capacity of 12 cups or more.

**Note: The Test Kitchen recommends 1 egg for either size recipe.

Nutrition Facts per slice: 172 cal., 4 g total fat (1 g sat. fat), 13 mg chol., 114 mg sodium, 30 g carbo., 5 g pro.

Maple Syrup Facts

Pure maple syrup is tapped from maple trees late in winter when their sap begins to flow, then boiled until thick. One gallon of syrup requires more than 30 gallons of sap. Lighter in taste and less expensive is maple-flavored syrup, which is a syrup, such as corn syrup, that has a small amount of maple syrup added. Syrups made from corn syrup plus maple extract are called pancake syrups.

Toasting the nuts brings out their rich flavor. If you like, decorate the glazed loaf with toasted sliced almonds.

Cranberry-Nut Sourdough Bread

PREP:
15 minutes

MAKES:
1½-pound recipe
(16 slices)

1½-POUND*	INGREDIENTS
1¼ cups	Sourdough Starter (page 106)
2 teaspoons	finely shredded orange peel
2 tablespoons	orange juice or water
1 tablespoon	cooking oil
3 cups	bread flour
1 tablespoon	sugar
¾ teaspoon	salt
1 teaspoon	active dry yeast
	or bread machine yeast
½ cup	snipped dried cranberries
½ cup	chopped almonds
	or walnuts, toasted
1 recipe	Powdered Sugar Glaze

① Add the ingredients, except the Powdered Sugar Glaze, to the machine according to the manufacturer's directions. Select the basic white bread cycle. Drizzle the cooled loaf with Powdered Sugar Glaze.

Powdered Sugar Glaze: In a small bowl stir together ½ cup sifted powdered sugar and ½ teaspoon vanilla. Stir in enough milk (2 to 3 teaspoons) to make a glaze of drizzling consistency.

*Note: For the 1½-pound loaf, the bread machine pan must have a capacity of 10 cups or more.

Nutrition Facts per slice: 191 cal., 5 g total fat (0 g sat. fat), 0 mg chol., 104 mg sodium, 35 g carbo., 5 g pro.

Serve this sensational raisin bread toasted and buttered for breakfast. Its sweet, warming aroma alone is enough to quickly lift spirits.

Raisin-Almond Sourdough Bread

1½-POUND*	INGREDIENTS	2-POUND*
1 cup	Sourdough Starter (page 106)	1⅓ cups
⅓ cup	water	½ cup
1	egg**	1
2 tablespoons	honey	3 tablespoons
1 tablespoon	margarine or butter, cut up	2 tablespoons
3 cups	bread flour	4 cups
1 teaspoon	finely shredded orange peel	1½ teaspoons
¾ teaspoon	salt	1 teaspoon
1 teaspoon	active dry yeast	1 teaspoon
	or bread machine yeast**	
½ cup	chopped almonds, toasted	⅔ cup
½ cup	dark raisins	⅔ cup

PREP:
15 minutes

MAKES:
1½-pound recipe
(20 slices)
OR
2-pound recipe
(27 slices)

1 Select the loaf size. Add the ingredients to the machine according to the manufacturer's directions. Select the basic white bread cycle.

*Note: For the 1½-pound loaf, the bread machine pan must have a capacity of 10 cups or more. For the 2-pound loaf, the bread machine pan must have a capacity of 12 cups or more.

**Note: The Test Kitchen recommends 1 egg and 1 teaspoon yeast for either size recipe.

Nutrition Facts per slice: 134 cal., 3 g total fat (0 g sat. fat), 11 mg chol., 91 mg sodium, 24 g carbo., 4 g pro.

This bread begs to be saved for a coffee break. The combination of coffee and almond brickle is perfect for a pick-me-up anytime.

Toffee Sourdough Bread

PREP:	1½-POUND*	INGREDIENTS	2-POUND*
10 minutes	2 teaspoons	instant coffee crystals	1 tablespoon
	2 tablespoons	milk or water	⅓ cup
MAKES:	1¼ cups	Sourdough Starter (page 106)	1½ cups
1½-pound recipe (18 slices)	2 tablespoons	margarine or butter, cut up**	2 tablespoons
OR	3 cups	bread flour	4 cups
2-pound recipe (24 slices)	4 teaspoons	sugar	2 tablespoons
	¾ teaspoon	salt	1 teaspoon
	1 teaspoon	active dry yeast	1¼ teaspoons
		or bread machine yeast	
	½ cup	almond brickle pieces	⅔ cup

1 Select the loaf size. In a small bowl dissolve the coffee crystals in the milk. Add the coffee mixture and the remaining ingredients to the machine according to the manufacturer's directions. Select the basic white bread cycle.

*Note: For the 1½-pound loaf, the bread machine pan must have a capacity of 10 cups or more. For the 2-pound loaf, the bread machine pan must have a capacity of 12 cups or more.

**Note: The Test Kitchen recommends 2 tablespoons margarine or butter for either size recipe.

Nutrition Facts per slice: 149 cal., 3 g total fat (0 g sat. fat), 2 mg chol., 132 mg sodium, 26 g carbo., 4 g pro.

Love bread pudding? Give your favorite recipe an elegant twist by using slices of this cinnamony coffee-and-nut loaf.

Hazelnut-Espresso Sourdough Bread

1½-POUND*	INGREDIENTS	2-POUND*
1 cup	Sourdough Starter** (page 106)	1 cup
⅓ cup	milk	½ cup
1	egg**	1
2 tablespoons	honey	3 tablespoons
1 tablespoon	margarine or butter, cut up	2 tablespoons
3 cups	bread flour	4 cups
1 tablespoon	instant espresso coffee powder or instant coffee crystals	4 teaspoons
¾ teaspoon	salt	1 teaspoon
¼ teaspoon	ground cinnamon	½ teaspoon
1 teaspoon	active dry yeast or bread machine yeast**	1 teaspoon
½ cup	chopped hazelnuts (filberts) or almonds, toasted	⅔ cup
1 recipe	Coffee Glaze	1 recipe

PREP:
15 minutes

MAKES:
1½-pound recipe
(20 slices)
OR
2-pound recipe
(27 slices)

1 Select the loaf size. Add the ingredients, except the Coffee Glaze, to the machine according to the manufacturer's directions. Select the basic white bread cycle. Drizzle the cooled loaf with Coffee Glaze.

Coffee Glaze: In a small bowl dissolve ½ teaspoon instant espresso coffee powder or instant coffee crystals in 2 teaspoons milk. Stir in 1 cup sifted powdered sugar and enough additional milk (1 to 2 teaspoons) to make a glaze of drizzling consistency.

*Note: For the 1½-pound loaf, the bread machine pan must have a capacity of 10 cups or more. For the 2-pound loaf, the bread machine pan must have a capacity of 12 cups or more.

**Note: The Test Kitchen recommends 1 cup Sourdough Starter, 1 egg, and 1 teaspoon yeast for either size recipe.

Nutrition Facts per slice: 149 cal., 3 g total fat (0 g sat. fat), 11 mg chol., 93 mg sodium, 26 g carbo., 4 g pro.

For a true sandwich meister, rye is the undisputed king of breads. Usurping the throne is this tasty rendition, tart from the starter and rich with cream cheese.

Cream Cheese Sourdough Bread

PREP:
10 minutes

MAKES:
1½-pound recipe
(16 slices)
OR
2-pound recipe
(22 slices)

1½-POUND*	INGREDIENTS	2-POUND*
1 cup	Sourdough Starter (page 106)	1¼ cups
⅓ cup	milk	½ cup
2 ounces	cream cheese, softened	3 ounces
2 teaspoons	cooking oil	1 tablespoon
2 teaspoons	honey	1 tablespoon
1¾ cups	bread flour	2½ cups
1¼ cups	rye flour	1½ cups
3 tablespoons	snipped fresh chives	¼ cup
2 tablespoons	gluten flour**	2 tablespoons
¾ teaspoon	salt	1 teaspoon
¾ teaspoon	caraway seeds	1 teaspoon
1 teaspoon	active dry yeast	1¼ teaspoons
	or bread machine yeast	

① Select the loaf size. Add the ingredients to the machine according to the manufacturer's directions. If available, select the whole grain cycle, or select the basic white bread cycle.

*Note: For the 1½-pound loaf, the bread machine pan must have a capacity of 10 cups or more. For the 2-pound loaf, the bread machine pan must have a capacity of 12 cups or more.

**Note: The Test Kitchen recommends 2 tablespoons gluten flour for either size recipe.

Nutrition Facts per slice: 133 cal., 2 g total fat (1 g sat. fat), 4 mg chol., 114 mg sodium, 24 g carbo., 4 g pro.

Served plain or with a drizzle of Powdered Sugar Glaze (page 237), these rolls are oh-so-yummy.

Sourdough Cinnamon Rolls

1½-POUND	INGREDIENTS	2-POUND
1 cup	Sourdough Starter (page 106)	1⅓ cups
⅓ cup	water*	⅓ cup
1	egg*	1
3 tablespoons	honey	¼ cup
1 tablespoon	margarine or butter, cut up	2 tablespoons
3 cups	bread flour	4 cups
¾ teaspoon	salt	1 teaspoon
1¼ teaspoons	active dry yeast	1¾ teaspoons
	or bread machine yeast	
½ cup	chopped pecans	⅔ cup
⅓ cup	granulated sugar	½ cup
2 tablespoons	brown sugar	3 tablespoons
1½ teaspoons	ground cinnamon	2 teaspoons
2 tablespoons	margarine or butter, melted	3 tablespoons
¼ cup	whipping cream	⅓ cup

PREP:
25 minutes

RISE:
30 minutes

BAKE:
20 minutes

MAKES:
1½-pound recipe
(12 rolls)
OR
2-pound recipe
(18 rolls)

① Select the recipe size. Add the first 8 ingredients to the machine according to the manufacturer's directions. Select the dough cycle. When cycle is complete, remove dough. Punch down. Cover and let rest for 10 minutes.

② Meanwhile, for filling, in a small bowl stir together the pecans, granulated sugar, brown sugar, and cinnamon.

③ *For the 1½-pound recipe:* Grease a 13×9×2-inch baking pan; set aside. On a lightly floured surface, roll the dough into a 12-inch square. Brush with the melted margarine and sprinkle with filling. Roll up into a spiral; seal edge. Cut into twelve 1-inch slices. Place cut sides down in the prepared baking pan.

④ Cover and let rise in a warm place about 30 minutes or until nearly double. Drizzle the whipping cream over rolls. Bake in a 375°F oven for 20 to 25 minutes or until golden brown. Cool in pan on a wire rack about 5 minutes; invert onto wire rack.

For the 2-pound recipe: Prepare as above, except roll the dough into an 18×12-inch rectangle. Fill and roll up, starting from a long side. Cut into eighteen 1-inch slices; place in 2 greased 8×8×2-inch baking pans or 9×1½-inch round baking pans. Continue as above.

*Note: The Test Kitchen recommends ⅓ cup water and 1 egg for either size recipe.

Nutrition Facts per roll: 281 cal., 9 g total fat (2 g sat. fat), 25 mg chol., 177 mg sodium, 44 g carbo., 7 g pro.

A chewy pretzel hot from a street cart is the ultimate comfort food in Philadelphia, where pretzels are prized. This version is extra-tangy, extra-easy, and extra-good.

Sourdough Baked Pretzels

PREP: 40 minutes	1½-POUND	INGREDIENTS	2-POUND
	1¼ cups	Sourdough Starter (page 106)	1¾ cups
BAKE: 18 minutes	2 tablespoons	milk	¼ cup
	1½ cups	bread flour	2 cups
	1⅓ cups	whole wheat flour	1¾ cups
MAKES: 1½-pound recipe (16 pretzels) OR 2-pound recipe (20 pretzels)	1 tablespoon	gluten flour	2 tablespoons
	1 tablespoon	sugar	4 teaspoons
	¾ teaspoon	salt	1 teaspoon
	1 teaspoon	active dry yeast or bread machine yeast	1¼ teaspoons
	1	slightly beaten egg	1
	1 tablespoon	water	1 tablespoon
		Coarse salt or sesame seeds (optional)	

1 Select the recipe size. Add the first 8 ingredients to the machine according to the manufacturer's directions. Select the dough cycle. When cycle is complete, remove dough. Punch down. Cover and let rest for 10 minutes. Grease large baking sheets; set aside.

2 On a lightly floured surface, roll the 1½-pound dough into a 14×8-inch rectangle. Cut into sixteen 14×½-inch strips. (Roll the 2-pound dough into a 14×10-inch rectangle; cut into twenty 14×½-inch strips.) Gently pull the strips into 16-inch ropes.

3 Shape each pretzel by crossing one end of a rope over the other to form a circle, overlapping about 4 inches from each end. Take one end of dough in each hand and twist once at the point where the dough overlaps. Carefully lift each end across to the edge of the circle opposite it. Tuck ends under edges to make a pretzel shape; moisten ends and press to seal. Place on the prepared baking sheets. *Do not let rise.*

4 In a small bowl combine egg and water; brush over pretzels. If desired, sprinkle with coarse salt. Bake in a 350°F oven for 18 to 20 minutes or until golden brown. Remove from baking sheets; cool on wire racks.

Nutrition Facts per pretzel: 120 cal., 1 g total fat (0 g sat. fat), 13 mg chol., 106 mg sodium, 24 g carbo., 5 g pro.

WHOLE GRAIN GOODNESS

All for one and one for all is the motto of this tasty round loaf that amply serves a crowd. For a giant picnic sandwich, fill it mile-high with cold cuts and cut into generous wedges.

Cracked Wheat Bread

PREP:	1½-POUND	INGREDIENTS	2-POUND
25 minutes			
	1 cup	water*	1 cup
RISE:	⅓ cup	cracked wheat	½ cup
45 minutes	1 cup	milk	1¼ cups
	2 tablespoons	cooking oil*	2 tablespoons
BAKE:	2 cups	whole wheat flour	2½ cups
35 minutes	1 cup	bread flour	1½ cups
	1 tablespoon	brown sugar	2 tablespoons
MAKES:	1 tablespoon	gluten flour	4 teaspoons
1½-pound recipe	¾ teaspoon	salt	1 teaspoon
(16 slices)	½ teaspoon	dried rosemary, crushed,	¾ teaspoon
OR		or	
2-pound recipe	1½ teaspoons	snipped fresh rosemary	1 tablespoon
(22 slices)	1¼ teaspoons	active dry yeast	1½ teaspoons
		or bread machine yeast	
	1	slightly beaten egg	1
	1 tablespoon	water	1 tablespoon
	1 tablespoon	fresh rosemary leaves (optional)	1 tablespoon

1 Select the recipe size. In a small saucepan bring the 1 cup water to boiling; remove from heat. Stir in the cracked wheat. Let stand for 3 minutes; drain well.

2 Add the drained cracked wheat and the next 9 ingredients to the machine according to the manufacturer's directions. Select the dough cycle. When cycle is complete, remove dough. Punch down. Cover and let rest for 10 minutes. Lightly grease a baking sheet; set aside.

3 On a lightly floured surface, shape the 1½- or 2-pound dough into a ball. Place on the prepared baking sheet. Flatten slightly to a 6-inch round loaf. Cover and let rise in a warm place about 45 minutes or until nearly double.

4 In a small bowl combine egg and the 1 tablespoon water; brush over loaf. If desired, sprinkle with fresh rosemary leaves. Bake in a 350°F oven for 35 to 40 minutes or until bread sounds hollow when lightly tapped. If necessary, cover loosely with foil the last 5 to 10 minutes to prevent overbrowning. Remove from baking sheet; cool on a wire rack.

*Note: The Test Kitchen recommends 1 cup water and 2 tablespoons oil for either size recipe.

Nutrition Facts per slice: 121 cal., 3 g total fat (1 g sat. fat), 14 mg chol., 113 mg sodium, 20 g carbo., 5 g pro.

A granary is where fresh grain is stored; hence, the word is fitting for this chewy, multigrain bread. Look for cracked wheat, millet, and wheat bran in larger supermarkets or health-food stores.

Granary Bread

1½-POUND	INGREDIENTS	2-POUND
1 cup	water*	1 cup
¼ cup	cracked wheat	⅓ cup
2 tablespoons	millet	3 tablespoons
1¼ cups	water	1¾ cups
2 tablespoons	molasses or honey*	2 tablespoons
2 teaspoons	shortening	1 tablespoon
2 cups	whole wheat flour	2⅔ cups
1 cup	bread flour	1⅓ cups
¼ cup	regular or quick-cooking rolled oats	⅓ cup
3 tablespoons	cornmeal	¼ cup
2 tablespoons	toasted wheat germ or unprocessed wheat bran*	2 tablespoons
1 tablespoon	gluten flour	4 teaspoons
¾ teaspoon	salt	1 teaspoon
1 teaspoon	active dry yeast or bread machine yeast	1½ teaspoons

PREP:
15 minutes

MAKES:
1½-pound recipe
(16 slices)
OR
2-pound recipe
(20 slices)

① Select the loaf size. In a small saucepan bring the 1 cup water to boiling; remove from heat. Stir in the cracked wheat and millet. Let stand for 5 minutes; drain well.

② Add the drained cracked wheat mixture and the remaining ingredients to the machine according to the manufacturer's directions. If available, select the whole grain cycle, or select the basic white bread cycle.

*Note: The Test Kitchen recommends 1 cup water, 2 tablespoons molasses, and 2 tablespoons wheat germ for either size recipe.

Nutrition Facts per slice: 124 cal., 1 g total fat (0 g sat. fat), 0 mg chol., 112 mg sodium, 25 g carbo., 4 g pro.

Put out a plate of pickles, slices of roast pork or beef, and this hearty, robust bread and you'll have a simple and wholly satisfying supper.

Roasted Garlic and Stout Bread

	1½-POUND	INGREDIENTS
	2 teaspoons	active dry yeast
		or bread machine yeast
	1 cup	stout or other dark beer
	½ cup	bread flour
	1 teaspoon	brown sugar
	1 tablespoon	shortening
	1 tablespoon	bottled minced roasted garlic
	1½ cups	bread flour
	1 cup	whole wheat flour
	2 tablespoons	brown sugar
	1 tablespoon	gluten flour
	¾ teaspoon	salt
		Yellow cornmeal

PREP:
25 minutes

STAND:
12 hours

RISE:
30 minutes

BAKE:
25 minutes

MAKES:
1½-pound recipe
(16 slices)

1 *To make the starter:* In a medium bowl dissolve the yeast in the stout. Stir in the ½ cup bread flour and the 1 teaspoon brown sugar just until smooth. Cover with plastic wrap. Let stand at room temperature (70°F to 80°F) for 12 to 24 hours or until mixture has a slightly fermented aroma, stirring two or three times.

2 *To finish the bread:* Add the starter and the next 7 ingredients to the machine according to the manufacturer's directions. Select the dough cycle. When cycle is complete, remove dough. Punch down. Cover and let rest for 10 minutes. Lightly grease a baking sheet and sprinkle with cornmeal; set aside.

3 On a lightly floured surface, shape the dough into a ball. Place on the prepared baking sheet. Flatten slightly to a 7-inch round loaf. Using a sharp knife, make three or four cuts about ¼ inch deep across top of loaf.

4 Cover and let rise in a warm place for 30 to 40 minutes or until nearly double. Bake in a 400°F oven about 25 minutes or until bread sounds hollow when lightly tapped. Remove from baking sheet; cool on a wire rack.

Nutrition Facts per slice: 112 cal., 1 g total fat (0 g sat. fat), 0 mg chol., 111 mg sodium, 21 g carbo., 4 g pro.

Bursting with flavor and nutrition, this loaf includes muesli, a tempting combination of rolled oats mixed with other cereals or grains, dried fruits, and nuts. Look for muesli in the cereal aisle of your supermarket.

Honey Grain Bread

1½-POUND	INGREDIENTS	2-POUND
1 cup	water	1⅓ cups
3 tablespoons	honey	¼ cup
2 tablespoons	margarine or butter, cut up	3 tablespoons
1⅔ cups	bread flour	2¼ cups
1⅓ cups	whole wheat flour	1⅔ cups
¾ cup	muesli	1 cup
¾ teaspoon	salt	1 teaspoon
¼ teaspoon	ground cinnamon	½ teaspoon
1 teaspoon	active dry yeast	1¼ teaspoons
	or bread machine yeast	

PREP:
10 minutes

MAKES:
1½-pound recipe
(16 slices)
OR
2-pound recipe
(22 slices)

1 Select the loaf size. Add the ingredients to the machine according to the manufacturer's directions. If available, select the whole grain cycle, or select the basic white bread cycle and, if available, the light color setting.

Nutrition Facts per slice: 133 cal., 2 g total fat (0 g sat. fat), 0 mg chol., 130 mg sodium, 25 g carbo., 4 g pro.

When making this slightly sweet, subtly nutty loaf, the Test Kitchen found that a blender, rather than a food processor, was best for grinding the flax seeds.

Hearty Wheat Bread with Flax Seeds

PREP: 10 minutes	1½-POUND*	INGREDIENTS	2-POUND*
	⅓ cup	flax seeds	½ cup
MAKES:	1 cup	milk	1⅓ cups
1½-pound recipe (16 slices)	1	egg(s)	2
OR	2 tablespoons	margarine or butter, cut up	3 tablespoons
2-pound recipe (22 slices)	2½ cups	bread flour	3⅓ cups
	¾ cup	whole wheat flour	1 cup
	3 tablespoons	packed brown sugar	¼ cup
	¾ teaspoon	salt	1 teaspoon
	1 teaspoon	active dry yeast or bread machine yeast	1¼ teaspoons

1 Select the loaf size. Place the flax seeds in a blender container. Cover and blend until flax seeds are ground.

2 Add the ingredients to the machine according to the manufacturer's directions, adding the ground flax seeds with the flours. If available, select the whole grain cycle, or select the basic white bread cycle.

*Note: For the 1½-pound loaf, the bread machine pan must have a capacity of 10 cups or more. For the 2-pound loaf, the bread machine pan must have a capacity of 12 cups or more.

Nutrition Facts per slice: 148 cal., 4 g total fat (1 g sat. fat), 14 mg chol., 140 mg sodium, 24 g carbo., 5 g pro.

Egg Options

It works well to use refrigerated or thawed frozen egg product in place of whole eggs. These products are a convenient option to fresh eggs, plus they are cholesterol-free. Egg whites are another no-cholesterol alternative to whole eggs. For healthful baking, keep these equations in mind:

1 egg = ¼ cup egg product   2 egg whites = 1 egg

Here's just the bread to make an egg salad sandwich into a deliciously tempting lunch.

Cracked Wheat and Honey Nut Bread

PREP:
20 minutes

MAKES:
1½-pound recipe
(16 slices)

1½-POUND	INGREDIENTS
1 cup	water
⅓ cup	cracked wheat
1¼ cups	milk
2 tablespoons	cooking oil
2 tablespoons	honey
2¼ cups	whole wheat flour
1¼ cups	bread flour
1 teaspoon	salt
1 teaspoon	active dry yeast
	or bread machine yeast
½ cup	walnuts or pecans, chopped

1 In a small saucepan bring the water to boiling; remove from heat. Stir in the cracked wheat. Let stand for 3 minutes; drain well.

2 Add the drained cracked wheat and the remaining ingredients to the machine according to the manufacturer's directions. If available, select the whole grain cycle, or select the basic white bread cycle.

Nutrition Facts per slice: 171 cal., 5 g total fat (0 g sat. fat), 2 mg chol., 210 mg sodium, 29 g carbo., 6 g pro.

This is a superb everyday, all-purpose loaf for sandwiches and terrific toast.

Whole Grain Bread

PREP:
10 minutes

MAKES:
1½-pound recipe
(16 slices)
OR
2-pound recipe
(22 slices)

1½-POUND*	INGREDIENTS	2-POUND*
1¼ cups	milk	1½ cups
1	egg(s)	2
4 teaspoons	molasses or honey	2 tablespoons
4 teaspoons	butter or margarine	2 tablespoons
2 cups	bread flour	2⅔ cups
1¼ cups	whole wheat flour	1½ cups
¾ cup	four-grain cereal flakes or cornflakes	1 cup
¾ teaspoon	salt	1 teaspoon
1 teaspoon	active dry yeast or bread machine yeast	1½ teaspoons
⅓ cup	shelled sunflower seeds or chopped pecans	½ cup

1 Select the loaf size. Add the ingredients to the machine according to the manufacturer's directions. If available, select the whole grain cycle, or select the basic white bread cycle.

*Note: For the 1½-pound loaf, the bread machine pan must have a capacity of 10 cups or more. For the 2-pound loaf, the bread machine pan must have a capacity of 12 cups or more.

Nutrition Facts per slice: 144 cal., 4 g total fat (1 g sat. fat), 17 mg chol., 135 mg sodium, 23 g carbo., 5 g pro.

Sage gives this old-world loaf, based on a recipe from the Italian province of Tuscany, a sensational herb flavor.

Italian Whole Wheat-Sage Bread

1½-POUND	INGREDIENTS	2-POUND
1 cup	water	1½ cups
1 tablespoon	olive oil or cooking oil	4 teaspoons
2 cups	bread flour	2⅔ cups
1 cup	whole wheat flour	1⅓ cups
2 teaspoons	snipped fresh sage	1 tablespoon
	or	
½ teaspoon	dried sage, crushed	1 teaspoon
1 teaspoon	sugar	1½ teaspoons
¾ teaspoon	salt	1 teaspoon
1 teaspoon	active dry yeast	1¼ teaspoons
	or bread machine yeast	

PREP:
10 minutes

MAKES:
1½-pound recipe
(16 slices)
OR
2-pound recipe
(22 slices)

1 Select the loaf size. Add the ingredients to the machine according to the manufacturer's directions. If available, select the whole grain cycle, or select the basic white bread cycle.

Nutrition Facts per slice: 97 cal., 1 g total fat (0 g sat. fat), 0 mg chol., 101 mg sodium, 18 g carbo., 3 g pro.

Savor the kick of black pepper, the sharpness of Parmesan, and the light smokiness of provolone in this whole wheat loaf. If you use aged provolone cheese, be sure to crumble it rather than shred it.

Pepper-Cheese Bread

PREP: 25 minutes	1½-POUND	INGREDIENTS	2-POUND
	1 cup	water	1⅓ cups
RISE: 30 minutes	2 tablespoons	olive oil or cooking oil	3 tablespoons
	2 cups	bread flour	2⅔ cups
BAKE: 35 minutes	1 cup	whole wheat flour	1⅓ cups
	1 teaspoon	cracked black pepper	1½ teaspoons
	¾ teaspoon	salt	1 teaspoon
MAKES: 1½-pound recipe (16 slices)	1 teaspoon	active dry yeast	1¼ teaspoons
		or bread machine yeast	
OR	½ cup	shredded provolone cheese	⅔ cup
2-pound recipe (22 slices)	¼ cup	grated Parmesan cheese	⅓ cup
	1	slightly beaten egg white	1
	1 tablespoon	water	1 tablespoon

1 Select the recipe size. Add the first 7 ingredients to the machine according to the manufacturer's directions. Select the dough cycle. When cycle is complete, remove dough. Punch down. Cover and let rest for 10 minutes. Grease a baking sheet; set aside.

2 *For the 1½-pound recipe:* On a lightly floured surface, roll the dough into a 12×10-inch rectangle. Sprinkle with the provolone and Parmesan cheeses. Starting from a long side, roll up into a spiral; seal edge. Pinch and pull ends to taper. Place loaf, seam side down, on the prepared baking sheet. Cover and let rise in a warm place for 30 to 45 minutes or until nearly double.

3 Using a sharp knife, make three or four diagonal cuts about ¼ inch deep across top of loaf. In a small bowl combine egg white and the 1 tablespoon water; brush some of the egg white mixture over loaf.

4 Bake in a 375°F oven for 15 minutes. Brush with the remaining egg white mixture. Bake for 20 to 25 minutes more or until bread sounds hollow when lightly tapped. Remove from baking sheet; cool on a wire rack.

For the 2-pound recipe: Prepare as above, except divide the dough in half. Roll each portion into a 10×8-inch rectangle. Sprinkle each rectangle with half of the provolone and Parmesan cheeses. Continue as above.

Nutrition Facts per slice: 124 cal., 4 g total fat (1 g sat. fat), 4 mg chol., 165 mg sodium, 18 g carbo., 5 g pro.

Every soup supper needs bread to complete the meal—and this is the one to use. Whole wheat flour makes it hearty, while tomato and oregano deliver goodness from the garden.

Tomato-Herb Loaf

1½-POUND	INGREDIENTS	2-POUND
⅔ cup	water	¾ cup
3 tablespoons	snipped dried tomatoes (not oil-packed)	¼ cup
½ cup	tomato sauce	¾ cup
1 tablespoon	margarine or butter	4 teaspoons
2 cups	bread flour	2⅔ cups
1 cup	whole wheat flour	1⅓ cups
1 tablespoon	brown sugar	2 tablespoons
1 teaspoon	dried oregano, crushed, or	1½ teaspoons
1 tablespoon	snipped fresh oregano	4 teaspoons
½ teaspoon	salt	¾ teaspoon
1 teaspoon	active dry yeast or bread machine yeast	1¼ teaspoons

PREP:
10 minutes

MAKES:
1½-pound recipe
(16 slices)
OR
2-pound recipe
(22 slices)

1 Select the loaf size. Add the ingredients to the machine according to the manufacturer's directions, adding the dried tomatoes with the water. If available, select the whole grain cycle, or select the basic white bread cycle.

Nutrition Facts per slice: 101 cal., 1 g total fat (0 g sat. fat), 0 mg chol., 136 mg sodium, 20 g carbo., 3 g pro.

Buying Dried Tomatoes

Dried tomatoes have gone mainstream. Once stocked only by upscale markets that imported them from Italy, these intensely flavored nuggets are now staples at every corner grocery, and are produced stateside. Common market forms include oil-packed and dry, in jars or bags, bulk and prepackaged. To chop them, as most recipes suggest, snip with scissors.

Whole-grain breads rank among those much-sought-after foods that can be described as "satisfying" and "low fat" in the same breath. This healthful loaf is full of robust wheat flavor—with a touch of honey for sweetness—and plenty of good-for-you grains too.

Seven-Grain Bread

PREP:	1½-POUND*	INGREDIENTS	2-POUND*
10 minutes	⅔ cup	water	¾ cup
	⅓ cup	applesauce	⅔ cup
MAKES:	1	egg**	1
1½-pound recipe (16 slices)	2 tablespoons	honey	3 tablespoons
OR	1¾ cups	whole wheat flour	2⅓ cups
2-pound recipe (20 slices)	¾ cup	bread flour	1 cup
	½ cup	seven-grain cereal	⅔ cup
	1 tablespoon	gluten flour	2 tablespoons
	1 teaspoon	salt	1¼ teaspoons
	1 teaspoon	active dry yeast or bread machine yeast	1½ teaspoons

1 Select the loaf size. Add the ingredients to the machine according to the manufacturer's directions. If available, select the whole grain cycle, or select the basic white bread cycle.

*Note: For the 1½-pound loaf, the bread machine pan must have a capacity of 10 cups or more. For the 2-pound loaf, the bread machine pan must have a capacity of 12 cups or more.

**Note: The Test Kitchen recommends 1 egg for either size recipe.

Nutrition Facts per slice: 100 cal., 1 g total fat (0 g sat. fat), 13 mg chol., 151 mg sodium, 20 g carbo., 4 g pro.

Gluten is Good

Because whole grain flours are low in gluten (the protein that helps give bread structure and height), our whole grain bread recipes often call for a little extra gluten flour to help the finished loaf attain the proper texture. Sometimes called wheat gluten, gluten flour is made by removing most of the starch from high-protein, hard wheat flour. If you can't find gluten flour at your supermarket, look for it at a health-food store. Store it in an airtight container in a cool, dry place up to five months, or freeze it up to one year.

Because there was a shortage of wood for fuel in Ireland, breads such as this one were traditionally baked over smoldering open peat fires. What makes this bread distinctive is the delicious pairing of savory caraway seeds with sweet raisins.

Whole Wheat Irish Bread

1½-POUND	INGREDIENTS
1¼ cups	buttermilk or sour milk*
2 tablespoons	cooking oil
1½ cups	whole wheat flour
1½ cups	bread flour
3 tablespoons	brown sugar
1 tablespoon	caraway seeds
¾ teaspoon	salt
1 teaspoon	active dry yeast
	or bread machine yeast
⅔ cup	dark raisins

PREP:
10 minutes

MAKES:
1½-pound recipe
(16 slices)

1 Add the ingredients to the machine according to the manufacturer's directions. If available, select the whole grain cycle, or select the basic white bread cycle.

*Note: To make 1¼ cups sour milk, place 3¾ teaspoons lemon juice or vinegar in a 2-cup liquid measuring cup. Add enough milk to measure 1¼ cups liquid; stir. Let stand for 5 minutes before using.

Nutrition Facts per slice: 138 cal., 2 g total fat (0 g sat. fat), 0 mg chol., 120 mg sodium, 27 g carbo., 5 g pro.

Dark anise seeds dot this oat loaf, adding a light and delicate hint of licorice. Try this bread toasted and lightly spread with Citrus Butter (page 264) for a marvelous morning treat.

Anise Wheat Bread

	1½-POUND	INGREDIENTS	2-POUND
PREP: 25 minutes	½ cup	regular or quick-cooking rolled oats	¾ cup
	¾ cup	milk	1 cup
MAKES: 1½-pound recipe (16 slices)	¼ cup	water*	¼ cup
OR	4 teaspoons	margarine or butter, cut up, or cooking oil	2 tablespoons
2-pound recipe (22 slices)	1¾ cups	bread flour	2 cups
	¾ cup	whole wheat flour	1 cup
	2 tablespoons	sugar	3 tablespoons
	¾ teaspoon	salt	1 teaspoon
	½ teaspoon	anise seeds	¾ teaspoon
	1¼ teaspoons	active dry yeast or bread machine yeast	1½ teaspoons

1 Select the loaf size. Spread the rolled oats in a shallow baking pan. Bake in a 350°F oven for 15 to 20 minutes or until light brown, stirring occasionally. Cool slightly. Transfer to a blender container or food processor bowl. Cover and blend or process until finely ground.

2 Add the ingredients to the machine according to the manufacturer's directions, adding the ground oats with the flours. If available, select the whole grain cycle, or select the basic white bread cycle.

*Note: The Test Kitchen recommends ¼ cup water for either size recipe.

Nutrition Facts per slice: 104 cal., 2 g total fat (0 g sat. fat), 1 mg chol., 118 mg sodium, 19 g carbo., 3 g pro.

What a combination! This cottage cheese and dill loaf tastes great when served with chicken, beef, or fish.

Dill-Onion Wheat Bread

1½-POUND*	INGREDIENTS
¾ cup	undrained, cream-style cottage cheese
½ cup	water
1	egg
1 tablespoon	margarine or butter
1½ cups	whole wheat flour
1½ cups	bread flour
1 tablespoon	dried minced onion
2 teaspoons	sugar
2 teaspoons	dried dill
	or
2 tablespoons	snipped fresh dill
¾ teaspoon	salt
1 teaspoon	active dry yeast or bread machine yeast

PREP:
10 minutes

MAKES:
1½-pound recipe
(16 slices)

① Add the ingredients to the machine according to the manufacturer's directions. If available, select the whole grain cycle, or select the basic white bread cycle.

*Note: The bread machine pan must have a capacity of 10 cups or more.

Nutrition Facts per slice: 116 cal., 2 g total fat (0 g sat. fat), 21 mg chol., 164 mg sodium, 20 g carbo., 6 g pro.

Wheat, oats, barley, and corn offer robust flavor in this nutritious loaf.

Four-Grain Bread

PREP:
25 minutes

MAKES:
1½-pound recipe
(16 slices)
OR
2-pound recipe
(22 slices)

1½-POUND	INGREDIENTS	2-POUND
⅓ cup	quick-cooking rolled oats	½ cup
⅓ cup	quick-cooking barley	½ cup
1¼ cups	water	1⅔ cups
2 tablespoons	margarine or butter, cut up, or cooking oil	3 tablespoons
1½ cups	bread flour	1⅔ cups
¾ cup	whole wheat flour	1 cup
⅓ cup	cornmeal	½ cup
1 tablespoon	sugar	2 tablespoons
1 tablespoon	gluten flour	4 teaspoons
¾ teaspoon	salt	1 teaspoon
1¼ teaspoons	active dry yeast or bread machine yeast	1½ teaspoons

1 Select the loaf size. Spread the rolled oats and barley in a shallow baking pan. Bake in a 350°F oven for 15 to 20 minutes or until light brown, stirring occasionally. Cool slightly. Transfer to a blender container or food processor bowl. Cover and blend or process until oat mixture is finely ground.

2 Add the ingredients to the machine according to the manufacturer's directions, adding the ground oat mixture with the flours. If available, select the whole grain cycle, or select the basic white bread cycle.

Nutrition Facts per slice: 123 cal., 2 g total fat (0 g sat. fat), 0 mg chol., 118 mg sodium, 23 g carbo., 4 g pro.

As a bonus, this hearty rosemary- and thyme-scented wheat bread offers the option of blending in shelled sunflower seeds. The seeds give the whole-grain bread a slightly crunchy texture.

Whole Wheat-Herb Bread

1½-POUND	INGREDIENTS	2-POUND
1 cup	milk	1⅓ cups
3 tablespoons	water	¼ cup
1 tablespoon	cooking oil	4 teaspoons
3 cups	whole wheat flour	4 cups
¼ cup	gluten flour	⅓ cup
4 teaspoons	sugar	2 tablespoons
1 teaspoon	dried thyme, crushed,	1¼ teaspoons
	or	
1 tablespoon	snipped fresh thyme	4 teaspoons
¾ teaspoon	salt	1 teaspoon
¼ teaspoon	dried rosemary, crushed,	½ teaspoon
	or	
1 teaspoon	snipped fresh rosemary	1½ teaspoons
1 teaspoon	active dry yeast	1¼ teaspoons
	or bread machine yeast	
¼ cup	shelled sunflower seeds	⅓ cup
	(optional)	

PREP:
10 minutes

MAKES:
1½-pound recipe
(16 slices)
OR
2-pound recipe
(22 slices)

1 Select the loaf size. Add the ingredients to the machine according to the manufacturer's directions. If available, select the whole grain cycle, or select the basic white bread cycle.

Nutrition Facts per slice: 105 cal., 2 g total fat (0 g sat. fat), 1 mg chol., 109 mg sodium, 19 g carbo., 5 g pro.

This thick-crusted bread gets added interest with a sprinkling of a trio of seeds. Bring it to the table with a big bowl of mushroom soup and a wedge of farmhouse cheddar cheese for a country-style Sunday night soup supper.

Country Seed Bread

PREP:
10 minutes

MAKES:
1½-pound recipe
(16 slices)
OR
2-pound recipe
(22 slices)

1½-POUND	INGREDIENTS	2-POUND
1 cup	milk	1⅓ cups
¼ cup	water	⅓ cup
4 teaspoons	honey	2 tablespoons
1 tablespoon	margarine or butter	4 teaspoons
1½ cups	whole wheat flour	2 cups
1¼ cups	bread flour	1¾ cups
½ cup	soy flour*	½ cup
1 tablespoon	gluten flour	4 teaspoons
1 teaspoon	flax seeds	1¼ teaspoons
1 teaspoon	sesame seeds	1¼ teaspoons
1 teaspoon	poppy seeds	1¼ teaspoons
¾ teaspoon	salt	1 teaspoon
1¼ teaspoons	active dry yeast	1½ teaspoons
	or bread machine yeast	

① Select the loaf size. Add the ingredients to the machine according to the manufacturer's directions. If available, select the whole grain cycle, or select the basic white bread cycle.

*Note: The Test Kitchen recommends ½ cup soy flour for either size recipe.

Nutrition Facts per slice: 114 cal., 2 g total fat (0 g sat. fat), 1 mg chol., 127 mg sodium, 20 g carbo., 5 g pro.

This herbed bread is so good you'll be tempted to finish it off in one day. Save a little for a scrumptious cheese strata the next morning.

Potato-Herb Wheat Bread

1½-POUND	INGREDIENTS
¾ cup	water
¾ cup	chopped, peeled potato
	Milk
4 teaspoons	honey
1 tablespoon	**cooking oil**
2 cups	bread flour
1 cup	**whole wheat flour**
3 tablespoons	nonfat dry milk powder
¾ teaspoon	**salt**
½ teaspoon	dried thyme, crushed
½ teaspoon	**dried oregano, crushed**
¼ teaspoon	dried rosemary, crushed
1 teaspoon	**active dry yeast**
	or bread machine yeast

PREP:
30 minutes

MAKES:
1½-pound recipe
(16 slices)

1 In a small saucepan combine the water and potato. Bring to boiling; reduce heat. Cover and simmer about 15 minutes or until potato is very tender. Do not drain. Mash potato in water; measure potato mixture. Add milk to equal 1¼ cups mixture. Cool slightly.

2 Add the potato mixture and the remaining ingredients to the machine according to the manufacturer's directions. If available, select the whole grain cycle, or select the basic white bread cycle.

Nutrition Facts per slice: 120 cal., 2 g total fat (0 g sat. fat), 0 mg chol., 110 mg sodium, 23 g carbo., 5 g pro.

Wild rice, with its nutty flavor and chewy texture, makes this wholesome loaf hard to resist.

Wild Rice and Oat Bran Bread

PREP:
10 minutes

MAKES:
1½-pound recipe
(16 slices)

1½-POUND	INGREDIENTS
1 cup	milk
¾ cup	cooked wild rice,
	well drained and cooled*
2 tablespoons	honey
2 tablespoons	shortening
2 cups	whole wheat flour
1 cup	bread flour
⅓ cup	oat bran
¾ teaspoon	salt
1 teaspoon	active dry yeast
	or bread machine yeast

1 Add the ingredients to the machine according to the manufacturer's directions. If available, select the whole grain cycle, or select the basic white bread cycle.

*Note: For ¾ cup cooked wild rice, start with ¾ cup water and ¼ cup uncooked wild rice. In a small saucepan bring water to boiling. Stir in wild rice; reduce heat to low. Cover and simmer about 40 minutes or just until rice is tender. Drain well; cool slightly.

Nutrition Facts per slice: 126 cal., 2 g total fat (0 g sat. fat), 2 mg chol., 113 mg sodium, 23 g carbo., 5 g pro.

The tender, light texture, the golden crust, and—of course—the perennially pleasing combination of mustard and dill combine for a loveable loaf indeed.

Mustard-Dill Loaf

1½-POUND*	INGREDIENTS	2-POUND*
1 cup	water	1¼ cups
2 tablespoons	Dijon-style mustard	3 tablespoons
1 tablespoon	shortening or cooking oil	2 tablespoons
2 cups	bread flour	2²/₃ cups
1 cup	whole wheat flour	1¹/₃ cups
1 tablespoon	brown sugar	4 teaspoons
1 teaspoon	dried dill	1¼ teaspoons
	or	
1 tablespoon	snipped fresh dill	4 teaspoons
³/₄ teaspoon	salt	1 teaspoon
1 teaspoon	active dry yeast	1¼ teaspoons
	or bread machine yeast	

PREP:
10 minutes

MAKES:
1½-pound recipe
(16 slices)
OR
2-pound recipe
(22 slices)

1 Select the loaf size. Add the ingredients to the machine according to the manufacturer's directions. If available, select the whole grain cycle, or select the basic white bread cycle.

*Note: For the 1½-pound loaf, the bread machine pan must have a capacity of 10 cups or more. For the 2-pound loaf, the bread machine pan must have a capacity of 12 cups or more.

Nutrition Facts per slice: 101 cal., 1 g total fat (0 g sat. fat), 0 mg chol., 121 mg sodium, 19 g carbo., 3 g pro.

Change the flavor of this hearty bread on a whim. If you like, use crushed anise seeds, fennel seeds, or poppy seeds in place of the caraway seeds.

Caraway Seed-Whole Wheat Bread

PREP:
10 minutes

MAKES:
1½-pound recipe
(16 slices)

1½-POUND	INGREDIENTS
1 cup	milk
1 tablespoon	cooking oil
1½ teaspoons	honey
2 cups	bread flour
1 cup	whole wheat flour
1½ teaspoons	sesame seeds, toasted
1½ teaspoons	caraway seeds, crushed
¾ teaspoon	salt
1 teaspoon	active dry yeast
	or bread machine yeast
3 tablespoons	shelled sunflower seeds

1 Add the ingredients to the machine according to the manufacturer's directions. If available, select the whole grain cycle, or select the basic white bread cycle.

Nutrition Facts per slice: 117 cal., 3 g total fat (0 g sat. fat), 2 mg chol., 110 mg sodium, 20 g carbo., 5 g pro.

If you don't keep cooked bacon pieces in the cupboard, substitute five slices of bacon. Cook the bacon until crisp, drain on paper towels, and crumble before using.

Bacon-Chive Bread

1½-POUND	INGREDIENTS
1¼ cups	milk
2 tablespoons	prepared mustard
1 tablespoon	shortening
2 cups	whole wheat flour
1 cup	bread flour
⅓ cup	cooked bacon pieces
3 tablespoons	snipped fresh chives
1 tablespoon	brown sugar
¾ teaspoon	salt
1 teaspoon	active dry yeast
	or bread machine yeast

PREP:
10 minutes

MAKES:
1½-pound recipe
(16 slices)

1 Add the ingredients to the machine according to the manufacturer's directions. If available, select the whole grain cycle, or select the basic white bread cycle.

Nutrition Facts per slice: 114 cal., 2 g total fat (0 g sat. fat), 2 mg chol., 198 mg sodium, 20 g carbo., 5 g pro.

Before storing fresh basil, cut ½ inch from the stems. Place the herb, stems submerged, in a jar of water and cover the tops with a loose-fitting plastic bag. Be sure to store basil at room temperature; it may blacken if kept in the refrigerator.

Cracked Wheat and Basil Bread

PREP:
15 minutes

MAKES:
1½-pound recipe
(16 slices)

1½-POUND	INGREDIENTS
1½ cups	buttermilk or sour milk*
2 tablespoons	shortening
2 cups	whole wheat flour
1 cup	bread flour
⅓ cup	cracked wheat
¼ cup	snipped fresh basil
	or
½ teaspoon	dried basil, crushed
1 tablespoon	brown sugar
¾ teaspoon	salt
1 teaspoon	active dry yeast
	or bread machine yeast

1 Add the ingredients to the machine according to the manufacturer's directions. If available, select the whole grain cycle, or select the basic white bread cycle.

*Note: To make 1½ cups sour milk, place 4½ teaspoons lemon juice or vinegar in a 2-cup liquid measuring cup. Add enough milk to measure 1½ cups liquid; stir. Let stand for 5 minutes before using.

Nutrition Facts per slice: 122 cal., 2 g total fat (0 g sat. fat), 2 mg chol., 126 mg sodium, 23 g carbo., 5 g pro.

If you can't find barley flour or barley meal, grind your own using regular barley. Place the barley in a blender container and cover and blend until finely ground.

Molasses-Barley Bread

PREP:
10 minutes

MAKES:
1½-pound recipe
(16 slices)

1½-POUND	INGREDIENTS
1 cup	water
3 tablespoons	molasses or brown sugar
2 tablespoons	cooking oil
2 cups	bread flour
½ cup	barley flour
½ cup	whole wheat flour
3 tablespoons	nonfat dry milk powder
1 teaspoon	salt
¾ teaspoon	ground cinnamon
1 teaspoon	active dry yeast
	or bread machine yeast

1 Add the ingredients to the machine according to the manufacturer's directions. If available, select the whole grain cycle, or select the basic white bread cycle.

Nutrition Facts per slice: 113 cal., 2 g total fat (0 g sat. fat), 0 mg chol., 156 mg sodium, 21 g carbo., 3 g pro.

Louisiana-style seasonings supply the spice for this rich and hearty bread made even better with whole wheat flour. It's sure to jazz up your everyday meals or Cajun-inspired dinners.

Cajun Whole Wheat Bread

PREP:
15 minutes

MAKES:
1½-pound recipe
(16 slices)
OR
2-pound recipe
(22 slices)

1½-POUND	INGREDIENTS	2-POUND
⅓ cup	chopped onion	½ cup
⅓ cup	chopped green sweet pepper	½ cup
4 teaspoons	chile oil or cooking oil	2 tablespoons
1½ teaspoons	Cajun seasoning	2 teaspoons
1 cup	milk	1⅓ cups
2 tablespoons	honey or mild-flavored molasses	3 tablespoons
2 cups	whole wheat flour	2⅔ cups
1 cup	bread flour	1⅓ cups
1 tablespoon	gluten flour	2 tablespoons
1 teaspoon	active dry yeast or bread machine yeast	1¼ teaspoons

1 Select the loaf size. In a small saucepan cook the onion and sweet pepper in hot oil until onion is tender, stirring occasionally. Stir in the Cajun seasoning; cook and stir over low heat for 30 seconds more. Cool slightly.

2 Add the onion mixture and the remaining ingredients to the machine according to the manufacturer's directions. If available, select the whole grain cycle, or select the basic white bread cycle.

Nutrition Facts per slice: 113 cal., 2 g total fat (0 g sat. fat), 1 mg chol., 26 mg sodium, 21 g carbo., 4 g pro.

The chili seasonings and kidney beans in this full-flavor loaf will remind you of your favorite bowl of red. Team it with plain grilled, broiled, or roasted meats or poultry.

Chili Bread

1½-POUND	INGREDIENTS
⅓ cup	chopped onion
⅓ cup	chopped green sweet pepper
4 teaspoons	cooking oil
1¼ teaspoons	chili powder
½ teaspoon	ground cumin
1 cup	milk
½ cup	drained, canned red
	kidney beans
2 cups	whole wheat flour
1 cup	bread flour
1 tablespoon	brown sugar
¾ teaspoon	salt
1 teaspoon	active dry yeast
	or bread machine yeast

PREP:
15 minutes

MAKES:
1½-pound recipe
(16 slices)

❶ In a small saucepan cook the onion and sweet pepper in hot oil until onion is tender, stirring occasionally. Stir in the chili powder and cumin; cook and stir over low heat for 1 minute more. Cool slightly.

❷ Add the onion mixture and the remaining ingredients to the machine according to the manufacturer's directions. If available, select the whole grain cycle, or select the basic white bread cycle.

Nutrition Facts per slice: 114 cal., 2 g total fat (0 g sat. fat), 2 mg chol., 125 mg sodium, 21 g carbo., 5 g pro.

Millet is a tiny round yellow cereal grain. It adds a chewy texture to this bread and a bit of nuttiness to the flavor. If you can't find it on your grocer's shelf, try a health-food store or Asian market.

Onion-Millet Bread

PREP:
10 minutes

MAKES:
1½-pound recipe
(16 slices)
OR
2-pound recipe
(22 slices)

1½-POUND	INGREDIENTS	2-POUND
1 cup	milk	1⅓ cups
2 tablespoons	water	3 tablespoons
1 tablespoon	cooking oil	4 teaspoons
2 cups	bread flour	2⅔ cups
1 cup	whole wheat flour	1⅓ cups
¼ cup	millet	⅓ cup
2 tablespoons	brown sugar	3 tablespoons
1 tablespoon	dried minced onion	4 teaspoons
¾ teaspoon	salt	1 teaspoon
⅛ teaspoon	garlic powder*	⅛ teaspoon
1 teaspoon	active dry yeast	1¼ teaspoons
	or bread machine yeast	

1 Select the loaf size. Add the ingredients to the machine according to the manufacturer's directions. If available, select the whole grain cycle, or select the basic white bread cycle.

*Note: The Test Kitchen recommends ⅛ teaspoon garlic powder for either size recipe.

Nutrition Facts per slice: 121 cal., 2 g total fat (0 g sat. fat), 1 mg chol., 109 mg sodium, 23 g carbo., 4 g pro.

Fennel seeds, with their licoricelike flavor, can take center stage in both sweet and savory dishes. Here, they complement coarsely ground black pepper for a loaf with plenty of gusto.

Pepper and Fennel Loaf

1½-POUND	INGREDIENTS
1¼ cups	milk
2 teaspoons	shortening
2 cups	whole wheat flour
1 cup	bread flour
1 tablespoon	brown sugar
1 teaspoon	fennel seeds
¾ teaspoon	salt
½ to 1 teaspoon	coarsely ground black pepper
1 teaspoon	active dry yeast
	or bread machine yeast

PREP:
10 minutes

MAKES:
1½-pound recipe
(16 slices)

1 Add the ingredients to the machine according to the manufacturer's directions. If available, select the whole grain cycle, or select the basic white bread cycle.

Nutrition Facts per slice: 72 cal., 2 g total fat (0 g sat. fat), 2 mg chol., 111 mg sodium, 14 g carbo., 3 g pro.

In days gone by, folks looked forward to the wheat harvest so they could mill new flour for breads like this one. The toasted wheat germ and hint of brown sugar make this loaf a cut above other whole wheat breads.

Harvest Bread

PREP:
10 minutes

MAKES:
1½-pound recipe
(16 slices)
OR
2-pound recipe
(22 slices)

1½-POUND*	INGREDIENTS	2-POUND*
1 cup	milk	1⅓ cups
1	egg(s)	2
2 tablespoons	margarine or butter, cut up	3 tablespoons
2½ cups	bread flour	3⅓ cups
¾ cup	whole wheat flour	1 cup
½ cup	toasted wheat germ	⅔ cup
3 tablespoons	packed brown sugar	¼ cup
¾ teaspoon	salt	1 teaspoon
1 teaspoon	active dry yeast	1¼ teaspoons
	or bread machine yeast	

1 Select the loaf size. Add the ingredients to the machine according to the manufacturer's directions. If available, select the whole grain cycle, or select the basic white bread cycle.

*Note: For the 1½-pound loaf, the bread machine pan must have a capacity of 10 cups or more. For the 2-pound loaf, the bread machine pan must have a capacity of 12 cups or more.

Nutrition Facts per slice: 143 cal., 3 g total fat (1 g sat. fat), 14 mg chol., 130 mg sodium, 24 g carbo., 5 g pro.

The light- and even-grained texture, the golden crust, and a heavenly scent of garlic make this bread a winner. It's so versatile: Serve it with soups in the winter or salads in the summer.

Roasted Garlic Wheat Bread

1½-POUND	INGREDIENTS	2-POUND
¾ cup	water	1 cup
⅓ cup	dairy sour cream	½ cup
1½ teaspoons	bottled minced roasted garlic	2 teaspoons
1½ cups	whole wheat flour	2 cups
1½ cups	bread flour	2 cups
2 teaspoons	gluten flour	1 tablespoon
1 teaspoon	sugar	1½ teaspoons
¾ teaspoon	salt	1 teaspoon
1 teaspoon	active dry yeast	1¼ teaspoons
	or bread machine yeast	

PREP:
10 minutes

MAKES:
1½-pound recipe
(16 slices)
OR
2-pound recipe
(22 slices)

1 Select the loaf size. Add the ingredients to the machine according to the manufacturer's directions. If available, select the whole grain cycle, or select the basic white bread cycle.

Nutrition Facts per slice: 99 cal., 1 g total fat (1 g sat. fat), 2 mg chol., 104 mg sodium, 18 g carbo., 4 g pro.

Garlic in Jars

Bottled minced and bottled chopped roasted garlic are new convenience products found in the produce section of the supermarket. One teaspoonful is the equivalent of two to three cloves of fresh roasted garlic. You get great garlic flavor with none of the fuss. Store opened jars in the refrigerator.

With this easy recipe, you can enjoy the enchanting flavors of fresh basil, pine nuts, and Parmesan cheese without going to the trouble of making pesto from scratch.

Pesto and Wheat Bread

PREP:
15 minutes

MAKES:
1½-pound recipe
(16 slices)

1½-POUND	INGREDIENTS
1¼ cups	water
2 tablespoons	cooking oil
2 cups	whole wheat flour
1 cup	bread flour
½ cup	snipped fresh basil
⅓ cup	grated Parmesan cheese
¼ cup	oat bran
1 tablespoon	brown sugar
¾ teaspoon	salt
1 teaspoon	active dry yeast
	or bread machine yeast
½ cup	pine nuts
	or slivered almonds, toasted

1 Add the ingredients to the machine according to the manufacturer's directions. If available, select the whole grain cycle, or select the basic white bread cycle.

Nutrition Facts per slice: 138 cal., 5 g total fat (2 g sat. fat), 2 mg chol., 146 mg sodium, 20 g carbo., 6 g pro.

Anise seeds have been used in cooking since ancient times and are hallmarks of cuisines from Italy to India to Southeast Asia. In this recipe, they marry with bulgur and walnuts to produce exquisite slices for everything from toast to tea sandwiches.

Walnut-Anise Bulgur Bread

1½-POUND	INGREDIENTS
¾ cup	water
⅓ cup	bulgur
1 cup plus 1 tablespoon	milk
2 teaspoons	shortening
2 cups	whole wheat flour
1 cup	bread flour
1 tablespoon	brown sugar
¾ teaspoon	salt
¾ teaspoon	anise seeds, crushed
1 teaspoon	active dry yeast or bread machine yeast
⅓ cup	chopped walnuts, toasted

PREP:
15 minutes

MAKES:
1½-pound recipe
(16 slices)

1 In a small saucepan bring the water to boiling; remove from heat. Stir in the bulgur. Let stand for 5 minutes; drain well.

2 Add the drained bulgur and the remaining ingredients to the machine according to the manufacturer's directions. If available, select the whole grain cycle, or select the basic white bread cycle.

Nutrition Facts per slice: 129 cal., 3 g total fat (0 g sat. fat), 2 mg chol., 111 mg sodium, 23 g carbo., 5 g pro.

When you're purchasing the shallots to make this inviting pesto-flavored bread, look for firm, well-shaped shallots with no sprouts. Avoid shriveled or wrinkled ones.

Basil-Shallot Braid

PREP:	1½-POUND	INGREDIENTS	2-POUND
30 minutes	³/₄ cup	milk	1 cup
RISE:	1	egg(s)	2
40 minutes	2 tablespoons	margarine or butter, cut up	3 tablespoons
BAKE:	1 tablespoon	water*	1 tablespoon
25 minutes	1½ cups	bread flour	2¼ cups
	1½ cups	whole wheat flour	2 cups
MAKES:	2 tablespoons	sugar	3 tablespoons
1½-pound recipe (16 slices)	³/₄ teaspoon	salt	1 teaspoon
OR	1 teaspoon	active dry yeast	1¼ teaspoons
2-pound recipe (24 slices)		or bread machine yeast	
	½ cup	finely chopped shallots	²/₃ cup
	1 tablespoon	olive oil or cooking oil	3 tablespoons
	½ cup	snipped fresh basil	²/₃ cup
	¼ cup	grated Parmesan cheese	¹/₃ cup
	¼ cup	pine nuts, toasted	¹/₃ cup

❶ Select the recipe size. Add the first 9 ingredients to the machine according to the manufacturer's directions. Select the dough cycle. When cycle is complete, remove dough. Punch down. Cover and let rest for 10 minutes. Meanwhile, for filling, in a small saucepan cook shallots in hot oil until tender, stirring occasionally. In a small bowl combine the shallot mixture, basil, Parmesan cheese, and pine nuts. Lightly grease a baking sheet; set aside.

❷ On a lightly floured surface, roll the 1½-pound dough into a 15×12-inch rectangle. Cut into three 15×4-inch strips. (Roll the 2-pound dough into a 17×12-inch rectangle; cut into three 17×4-inch strips.) Spread one-third of the filling down the center of each strip; moisten edges. Bring long edges together over filling and pinch to seal.

❸ To shape, line up the ropes, 1 inch apart, on the prepared baking sheet. Starting in the middle, loosely braid by bringing the left rope under the center rope. Bring the right rope under the new center rope. Repeat to the end. On the other end, braid by bringing the outside ropes alternately over the center rope to center. Press ends together to seal; tuck under loaf. Cover and let rise in a warm place about 40 minutes or until nearly double.

❹ Bake in a 350°F oven about 25 minutes or until bread sounds hollow when lightly tapped. If necessary, cover loosely with foil the last 5 minutes to prevent overbrowning. Remove from baking sheet; cool on a wire rack.

*Note: The Test Kitchen recommends 1 tablespoon water for either size recipe.

Nutrition Facts per slice: 146 cal., 5 g total fat (1 g sat. fat), 15 mg chol., 157 mg sodium, 21 g carbo., 5 g pro.

No need to wait for blueberry season to make this wholesome loaf. Dried blueberries are available year-round in many supermarkets—look for them in the produce aisle.

Blueberry-Granola Wheat Bread

1½-POUND	INGREDIENTS	2-POUND
1¼ cups	milk	1½ cups
½ cup	dried blueberries	⅔ cup
1 tablespoon	shortening or cooking oil	4 teaspoons
2 cups	whole wheat flour	2⅔ cups
1 cup	bread flour	1⅓ cups
½ cup	granola	⅔ cup
1 tablespoon	gluten flour	4 teaspoons
1 tablespoon	brown sugar	4 teaspoons
¾ teaspoon	salt	1 teaspoon
1 teaspoon	active dry yeast	1¼ teaspoons
	or bread machine yeast	

PREP:
20 minutes

MAKES:
1½-pound recipe
(16 slices)
OR
2-pound recipe
(22 slices)

1 Select the loaf size. Place the milk in a microwave-safe liquid measuring cup or bowl. Microwave, uncovered, on 100-percent power (high) for 1 minute. Add the milk to the machine; add the dried blueberries. Let stand for 10 minutes.

2 Add the remaining ingredients to the machine according to the manufacturer's directions. If available, select the whole grain cycle, or select the basic white bread cycle.

Nutrition Facts per slice: 145 cal., 3 g total fat (1 g sat. fat), 1 mg chol., 120 mg sodium, 27 g carbo., 4 g pro.

Cardamom, a member of the ginger family, gives this bread a spicy-sweet flavor. One taste and you'll appreciate why the Far East spice trade changed the Western world.

Cardamom-Apple Bread

PREP:
15 minutes

MAKES:
1½-pound recipe
(16 slices)

1½-POUND	INGREDIENTS
¾ cup	water
⅓ cup	shredded apple
2 tablespoons	honey
1 tablespoon	margarine or butter
1½ cups	whole wheat flour
1½ cups	bread flour
1½ teaspoons	finely shredded orange peel
¾ teaspoon	salt
½ teaspoon	ground cardamom
1 teaspoon	active dry yeast
	or bread machine yeast
⅓ cup	dark raisins (optional)

1 Add the ingredients to the machine according to the manufacturer's directions. If available, select the whole grain cycle, or select the basic white bread cycle.

Nutrition Facts per slice: 110 cal., 2 g total fat (0 g sat. fat), 0 mg chol., 110 mg sodium, 23 g carbo., 3 g pro.

Spice Buying Tips

Spices, such as cardamom, are often available whole or ground. Ground spices lose their flavor fairly quickly (in about six months), so buying ground spices in small quantities makes sense. Whole spices can be stored longer and ground as needed. Keep all spices in airtight containers in a cool, dark place.

Legend has it that the original "anadama" bread was made by a man frustrated with his wife's less-than-competent baking skills. In desperation, he made his own bread while mumbling "Anna—damn her."

Fennel-Orange Anadama Bread

1½-POUND	INGREDIENTS	2-POUND
½ cup	milk	¾ cup
⅓ cup	water	½ cup
3 tablespoons	molasses	¼ cup
1 tablespoon	margarine or butter, cut up	2 tablespoons
2 cups	bread flour	2⅔ cups
¾ cup	whole wheat flour	1 cup
½ cup	cornmeal	⅔ cup
4 teaspoons	gluten flour	2 tablespoons
1½ teaspoons	fennel seeds, crushed	2 teaspoons
¾ teaspoon	salt	1 teaspoon
½ teaspoon	finely shredded orange peel	1 teaspoon
1¼ teaspoons	active dry yeast	1½ teaspoons
	or bread machine yeast	

PREP:
10 minutes

MAKES:
1½-pound recipe
(16 slices)
OR
2-pound recipe
(22 slices)

1 Select the loaf size. Add the ingredients to the machine according to the manufacturer's directions. If available, select the whole grain cycle, or select the basic white bread cycle.

Nutrition Facts per slice: 120 cal., 1 g total fat (0 g sat. fat), 1 mg chol., 124 mg sodium, 23 g carbo., 4 g pro.

Hosting an open house or tea? Here's an idea for a quick nibble. Cut slices of this delectable loaf into fancy shapes with hors d'oeuvre cutters. Spread the shapes with pineapple-flavored cream cheese or lemon curd and top with a pecan or walnut half.

Maple and Wheat Nut Bread

PREP:
15 minutes

MAKES:
1½-pound recipe
(16 slices)

1½-POUND	INGREDIENTS
1 cup	milk
3 tablespoons	maple-flavored syrup
2 teaspoons	shortening
2 cups	whole wheat flour
1 cup	bread flour
³/₄ teaspoon	salt
1 teaspoon	active dry yeast
	or bread machine yeast
¹/₂ cup	chopped pecans
	or walnuts, toasted

1 Add the ingredients to the machine according to the manufacturer's directions. If available, select the whole grain cycle, or select the basic white bread cycle.

Nutrition Facts per slice: 132 cal., 3 g total fat (0 g sat. fat), 2 mg chol., 116 mg sodium, 21 g carbo., 5 g pro.

Micro-Toasting Nuts

Did you know that nuts can be "toasted" in the microwave oven? Place ¹/₂ to 1 cup nuts in a microwave-safe 2-cup liquid measuring cup. Microwave, uncovered, on 100-percent power (high) until light brown, stirring after 2 minutes, then every 30 seconds. Microwave for 2 to 4 minutes more, watching carefully. Nuts will continue to toast as they stand.

As you shred the lemon peel for this fresh-tasting bread, use only the yellow outer peel; the white part is too bitter.

Lemony Granola Bread

1¹⁄₂-POUND	INGREDIENTS	2-POUND
1¼ cups	water	1¹⁄₂ cups
3 tablespoons	margarine or butter, cut up	¼ cup
2 cups	bread flour	2²⁄₃ cups
1¹⁄₂ cups	granola with raisins	2 cups
1 cup	whole wheat flour	1¹⁄₃ cups
¼ cup	nonfat dry milk powder	¹⁄₃ cup
1 teaspoon	finely shredded lemon peel	1¹⁄₂ teaspoons
³⁄₄ teaspoon	salt	1 teaspoon
1 teaspoon	active dry yeast	1¼ teaspoons
	or bread machine yeast	

PREP:
10 minutes

MAKES:
1¹⁄₂-pound recipe
(16 slices)
OR
2-pound recipe
(22 slices)

❶ Select the loaf size. Add the ingredients to the machine according to the manufacturer's directions. If available, select the whole grain cycle, or select the basic white bread cycle.

Nutrition Facts per slice: 158 cal., 4 g total fat (2 g sat. fat), 0 mg chol., 154 mg sodium, 26 g carbo., 5 g pro.

Molasses, sunflower seeds, and raisins are an awesome taste trio in this hearty oat bread.

Sunflower and Grains Bread

PREP:
25 minutes

MAKES:
1½-pound recipe
(16 slices)

1½-POUND	INGREDIENTS
½ cup	regular or quick-cooking rolled oats
1 cup plus 2 tablespoons	buttermilk
2 tablespoons	honey or molasses
1 tablespoon	cooking oil
2 cups	bread flour
½ cup	whole wheat flour
¾ teaspoon	salt
1 teaspoon	active dry yeast or bread machine yeast
½ cup	shelled sunflower seeds
¼ cup	dark raisins

1 Spread the rolled oats in a shallow baking pan. Bake in a 350°F oven for 15 to 20 minutes or until light brown, stirring occasionally. Cool slightly.

2 Add the ingredients to the machine according to the manufacturer's directions, adding the oats with flours. If available, select the whole grain cycle, or select the basic white bread cycle.

Nutrition Facts per slice: 146 cal., 3 g total fat (0 g sat. fat), 0 mg chol., 120 mg sodium, 24 g carbo., 5 g pro.

The art of fermentation finds its ultimate expression in this savory whole grain yeast bread boosted with cherry stout and brightened with morsels of dried tart cherries.

Fruit and Beer Bread

1½-POUND	INGREDIENTS	2-POUND
1 cup	cherry stout	1¼ cups
	or mild-flavored beer	
2 tablespoons	water	3 tablespoons
1 tablespoon	margarine or butter	4 teaspoons
2 cups	bread flour	2½ cups
1 cup	whole wheat flour	1½ cups
4 teaspoons	sugar	2 tablespoons
1 teaspoon	dried savory, crushed,	1¼ teaspoons
	or	
1 tablespoon	snipped fresh savory	4 teaspoons
¾ teaspoon	salt	1 teaspoon
1 teaspoon	active dry yeast	1¼ teaspoons
	or bread machine yeast	
½ cup	snipped dried tart cherries	⅔ cup

PREP:
15 minutes

MAKES:
1½-pound recipe
(16 slices)
OR
2-pound recipe
(22 slices)

1 Select the loaf size. Add the ingredients to the machine according to the manufacturer's directions. If available, select the whole grain cycle, or select the basic white bread cycle.

Nutrition Facts per slice: 117 cal., 1 g total fat (0 g sat. fat), 0 mg chol., 110 mg sodium, 23 g carbo., 3 g pro.

Make sure the granola you use doesn't include golden raisins or dried apricots, peaches, or apples because the sulfur used to keep these fruits light may inhibit the performance of the yeast.

Date-Granola Bread

PREP:	1½-POUND	I N G R E D I E N T S
15 minutes	1¼ cups	buttermilk or sour milk*
	2 tablespoons	honey
MAKES:	1 tablespoon	margarine or butter
1½-pound recipe (16 slices)	2 cups	bread flour
	1½ cups	whole wheat flour
	²/₃ cup	granola
	¾ teaspoon	salt
	1 teaspoon	active dry yeast
		or bread machine yeast
	⅓ cup	chopped pecans
	⅓ cup	chopped pitted dates

1 Add the ingredients to the machine according to the manufacturer's directions. If available, select the whole grain cycle, or select the basic white bread cycle and, if available, the light color setting.

*Note: To make 1¼ cups sour milk, place 3¾ teaspoons lemon juice or vinegar in a 2-cup liquid measuring cup. Add enough milk to measure 1¼ cups liquid; stir. Let stand for 5 minutes before using.

Nutrition Facts per slice: 174 cal., 5 g total fat (2 g sat. fat), 2 mg chol., 149 mg sodium, 30 g carbo., 5 g pro.

You'll find this fun-to-eat bread chock-full of apple, nuts, and raisins. For a tart apple flavor use Granny Smith or Northern Spy apples; for a sweeter flavor opt for Golden Delicious or Gala.

Chunky Apple Bread

1½-POUND	INGREDIENTS
1¼ cups	apple juice
¾ cup	finely chopped, peeled apple
2 tablespoons	margarine or butter, cut up
2 cups	bread flour
1½ cups	whole wheat flour
¾ cup	regular or quick-cooking rolled oats
1 tablespoon	sugar
¾ teaspoon	salt
½ teaspoon	ground cinnamon
1 teaspoon	active dry yeast or bread machine yeast
⅓ cup	chopped walnuts
⅓ cup	dark raisins (optional)

PREP:
15 minutes

MAKES:
1½-pound recipe
(16 slices)

1 Add the ingredients to the machine according to the manufacturer's directions. If available, select the whole grain cycle, or select the basic white bread cycle.

Nutrition Facts per slice: 164 cal., 3 g total fat (0 g sat. fat), 0 mg chol., 114 mg sodium, 29 g carbo., 5 g pro.

For a new take on Grandma's favorite, try this updated yeast version. You'll love the bits of oats and rich honey flavor in every bite.

Banana-Nut Oatmeal Bread

PREP:
25 minutes

MAKES:
1½-pound recipe
(16 slices)

1½-POUND*	INGREDIENTS
⅓ cup	quick-cooking or regular rolled oats
⅔ cup	buttermilk or sour milk**
½ cup	mashed ripe banana
1	egg
2 tablespoons	margarine or butter, cut up
4 teaspoons	honey
2 cups	bread flour
1 cup plus 2 tablespoons	whole wheat flour
¾ teaspoon	salt
¾ teaspoon	ground cinnamon
¼ teaspoon	ground nutmeg
1 teaspoon	active dry yeast or bread machine yeast
⅓ cup	chopped walnuts

1 Spread the rolled oats in a shallow baking pan. Bake in a 350°F oven for 15 to 20 minutes or until light brown, stirring occasionally. Cool slightly.

2 Add the ingredients to the machine according to the manufacturer's directions, adding the oats with flours. If available, select the whole grain cycle, or select the basic white bread cycle.

*Note: The bread machine pan must have a capacity of 10 cups or more.

**Note: To make ⅔ cup sour milk, place 2 teaspoons lemon juice or vinegar in a 1-cup liquid measuring cup. Add enough milk to measure ⅔ cup liquid; stir. Let stand for 5 minutes before using.

Nutrition Facts per slice: 150 cal., 5 g total fat (0 g sat. fat), 21 mg chol., 132 mg sodium, 24 g carbo., 6 g pro.

It used to be that cranberry bread was only a fall or holiday treat. But with dried cranberries, you can enjoy this spicy loaf anytime.

Spiced Maple and Cranberry Bread

PREP:
15 minutes

MAKES:
1½-pound recipe
(16 slices)

1½-POUND	INGREDIENTS
1 cup	milk
¼ cup	maple-flavored syrup
2 tablespoons	margarine or butter, cut up
2 cups	whole wheat flour
1 cup	bread flour
¾ teaspoon	salt
½ teaspoon	apple pie spice
1 teaspoon	active dry yeast
	or bread machine yeast
⅔ cup	snipped dried cranberries

1 Add the ingredients to the machine according to the manufacturer's directions. If available, select the whole grain cycle, or select the basic white bread cycle.

Nutrition Facts per slice: 135 cal., 2 g total fat (0 g sat. fat), 2 mg chol., 132 mg sodium, 27 g carbo., 5 g pro.

The enticing aroma of this delicious loaf will lure hungry appetites to your kitchen. When lunch rolls around, it makes a terrific peanut butter and jelly sandwich.

Pineapple-Carrot Bread

PREP:
15 minutes

MAKES:
1½-pound recipe
(16 slices)
OR
2-pound recipe
(22 slices)

1½-POUND	INGREDIENTS	2-POUND
¾ cup	buttermilk or sour milk*	1 cup
1 (8-ounce) can	crushed pineapple (juice pack), well drained	1 (15¼-ounce) can
½ cup	coarsely shredded carrot	⅔ cup
1 tablespoon	shortening or cooking oil	4 teaspoons
2 cups	whole wheat flour	2⅔ cups
1 cup	bread flour	1⅓ cups
1 tablespoon	brown sugar	4 teaspoons
¾ teaspoon	salt	1 teaspoon
1 teaspoon	active dry yeast or bread machine yeast	1¼ teaspoons

① Select the loaf size. Add the ingredients to the machine according to the manufacturer's directions, adding the pineapple with the buttermilk. If available, select the whole grain cycle, or select the basic white bread cycle.

*Note: To make ¾ cup sour milk, place 2¼ teaspoons lemon juice or vinegar in a 1-cup liquid measuring cup. Add enough milk to measure ¾ cup liquid; stir. To make 1 cup sour milk, place 1 tablespoon lemon juice or vinegar in a 1-cup liquid measuring cup. Add enough milk to measure 1 cup liquid; stir. Let stand for 5 minutes before using.

Nutrition Facts per slice: 107 cal., 1 g total fat (0 g sat. fat), 0 mg chol., 116 mg sodium, 21 g carbo., 4 g pro.

Easy-to-Use Buttermilk Powder

If you use buttermilk infrequently but you appreciate its virtues for baking, use buttermilk powder instead of liquid buttermilk. It tenderizes in exactly the same way and has a long shelf life. In general, reconstitute with water before using as directed on the label.

Coriander seeds taste like a blend of lemon, sage, and caraway. Ground and mixed with a medley of spices and honey, they add unique flavor nuances to this first-rate bread.

Coriander-Honey Grain Bread

1½-POUND*	INGREDIENTS
1¼ cups	milk
1	egg
1 tablespoon	honey
1 tablespoon	margarine or butter
2½ cups	bread flour
1 cup	whole wheat flour
1 teaspoon	ground coriander
¾ teaspoon	salt
½ teaspoon	ground cinnamon
¼ teaspoon	ground cloves
⅛ teaspoon	ground ginger
1 teaspoon	active dry yeast
	or bread machine yeast

PREP:
10 minutes

MAKES:
1½-pound recipe
(16 slices)

1 Add the ingredients to the machine according to the manufacturer's directions. If available, select the whole grain cycle, or select the basic white bread cycle.

Note: The bread machine pan must have a capacity of 10 cups or more.

Nutrition Facts per slice: 126 cal., 2 g total fat (0 g sat. fat), 21 mg chol., 125 mg sodium, 23 g carbo., 5 g pro.

This rye bread is unlike any you'll find at the store. It's loaded with onion and features a unique combination of anise and caraway seeds.

Onion Rye Bread

PREP: 20 minutes	1½-POUND	INGREDIENTS
	²/₃ cup	milk
RISE: 30 minutes	²/₃ cup	finely chopped onion
	1	egg
BAKE: 30 minutes	¼ cup	margarine or butter, cut up
	1 tablespoon	water
MAKES: 1½-pound recipe (16 slices)	1¾ cups	bread flour
	1¼ cups	rye flour
	¼ cup	packed brown sugar
	1 tablespoon	anise seeds
	1 tablespoon	caraway seeds
	1 teaspoon	salt
	2½ teaspoons	active dry yeast or bread machine yeast

1 Add the ingredients to the machine according to the manufacturer's directions. Select the dough cycle. When the cycle is complete, remove dough. Punch down. Cover and let rest for 10 minutes.

2 Grease a 9×5×3- or 8×4×2-inch loaf pan. On a lightly floured surface, shape the dough into a loaf, pinching and tucking the edges under the loaf. Place in the prepared loaf pan. Cover and let rise in a warm place about 30 minutes or until nearly double.

3 Bake in a 375°F oven for 30 to 35 minutes or until bread sounds hollow when lightly tapped. Remove from pan; cool on a wire rack.

Nutrition Facts per slice: 138 cal., 4 g total fat (1 g sat. fat), 14 mg chol., 188 mg sodium, 22 g carbo., 4 g pro.

Stone-ground mustard gives zip to this flavorful rye. Its dense, even texture makes it sandwich-worthy.

Mustard Rye Bread

1½-POUND	INGREDIENTS	2-POUND
1¼ cups	water	1½ cups
¼ cup	stone-ground mustard	⅓ cup
1 tablespoon	shortening	2 tablespoons
2 cups	bread flour	2⅔ cups
1½ cups	rye flour	2 cups
2 tablespoons	gluten flour	3 tablespoons
1 tablespoon	brown sugar	4 teaspoons
1 teaspoon	caraway seeds*	1 teaspoon
¾ teaspoon	salt	1 teaspoon
1 teaspoon	active dry yeast	1¼ teaspoons
	or bread machine yeast	

PREP:
10 minutes

MAKES:
1½-pound recipe
(16 slices)
OR
2-pound recipe
(22 slices)

1 Select the loaf size. Add the ingredients to the machine according to the manufacturer's directions. If available, select the whole grain cycle, or select the basic white bread cycle.

*Note:: The Test Kitchen recommends 1 teaspoon caraway seeds for either size recipe.

Nutrition Facts per slice: 114 cal., 2 g total fat (0 g sat. fat), 0 mg chol., 152 mg sodium, 21 g carbo., 4 g pro.

Orange peel adds a hint of citrus flavor to this fresh-baked masterpiece.

Rye-Anise Loaf

PREP:
10 minutes

MAKES:
1½-pound recipe
(16 slices)
OR
2-pound recipe
(22 slices)

1½-POUND*	INGREDIENTS	2-POUND*
½ cup	milk	¾ cup
¼ cup	water	⅓ cup
1	egg**	1
2 tablespoons	margarine or butter, cut up, or shortening	3 tablespoons
2 cups	bread flour	2⅔ cups
1 cup	rye flour	1⅔ cups
3 tablespoons	packed brown sugar	¼ cup
1 tablespoon	gluten flour	4 teaspoons
2 teaspoons	anise seeds, slightly crushed	1 tablespoon
1½ teaspoons	finely shredded orange peel	2 teaspoons
¾ teaspoon	salt	1 teaspoon
1½ teaspoons	active dry yeast or bread machine yeast	1¾ teaspoons

1 Select the loaf size. Add the ingredients to the machine according to the manufacturer's directions. If available, select the whole grain cycle, or select the basic white bread cycle and, if available, the light color setting.

*Note: For the 1½-pound loaf, the bread machine pan must have a capacity of 10 cups or more. For the 2-pound loaf, the bread machine pan must have a capacity of 12 cups or more.

**Note: The Test Kitchen recommends 1 egg for either size recipe.

Nutrition Facts per slice: 118 cal., 2 g total fat (1 g sat. fat), 14 mg chol., 126 mg sodium, 20 g carbo., 4 g pro.

Although molasses is the traditional flavoring for pumpernickel bread, this raisin-stuffed version has two other seasoning boosters—a touch of cocoa powder and a sprinkling of caraway seeds.

Raisin-Pumpernickel Bread

PREP:
10 minutes

MAKES:
1½-pound recipe
(16 slices)

1½-POUND	INGREDIENTS
1⅓ cups	milk
2 tablespoons	molasses
1 tablespoon	cooking oil
2 cups	bread flour
1 cup	whole wheat flour
½ cup	rye flour
2 tablespoons	unsweetened cocoa powder
1 tablespoon	gluten flour
1½ teaspoons	caraway seeds
¾ teaspoon	salt
1 teaspoon	active dry yeast
	or bread machine yeast
⅓ cup	dark raisins

1 Add the ingredients to the machine according to the manufacturer's directions. If available, select the whole grain cycle, or select the basic white bread cycle.

Nutrition Facts per slice: 137 cal., 2 g total fat (0 g sat. fat), 2 mg chol., 114 mg sodium, 26 g carbo., 5 g pro.

You'll have bragging rights equal to those of even the best bread bakers when you serve this wholesome loaf brimming with sunflower seeds and raisins.

Whole Grain Sunflower Bread

PREP:
10 minutes

MAKES:
1½-pound recipe
(16 slices)

1½-POUND	INGREDIENTS
1½ cups	milk
2 tablespoons	cooking oil
1 tablespoon	honey
2½ cups	bread flour
¾ cup	rye flour
¾ cup	whole wheat flour
¾ teaspoon	salt
1 teaspoon	active dry yeast
	or bread machine yeast
3 tablespoons	dark raisins
3 tablespoons	shelled sunflower seeds

1 Add the ingredients to the machine according to the manufacturer's directions. If available, select the whole grain cycle, or select the basic white bread cycle.

Nutrition Facts per slice: 158 cal., 3 g total fat (0 g sat. fat), 2 mg chol., 113 mg sodium, 29 g carbo., 5 g pro.

This aromatic loaf would make a good choice for something special to serve alongside an appetizer tray of cheeses, smoked salmon, and savory spreads.

Scandinavian Lemon-Dill Rye Bread

1½-POUND	INGREDIENTS
2 teaspoons	active dry yeast
	or bread machine yeast
¾ cup	warm water (105°F to 115°F)
¾ cup	bread flour
1 teaspoon	sugar
⅓ cup	water
1 tablespoon	olive oil
1¼ cups	bread flour
¾ cup	rye flour
¼ cup	cornmeal
4 teaspoons	gluten flour
2 teaspoons	dill seeds
2 teaspoons	dried minced onion
1½ teaspoons	finely shredded lemon peel
¾ teaspoon	salt

PREP:
25 minutes

STAND:
12 hours

RISE:
30 minutes

BAKE:
25 minutes

MAKES:
1½-pound recipe
(16 slices)

1 *To make the starter:* In a medium bowl dissolve the yeast in the ¾ cup warm water. Stir in the ¾ cup bread flour and sugar just until smooth. Cover with plastic wrap. Let stand at room temperature (70°F to 80°F) for 12 to 24 hours or until mixture has a slightly fermented aroma, stirring two or three times.

2 *To finish the bread:* Add the starter and the remaining ingredients to the machine according to the manufacturer's directions. Select the dough cycle. When cycle is complete, remove dough. Punch down. Cover and let rest for 10 minutes. Lightly grease a baking sheet and sprinkle with additional cornmeal; set aside.

3 On a lightly floured surface, shape the dough into a ball. Place on the prepared baking sheet. Flatten slightly to a 6-inch round loaf. Using a sharp knife, make several cuts about ¼ inch deep across top of loaf. Cover and let rise in a warm place for 30 to 45 minutes or until nearly double.

4 Bake in a 400°F oven about 25 minutes or until bread sounds hollow when lightly tapped. Remove from baking sheet; cool on a wire rack.

Nutrition Facts per slice: 102 cal., 1 g total fat (0 g sat. fat), 0 mg chol., 110 mg sodium, 19 g carbo., 3 g pro.

"Brew-in-a-bread" describes this finely textured rye. The flavors of beer and caraway upgrade a simple roast pork or beef sandwich to new heights.

Stout Rye Bread

PREP:
10 minutes

MAKES:
1½-pound recipe
(16 slices)
OR
2-pound recipe
(22 slices)

1½-POUND	INGREDIENTS	2-POUND
1 cup	stout or other dark beer	1¼ cups
1 tablespoon	shortening*	1 tablespoon
2 cups	bread flour	2⅔ cups
1 cup	rye flour	1⅓ cups
2 tablespoons	gluten flour*	2 tablespoons
1 tablespoon	brown sugar	4 teaspoons
1 teaspoon	caraway seeds*	1 teaspoon
¾ teaspoon	salt	1 teaspoon
1 teaspoon	active dry yeast	1½ teaspoons
	or bread machine yeast	

1 Select the loaf size. Add the ingredients to the machine according to the manufacturer's directions. If available, select the whole grain cycle, or select the basic white bread cycle.

*Note: The Test Kitchen recommends 1 tablespoon shortening, 2 tablespoons gluten flour, and 1 teaspoon caraway seeds for either size recipe.

Nutrition Facts per slice: 105 cal., 1 g total fat (0 g sat. fat), 0 mg chol., 102 mg sodium, 19 g carbo., 3 g pro.

Beer and Bread Duo

There is no doubt that beer and bread have a special affinity—pass the pretzels, please. A foamy brew with a pub-goer's lunch of crusty bread and cheese is a famous menu marriage. Another is rye bread, smoked meats, and dark, full-bodied stout, an ale with lots of malt. A good rule of thumb: Light beers pair well with light foods; robust brews require hearty dishes.

SWEET BREAD TREASURES

Bursting with a trio of terrific flavors, this bread will be a sure-fire hit on a brunch table. Try it slathered with orange marmalade to heighten its citrusy appeal.

Orange-Hazelnut-Blueberry Bread

PREP:	1½-POUND*	INGREDIENTS	2-POUND*
20 minutes	¾ cup	milk	1 cup
	½ cup	dried blueberries	⅔ cup
MAKES:	1	egg**	1
1½-pound recipe (16 slices)	2 tablespoons	margarine or butter, cut up	3 tablespoons
OR	3 cups	bread flour	4 cups
2-pound recipe (24 slices)	3 tablespoons	packed brown sugar	¼ cup
	1 tablespoon	finely shredded orange peel	4 teaspoons
	¾ teaspoon	salt	1 teaspoon
	1¼ teaspoons	active dry yeast or bread machine yeast	1½ teaspoons
	⅓ cup	chopped hazelnuts (filberts), toasted	½ cup
	1 recipe	Orange Icing (optional)	1 recipe

1 Select the loaf size. Add the milk and dried blueberries to machine. Let stand for 10 minutes.

2 Add the remaining ingredients, except the Orange Icing, to the machine according to the manufacturer's directions. Select the basic white bread cycle and, if available, the light color setting. If desired, drizzle the cooled loaf with Orange Icing.

Orange Icing: In a small bowl stir together ½ cup sifted powdered sugar and enough orange juice (1 to 3 teaspoons) to make an icing of drizzling consistency.

*Note: For the 1½-pound loaf, the bread machine pan must have a capacity of 10 cups or more. For the 2-pound loaf, the bread machine pan must have a capacity of 12 cups or more.

**Note: The Test Kitchen recommends 1 egg for either size recipe.

Nutrition Facts per slice: 166 cal., 4 g total fat (1 g sat. fat), 14 mg chol., 137 mg sodium, 27 g carbo., 5 g pro.

Handling Hazelnuts

Toasting hazelnuts (filberts) deepens their rich flavor and loosens their bitter, paper-thin brown skin so you can more easily remove it. Toast nuts on a baking sheet in a 350°F oven for 10 to 15 minutes or until the nuts are aromatic, stirring once or twice. Place toasted nuts on a clean kitchen towel and rub off the skin (some skin may remain).

Become a hero to the blueberry muffin fans in your home. For an old-fashioned breakfast, serve toasted slices of this blueberry-studded bread with scrambled eggs and bacon.

Blueberry Muffin Bread

1½-POUND*	INGREDIENTS	2-POUND*
¾ cup	milk	1 cup
1	egg**	1
3 tablespoons	water	¼ cup
2 tablespoons	margarine or butter, cut up	3 tablespoons
3 cups	bread flour	4 cups
3 tablespoons	sugar	¼ cup
¾ teaspoon	salt	1 teaspoon
¼ teaspoon	ground nutmeg	½ teaspoon
1 teaspoon	active dry yeast	1¼ teaspoons
	or bread machine yeast	
⅓ cup	dried blueberries	½ cup
1 recipe	Powdered Sugar Glaze	1 recipe
	(optional)	

PREP:
10 minutes

MAKES:
1½-pound recipe
(16 slices)
OR
2-pound recipe
(22 slices)

1 Select the loaf size. Add the ingredients, except the Powdered Sugar Glaze, to the machine according to the manufacturer's directions. Select the basic white bread cycle. If desired, drizzle the cooled loaf with Powdered Sugar Glaze.

Powdered Sugar Glaze: In a small bowl stir together ½ cup sifted powdered sugar and enough milk (1 to 2 teaspoons) to make a glaze of drizzling consistency.

*Note: For the 1½-pound loaf, the bread machine pan must have a capacity of 10 cups or more. For the 2-pound loaf, the bread machine pan must have a capacity of 12 cups or more.

**Note: The Test Kitchen recommends 1 egg for either size recipe.

Nutrition Facts per slice: 140 cal., 2 g total fat (1 g sat. fat), 14 mg chol., 127 mg sodium, 25 g carbo., 4 g pro.

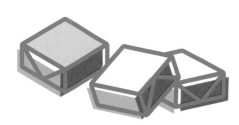

Drop everything—and make this recipe as soon as you can! The remarkable bread boasts a nicely rounded top, wonderful moistness and texture, and an irresistible lemon flavor.

Lemon Drop Bread

PREP:
15 minutes

MAKES:
1½-pound recipe
(16 slices)
OR
2-pound recipe
(22 slices)

1½-POUND	INGREDIENTS	2-POUND
¼ cup	coarsely crushed lemon drops	⅓ cup
¾ cup	milk	1 cup
1	egg*	1
2 tablespoons	frozen lemonade concentrate, thawed	3 tablespoons
2 tablespoons	margarine or butter, cut up	3 tablespoons
3 cups	bread flour	4 cups
2 tablespoons	sugar	3 tablespoons
1½ teaspoons	finely shredded lemon peel	2 teaspoons
¾ teaspoon	salt	1 teaspoon
1 teaspoon	active dry yeast or bread machine yeast	1¼ teaspoons
1 recipe	Lemon Icing	1 recipe

1 Select the loaf size. Set aside 1 tablespoon of the crushed lemon drops. Add the ingredients, except the Lemon Icing, to the machine according to the manufacturer's directions, adding the remaining crushed lemon drops with the flour. Select the basic white bread cycle.

2 Drizzle the cooled loaf with Lemon Icing and sprinkle with the reserved crushed lemon drops.

Lemon Icing: In a small bowl stir together ½ cup sifted powdered sugar, 1 teaspoon lemon juice, and ¼ teaspoon vanilla. Stir in enough milk (1 to 2 teaspoons) to make an icing of drizzling consistency.

*Note: The Test Kitchen recommends 1 egg for either size recipe.

Nutrition Facts per slice: 168 cal., 2 g total fat (1 g sat. fat), 14 mg chol., 139 mg sodium, 32 g carbo., 4 g pro.

Cranberries add a pleasantly tart counterpoint to the subtle wheat flavor of this loaf, while the Orange Icing lends a touch of sweetness.

Orange-Glazed Cranberry Nut Bread

1½-POUND*	INGREDIENTS	2-POUND*
¾ cup	milk	1 cup
1	egg**	1
3 tablespoons	margarine or butter, cut up	¼ cup
2 tablespoons	water	¼ cup
2 cups	bread flour	2⅔ cups
1 cup	whole wheat flour	1⅓ cups
3 tablespoons	sugar	¼ cup
2 teaspoons	finely shredded orange peel	2½ teaspoons
¾ teaspoon	salt	1 teaspoon
1 teaspoon	active dry yeast	1½ teaspoons
	or bread machine yeast	
¾ cup	snipped dried cranberries	1 cup
⅓ cup	chopped walnuts, toasted	½ cup
1 recipe	Orange Icing	1 recipe

PREP:
15 minutes

MAKES:
1½-pound recipe
(16 slices)
OR
2-pound recipe
(22 slices)

1 Select the loaf size. Add the ingredients, except the Orange Icing, to the machine according to the manufacturer's directions. If available, select the whole grain cycle, or select the basic white bread cycle. Frost the cooled loaf with Orange Icing.

Orange Icing: In a small bowl stir together ½ cup sifted powdered sugar and ¼ teaspoon vanilla. Stir in enough orange juice (1 to 3 teaspoons) to make an icing of spreading consistency.

*Note: For the 1½-pound loaf, the bread machine pan must have a capacity of 10 cups or more. For the 2-pound loaf, the bread machine pan must have a capacity of 12 cups or more.

**Note: The Test Kitchen recommends 1 egg for either size recipe.

Nutrition Facts per slice: 172 cal., 5 g total fat (1 g sat. fat), 14 mg chol., 145 mg sodium, 29 g carbo., 4 g pro.

Here's a great way to use up that overripe banana on your shelf! Serve the loaf freshly made with a fruited chicken salad for a weekend lunch—and toast leftovers for a teatime treat.

Strawberry-Banana Bread

PREP:
15 minutes

MAKES:
1½-pound recipe
(16 slices)
OR
2-pound recipe
(22 slices)

1½-POUND	INGREDIENTS	2-POUND
⅓ cup	milk	½ cup
⅓ cup	mashed ripe banana	½ cup
¼ cup	strawberry preserves	⅓ cup
1	egg*	1
2 tablespoons	margarine or butter, cut up	3 tablespoons
1 tablespoon	water	4 teaspoons
3 cups	bread flour	4 cups
¾ teaspoon	salt	1 teaspoon
1 teaspoon	active dry yeast	1¼ teaspoons
	or bread machine yeast	
½ cup	chopped pecans, toasted	⅔ cup

① Select the loaf size. Add the ingredients to the machine according to the manufacturer's directions. Select the basic white bread cycle.

*Note: The Test Kitchen recommends 1 egg for either size recipe.

Nutrition Facts per slice: 157 cal., 5 g total fat (1 g sat. fat), 14 mg chol., 134 mg sodium, 25 g carbo., 4 g pro.

Cut to Order

If your kids love bread as a snack, really impress them by cutting slices into fun shapes with cookie cutters. Keep an assortment of cutters, such as hearts, bears, and bunnies, handy and let them choose their own shapes. You can even cut their peanut butter and jelly sandwiches into fanciful shapes.

Bread? Dessert? Does it matter what you call it when chocolate and cherries costar in one loaf? This is a great antidote for a midafternoon slump.

Chocolate-Cherry Bread

1½-POUND*	INGREDIENTS	2-POUND*
³/₄ cup	milk	1 cup
1	egg**	1
2 tablespoons	water	3 tablespoons
1 tablespoon	margarine or butter	4 teaspoons
¹/₄ teaspoon	almond extract**	¹/₄ teaspoon
3 cups	bread flour	4 cups
2 tablespoons	sugar	3 tablespoons
³/₄ teaspoon	salt	1 teaspoon
1 teaspoon	active dry yeast	1¹/₄ teaspoons
	or bread machine yeast	
¹/₃ cup	dried cherries, snipped	¹/₂ cup
¹/₃ cup	semisweet chocolate pieces,	¹/₂ cup
	chilled	

PREP:
15 minutes

MAKES:
1½-pound recipe
(20 slices)
OR
2-pound recipe
(27 slices)

1 Select the loaf size. Add the ingredients to the machine according to the manufacturer's directions. Select the basic white bread cycle.

*Note: For the 1½-pound loaf, the bread machine pan must have a capacity of 10 cups or more. For the 2-pound loaf, the bread machine pan must have a capacity of 12 cups or more.

**Note: The Test Kitchen recommends 1 egg and ¼ teaspoon almond extract for either size recipe.

Nutrition Facts per slice: 113 cal., 2 g total fat (0 g sat. fat), 11 mg chol., 95 mg sodium, 20 g carbo., 3 g pro.

Machines Produce Different Effects

Depending on the brand, bread machines often will produce different end products. For example, in one bread machine, the Test Kitchen found that chilled chocolate chips would create a swirled bread while another bread machine created a solid-color bread. Either way, this bread tastes delicious.

Buttery-tasting macadamia nuts combine with divine white chocolate to create the ultimate of breads. For a special touch, it's finished off with a drizzle of white and dark chocolate glazes.

Macadamia-White Chocolate Bread

PREP:	1½-POUND*	INGREDIENTS	2-POUND*
15 minutes	⅔ cup	milk	¾ cup
	1	egg(s)	2
MAKES:	2 tablespoons	water	¼ cup
1½-pound recipe (18 slices)	2 tablespoons	margarine or butter, cut up**	2 tablespoons
OR	3 cups	bread flour	4 cups
2-pound recipe (24 slices)	2 tablespoons	sugar**	2 tablespoons
	¾ teaspoon	salt	1 teaspoon
	1 teaspoon	active dry yeast	1¼ teaspoons
		or bread machine yeast	
	½ cup	chopped macadamia nuts	⅔ cup
	2 ounces	white baking bar, chopped	3 ounces
	1 recipe	White Chocolate Glaze	1 recipe
	1 recipe	Dark Chocolate Glaze	1 recipe

1 Select the loaf size. Add the first 10 ingredients to the machine according to the manufacturer's directions. Select the basic white bread cycle. Drizzle the cooled loaf with White Chocolate Glaze and Dark Chocolate Glaze.

White Chocolate Glaze: In a small saucepan heat 1 ounce white baking bar, cut up, and 1 teaspoon shortening over low heat until melted, stirring constantly.

Dark Chocolate Glaze: In a small saucepan heat 1 ounce semisweet chocolate, cut up, and 1 teaspoon shortening over low heat until melted, stirring constantly.

*Note: For the 1½-pound loaf, the bread machine pan must have a capacity of 10 cups or more. For the 2-pound loaf, the bread machine pan must have a capacity of 12 cups or more.

**Note: The Test Kitchen recommends 2 tablespoons margarine or butter and 2 tablespoons sugar for either size recipe.

Nutrition Facts per slice: 173 cal., 7 g total fat (2 g sat. fat), 14 mg chol., 118 mg sodium, 23 g carbo., 4 g pro.

Serve this golden loaf sliced and lightly toasted for a weekend breakfast treat. The Browned Butter Glaze adds an extra-special finishing touch.

Lemon Breakfast Bread

1½-POUND*	INGREDIENTS	2-POUND*
½ cup	milk	⅔ cup
½ cup	mashed cooked potato**	⅔ cup
⅓ cup	water	½ cup
¼ cup	margarine or butter, cut up	⅓ cup
1	egg***	1
3 cups	bread flour	4 cups
¼ cup	sugar	⅓ cup
1 teaspoon	finely shredded lemon peel	1½ teaspoons
¾ teaspoon	salt	1 teaspoon
1 teaspoon	active dry yeast	1¼ teaspoons
	or bread machine yeast	
1 recipe	Browned Butter Glaze	1 recipe

PREP:
15 minutes

MAKES:
1½-pound recipe
(18 slices)
OR
2-pound recipe
(24 slices)

1 Select the loaf size. Add the ingredients, except the Browned Butter Glaze, to the machine according to the manufacturer's directions. Select the basic white bread cycle. Drizzle the cooled loaf with Browned Butter Glaze.

Browned Butter Glaze: In a small saucepan heat 1 tablespoon butter until golden brown. Stir in 1 cup sifted powdered sugar and ½ teaspoon vanilla. Stir in enough milk (about 1 tablespoon) to make a glaze of drizzling consistency. Use immediately (glaze will appear thin, but it sets up quickly when drizzled on loaf).

*Note: For the 1½-pound loaf, the bread machine pan must have a capacity of 10 cups or more. For the 2-pound loaf, the bread machine pan must have a capacity of 12 cups or more.

**Note: For ½ or ⅔ cup mashed cooked potato, peel and cut up 1 medium to large potato. In a covered small saucepan cook potato in boiling water about 15 minutes or until potato is very tender. Drain. Mash with a potato masher; cool slightly. Measure the amount needed.

***Note: The Test Kitchen recommends 1 egg for either size recipe.

Nutrition Facts per slice: 157 cal., 4 g total fat (1 g sat. fat), 14 mg chol., 133 mg sodium, 27 g carbo., 4 g pro.

Dried cherries and walnuts give this bread texture, while shredded orange peel adds a citrus flavor. Orange-Ginger Butter (page 265) is a great serve-along.

Walnut-Cherry Bread

PREP:
15 minutes

MAKES:
1½-pound recipe
(16 slices)
OR
2-pound recipe
(22 slices)

1½-POUND	INGREDIENTS	2-POUND
¾ cup	milk	1 cup
¼ cup	water	⅓ cup
¼ cup	light-colored corn syrup	⅓ cup
2 tablespoons	walnut oil or cooking oil	3 tablespoons
3 cups	bread flour	4 cups
1 teaspoon	finely shredded orange peel or lemon peel	1½ teaspoons
¾ teaspoon	salt	1 teaspoon
1¼ teaspoons	active dry yeast or bread machine yeast	1½ teaspoons
¾ cup	snipped dried tart cherries or cranberries	1 cup
⅓ cup	chopped walnuts, toasted	½ cup

1 Select the loaf size. Add the ingredients to the machine according to the manufacturer's directions. Select the basic white bread cycle.

Nutrition Facts per slice: 164 cal., 4 g total fat (0 g sat. fat), 1 mg chol., 110 mg sodium, 28 g carbo., 4 g pro.

Not all fresh foods hibernate in wintertime. Showcase one of the season's best—juicy pears—in this company-worthy bread. Apple juice or pear nectar lends sweetness.

Pear Loaf

1½-POUND	INGREDIENTS	2-POUND
½ cup	milk	⅔ cup
⅓ cup	apple juice or pear nectar*	⅓ cup
¾ cup	chopped peeled pear**	1 cup
4 teaspoons	margarine or butter, cut up	2 tablespoons
3 cups	bread flour	4 cups
2 tablespoons	brown sugar	3 tablespoons
¾ teaspoon	salt	1 teaspoon
½ teaspoon	finely shredded lemon peel	¾ teaspoon
1 teaspoon	active dry yeast	1¼ teaspoons
	or bread machine yeast	
⅓ cup	chopped almonds, toasted	½ cup

PREP:
15 minutes

MAKES:
1½-pound recipe
(16 slices)
OR
2-pound recipe
(22 slices)

① Select the loaf size. Add the ingredients to the machine according to the manufacturer's directions, adding the pear with the liquid. Select the basic white bread cycle.

*Note: The Test Kitchen recommends ⅓ cup apple juice or pear nectar for either size recipe.

**Note: Choose a firm, ripe pear. You may need to adjust the flour or juice if the pear is unripe or if it is very ripe and juicy.

Nutrition Facts per slice: 134 cal., 3 g total fat (0 g sat. fat), 1 mg chol., 116 mg sodium, 23 g carbo., 4 g pro.

Working with Fresh Pears

A pear is ripe when it yields to slight pressure at the stem end. If too firm, ripen pears in a paper bag for a day or two. To peel a pear, trim off stem and blossom ends, then remove the skin with a small paring knife. To chop, halve the peeled pear and scoop out the core. Slice each half. Stack the slices and cut lengthwise, then crosswise. Use immediately or the flesh will discolor.

Vibrant green pistachios dot this light, moist, chocolatey loaf. The yummy chocolate glaze is not mandatory, of course, but is highly recommended! If you like, sprinkle with additional pistachios.

Chocolate-Pistachio Bread

PREP: 15 minutes	1½-POUND*	INGREDIENTS	2-POUND*
	¾ cup	milk	1 cup
MAKES:	1	egg**	1
1½-pound recipe (20 slices)	3 tablespoons	water	¼ cup
OR	4 teaspoons	margarine or butter, cut up	2 tablespoons
2-pound recipe (27 slices)	1 teaspoon	vanilla	1½ teaspoons
	3 cups	bread flour	4 cups
	3 tablespoons	sugar	¼ cup
	2 tablespoons	unsweetened cocoa powder	3 tablespoons
	¾ teaspoon	salt	1 teaspoon
	1 teaspoon	active dry yeast or bread machine yeast	1¼ teaspoons
	½ cup	chopped pistachio nuts	⅔ cup
	1 recipe	Chocolate Glaze	1 recipe

1 Select the loaf size. Add the ingredients, except the Chocolate Glaze, to the machine according to the manufacturer's directions. Select the basic white bread cycle.

2 Drizzle cooled loaf with Chocolate Glaze. If desired, sprinkle with additional pistachio nuts.

Chocolate Glaze: In a small bowl stir together ½ cup sifted powdered sugar, 1 tablespoon unsweetened cocoa powder, and ¼ teaspoon vanilla. Stir in enough milk (1 to 2 teaspoons) to make a glaze of drizzling consistency.

*Note: For the 1½-pound loaf, the bread machine pan must have a capacity of 10 cups or more. For the 2-pound loaf, the bread machine pan must have a capacity of 12 cups or more.

**Note: The Test Kitchen recommends 1 egg for either size recipe.

Nutrition Facts per slice: 130 cal., 3 g total fat (1 g sat. fat), 11 mg chol., 98 mg sodium, 21 g carbo., 4 g pro.

If your weakness is chocolate, you will adore this bread. It features the tastes of cocoa, semisweet chocolate pieces, and strawberry flavors. What more could you ask for?

Chocolate-Strawberry Bread

1½-POUND*	INGREDIENTS	2-POUND*
²/₃ cup	milk	³/₄ cup
¹/₄ cup	water	¹/₃ cup
¹/₄ cup	strawberry preserves	¹/₃ cup
1	egg**	1
2 tablespoons	margarine or butter, cut up	3 tablespoons
¹/₂ teaspoon	strawberry extract	³/₄ teaspoon
3 cups	bread flour	4 cups
2 tablespoons	unsweetened cocoa powder	3 tablespoons
³/₄ teaspoon	salt	1 teaspoon
1 teaspoon	active dry yeast	1¹/₂ teaspoons
	or bread machine yeast	
¹/₄ cup	miniature semisweet chocolate	¹/₃ cup
	pieces	

PREP:
10 minutes

MAKES:
1½-pound recipe
(16 slices)
OR
2-pound recipe
(22 slices)

❶ Select the loaf size. Add the ingredients to the machine according to the manufacturer's directions. Select the basic white bread cycle.

*Note: For the 1½-pound loaf, the bread machine pan must have a capacity of 10 cups or more. For the 2-pound loaf, the bread machine pan must have a capacity of 12 cups or more.

**Note: The Test Kitchen recommends 1 egg for either size recipe.

Nutrition Facts per slice: 145 cal., 3 g total fat (1 g sat. fat), 14 mg chol., 127 mg sodium, 25 g carbo., 4 g pro.

Selecting Fruit Spreads

When it comes to picking fruit spreads, mind your p's and j's. Jellies are firm, translucent spreads made of fruit juices boiled with sugar. Jams are mashed fruit cooked with sugar until thick. Preserves resemble jams but have larger chunks of fruit.

Looking to win over a chocolate-lover's heart? This loaf offers a delightful way to savor great fudgy favors.

Double Chocolate Bread

	1½-POUND*	INGREDIENTS	2-POUND*
PREP: 10 minutes	¾ cup	milk	1 cup
	1	egg(s)	2
MAKES: 1½-pound recipe (16 slices) OR 2-pound recipe (24 slices)	2 tablespoons	water**	2 tablespoons
	1 tablespoon	margarine or butter, cut up	2 tablespoons
	1½ teaspoons	vanilla	2 teaspoons
	3 cups	bread flour	4 cups
	3 tablespoons	packed brown sugar	¼ cup
	4 teaspoons	unsweetened cocoa powder	2 tablespoons
	¾ teaspoon	salt	1 teaspoon
	1 teaspoon	active dry yeast	1¼ teaspoons
		or bread machine yeast	
	⅔ cup	semisweet chocolate pieces	1 cup

1 Select the loaf size. Add the ingredients to the machine according to the manufacturer's directions. Select the basic white bread cycle and, if available, the light color setting.

*Note: For the 1½-pound loaf, the bread machine pan must have a capacity of 10 cups or more. For the 2-pound loaf, the bread machine pan must have a capacity of 12 cups or more.

**Note: The Test Kitchen recommends 2 tablespoons water for either size recipe.

Nutrition Facts per slice: 154 cal., 4 g total fat (1 g sat. fat), 14 mg chol., 128 mg sodium, 23 g carbo., 4 g pro.

Indulge your love of chocolate and cashews in this sweet and satisfying bread. Get creative—try it in your favorite bread pudding recipe or as French toast topped with a fresh strawberry sauce.

Chocolate-Cashew Loaf

1½-POUND*	INGREDIENTS	2-POUND*
¾ cup	milk	1 cup
1	egg**	1
3 tablespoons	water	¼ cup
3 tablespoons	honey	¼ cup
4 teaspoons	margarine or butter, cut up	2 tablespoons
1 teaspoon	vanilla	1½ teaspoons
3 cups	bread flour	4 cups
2 tablespoons	unsweetened cocoa powder	3 tablespoons
¾ teaspoon	salt	1 teaspoon
1 teaspoon	active dry yeast	1¼ teaspoons
	or bread machine yeast	
½ cup	coarsely chopped cashews	⅔ cup
	or peanuts	

PREP:
15 minutes

MAKES:
1½-pound recipe
(16 slices)
OR
2-pound recipe
(22 slices)

1 Select the loaf size. Add the ingredients to the machine according to the manufacturer's directions. Select the basic white bread cycle.

*Note: For the 1½-pound loaf, the bread machine pan must have a capacity of 10 cups or more. For the 2-pound loaf, the bread machine pan must have a capacity of 12 cups or more.

**Note: The Test Kitchen recommends 1 egg for either size recipe.

Nutrition Facts per slice: 155 cal., 4 g total fat (1 g sat. fat), 14 mg chol., 159 mg sodium, 24 g carbo., 5 g pro.

Depending on how thoroughly your bread machine melts the chocolate, this scrumptious loaf may be marbled, flecked, or uniform in color.

Chocolate Chip-Coconut Bread

PREP:
15 minutes

MAKES:
1½-pound recipe
(16 slices)
OR
2-pound recipe
(22 slices)

1½-POUND*	INGREDIENTS	2-POUND*
³/₄ cup	milk	1 cup
1	egg**	1
2 tablespoons	water	3 tablespoons
1 tablespoon	margarine or butter	4 teaspoons
1 teaspoon	vanilla	1½ teaspoons
3 cups	bread flour	4 cups
2 tablespoons	sugar	3 tablespoons
³/₄ teaspoon	salt	1 teaspoon
1 teaspoon	active dry yeast	1¼ teaspoons
	or bread machine yeast	
¹/₃ cup	semisweet chocolate pieces	¹/₂ cup
¹/₃ cup	coconut, toasted	¹/₂ cup

1 Select the loaf size. Add the ingredients to the machine according to the manufacturer's directions. Select the basic white bread cycle.

*Note: For the 1½-pound loaf, the bread machine pan must have a capacity of 10 cups or more. For the 2-pound loaf, the bread machine pan must have a capacity of 12 cups or more.

**Note: The Test Kitchen recommends 1 egg for either size recipe.

Nutrition Facts per slice: 144 cal., 4 g total fat (0 g sat. fat), 14 mg chol., 123 mg sodium, 24 g carbo., 4 g pro.

The fun pink color of this sweet bread comes from maraschino cherry juice. Top off slices with a dab of Chocolate-Nut Spread (page 265)—a delectable combo!

Cherry-Almond Bread

1½-POUND	INGREDIENTS	2-POUND
³/₄ cup	milk	1 cup
¹/₂ cup	maraschino cherries, halved	²/₃ cup
¹/₄ cup	maraschino cherry juice	¹/₃ cup
4 teaspoons	margarine or butter, cut up	2 tablespoons
¹/₄ teaspoon	almond extract*	¹/₄ teaspoon
3 cups	bread flour	4 cups
¹/₄ cup	chopped almonds	¹/₃ cup
1 tablespoon	sugar	4 teaspoons
³/₄ teaspoon	salt	1 teaspoon
1 teaspoon	active dry yeast	1¹/₄ teaspoons
	or bread machine yeast	

PREP:
15 minutes

MAKES:
1½-pound recipe
(18 slices)
OR
2-pound recipe
(24 slices)

1 Select the loaf size. Add the ingredients to the machine according to the manufacturer's directions, adding the cherries with the milk and the almonds with the flour. Select the basic white bread cycle.

*Note: The Test Kitchen recommends ¹/₄ teaspoon almond extract for either size recipe.

Nutrition Facts per slice: 116 cal., 2 g total fat (0 g sat. fat), 1 mg chol., 105 mg sodium, 20 g carbo., 4 g pro.

Maraschino Cherry Facts

Maraschino cherries really do grow on trees. The name comes from *marasca,* Italian for the variety of cherry whose juice is fermented to make maraschino cordial. The preserved cherries that garnish drinks, cakes, cookies, and breads taste like the cordial, but are nonalcoholic.

Here's one bread that really lives up to its name. Not only is it a perfect partner to a cup of tea, but the ingredients include tea and other traditional accompaniments for tea.

Sweet Lemon Tea Bread

PREP:
10 minutes

MAKES:
1½-pound recipe
(18 slices)

OR

2-pound recipe
(24 slices)

1½-POUND*	INGREDIENTS	2-POUND*
²/₃ cup	milk	³/₄ cup
¹/₄ cup	water	¹/₃ cup
2 tablespoons	instant tea powder	3 tablespoons
1	egg**	1
2 tablespoons	margarine or butter, cut up	3 tablespoons
3 cups	bread flour	4 cups
3 tablespoons	sugar	¹/₄ cup
2 teaspoons	finely shredded lemon peel	1 tablespoon
³/₄ teaspoon	salt	1 teaspoon
¹/₂ teaspoon	ground cardamom	³/₄ teaspoon
1 teaspoon	active dry yeast	1¹/₄ teaspoons
	or bread machine yeast	

1 Select the loaf size. Add the ingredients to the machine according to the manufacturer's directions, adding the tea powder with the liquid. Select the basic white bread cycle.

*Note: For the 1½-pound loaf, the bread machine pan must have a capacity of 10 cups or more. For the 2-pound loaf, the bread machine pan must have a capacity of 12 cups or more.

**Note: The Test Kitchen recommends 1 egg for either size recipe.

Nutrition Facts per slice: 112 cal., 2 g total fat (0 g sat. fat), 13 mg chol., 113 mg sodium, 19 g carbo., 3 g pro.

This bread gets a double whammy of citrus with lemon and orange. The crowning glory is an orange glaze for extra citrus flavor.

Citrus Loaf

1½-POUND*	INGREDIENTS	2-POUND*
⅔ cup	water**	⅔ cup
⅓ cup	orange juice	½ cup
1	egg**	1
2 tablespoons	margarine or butter, cut up	3 tablespoons
3 cups	bread flour	4 cups
3 tablespoons	sugar	¼ cup
1 teaspoon	finely shredded lemon peel	1½ teaspoons
¾ teaspoon	salt	1 teaspoon
½ teaspoon	finely shredded orange peel	1 teaspoon
1 teaspoon	active dry yeast	1¼ teaspoons
	or bread machine yeast	
1 recipe	Citrus Glaze	1 recipe

PREP:
15 minutes

MAKES:
1½-pound recipe
(20 slices)
OR
2-pound recipe
(27 slices)

1 Select the loaf size. Add the ingredients, except the Citrus Glaze, to the machine according to the manufacturer's directions. Select the basic white bread cycle. Frost the cooled loaf with Citrus Glaze.

Citrus Glaze: In a small bowl stir together 1 cup sifted powdered sugar and ½ teaspoon finely shredded orange peel. Stir in enough orange juice (3 to 4 teaspoons) to make a glaze of spreading consistency.

*Note: For the 1½-pound loaf, the bread machine pan must have a capacity of 10 cups or more. For the 2-pound loaf, the bread machine pan must have a capacity of 12 cups or more.

**Note: The Test Kitchen recommends ⅔ cup water and 1 egg for either size recipe.

Nutrition Facts per slice: 118 cal., 2 g total fat (0 g sat. fat), 11 mg chol., 97 mg sodium, 22 g carbo., 3 g pro.

Candied lemon peel and crystallized ginger add hints of sophistication to this delicate bread.

Gingered Lemon Bread

PREP:
15 minutes

MAKES:
1½-pound recipe
(20 slices)
OR
2-pound recipe
(27 slices)

1½-POUND*	INGREDIENTS	2-POUND*
¾ cup	milk	1 cup
1	egg**	1
2 tablespoons	water	¼ cup
2 tablespoons	margarine or butter, cut up	3 tablespoons
3 cups	bread flour	4 cups
2 tablespoons	brown sugar	3 tablespoons
¾ teaspoon	salt	1 teaspoon
1 teaspoon	active dry yeast	1¼ teaspoons
	or bread machine yeast	
⅓ cup	coarsely chopped candied lemon peel	½ cup
2 tablespoons	coarsely snipped crystallized ginger	3 tablespoons

❶ Select the loaf size. Add the ingredients to the machine according to the manufacturer's directions. Select the basic white bread cycle.

*Note: For the 1½-pound loaf, the bread machine pan must have a capacity of 10 cups or more. For the 2-pound loaf, the bread machine pan must have a capacity of 12 cups or more.

**Note: The Test Kitchen recommends 1 egg for either size recipe.

Nutrition Facts per slice: 110 cal., 2 g total fat (0 g sat. fat), 11 mg chol., 102 mg sodium, 20 g carbo., 3 g pro.

Sour cream adds richness, lemon peel supplies flavor, and poppy seeds lend crunchy texture. Sliced thin and cut into decorative shapes, this bread is worthy of a place on a special tea tray.

Poppy Seed Tea Bread

1½-POUND*	INGREDIENTS	2-POUND*
⅔ cup	milk	¾ cup
⅓ cup	dairy sour cream	½ cup
1	egg**	1
3 tablespoons	margarine or butter, cut up	¼ cup
3 cups	bread flour	4 cups
¼ cup	sugar	⅓ cup
2 tablespoons	poppy seeds	3 tablespoons
1 tablespoon	finely shredded lemon peel	4 teaspoons
¾ teaspoon	salt	1 teaspoon
1 teaspoon	active dry yeast	1¼ teaspoons
	or bread machine yeast	

PREP:
10 minutes

MAKES:
1½-pound recipe
(16 slices)
OR
2-pound recipe
(22 slices)

1 Select the loaf size. Add the ingredients to the machine according to the manufacturer's directions. Select the basic white bread cycle.

*Note: For the 1½-pound loaf, the bread machine pan must have a capacity of 10 cups or more. For the 2-pound loaf, the bread machine pan must have a capacity of 12 cups or more.

**Note: The Test Kitchen recommends 1 egg for either size recipe.

Nutrition Facts per slice: 151 cal., 5 g total fat (1 g sat. fat), 16 mg chol., 137 mg sodium, 23 g carbo., 4 g pro.

This tart and sweet loaf has a delicate, golden brown crust and can rise to any occasion.
Serve slices on a doily-lined plate and voila: It's an instant party!

Lemony Molasses Bread

PREP:
15 minutes

MAKES:
1½-pound recipe
(16 slices)
OR
2-pound recipe
(22 slices)

1½-POUND*	INGREDIENTS	2-POUND*
¾ cup	milk**	¾ cup
1	egg(s)	2
2 tablespoons	water	3 tablespoons
2 tablespoons	mild-flavored molasses	3 tablespoons
2 tablespoons	margarine or butter, cut up**	2 tablespoons
3 cups	bread flour	4 cups
1 teaspoon	finely shredded lemon peel	1½ teaspoons
¾ teaspoon	salt	1 teaspoon
1¼ teaspoons	active dry yeast	1¼ teaspoons
	or bread machine yeast**	
½ cup	chopped pecans, toasted	⅔ cup

1 Select the loaf size. Add the ingredients to the machine according to the manufacturer's directions. Select the basic white bread cycle.

*Note: For the 1½-pound loaf, the bread machine pan must have a capacity of 10 cups or more. For the 2-pound loaf, the bread machine pan must have a capacity of 12 cups or more.

**Note: The Test Kitchen recommends ¾ cup milk, 2 tablespoons margarine or butter, and 1¼ teaspoons yeast for either size recipe.

Nutrition Facts per slice: 146 cal., 5 g total fat (1 g sat. fat), 14 mg chol., 127 mg sodium, 22 g carbo., 4 g pro.

Just for the fun of it, treat coworkers to slices of this nutty sweet bread. It's a coffee-break champ if there ever was one!

Peanut Wheat Bread

1½-POUND*	INGREDIENTS	2-POUND*
½ cup	milk	¾ cup
¼ cup	water	⅓ cup
¼ cup	peanut butter	⅓ cup
1	egg**	1
3 tablespoons	honey	¼ cup
2½ cups	bread flour	3⅓ cups
½ cup	whole wheat flour	⅔ cup
¾ teaspoon	salt	1 teaspoon
1¼ teaspoons	active dry yeast	1½ teaspoons
	or bread machine yeast	
1 recipe	Chocolate Icing	1 recipe
1 tablespoon	chopped honey-roasted peanuts**	1 tablespoon

PREP:
15 minutes

MAKES:
1½-pound recipe
(16 slices)
OR
2-pound recipe
(22 slices)

1 Select the loaf size. Add the first 9 ingredients to the machine according to the manufacturer's directions. Select the basic white bread cycle and, if available, the light color setting.

2 Drizzle the cooled loaf with Chocolate Icing and sprinkle with honey-roasted peanuts.

Chocolate Icing: In a small bowl stir together 1 cup sifted powdered sugar and 2 tablespoons unsweetened cocoa powder. Stir in enough milk (1 to 2 tablespoons) to make an icing of drizzling consistency.

*Note: For the 1½-pound loaf, the bread machine pan must have a capacity of 10 cups or more. For the 2-pound loaf, the bread machine pan must have a capacity of 12 cups or more.

**Note: The Test Kitchen recommends 1 egg and 1 tablespoon honey-roasted peanuts for either size recipe.

Nutrition Facts per slice: 165 cal., 3 g total fat (1 g sat. fat), 14 mg chol., 139 mg sodium, 30 g carbo., 5 g pro.

This blue-ribbon recipe combines the wonderful flavors of chocolate and hazelnut. Look for the secret ingredient—chocolate-hazelnut spread—next to the peanut butter in the supermarket.

Chocolate-Hazelnut Loaf

PREP:
15 minutes

MAKES:
1½-pound recipe
(16 slices)
OR
2-pound recipe
(22 slices)

1½-POUND*	INGREDIENTS	2-POUND*
½ cup	milk	⅔ cup
¼ cup	water	⅓ cup
¼ cup	chocolate-hazelnut spread	⅓ cup
1	egg**	1
3 cups	bread flour	4 cups
2 tablespoons	sugar	3 tablespoons
¾ teaspoon	salt	1 teaspoon
1¼ teaspoons	active dry yeast	1½ teaspoons
	or bread machine yeast	
⅓ cup	chopped hazelnuts (filberts), toasted	½ cup

1 Select the loaf size. Add the ingredients to the machine according to the manufacturer's directions. Select the basic white bread cycle. If desired, serve the cooled loaf with additional chocolate-hazelnut spread.

*Note: For the 1½-pound loaf, the bread machine pan must have a capacity of 10 cups or more. For the 2-pound loaf, the bread machine pan must have a capacity of 12 cups or more.

**Note: The Test Kitchen recommends 1 egg for either size recipe.

Nutrition Facts per slice: 143 cal., 4 g total fat (0 g sat. fat), 14 mg chol., 312 mg sodium, 23 g carbo., 4 g pro.

The rich flavors of this loaf make it a real crowd-pleaser. Top it with peanut butter and sliced banana for a great lunchtime sandwich.

Chocolate Malt Bread

1½-POUND*	INGREDIENTS	2-POUND*
½ cup	milk	¾ cup
1	egg**	1
3 tablespoons	water	¼ cup
4 teaspoons	margarine or butter, cut up	2 tablespoons
3 cups	bread flour	4 cups
⅓ cup	instant chocolate malted milk powder	½ cup
2 tablespoons	sugar	3 tablespoons
¾ teaspoon	salt	1 teaspoon
1 teaspoon	active dry yeast or bread machine yeast	1¼ teaspoons

PREP:
10 minutes

MAKES:
1½-pound recipe
(18 slices)
OR
2-pound recipe
(24 slices)

1 Select the loaf size. Add the ingredients to the machine according to the manufacturer's directions. Select the basic white bread cycle.

*Note: For the 1½-pound loaf, the bread machine pan must have a capacity of 10 cups or more. For the 2-pound loaf, the bread machine pan must have a capacity of 12 cups or more.

**Note: The Test Kitchen recommends 1 egg for either size recipe.

Nutrition Facts per slice: 121 cal., 2 g total fat (0 g sat. fat), 13 mg chol., 118 mg sodium, 23 g carbo., 4 g pro.

About Malt Powder

Malt powder is made of a grain, which typically is barley, that is soaked, sprouted, dried, and then ground into a powder that tastes slightly sweet. The powder is used in making vinegar and malted milk powder, in brewing beer, and in distilling liquor.

This recipe produces a loaf that's not too sweet, not too tart, and prettily dotted with the starring ingredients.

Poppy Seed-Cranberry Bread

PREP:
10 minutes

MAKES:
1½-pound recipe
(16 slices)
OR
2-pound recipe
(22 slices)

1½-POUND*	INGREDIENTS	2-POUND*
¾ cup	water	1 cup
1	egg**	1
3 tablespoons	honey	¼ cup
1 tablespoon	margarine or butter	4 teaspoons
3 cups	bread flour	4 cups
1 teaspoon	finely shredded orange peel	1½ teaspoons
1 teaspoon	poppy seeds	1¼ teaspoons
¾ teaspoon	salt	1 teaspoon
1 teaspoon	active dry yeast	1¼ teaspoons
	or bread machine yeast	
½ cup	dried cranberries	¾ cup

1 Select the loaf size. Add the ingredients to the machine according to the manufacturer's directions. Select the basic white bread cycle.

*Note: For the 1½-pound loaf, the bread machine pan must have a capacity of 10 cups or more. For the 2-pound loaf, the bread machine pan must have a capacity of 12 cups or more.

**Note: The Test Kitchen recommends 1 egg for either size recipe.

Nutrition Facts per slice: 129 cal., 2 g total fat (0 g sat. fat), 13 mg chol., 123 mg sodium, 25 g carbo., 4 g pro.

Orange-flavored dried plums infuse this oat-and-nut bread with remarkable sweetness and flavor.

Orange-Dried Plum Bread

1½-POUND	INGREDIENTS	2-POUND
1 cup	water	1¼ cups
1 tablespoon	margarine or butter	4 teaspoons
3 cups	bread flour	4 cups
⅓ cup	regular or quick-cooking rolled oats	½ cup
1 tablespoon	brown sugar	4 teaspoons
¾ teaspoon	salt	1 teaspoon
1¼ teaspoons	active dry yeast or bread machine yeast	1½ teaspoons
¾ cup	snipped orange-flavored, pitted, dried plums (prunes)	1 cup
⅓ cup	chopped almonds, toasted	½ cup

PREP:
15 minutes

MAKES:
1½-pound recipe
(16 slices)
OR
2-pound recipe
(22 slices)

❶ Select the loaf size. Add the ingredients to the machine according to the manufacturer's directions. Select the basic white bread cycle.

Nutrition Facts per slice: 145 cal., 3 g total fat (0 g sat. fat), 0 mg chol., 119 mg sodium, 26 g carbo., 4 g pro.

For an extra burst of sweetness, use sweet rather than dry sherry in this spiraled loaf.

Sherried Date Bread

PREP:
15 minutes

MAKES:
1½-pound recipe
(16 slices)

1½-POUND	INGREDIENTS
1 cup	white grape juice
¼ cup	dry sherry
	or orange juice
4 teaspoons	margarine or butter
3 cups	bread flour
¾ teaspoon	salt
¼ teaspoon	ground cinnamon
1 teaspoon	active dry yeast
	or bread machine yeast
½ cup	snipped pitted whole dates
⅓ cup	chopped pecans, toasted

1 Add the ingredients to the machine according to the manufacturer's directions. Select the basic white bread cycle.

Nutrition Facts per slice: 152 cal., 3 g total fat (0 g sat. fat), 0 mg chol., 114 mg sodium, 26 g carbo., 3 g pro.

Does Tuscany suddenly beckon? This bread is likely why. From out of a rustic Italian farm kitchen comes its earthy flavors of whole grains, sweet dried figs, and toasted pine nuts.

Fig and Pine Nut Bread

1½-POUND*	INGREDIENTS	2-POUND*
⅔ cup	milk	¾ cup
1	egg**	1
3 tablespoons	margarine or butter, cut up	¼ cup
2 tablespoons	water	3 tablespoons
2 cups	bread flour	2⅔ cups
1 cup	whole wheat flour	1⅓ cups
3 tablespoons	sugar	¼ cup
¾ teaspoon	salt	1 teaspoon
⅛ teaspoon	ground nutmeg	¼ teaspoon
1 teaspoon	active dry yeast	1½ teaspoons
	or bread machine yeast	
⅔ cup	dried figs, cut into thin strips	¾ cup
¼ cup	pine nuts, toasted	⅓ cup

PREP:
15 minutes

MAKES:
1½-pound recipe
(16 slices)
OR
2-pound recipe
(22 slices)

1 Select the loaf size. Add the ingredients to the machine according to the manufacturer's directions. If available, select the whole grain cycle, or select the basic white bread cycle.

*Note: For the 1½-pound loaf, the bread machine pan must have a capacity of 10 cups or more. For the 2-pound loaf, the bread machine pan must have a capacity of 12 cups or more.

**Note: The Test Kitchen recommends 1 egg for either size recipe.

Nutrition Facts per slice: 160 cal., 4 g total fat (1 g sat. fat), 14 mg chol., 136 mg sodium, 27 g carbo., 5 g pro.

Grating Fresh Nutmeg

Slightly sweet and spicy nutmeg is amazingly intense when freshly grated from the whole kernel with an inexpensive grater found in the gadget section of cookware shops. Tinned steel nutmeg graters have one flat side and one curved grating side. Nutmeg mills work like a pepper mill: Drop in the whole nutmeg, turn the crank, and shave the spice.

Celebrate fall harvest with this bread. The fresh tart apples combine with the sweet almond brickle to create a loaf that tastes a bit like candied apple.

Apple-Brickle Bread

PREP:	1½-POUND*	INGREDIENTS	2-POUND*
15 minutes	⅔ cup	milk**	⅔ cup
	½ cup	chopped peeled apple	⅔ cup
MAKES:	1	egg(s)	2
1½-pound recipe (18 slices)	2 tablespoons	water**	2 tablespoons
OR	2 tablespoons	margarine or butter, cut up**	2 tablespoons
2-pound recipe (24 slices)	3 cups	bread flour	4 cups
	2 tablespoons	sugar	3 tablespoons
	¾ teaspoon	salt	1 teaspoon
	½ teaspoon	ground cinnamon	¾ teaspoon
	1 teaspoon	active dry yeast or bread machine yeast	1¼ teaspoons
	⅓ cup	almond brickle pieces	½ cup

1 Select the loaf size. Add the ingredients to the machine according to the manufacturer's directions, adding the apple with the milk. Select the basic white bread cycle.

*Note: For the 1½-pound loaf, the bread machine pan must have a capacity of 10 cups or more. For the 2-pound loaf, the bread machine pan must have a capacity of 12 cups or more.

**Note: The Test Kitchen recommends ⅔ cup milk, 2 tablespoons water, and 2 tablespoons margarine or butter for either size recipe.

Nutrition Facts per slice: 127 cal., 3 g total fat (0 g sat. fat), 14 mg chol., 130 mg sodium, 21 g carbo., 4 g pro.

Give your kids a sweet send-off to school with this bread topped with Nut 'n' Honey Butter (page 264). The sweetly spiced loaf is flavored with apple cider and applesauce.

Oatmeal-Applesauce Bread

1½-POUND*	INGREDIENTS	2-POUND*
³/₄ cup	apple cider or apple juice	1 cup
¹/₂ cup	applesauce**	¹/₂ cup
1 tablespoon	margarine or butter	4 teaspoons
3 cups	bread flour	4 cups
¹/₃ cup	regular or quick-cooking rolled oats	¹/₂ cup
1 tablespoon	brown sugar	4 teaspoons
³/₄ teaspoon	salt	1 teaspoon
¹/₄ teaspoon	apple pie spice	¹/₂ teaspoon
1 teaspoon	active dry yeast or bread machine yeast	1¹/₄ teaspoons

PREP:
10 minutes

MAKES:
1½-pound recipe (18 slices)
OR
2-pound recipe (24 slices)

1 Select the loaf size. Add the ingredients to the machine according to the manufacturer's directions. Select the basic white bread cycle.

*Note: For the 1½-pound loaf, the bread machine pan must have a capacity of 10 cups or more. For the 2-pound loaf, the bread machine pan must have a capacity of 12 cups or more.

**Note: The Test Kitchen recommends ½ cup applesauce for either size recipe.

Nutrition Facts per slice: 108 cal., 1 g total fat (0 g sat. fat), 0 mg chol., 98 mg sodium, 21 g carbo., 3 g pro.

Moist and delicious, this appealing bread has graced American dinner tables for generations.

Apple Butter Bread

	1½-POUND*	INGREDIENTS	2-POUND*
PREP: 10 minutes	½ cup	milk	⅔ cup
	⅓ cup	apple butter	½ cup
MAKES: 1½-pound recipe (16 slices) OR 2-pound recipe (22 slices)	¼ cup	water	⅓ cup
	1	egg**	1
	4 teaspoons	margarine or butter, cut up	2 tablespoons
	3 cups	bread flour	4 cups
	¾ teaspoon	salt	1 teaspoon
	½ teaspoon	apple pie spice or ground allspice	¾ teaspoon
	1 teaspoon	active dry yeast or bread machine yeast	1¼ teaspoons

1 Select the loaf size. Add the ingredients to the machine according to the manufacturer's directions. Select the basic white bread cycle.

*Note: For the 1½-pound loaf, the bread machine pan must have a capacity of 10 cups or more. For the 2-pound loaf, the bread machine pan must have a capacity of 12 cups or more.

**Note: The Test Kitchen recommends 1 egg for either size recipe.

Nutrition Facts per slice: 123 cal., 2 g total fat (0 g sat. fat), 14 mg chol., 120 mg sodium, 22 g carbo., 4 g pro.

Homemade Apple Pie Spice

In a pinch, you can blend apple pie spice from spices you probably have on hand. For 1 teaspoon apple pie spice, combine ½ teaspoon ground cinnamon, ¼ teaspoon ground nutmeg, ⅛ teaspoon ground allspice, and a dash of ground cloves or ginger.

Here's a twist to Mom's apple pie. If you love apples and nuts, try them in a new venue—an impressive sweet bread made moist with applesauce and munchy with chopped nuts.

Apple-Walnut Bread

1½-POUND*	INGREDIENTS	2-POUND*
²/₃ cup	water**	²/₃ cup
1	egg(s)	2
¼ cup	applesauce	⅓ cup
2 tablespoons	margarine or butter, cut up**	2 tablespoons
3 cups	bread flour	4 cups
2 tablespoons	sugar	3 tablespoons
¾ teaspoon	salt	1 teaspoon
1 teaspoon	active dry yeast	1 teaspoon
	or bread machine yeast**	
½ cup	chopped walnuts	²/₃ cup

PREP:
15 minutes

MAKES:
1½-pound recipe
(18 slices)
OR
2-pound recipe
(24 slices)

1 Select the loaf size. Add the ingredients to the machine according to the manufacturer's directions. Select the basic white bread cycle.

*Note: For the 1½-pound loaf, the bread machine pan must have a capacity of 10 cups or more. For the 2-pound loaf, the bread machine pan must have a capacity of 12 cups or more.

**Note: The Test Kitchen recommends ²/₃ cup water, 2 tablespoons margarine or butter, and 1 teaspoon yeast for either size recipe.

Nutrition Facts per slice: 128 cal., 4 g total fat (1 g sat. fat), 12 mg chol., 108 mg sodium, 19 g carbo., 4 g pro.

Almond extract delicately flavors this loaf, and peach baby food makes preparation super simple.

Peaches and Cream Loaf

PREP:
10 minutes

MAKES:
1½-pound recipe
(16 slices)
OR
2-pound recipe
(22 slices)

1½-POUND	INGREDIENTS	2-POUND
1 cup	peach baby food	1⅓ cups
3 tablespoons	whipping cream	¼ cup
1 tablespoon	margarine or butter, cut up	2 tablespoons
¼ teaspoon	almond extract*	¼ teaspoon
3 cups	bread flour	4 cups
1 tablespoon	sugar	4 teaspoons
¾ teaspoon	salt	1 teaspoon
1 teaspoon	active dry yeast	1¼ teaspoons
	or bread machine yeast	

1 Select the loaf size. Add the ingredients to the machine according to the manufacturer's directions. Select the basic white bread cycle.

*Note: The Test Kitchen recommends ¼ teaspoon almond extract for either size recipe.

Nutrition Facts per slice: 123 cal., 2 g total fat (1 g sat. fat), 4 mg chol., 111 mg sodium, 22 g carbo., 3 g pro.

Showcase this golden loaf for brunch accompanied by your favorite preserve or marmalade.

Orange-Cinnamon Loaf

1½-POUND*	INGREDIENTS	2-POUND*
½ cup	buttermilk or sour milk***	⅔ cup
⅓ cup	water	½ cup
1	egg**	1
3 tablespoons	margarine or butter, cut up	¼ cup
3 cups	bread flour	4 cups
3 tablespoons	sugar	¼ cup
2 teaspoons	finely shredded orange peel	2½ teaspoons
¾ teaspoon	salt	1 teaspoon
¾ teaspoon	ground cinnamon	1 teaspoon
1 teaspoon	active dry yeast	1½ teaspoons
	or bread machine yeast	
1 recipe	Orange Glaze	1 recipe

PREP:
15 minutes

MAKES:
1½-pound recipe
(16 slices)
OR
2-pound recipe
(22 slices)

① Select the loaf size. Add the ingredients, except the Orange Glaze, to the machine according to the manufacturer's directions. Select the basic white bread cycle. Drizzle the cooled loaf with Orange Glaze.

Orange Glaze: In a small bowl stir together 1 cup sifted powdered sugar and 1 teaspoon vanilla. Stir in enough orange juice (4 to 6 teaspoons) to make a glaze of drizzling consistency.

*Note: For the 1½-pound loaf, the bread machine pan must have a capacity of 10 cups or more. For the 2-pound loaf, the bread machine pan must have a capacity of 12 cups or more.

**Note: The Test Kitchen recommends 1 egg for either size recipe.

***Note: To make ½ cup sour milk, place 1½ teaspoons lemon juice or vinegar in a 1-cup liquid measuring cup. Add enough milk to measure ½ cup liquid; stir. To make ⅔ cup sour milk, place 2 teaspoons lemon juice or vinegar in a 1-cup liquid measuring cup. Add enough milk to measure ⅔ cup liquid; stir. Let stand for 5 minutes before using.

Nutrition Facts per slice: 155 cal., 3 g total fat (1 g sat. fat), 14 mg chol., 134 mg sodium, 28 g carbo., 4 g pro.

Swap lemon or tangerine peel for the orange peel and this honey-sweetened loaf takes on an exciting new flavor.

Orange-Sherry Bread

1½-POUND	INGREDIENTS
1 cup	milk
3 tablespoons	dry sherry or orange juice
3 tablespoons	honey
2 tablespoons	margarine or butter, cut up
1½ cups	bread flour
1½ cups	whole wheat flour
2 teaspoons	finely shredded orange peel
¾ teaspoon	salt
1 teaspoon	active dry yeast
	or bread machine yeast
½ cup	dark raisins

1 Add the ingredients to the machine according to the manufacturer's directions. If available, select the whole grain cycle, or select the basic white bread cycle and, if available, the light color setting.

Nutrition Facts per slice: 132 cal., 2 g total fat (0 g sat. fat), 2 mg chol., 122 mg sodium, 26 g carbo., 5 g pro.

Jump start your day with the nutritious goodness of this flavor-packed loaf. Fiber-rich bran coupled with the natural sweetness of maple makes this a healthful and delicious choice.

Maple-Bran Breakfast Bread

1½-POUND	INGREDIENTS	2-POUND
¾ cup	milk	1 cup
3 tablespoons	maple-flavored syrup	¼ cup
	or pure maple syrup	
2 tablespoons	margarine or butter, cut up	3 tablespoons
2 tablespoons	water*	2 tablespoons
2½ cups	bread flour	3⅓ cups
¾ cup	whole bran cereal	1 cup
2 teaspoons	gluten flour*	2 teaspoons
¾ teaspoon	salt	1 teaspoon
1¼ teaspoons	active dry yeast	1½ teaspoons
	or bread machine yeast	
¼ cup	chopped walnuts, toasted	⅓ cup

PREP:
15 minutes

MAKES:
1½-pound recipe
(16 slices)
OR
2-pound recipe
(22 slices)

1 Select the loaf size. Add the ingredients to the machine according to the manufacturer's directions, adding the bran cereal with the flour. Select the basic white bread cycle.

*Note: The Test Kitchen recommends 2 tablespoons water and 2 teaspoons gluten flour for either size recipe.

Nutrition Facts per slice: 123 cal., 3 g total fat (1 g sat. fat), 1 mg chol., 145 mg sodium, 21 g carbo., 4 g pro.

Use It in French Toast

When life gives you leftover bread, make French toast! Here's one way: In a small bowl combine 2 slightly beaten eggs, ½ cup milk, and ½ teaspoon vanilla. Lay 3 or 4 thick, day-old bread slices in a shallow dish and pour egg mixture over; let bread soak about 15 minutes, turning slices once. Drain. Cook bread in butter or oil in a hot skillet for 2 to 3 minutes on both sides or until golden brown. Serve warm with maple syrup.

Serve this wonderfully spiced loaf with fresh fruit as a snack or dessert.

Anise Bread

PREP:
10 minutes

MAKES:
1½-pound recipe
(16 slices)

1½-POUND*	INGREDIENTS
½ cup	milk
½ cup	orange juice
1	egg
2 tablespoons	margarine or butter, cut up
3 cups	bread flour
4 teaspoons	brown sugar
1½ teaspoons	anise seeds
¾ teaspoon	salt
¾ teaspoon	finely shredded lemon peel
¾ teaspoon	finely shredded orange peel
⅛ teaspoon	ground mace
⅛ teaspoon	ground nutmeg
1 teaspoon	active dry yeast
	or bread machine yeast

1 Add the ingredients to the machine according to the manufacturer's directions. Select the basic white bread cycle.

*Note: The bread machine pan must have a capacity of 10 cups or more.

Nutrition Facts per slice: 123 cal., 2 g total fat (0 g sat. fat), 21 mg chol., 123 mg sodium, 21 g carbo., 5 g pro.

Experiment with Anise

If you've never tried anise seeds, here's your chance. The anise seed comes from the anise plant, which is a member of the parsley family. The distinctive licorice flavor is enjoyed in candies as well as savory dishes. It is often used in Southeast Asian cuisine. Look for anise seeds in the spice section of the supermarket.

This recipe recalls the shoo-fly pie, a Pennsylvania Dutch classic that according to some, was so named because its molasses-and-brown-sugar sweetness attracted flies. Our shoo-fly-pie flavored bread will prove equally attractive—and to less irritating creatures too!

Shoo-Fly Pie Bread

1½-POUND	INGREDIENTS	2-POUND
1 cup	milk	1⅓ cups
3 tablespoons	molasses	¼ cup
2 tablespoons	shortening or cooking oil	3 tablespoons
2 cups	bread flour	2⅔ cups
1 cup	whole wheat flour	1⅓ cups
1 tablespoon	gluten flour	4 teaspoons
1 tablespoon	brown sugar	4 teaspoons
¾ teaspoon	salt	1 teaspoon
1¼ teaspoons	active dry yeast	1½ teaspoons
	or bread machine yeast	

PREP:
10 minutes

MAKES:
1½-pound recipe
(16 slices)
OR
2-pound recipe
(22 slices)

1 Select the loaf size. Add the ingredients to the machine according to the manufacturer's directions. If available, select the whole grain cycle, or select the basic white bread cycle.

Nutrition Facts per slice: 125 cal., 2 g total fat (1 g sat. fat), 1 mg chol., 119 mg sodium, 22 g carbo., 4 g pro.

You don't have to wait until the winter holidays for cranberries. Fortunately dried cranberries are available year-round. Look for them in the produce section or dried fruit section of the supermarket.

Chocolate-Cranberry Nut Bread

	1½-POUND*	INGREDIENTS	2-POUND*
PREP: 15 minutes	⅔ cup	milk**	⅔ cup
	1	egg(s)	2
MAKES:	¼ cup	water	⅓ cup
1½-pound recipe (16 slices)	2 tablespoons	honey	3 tablespoons
OR	2 tablespoons	margarine or butter, cut up**	2 tablespoons
2-pound recipe (22 slices)	3 cups	bread flour	4 cups
	¾ teaspoon	salt	1 teaspoon
	1¼ teaspoons	active dry yeast	1½ teaspoons
		or bread machine yeast	
	½ cup	chopped hazelnuts (filberts)	⅔ cup
	½ cup	dried cranberries	⅔ cup
	⅓ cup	miniature semisweet chocolate pieces	½ cup

❶ Select the loaf size. Add the ingredients to the machine according to the manufacturer's directions. Select the basic white bread cycle.

*Note: For the 1½-pound loaf, the bread machine pan must have a capacity of 10 cups or more. For the 2-pound loaf, the bread machine pan must have a capacity of 12 cups or more.

**Note: The Test Kitchen recommends ⅔ cup milk and 2 tablespoons margarine or butter for either size recipe.

Nutrition Facts per slice: 175 cal., 6 g total fat (1 g sat. fat), 14 mg chol., 127 mg sodium, 27 g carbo., 5 g pro.

Bowl 'em over tomorrow morning! Instead of the same ordinary bowl of cold cereal, serve up slices of a granola-flecked fruit bread that also makes tasty toast.

Cranberry-Granola Bread

1½-POUND	INGREDIENTS	2-POUND
1¼ cups	buttermilk or sour milk**	1⅔ cups
2 tablespoons	honey	3 tablespoons
1 tablespoon	margarine or butter*	1 tablespoon
1½ cups	bread flour	2 cups
1½ cups	whole wheat flour	2 cups
1 tablespoon	gluten flour	2 tablespoons
¾ teaspoon	salt	1 teaspoon
1 teaspoon	active dry yeast	1¼ teaspoons
	or bread machine yeast	
⅔ cup	granola	¾ cup
½ cup	dried cranberries	¾ cup
¼ cup	chopped almonds, toasted	⅓ cup

PREP:
15 minutes

MAKES:
1½-pound recipe
(16 slices)
OR
2-pound recipe
(22 slices)

1 Select the loaf size. Add the ingredients to the machine according to the manufacturer's directions. If available, select the whole grain cycle, or select the basic white bread cycle.

*Note: The Test Kitchen recommends 1 tablespoon margarine or butter for either size recipe.

**Note: To make 1¼ cups sour milk, place 3¾ teaspoons lemon juice or vinegar in a 2-cup liquid measuring cup. Add enough milk to measure 1¼ cups liquid; stir. To make 1⅔ cups sour milk, place 5 teaspoons lemon juice or vinegar in a 2-cup liquid measuring cup. Add enough milk to measure 1⅔ cups liquid; stir. Let stand for 5 minutes before using.

Nutrition Facts per slice: 154 cal., 3 g total fat (1 g sat. fat), 1 mg chol., 140 mg sodium, 27 g carbo., 5 g pro.

All About Granola

Hitting its height in popularity in the '70s, the breakfast cereal granola generally contains a variety of grains (one of which is usually oats), nuts, and dried fruit. It often contains oil and honey and is toasted for a crunchy texture. Added to breads, granola boosts the fiber and nutrition.

What better way to enjoy chocolate than combining it with the rich fruity flavor of banana?
Save your ripe bananas and put them to good use in this mini chocolate chip-filled loaf.

Banana-Chocolate Chip Bread

	1½-POUND*	INGREDIENTS	2-POUND*
PREP: 10 minutes	½ cup	mashed ripe banana	⅔ cup
	½ cup	milk**	½ cup
MAKES:	1	egg(s)	2
1½-pound recipe (16 slices)	2 tablespoons	margarine or butter, cut up**	2 tablespoons
OR	3 cups	bread flour	4 cups
2-pound recipe (22 slices)	2 tablespoons	brown sugar	3 tablespoons
	¾ teaspoon	salt	1 teaspoon
	1 teaspoon	active dry yeast or bread machine yeast	1¼ teaspoons
	⅓ cup	miniature semisweet chocolate pieces	½ cup

1 Select the loaf size. Add the ingredients to the machine according to the manufacturer's directions. Select the basic white bread cycle.

*Note: For the 1½-pound loaf, the bread machine pan must have a capacity of 10 cups or more. For the 2-pound loaf, the bread machine pan must have a capacity of 12 cups or more.

**Note: The Test Kitchen recommends ½ cup milk and 2 tablespoons margarine or butter for either size recipe.

Nutrition Facts per slice: 145 cal., 3 g total fat (1 g sat. fat), 14 mg chol., 126 mg sodium, 25 g carbo., 4 g pro.

Capture the flavors of the tropics in this sweet loaf. Banana and candied pineapple make it a family favorite, especially when spread with peanut butter or drizzled with honey.

Pineapple-Banana Loaf

1½-POUND*	INGREDIENTS	2-POUND*
½ cup	buttermilk or sour milk***	⅔ cup
½ cup	mashed ripe banana	⅔ cup
1	egg**	1
1 tablespoon	margarine or butter	4 teaspoons
1 teaspoon	vanilla	1½ teaspoons
3 cups	bread flour	4 cups
3 tablespoons	sugar	¼ cup
¾ teaspoon	salt	1 teaspoon
1 teaspoon	active dry yeast	1¼ teaspoons
	or bread machine yeast	
¼ cup	chopped candied pineapple	⅓ cup
¼ cup	chopped pecans	⅓ cup
	or walnuts, toasted	

PREP:
15 minutes

MAKES:
1½-pound recipe
(20 slices)
OR
2-pound recipe
(27 slices)

1 Select the loaf size. Add the ingredients to the machine according to the manufacturer's directions. Select the basic white bread cycle.

*Note: For the 1½-pound loaf, the bread machine pan must have a capacity of 10 cups or more. For the 2-pound loaf, the bread machine pan must have a capacity of 12 cups or more.

**Note: The Test Kitchen recommends 1 egg for either size recipe.

***Note: To make ½ cup sour milk, place 1½ teaspoons lemon juice or vinegar in a 1-cup liquid measuring cup. Add enough milk to measure ½ cup liquid; stir. To make ⅔ cup sour milk, place 2 teaspoons lemon juice or vinegar in a 1-cup liquid measuring cup. Add enough milk to measure ⅔ cup liquid; stir. Let stand for 5 minutes before using.

Nutrition Facts per slice: 117 cal., 2 g total fat (0 g sat. fat), 11 mg chol., 97 mg sodium, 21 g carbo., 3 g pro.

Keep Candied Fruit From Clumping

Bits of sticky candied fruit will sometimes clump together in a dough no matter how thoroughly it's kneaded. For more even distribution, first toss the chopped pieces in a little of the flour from the recipe, then add them with the rest of the ingredients as directed.

Double your pleasure with the fusion of carrot and pineapple flavors. The cakelike appearance and cream cheese topping makes it so versatile you may want to serve it for dessert.

Carrot-Pineapple Bread

PREP:	1½-POUND*	INGREDIENTS	2-POUND*
15 minutes	1 (8-ounce) can	crushed pineapple (juice pack), undrained**	1 (8-ounce) can
MAKES:	⅓ cup	finely shredded carrot	½ cup
1½-pound recipe (18 slices)	1	egg(s)	2
OR	2 tablespoons	margarine or butter, cut up**	2 tablespoons
2-pound recipe (24 slices)	3 cups	bread flour	4 cups
	2 tablespoons	sugar	3 tablespoons
	¾ teaspoon	salt	1 teaspoon
	½ teaspoon	ground ginger	¾ teaspoon
	1 teaspoon	active dry yeast or bread machine yeast	1¼ teaspoons
	1 recipe	Cream Cheese Glaze	1 recipe

❶ Select the loaf size. Add the ingredients, except the Cream Cheese Glaze, to the machine according to the manufacturer's directions. Select the basic white bread cycle.

❷ Spoon the Cream Cheese Glaze over cooled loaf, allowing some of the glaze to flow down sides of bread.

Cream Cheese Glaze: In a small bowl stir together one-fourth of an 8-ounce tub cream cheese and 1 tablespoon sugar. Stir in enough milk (4 to 5 teaspoons) to make a glaze of drizzling consistency.

*Note: For the 1½-pound loaf, the bread machine pan must have a capacity of 10 cups or more. For the 2-pound loaf, the bread machine pan must have a capacity of 12 cups or more.

**Note: The Test Kitchen recommends one 8-ounce can pineapple and 2 tablespoons margarine or butter for either size recipe.

Nutrition Facts per slice: 136 cal., 3 g total fat (1 g sat. fat), 17 mg chol., 128 mg sodium, 22 g carbo., 4 g pro.

If eating at a kitchen island is all the island living you're doing these days, take a tropical trip via a moist, sweet bread with all the appropriate flavors—coconut, pineapple, and macadamia nuts.

Hawaiian Isle Bread

1½-POUND*	INGREDIENTS	2-POUND*
¾ cup	milk	1 cup
1	egg**	1
2 tablespoons	water	3 tablespoons
1 tablespoon	margarine or butter	4 teaspoons
1 teaspoon	vanilla	1½ teaspoons
¼ teaspoon	coconut extract**	¼ teaspoon
3 cups	bread flour	4 cups
2 tablespoons	sugar	3 tablespoons
¾ teaspoon	salt	1 teaspoon
1 teaspoon	active dry yeast	1¼ teaspoons
	or bread machine yeast	
½ cup	coarsely snipped candied	⅔ cup
	pineapple	
½ cup	coconut, toasted	⅔ cup
1 recipe	Powdered Sugar Glaze	1 recipe
2 tablespoons	chopped macadamia nuts**	2 tablespoons

PREP:
15 minutes

MAKES:
1½-pound recipe
(18 slices)
OR
2-pound recipe
(24 slices)

❶ Select the loaf size. Add the first 12 ingredients to the machine according to the manufacturer's directions. Select the basic white bread cycle.

❷ Drizzle the cooled loaf with Powdered Sugar Glaze and sprinkle with macadamia nuts.

Powdered Sugar Glaze: In a small bowl stir together 1 cup sifted powdered sugar and ½ teaspoon vanilla. Stir in enough milk (3 to 4 teaspoons) to make a glaze of drizzling consistency.

*Note: For the 1½-pound loaf, the bread machine pan must have a capacity of 10 cups or more. For the 2-pound loaf, the bread machine pan must have a capacity of 12 cups or more.

**Note: The Test Kitchen recommends 1 egg, ¼ teaspoon coconut extract, and 2 tablespoons nuts for either size recipe.

Nutrition Facts per slice: 161 cal., 3 g total fat (0 g sat. fat), 13 mg chol., 111 mg sodium, 29 g carbo., 4 g pro.

The simple addition of golden honey and licorice-flavored anise seeds catapults this whole wheat bread from plain ol' good to excellent.

Honey-Anise Bread

	1½-POUND*	INGREDIENTS	2-POUND*
PREP: 10 minutes	1 cup	milk	1¼ cups
	2 tablespoons	honey	3 tablespoons
MAKES: 1½-pound recipe (16 slices)	1 tablespoon	water	2 tablespoons
	1 tablespoon	margarine or butter, cut up	2 tablespoons
	1½ cups	bread flour	2 cups
OR	1½ cups	whole wheat flour	2 cups
2-pound recipe (22 slices)	1 tablespoon	anise seeds, crushed	4 teaspoons
	2 teaspoons	gluten flour	1 tablespoon
	¾ teaspoon	salt	1 teaspoon
	1 teaspoon	active dry yeast or bread machine yeast	1¼ teaspoons

1 Select the loaf size. Add the ingredients to the machine according to the manufacturer's directions. If available, select the whole grain cycle, or select the basic white bread cycle.

*Note: For the 1½-pound loaf, the bread machine pan must have a capacity of 10 cups or more. For the 2-pound loaf, the bread machine pan must have a capacity of 12 cups or more.

Nutrition Facts per slice: 110 cal., 2 g total fat (0 g sat. fat), 1 mg chol., 117 mg sodium, 21 g carbo., 4 g pro.

Home is where the heart is—and nothing says "home" better than this blissful bread. Packed full of good-for-you raisins and flavored with graham flour, it's the ultimate old-fashioned bread.

Cinnamon-Raisin Graham Bread

1½-POUND*	INGREDIENTS	2-POUND*
1 cup	water	1⅓ cups
3 tablespoons	honey	¼ cup
2 tablespoons	margarine or butter, cut up	3 tablespoons
2 cups	bread flour	2¾ cups
1 cup	graham (coarse whole wheat) flour	1¼ cups
1 tablespoon	gluten flour	4 teaspoons
¾ teaspoon	salt	1 teaspoon
¾ teaspoon	ground cinnamon	1 teaspoon
1 teaspoon	active dry yeast or bread machine yeast**	1 teaspoon
⅓ cup	dark raisins	½ cup

PREP:
10 minutes

MAKES:
1½-pound recipe
(16 slices)
OR
2-pound recipe
(22 slices)

1 Select the loaf size. Add the ingredients to the machine according to the manufacturer's directions. If available, select the whole grain cycle, or select the basic white bread cycle.

***Note:** For the 1½-pound loaf, the bread machine pan must have a capacity of 10 cups or more. For the 2-pound loaf, the bread machine pan must have a capacity of 12 cups or more.

****Note:** The Test Kitchen recommends 1 teaspoon yeast for either size recipe.

Nutrition Facts per slice: 124 cal., 2 g total fat (0 g sat. fat), 0 mg chol., 118 mg sodium, 24 g carbo., 4 g pro.

Graham Flour Origins

Graham flour got its name from its developer, the Rev. Sylvester Graham, a health advocate from Connecticut during the 1800s. Graham flour is whole wheat flour that is slightly coarser than regular ground whole wheat flour. You may use graham flour interchangeably with regular whole wheat flour in recipes.

You won't have to wait until the pears are ripe and juicy. This recipe utilizes sweet, juicy canned pears. Mash the drained pears well before adding them to the machine.

French Pear Bread

PREP:	1½-POUND*	INGREDIENTS	2-POUND*
10 minutes	¾ cup	mashed, drained canned pears (juice pack)	1 cup
MAKES:	¼ cup	water	⅓ cup
1½-pound recipe (20 slices)	1	egg**	1
OR	1 tablespoon	honey	4 teaspoons
2-pound recipe (27 slices)	3 cups	bread flour	4 cups
	¾ teaspoon	salt	1 teaspoon
	⅛ teaspoon	black pepper	¼ teaspoon
	1 teaspoon	active dry yeast or bread machine yeast	1¼ teaspoons

❶ Select the loaf size. Add the ingredients to the machine according to the manufacturer's directions. Select the basic white bread cycle.

*Note: For the 1½-pound loaf, the bread machine pan must have a capacity of 10 cups or more. For the 2-pound loaf, the bread machine pan must have a capacity of 12 cups or more.

**Note: The Test Kitchen recommends 1 egg for either size recipe.

Nutrition Facts per slice: 89 cal., 1 g total fat (0 g sat. fat), 11 mg chol., 84 mg sodium, 18 g carbo., 3 g pro.

Flavored coffee powder lends this fanciful bread mocha and almond accents, plus creaminess and a hint of sweetness.

Café Almond Bread

1½-POUND*	INGREDIENTS	2-POUND*
²/₃ cup	milk	³/₄ cup
¹/₄ cup	water	¹/₃ cup
1	egg**	1
2 tablespoons	margarine or butter, cut up	3 tablespoons
3 cups	bread flour	4 cups
3 tablespoons	sugar	¹/₄ cup
2 tablespoons	instant Roman- or Swiss-style coffee powder	3 tablespoons
³/₄ teaspoon	salt	1 teaspoon
1 teaspoon	active dry yeast or bread machine yeast	1¹/₄ teaspoons
¹/₂ cup	coarsely chopped almonds, toasted	²/₃ cup

PREP:
15 minutes

MAKES:
1½-pound recipe
(20 slices)
OR
2-pound recipe
(27 slices)

1 Select the loaf size. Add the ingredients to the machine according to the manufacturer's directions. Select the basic white bread cycle and, if available, the light color setting.

*Note: For the 1½-pound loaf, the bread machine pan must have a capacity of 10 cups or more. For the 2-pound loaf, the bread machine pan must have a capacity of 12 cups or more.

**Note: The Test Kitchen recommends 1 egg for either size loaf.

Nutrition Facts per slice: 116 cal., 3 g total fat (1 g sat. fat), 11 mg chol., 101 mg sodium, 18 g carbo., 4 g pro.

The best PB&J sandwich starts here. This tasty bread is peanutty with a capital "P"—peanut butter, dry-roasted peanuts, and a peanut glaze for triple peanut power.

Peanut Butter-Honey Bread

	1½-POUND*	INGREDIENTS	2-POUND*
PREP: 15 minutes	½ cup	milk	¾ cup
	¼ cup	water	⅓ cup
MAKES:	¼ cup	peanut butter	⅓ cup
1½-pound recipe (16 slices)	1	egg**	1
OR	3 tablespoons	honey	¼ cup
2-pound recipe (22 slices)	3 cups	bread flour	4 cups
	¾ teaspoon	salt	1 teaspoon
	1¼ teaspoons	active dry yeast	1½ teaspoons
		or bread machine yeast	
	⅓ cup	chopped dry-roasted peanuts	½ cup
	1 recipe	Peanut Butter Glaze	1 recipe

1 Select the loaf size. Add the ingredients, except the Peanut Butter Glaze, to the machine according to the manufacturer's directions. Select the basic white bread cycle. Drizzle the cooled loaf with Peanut Butter Glaze.

Peanut Butter Glaze: In a small bowl stir together 1 cup sifted powdered sugar and 2 tablespoons peanut butter. Stir in enough milk (1 to 2 tablespoons) to make a glaze of drizzling consistency.

*Note: For the 1½-pound loaf, the bread machine pan must have a capacity of 10 cups or more. For the 2-pound loaf, the bread machine pan must have a capacity of 12 cups or more.

**Note: The Test Kitchen recommends 1 egg for either size recipe.

Nutrition Facts per slice: 192 cal., 5 g total fat (1 g sat. fat), 14 mg chol., 162 mg sodium, 31 g carbo., 6 g pro.

Instant coffee and caramel ice cream topping give this bread its appealing aroma and taste. It's sweet, but not too sweet, and will be popular with coffee fans.

Caramel-Cappuccino Loaf

1½-POUND*	INGREDIENTS	2-POUND*
4 teaspoons	instant coffee crystals	2 tablespoons
¼ cup	water	⅓ cup
⅓ cup	milk	½ cup
¼ cup	caramel ice cream topping	⅓ cup
1	egg**	1
2 tablespoons	margarine or butter, cut up	3 tablespoons
3 cups	bread flour	4 cups
¾ teaspoon	salt	1 teaspoon
1¼ teaspoons	active dry yeast	1½ teaspoons
	or bread machine yeast	

PREP:
10 minutes

MAKES:
1½-pound recipe
(20 slices)
OR
2-pound recipe
(27 slices)

1 Select the loaf size. In a small bowl dissolve the coffee crystals in the water. Add the coffee mixture and the remaining ingredients to the machine according to the manufacturer's directions. Select the basic white bread cycle.

*Note: For the 1½-pound loaf, the bread machine pan must have a capacity of 10 cups or more. For the 2-pound loaf, the bread machine pan must have a capacity of 12 cups or more.

**Note: The Test Kitchen recommends 1 egg for either size recipe.

Nutrition Facts per slice: 102 cal., 2 g total fat (0 g sat. fat), 11 mg chol., 114 mg sodium, 18 g carbo., 3 g pro.

Die-hard peanut butter fans will appreciate this crunchy, flavorful loaf. Serve with a steaming cup of hot cocoa—morning, noon, or night.

Peanut Butter Snack Bread

PREP:
15 minutes

MAKES:
1½-pound recipe
(16 slices)
OR
2-pound recipe
(22 slices)

1½-POUND*	INGREDIENTS	2-POUND*
1 cup plus 2 tablespoons	milk	1¼ cups
⅓ cup	peanut butter	½ cup
1	egg(s)	2
3 cups	bread flour	4 cups
2 tablespoons	sugar	3 tablespoons
¾ teaspoon	salt	1 teaspoon
1 teaspoon	active dry yeast or bread machine yeast	1¼ teaspoons
¾ cup	chopped peanuts	1 cup

1 Select the loaf size. Add the ingredients to the machine according to the manufacturer's directions. Select the basic white bread cycle.

*Note: For the 1½-pound loaf, the bread machine pan must have a capacity of 10 cups or more. For the 2-pound loaf, the bread machine pan must have a capacity of 12 cups or more.

Nutrition Facts per slice: 184 cal., 7 g total fat (1 g sat. fat), 15 mg chol., 194 mg sodium, 24 g carbo., 7 g pro.

Inventing Peanut Butter

Don't tell your kids, but peanut butter was invented by a doctor as a health food. A St. Louis physician first thought to grind peanuts to a tasty paste at the turn of the 19th century and told the world about it at the 1904 St. Louis World's Fair. Its popularity quickly soared as a sandwich spread, especially with grape jelly.

To make sandwiches, omit the Amaretto Glaze and team this nutty bread with ham or turkey.
You'll be delighted with the balance of sweet and savory.

Hazelnut-Amaretto Loaf

1½-POUND*	INGREDIENTS
1 cup	milk
1	egg
3 tablespoons	margarine or butter, cut up
2 tablespoons	amaretto or hazelnut liqueur
	or orange juice
3 cups	bread flour
3 tablespoons	sugar
³/₄ teaspoon	salt
1 teaspoon	active dry yeast
	or bread machine yeast
³/₄ cup	chopped hazelnuts (filberts)
	or almonds, toasted
1 recipe	Amaretto Glaze

PREP:
15 minutes

MAKES:
1½-pound recipe
(16 slices)

1 Add the ingredients, except the Amaretto Glaze, to the machine according to the manufacturer's directions. Select the basic white bread cycle.

2 Drizzle the cooled loaf with Amaretto Glaze. If desired, sprinkle with additional hazelnuts or almonds.

Amaretto Glaze: In a small bowl stir together ½ cup sifted powdered sugar and 1 tablespoon amaretto or hazelnut liqueur or ½ teaspoon almond extract. Stir in enough milk (1 to 2 teaspoons) to make a glaze of drizzling consistency.

*Note: The bread machine pan must have a capacity of 10 cups or more.

Nutrition Facts per slice: 195 cal., 6 g total fat (2 g sat. fat), 21 mg chol., 140 mg sodium, 29 g carbo., 5 g pro.

Black walnuts and dried blueberries create a taste sensation to behold. Vary the recipe another time by using dried cherries and English walnuts.

Blueberry-Black Walnut Bread

PREP:
15 minutes

MAKES:
1½-pound recipe
(18 slices)
OR
2-pound recipe
(24 slices)

1½-POUND*	INGREDIENTS	2-POUND*
½ cup	milk	⅔ cup
½ cup	vanilla yogurt	⅔ cup
1	egg**	1
2 tablespoons	margarine or butter, cut up**	2 tablespoons
3 cups	bread flour	4 cups
¾ teaspoon	salt	1 teaspoon
1 teaspoon	active dry yeast	1¼ teaspoons
	or bread machine yeast	
⅓ cup	dried blueberries	½ cup
⅓ cup	chopped black walnuts	½ cup

1 Select the loaf size. Add the ingredients to the machine according to the manufacturer's directions. Select the basic white bread cycle.

*Note: For the 1½-pound loaf, the bread machine pan must have a capacity of 10 cups or more. For the 2-pound loaf, the bread machine pan must have a capacity of 12 cups or more.

**Note: The Test Kitchen recommends 1 egg and 2 tablespoons margarine or butter for either size recipe.

Nutrition Facts per slice: 135 cal., 4 g total fat (1 g sat. fat), 13 mg chol., 115 mg sodium, 21 g carbo., 4 g pro.

Browning Bread

If you notice your baking bread starting to get too brown, cover it with foil to reflect some of the dry heat away from the bread's surface. This prevents overbrowning while allowing the inside to finish cooking. Breads containing some sugar and butter are most likely to need this preventive measure.

Kuchen was first made in Germany and was a favorite for breakfast as well as for dessert. But today, cooks in many other European countries as well as in the United States claim it as their own—filling it either with fruit, preserves, or cheese.

Streusel Kuchen

1½-POUND	INGREDIENTS
1 cup	milk
1	egg
1 tablespoon	margarine or butter
3 cups	bread flour
3 tablespoons	sugar
³/₄ teaspoon	salt
1 teaspoon	active dry yeast
	or bread machine yeast
¹/₂ cup	orange marmalade
	or
³/₄ cup	blueberries (optional)
3 tablespoons	brown sugar
2 tablespoons	margarine or butter, softened
4 teaspoons	all-purpose flour or bread flour
³/₄ teaspoon	ground cinnamon
¹/₂ cup	walnuts or almonds, chopped
1 cup	sifted powdered sugar
4 to 5 teaspoons	milk

PREP:
25 minutes

RISE:
30 minutes

BAKE:
25 minutes

MAKES:
1½-pound recipe
(12 servings)

1 Add the first 7 ingredients to the machine according to the manufacturer's directions. Select the dough cycle. When cycle is complete, remove dough. Punch down. Cover and let rest for 10 minutes. Grease a 9×9×2-inch baking pan; set aside.

2 Divide the dough in half. Press 1 portion of dough into the prepared baking pan. If desired, top with orange marmalade. In a small bowl stir together brown sugar, the softened margarine, all-purpose flour, and cinnamon; stir in nuts. Sprinkle half of the nut mixture over the dough in pan.

3 On a lightly floured surface, roll the remaining dough into a 9-inch square; place on top of dough in pan. Sprinkle with the remaining nut mixture. Cover and let rise in a warm place for 30 to 40 minutes or until nearly double. Bake in a 350°F oven for 25 to 30 minutes or until golden brown. If necessary, cover loosely with foil the last 5 minutes to prevent overbrowning. Cool in pan on a wire rack.

4 For icing, in a small bowl stir together powdered sugar and enough of the 4 to 5 teaspoons milk to make an icing of drizzling consistency. Drizzle the icing over kuchen.

Nutrition Facts per serving: 450 cal., 11 g total fat (2 g sat. fat), 42 mg chol., 285 mg sodium, 80 g carbo., 11 g pro.

A bread such as this one, in which balls of yeast dough are dipped in margarine or butter and a sweet coating and then layered and baked, is sometimes called monkey bread.

Hungarian Coffee Cake

	1½-POUND	INGREDIENTS
PREP: 35 minutes	1 cup	buttermilk or sour milk*
	1	egg
RISE: 30 minutes	3 tablespoons	margarine or butter, cut up
	3¾ cups	bread flour
BAKE: 25 minutes	3 tablespoons	sugar
	1½ teaspoons	finely shredded orange peel
MAKES: 1½-pound recipe (16 servings)	¾ teaspoon	salt
	1 teaspoon	active dry yeast
		or bread machine yeast
	½ cup	raisins, dried cherries,
		or dried blueberries
	⅓ cup	sugar
	⅓ cup	chopped almonds or pecans, toasted
	1¼ teaspoons	ground cinnamon
	3 tablespoons	margarine or butter, melted

1 Add the first 8 ingredients to the machine according to the manufacturer's directions. Select the dough cycle. When cycle is complete, remove dough. On a lightly floured surface, gently knead the raisins into dough. Cover and let rest for 10 minutes. Lightly grease a 12-cup ring mold or fluted tube pan; set aside.

2 Divide the dough into 30 portions. Shape each portion into a smooth ball. In a small bowl combine the ⅓ cup sugar, almonds, and cinnamon. Dip each ball into the melted margarine; dip into sugar mixture to coat. Arrange half of the coated balls in the bottom of the prepared pan. Add the remaining coated balls, positioning them between the balls in the first layer. Drizzle with any remaining melted margarine and sprinkle with any remaining sugar mixture. Cover and let rise in a warm place for 30 to 45 minutes or until nearly double.

3 Bake in a 350°F oven for 25 to 30 minutes or until top is light brown. If necessary, cover loosely with foil the last 10 minutes to prevent overbrowning. Cool in pan on a wire rack for 1 minute. Invert onto a serving plate. Serve warm.

***Note:** To make 1 cup sour milk, place 1 tablespoon lemon juice or vinegar in a 1-cup liquid measuring cup. Add enough milk to measure 1 cup liquid; stir. Let stand 5 minutes before using.

Nutrition Facts per serving: 216 cal., 8 g total fat (2 g sat. fat), 21 mg chol., 173 mg sodium, 33 g carbo., 6 g pro.

If you don't want to take the time to weave the strips of dough over and under each other, arrange the number of strips you want to run lengthwise in the pan, then top with the remaining strips going in the opposite direction, forming a basket-weave pattern.

Lattice Coffee Cake

1½-POUND	INGREDIENTS	2-POUND
¾ cup	milk	1 cup
2	egg yolks	3
2 tablespoons	margarine or butter, cut up	3 tablespoons
3 cups	bread flour	4 cups
¼ cup	packed brown sugar	⅓ cup
¾ teaspoon	salt	1 teaspoon
½ teaspoon	ground mace	¾ teaspoon
1½ teaspoons	active dry yeast	2 teaspoons
	or bread machine yeast	
⅓ cup	apricot, pineapple,	½ cup
	or strawberry preserves	
¼ cup	chopped almonds	⅓ cup
3 tablespoons	margarine or butter, softened	¼ cup

PREP:
40 minutes

RISE:
1 hour

BAKE:
20 minutes

MAKES:
1½-pound recipe
(12 servings)
OR
2-pound recipe
(16 servings)

❶ Select the recipe size. Add the first 8 ingredients to the machine according to the manufacturer's directions. Select the dough cycle. When cycle is complete, remove dough. Punch down. Cover and let rest for 10 minutes.

❷ *For the 1½-pound recipe:* Grease an 11×7×1½-inch baking pan. Press two-thirds of the dough into the prepared baking pan. For filling, in a small bowl combine the preserves, almonds, and softened margarine; spread over dough in pan.

❸ On a lightly floured surface, roll the remaining dough into an 11×6-inch rectangle. Cut into twelve 11×½-inch strips. Weave the strips over filling in a lattice pattern. Trim ends; press against bottom dough to seal. Cover and let rise in a warm place about 1 hour or until nearly double.

❹ Bake in a 375°F oven for 20 to 25 minutes or until golden brown. If necessary, cover loosely with foil the last 10 minutes to prevent overbrowning. Cool slightly in pan on a wire rack. Serve warm.

For the 2-pound recipe: Prepare as above, except press two-thirds of the dough into a greased 13×9×2-inch baking pan. Roll the remaining dough into a 13×7-inch rectangle; cut into fourteen 13×½-inch strips. Continue as above.

Nutrition Facts per serving: 236 cal., 8 g total fat (2 g sat. fat), 37 mg chol., 201 mg sodium, 36 g carbo., 6 g pro.

As the bread machine does its work, the chocolate pieces melt, creating a rich, fudgy dough to encase the nutty chocolate filling.

Chocolate-Walnut Swirl Loaves

	1½-POUND	I N G R E D I E N T S
PREP: 25 minutes	½ cup	milk
	2	eggs
RISE: 30 minutes	¼ cup	water
	2 tablespoons	margarine or butter, cut up
BAKE: 30 minutes	½ teaspoon	vanilla
	2 cups	bread flour
MAKES: 1½-pound recipe (32 slices)	1 cup	whole wheat flour
	⅓ cup	sugar
	½ teaspoon	salt
	½ teaspoon	ground cinnamon
	1½ teaspoons	active dry yeast
		or bread machine yeast
	1 cup	semisweet chocolate pieces
	¼ cup	chopped walnuts
	1 teaspoon	shortening

❶ Add the first 11 ingredients and ½ cup of the chocolate pieces to the machine according to the manufacturer's directions. Select the dough cycle. When cycle is complete, remove dough. Punch down. Cover and let rest for 10 minutes. Grease two 8×4×2-inch loaf pans; set aside.

❷ Divide the dough in half. On a lightly floured surface, roll each portion into a 10×7-inch rectangle. Sprinkle each rectangle with 2 tablespoons chocolate pieces and 2 tablespoons walnuts; press lightly. Starting from a short side, roll up into a spiral; seal seam and ends. Place loaves, seam sides down, in the prepared loaf pans. Cover and let rise in a warm place for 30 to 45 minutes or until nearly double.

❸ Bake in a 350°F oven about 30 minutes or until bread sounds hollow when lightly tapped. If necessary, cover loosely with foil the last 10 minutes to prevent overbrowning. Remove from pans; cool slightly on wire racks.

❹ In a small saucepan combine the remaining chocolate pieces and the shortening. Heat over low heat until melted, stirring constantly. Drizzle the melted chocolate over loaves. Cool on wire racks.

Nutrition Facts per slice: 99 cal., 4 g total fat (1 g sat. fat), 14 mg chol., 51 mg sodium, 13 g carbo., 2 g pro.

This elegant daisy-shaped loaf is chock-full of nuts and cinnamon, making it ideal for delighting friends or family at your next gathering.

Raisin-Pecan Coffee Bread

1½-POUND	INGREDIENTS
½ cup	milk
2	eggs
¼ cup	butter or margarine, cut up
3 tablespoons	water
3 cups	bread flour
3 tablespoons	granulated sugar
½ teaspoon	salt
2¼ teaspoons	active dry yeast
	or bread machine yeast
3 tablespoons	butter or margarine, melted
⅓ cup	packed brown sugar
⅓ cup	raisins
⅓ cup	chopped pecans
1 teaspoon	ground cinnamon
1 recipe	Buttery Vanilla Glaze

PREP:
30 minutes

RISE:
20 minutes

BAKE:
20 minutes

MAKES:
1½-pound recipe
(12 servings)

1 Add the first 8 ingredients to the machine according to the manufacturer's directions. Select the dough cycle. When cycle is complete, remove dough. Punch down. Cover and let rest for 10 minutes.

2 Line a large baking sheet with foil and grease foil. Place the dough on the prepared baking sheet and roll into a 12-inch circle. Brush with the melted butter. Cut the dough, cutting from the edge of dough to within 2 inches of the center, into 12 wedges.

3 For filling, in a small bowl combine brown sugar, raisins, pecans, and cinnamon. Sprinkle the filling over dough. Starting at the wide end of each wedge, roll up toward the center of bread. Gently turn each wedge slightly so the same side of all wedges faces upward. Transfer the shaped bread still on foil to a 9×1½-inch round baking pan. Cover and let rise in a warm place about 20 minutes or until nearly double.

4 Bake in a 375°F oven for 20 to 25 minutes or until golden brown. Remove from pan; cool slightly on a wire rack. Drizzle with Buttery Vanilla Glaze. Serve warm.

Buttery Vanilla Glaze: In a small bowl stir together 1 cup sifted powdered sugar, 1 tablespoon milk, 1½ teaspoons melted butter or margarine, and ½ teaspoon vanilla. Stir in enough additional milk, 1 teaspoon at a time, to make a glaze of drizzling consistency.

Nutrition Facts per serving: 311 cal., 11 g total fat (5 g sat. fat), 57 mg chol., 195 mg sodium, 47 g carbo., 6 g pro.

The subtle sweetness of apple and the crunchiness of walnuts deliciously counterbalance the pungent flavor of blue cheese in this sophisticated coffee ring. Serve it with a chef's or cobb salad.

Apple-Walnut-Blue Cheese Burst

PREP:	1½-POUND	INGREDIENTS	2-POUND
25 minutes	¾ cup	buttermilk or sour milk (page 184)	1 cup
RISE:	1	egg(s)	2
45 minutes	¼ cup	margarine or butter, cut up	⅓ cup
BAKE:	2⅓ cups	bread flour	3¼ cups
30 minutes	⅔ cup	whole wheat flour	¾ cup
	2 tablespoons	granulated sugar	3 tablespoons
MAKES:	¾ teaspoon	salt	1 teaspoon
1½-pound recipe (16 servings)	1 teaspoon	active dry yeast	1¼ teaspoons
OR		or bread machine yeast	
2-pound recipe (22 servings)	1 cup	chopped, peeled cooking apples	1½ cups
	¾ cup	crumbled blue cheese	1 cup
	⅓ cup	chopped walnuts, toasted	½ cup
	2 tablespoons	brown sugar	3 tablespoons

❶ Select the recipe size. Add the first 8 ingredients to the machine according to the manufacturer's directions. Select the dough cycle. When cycle is complete, remove dough. Punch down. Cover and let rest for 10 minutes.

❷ Meanwhile, for filling, in a medium bowl combine the apples, blue cheese, walnuts, and brown sugar.

❸ *For the 1½-pound recipe:* Grease a large baking sheet; set aside. On a lightly floured surface, roll the dough into an 18×12-inch rectangle. Spread with the filling. Starting from a long side, roll up into a spiral; seal edge. Place seam side down on the prepared baking sheet. Bring ends together to form a ring. Moisten ends; pinch together to seal ring. Using kitchen scissors or a sharp knife, make a cut from the outside edge toward center, leaving about ½ inch attached. Repeat around the edge at 1- to 1½-inch intervals. Gently pull apart each slice. Cover and let rise in a warm place for 45 to 60 minutes or until nearly double.

❹ Bake in a 350°F oven for 30 to 35 minutes or until bread sounds hollow when lightly tapped. If necessary, cover loosely with foil the last 10 to 15 minutes to prevent overbrowning. Remove from baking sheet; cool on a wire rack.

For the 2-pound recipe: Prepare as above, except roll dough into a 20×16-inch rectangle. Fill and shape as above and place on a greased extra-large baking sheet. Continue as above.

Nutrition Facts per serving: 179 cal., 7 g total fat (2 g sat. fat), 19 mg chol., 239 mg sodium, 24 g carbo., 6 g pro.

A kissing cousin to monkey bread, this raisin-studded ring is made from balls of dough coated in sugar and nutmeg. The balls are stacked in a fluted tube pan and baked.

Raisin Bubble Ring

1½-POUND	INGREDIENTS	2-POUND
²/₃ cup	milk	³/₄ cup
¹/₄ cup	water	¹/₃ cup
¹/₄ cup	margarine or butter, cut up	¹/₃ cup
1	egg*	1
3 cups	bread flour	4 cups
3 tablespoons	sugar	¹/₄ cup
1½ teaspoons	finely shredded orange peel	2 teaspoons
³/₄ teaspoon	salt	1 teaspoon
¹/₄ teaspoon	ground nutmeg	¹/₂ teaspoon
1½ teaspoons	active dry yeast	2 teaspoons
	or bread machine yeast	
³/₄ cup	dark raisins	1 cup
¹/₂ cup	sugar	²/₃ cup
¹/₄ teaspoon	ground nutmeg	¹/₂ teaspoon
3 tablespoons	margarine or butter, melted	¹/₄ cup

PREP:
30 minutes

RISE:
30 minutes

BAKE:
35 minutes

MAKES:
1½-pound recipe
(12 servings)
OR
2-pound recipe
(16 servings)

1 Select the recipe size. Add the first 11 ingredients to the machine according to the manufacturer's directions. Select the dough cycle. When cycle is complete, remove dough. Punch down. Cover and let rest for 10 minutes. Grease a 10-inch fluted tube pan; set aside.

2 Divide the 1½-pound dough into 24 portions (divide the 2-pound dough into 32 portions). Shape each portion into a smooth ball.

3 In a small bowl stir together the ½ or ²/₃ cup sugar and ¼ or ½ teaspoon nutmeg. Dip each ball into the melted margarine; dip into the sugar mixture to coat. Arrange half of the coated balls in the bottom of the prepared tube pan. Add the remaining coated balls, positioning them between the balls in the first layer. Drizzle with any remaining melted margarine and sprinkle with any remaining sugar mixture. Cover and let rise in a warm place about 30 minutes or until nearly double.

4 Bake in a 325°F oven for 35 to 40 minutes or until bread sounds hollow when lightly tapped. If necessary, cover loosely with foil the last 10 minutes to prevent overbrowning. Cool in pan on a wire rack for 1 minute. Invert onto a serving plate. Serve warm.

*Note: The Test Kitchen recommends 1 egg for either size recipe.

Nutrition Facts per serving: 270 cal., 8 g total fat (2 g sat. fat), 19 mg chol., 225 mg sodium, 45 g carbo., 6 g pro.

A lemon-accented triple-berry puree takes center stage in this spectacular lattice-topped number. In berry season, make a couple of loaves to give as gifts.

Mixed Berry Coffee Cake

PREP:
30 minutes

RISE:
30 minutes

BAKE:
25 minutes

MAKES:
1½-pound recipe
(12 servings)

1½-POUND	INGREDIENTS
½ cup	milk
¼ cup	water
1	egg
2 tablespoons	margarine or butter, cut up
3 cups	bread flour
2 tablespoons	granulated sugar
¾ teaspoon	salt
¼ teaspoon	ground nutmeg
1 teaspoon	active dry yeast
	or bread machine yeast
½ cup	strawberries
½ cup	raspberries
½ cup	blackberries
¼ cup	granulated sugar
2 teaspoons	cornstarch
½ teaspoon	finely shredded lemon peel
	Sifted powdered sugar

➊ Add the first 9 ingredients to the machine according to the manufacturer's directions. Select the dough cycle. When cycle is complete, remove dough. Punch down. Cover and let rest for 10 minutes.

➋ Meanwhile, for filling, in a food processor bowl or blender container combine berries; cover and process or blend until nearly smooth. Press the berries through a sieve and discard seeds. In a medium saucepan stir together the ¼ cup granulated sugar and cornstarch. Stir in sieved berries. Cook and stir until thickened and bubbly. Stir in lemon peel.

➌ Grease an 11-inch tart pan; set aside. Divide the dough in half. Press 1 portion into the prepared tart pan, stopping and letting dough rest a few minutes occasionally. Spread with the filling to within ½ inch of edges. On a lightly floured surface, roll the remaining dough into an 11-inch circle; cut into ¾-inch strips. Weave the strips over filling in a lattice pattern. Trim ends as necessary; press against bottom dough to seal.

➍ Cover and let rise in a warm place about 30 minutes or until nearly double. Bake in a 375°F oven about 25 minutes or until golden brown. If necessary, cover loosely with foil the last 10 minutes to prevent overbrowning. Cool slightly in pan on a wire rack. Sprinkle with powdered sugar. Serve warm.

Nutrition Facts per serving: 189 cal., 3 g total fat (1 g sat. fat), 19 mg chol., 167 mg sodium, 35 g carbo., 5 g pro.

The red ribbon running through this coffee cake is conveniently made from raspberry preserves. The streusel topping is a buttery, cinnamon mixture that will melt in your mouth.

Raspberry Ribbon Coffee Bread

1½-POUND	INGREDIENTS	2-POUND
⅔ cup	milk	¾ cup
⅓ cup	butter or margarine, cut up	½ cup
1	egg(s)	2
2 tablespoons	water*	2 tablespoons
3 cups	bread flour	4 cups
⅓ cup	granulated sugar	½ cup
¾ teaspoon	salt	1 teaspoon
1¼ teaspoons	active dry yeast	1½ teaspoons
	or bread machine yeast	
⅓ cup	seedless red raspberry preserves	½ cup
	or apple butter	
¼ cup	all-purpose flour	⅓ cup
	or bread flour	
¼ cup	packed brown sugar	⅓ cup
½ teaspoon	ground cinnamon	1 teaspoon
3 tablespoons	butter	¼ cup

PREP:
25 minutes

RISE:
1 hour

BAKE:
50 minutes

MAKES:
1½-pound recipe
(16 slices)
OR
2-pound recipe
(20 slices)

1 Select the recipe size. Add the first 8 ingredients to the machine according to the manufacturer's directions. Select the dough cycle. When cycle is complete, remove dough. Punch down. Cover and let rest for 10 minutes. Grease a 10-inch tube pan; set aside.

2 On a lightly floured surface, roll the 1½-pound dough into a 16×8-inch rectangle (roll the 2-pound dough into a 16×10-inch rectangle). Spread with the preserves. Starting from a long side, roll up into a spiral; seal edge. Bring ends together to form a ring. Moisten ends; pinch together to seal ring. Place in the prepared tube pan. Cover and let rise in a warm place for 1 to 1¼ hours or until nearly double.

3 Meanwhile, for streusel topping, in a small bowl stir together all-purpose flour, brown sugar, and cinnamon. Using a pastry blender, cut in the 3 tablespoons or ¼ cup butter until mixture resembles coarse crumbs. Brush the top of the dough with a little additional milk; sprinkle with the streusel topping.

4 Bake in a 350°F oven about 50 minutes or until golden brown. If necessary, cover loosely with foil the last 10 minutes to prevent overbrowning. Cool in pan on a wire rack for 15 minutes. Remove from pan; cool slightly on wire rack. Serve warm or cool.

***Note:** The Test Kitchen recommends 2 tablespoons water for either size recipe.

Nutrition Facts per slice: 208 cal., 7 g total fat (4 g sat. fat), 37 mg chol., 182 mg sodium, 32 g carbo., 4 g pro.

Offer up nourishment for the body and the soul with this special hand-rolled bread. The golden spiral loaves offer a brown sugar-sweetened walnut filling. It is the ultimate in comfort food.

Walnut-Filled Loaves

	1½-POUND	INGREDIENTS	2-POUND
PREP: 30 minutes	¾ cup	milk	1 cup
RISE: 30 minutes	1	egg(s)	2
	3 tablespoons	margarine or butter, cut up	¼ cup
BAKE: 30 minutes	3 cups	bread flour	4 cups
	¼ cup	granulated sugar	⅓ cup
MAKES: 1½-pound recipe (32 slices)	¾ teaspoon	salt	1 teaspoon
	1 teaspoon	active dry yeast	1¼ teaspoons
OR		or bread machine yeast	
2-pound recipe (48 slices)	2 cups	ground walnuts	3 cups
	⅓ cup	packed brown sugar	½ cup
	3 tablespoons	granulated sugar	¼ cup
	1 tablespoon	margarine or butter, softened	2 tablespoons
	4 teaspoons	milk	2 tablespoons
	¼ teaspoon	vanilla	½ teaspoon
	1	slightly beaten egg	1
	1 tablespoon	water	1 tablespoon

1 Select the recipe size. Add the first 7 ingredients to the machine according to the manufacturer's directions. Select the dough cycle. When cycle is complete, remove dough. Punch down. Cover and let rest for 10 minutes. Meanwhile, for filling, in a medium bowl stir together walnuts, brown sugar, and the 3 tablespoons or ¼ cup granulated sugar. Stir in softened margarine, the 4 teaspoons or 2 tablespoons milk, and vanilla.

2 *For the 1½-pound recipe:* Grease a large baking sheet; set aside. Divide the dough in half. On a lightly floured surface, roll each portion into a 16×10-inch rectangle. Spread each rectangle with half of the filling almost to the edges. Starting from a long side, loosely roll up into a spiral. In a small bowl combine the beaten egg and water. Moisten edge of dough with some of the egg mixture; pinch firmly to seal. Place loaves, seam sides down, on the prepared baking sheet, tucking ends under loaves. Prick tops with a fork.

3 Cover and let rise in a warm place about 30 minutes or until nearly double. Brush with the remaining egg mixture. Bake in a 350°F oven about 30 minutes or until bread sounds hollow when lightly tapped. If necessary, cover loosely with foil the last 15 minutes to prevent overbrowning. Remove from baking sheet; cool on wire racks.

For the 2-pound recipe: Prepare as above, except divide the dough and filling into thirds. Fill and shape as above and place on 2 greased large baking sheets. Continue as above.

Nutrition Facts per slice: 133 cal., 7 g total fat (1 g sat. fat), 14 mg chol., 75 mg sodium, 16 g carbo., 3 g pro.

Dried blueberries and a cinnamon and brown sugar streusel make an exquisite filling for this rich dough.

Blueberry Tea Ring

1½-POUND	INGREDIENTS	2-POUND
³/₄ cup	milk	1 cup
¹/₄ cup	water	¹/₃ cup
¹/₄ cup	butter or margarine, cut up	¹/₃ cup
1	egg*	1
3¹/₂ cups	bread flour	4²/₃ cups
¹/₄ cup	granulated sugar	¹/₃ cup
³/₄ teaspoon	salt	1 teaspoon
1 teaspoon	active dry yeast	1¹/₄ teaspoons
	or bread machine yeast	
¹/₃ cup	packed brown sugar	¹/₂ cup
3 tablespoons	all-purpose flour or bread flour	¹/₄ cup
1 teaspoon	ground cinnamon	1¹/₄ teaspoons
3 tablespoons	butter	¹/₄ cup
¹/₂ cup	dried blueberries	²/₃ cup
1 recipe	Almond Glaze (page 307)	1 recipe

PREP:
35 minutes

RISE:
45 minutes

BAKE:
30 minutes

MAKES:
1½-pound recipe
(16 servings)
OR
2-pound recipe
(24 servings)

1 Select recipe size. Add first 8 ingredients to machine according to manufacturer's directions. Select dough cycle. When complete, remove dough. Punch down. Cover; let rest 10 minutes.

2 Meanwhile, for filling, stir together brown sugar, all-purpose flour, and cinnamon. Cut in the 3 tablespoons or ¹/₄ cup butter until mixture resembles coarse crumbs. In a small saucepan bring 1 cup water to boiling; remove from heat. Add dried blueberries; let stand for 5 minutes. Drain blueberries; pat dry with paper towels. Grease a large baking sheet; set aside.

3 On a lightly floured surface, roll the 1½-pound dough into a 15×9-inch rectangle (roll the 2-pound dough into an 18×10-inch rectangle). Sprinkle with the filling and blueberries. Starting from a long side, roll up into a spiral; seal edge. Place seam side down on the prepared baking sheet. Bring ends together to form a ring. Moisten ends; pinch together to seal ring. Using kitchen scissors or a sharp knife, make a cut from the outside edge toward center, leaving about 1 inch attached. Repeat around the edge at 1-inch intervals. Gently turn each slice slightly so the same side of all slices faces upward.

4 Cover and let rise in a warm place for 45 to 60 minutes or until nearly double. Bake in a 350°F oven for 30 to 35 minutes or until bread sounds hollow when lightly tapped (center may be lighter in color). If necessary, cover loosely with foil the last 5 to 10 minutes to prevent overbrowning. Remove from baking sheet; cool on a wire rack. Drizzle with Almond Glaze.

*Note: The Test Kitchen recommends 1 egg for either size recipe.

Nutrition Facts per serving: 250 cal., 6 g total fat (1 g sat. fat), 14 mg chol., 171 mg sodium, 44 g carbo., 5 g pro.

Leave it to the bread machine to offer an easy variation on a traditionally difficult recipe. With its many layers of thin dough, apple strudel is often a bit tricky to make—but here, all the yummy flavors of the filling are simply rolled up into a luscious loaf.

Apple Strudel Bread

	1½-POUND	INGREDIENTS
PREP: 35 minutes	¾ cup	milk
	⅓ cup	margarine or butter, cut up
RISE: 45 minutes	1	egg
	3¼ cups	bread flour
BAKE: 30 minutes	⅓ cup	granulated sugar
	¾ teaspoon	salt
MAKES: 1½-pound recipe (16 slices)	1 teaspoon	active dry yeast or bread machine yeast
	3 cups	thinly sliced, peeled apples
	½ cup	packed brown sugar
	½ cup	raisins
	4 teaspoons	all-purpose flour or bread flour
	1 teaspoon	ground cinnamon
	3 tablespoons	margarine or butter, softened
	1 recipe	Powdered Sugar Glaze

1 Add the first 7 ingredients to the machine according to the manufacturer's directions. Select the dough cycle. When cycle is complete, remove dough. Punch down. Cover and let rest for 10 minutes.

2 Meanwhile, for filling, in a medium bowl combine apples, brown sugar, raisins, all-purpose flour, and cinnamon. Line a 15×10×1-inch baking pan with foil and grease foil; set aside.

3 On a lightly floured surface, roll the dough into a 24×12-inch rectangle. Brush with the softened margarine. Starting about 2 inches from a long side, spoon the filling in a 3-inch band across dough. Starting from the long side, carefully roll up into a spiral; seal seam and ends. Carefully place loaf, seam side down, in the prepared baking pan, curving to form a crescent shape.

4 Cover and let rise in a warm place about 45 minutes or until nearly double. Bake in a 350°F oven for 30 to 35 minutes or until golden brown. Remove from pan; cool on a wire rack. Drizzle with Powdered Sugar Glaze.

Powdered Sugar Glaze: In a small bowl stir together ¾ cup sifted powdered sugar and ¼ teaspoon vanilla. Stir in enough milk (2 to 4 teaspoons) to make a glaze of drizzling consistency.

Nutrition Facts per slice: 251 cal., 7 g total fat (1 g sat. fat), 13 mg chol., 187 mg sodium, 44 g carbo., 4 g pro.

Cinnamon is the inside bark of an evergreen tree that grows in the tropics. The bark dries in tight rolls that are then sold as cinnamon sticks or pulverized to make ground cinnamon. The darker the ground cinnamon you use in a braid like this one, the richer the flavor.

Cinnamon-Sugar Braid

1½-POUND	INGREDIENTS	2-POUND
¾ cup	milk	1 cup
¼ cup	margarine or butter, cut up	⅓ cup
1	egg*	1
3 cups	bread flour	4 cups
¼ cup	sugar	⅓ cup
1 teaspoon	ground cinnamon	1¼ teaspoons
¾ teaspoon	salt	1 teaspoon
⅛ teaspoon	ground nutmeg	¼ teaspoon
1¼ teaspoons	active dry yeast	1½ teaspoons
	or bread machine yeast	
1	slightly beaten egg	1
1 tablespoon	sugar	4 teaspoons
¼ teaspoon	ground cinnamon	½ teaspoon

PREP:
30 minutes

RISE:
45 minutes

BAKE:
20 minutes

MAKES:
1½-pound recipe
(16 slices)
OR
2-pound recipe
(22 slices)

❶ Select the recipe size. Add the first 9 ingredients to the machine according to the manufacturer's directions. Select the dough cycle. When cycle is complete, remove dough. Punch down. Cover and let rest for 10 minutes. Grease a large baking sheet; set aside.

❷ *For the 1½-pound recipe:* Divide the dough into thirds. On a lightly floured surface, roll each portion into an 18-inch rope. To shape, line up the ropes, 1 inch apart, on the prepared baking sheet. Starting in the middle, loosely braid by bringing the left rope under the center rope. Bring the right rope under the new center rope. Repeat to the end. On the other end, braid by bringing the outside ropes alternately over the center rope to center. Press ends together to seal; tuck under loaf.

❸ Cover and let rise in a warm place about 45 minutes or until nearly double. Brush with the beaten egg. In a small bowl combine the 1 tablespoon or 4 teaspoons sugar and the ¼ or ½ teaspoon cinnamon; sprinkle over loaf.

❹ Bake in a 350°F oven for 20 to 30 minutes or until golden brown. Remove from baking sheet; cool on a wire rack.

For the 2-pound recipe: Prepare as above, except divide the dough into fourths. Roll each portion into a 14-inch rope. Line up 2 ropes, 1 inch apart, on the prepared baking sheet. Loosely twist the ropes together; tuck ends under loaf. Repeat with the remaining 2 ropes. Continue as above.

*Note: The Test Kitchen recommends 1 egg for either size recipe.

Nutrition Facts per slice: 150 cal., 4 g total fat (1 g sat. fat), 27 mg chol., 148 mg sodium, 23 g carbo., 4 g pro.

Chocolate-hazelnut spread makes the filling for this fabulous ring as easy as opening a jar. Look for it with the peanut butter.

Chocolate-Hazelnut Ring

	1½-POUND	INGREDIENTS	2-POUND
PREP: 30 minutes	²/₃ cup	milk	³/₄ cup
RISE: 45 minutes	1	egg*	1
	3 tablespoons	margarine or butter, cut up	¼ cup
BAKE: 30 minutes	2 tablespoons	water	3 tablespoons
	3 cups	bread flour	4 cups
MAKES:	¼ cup	sugar	⅓ cup
1½-pound recipe (16 servings)	³/₄ teaspoon	salt	1 teaspoon
OR	1¼ teaspoons	active dry yeast	1½ teaspoons
2-pound recipe (22 servings)		or bread machine yeast	
	⅓ cup	chocolate-hazelnut spread	½ cup
	⅓ cup	chopped hazelnuts (filberts)	½ cup
	1 recipe	Chocolate-Hazelnut Icing	1 recipe

1 Select the recipe size. Add the first 8 ingredients to the machine according to the manufacturer's directions. Select the dough cycle. When cycle is complete, remove dough. Punch down. Cover and let rest for 10 minutes. Grease a large baking sheet; set aside.

2 On a lightly floured surface, roll the 1½-pound dough into a 15×10-inch rectangle (roll the 2-pound dough into an 18×10-inch rectangle). Spread with the chocolate-hazelnut spread and sprinkle with hazelnuts.

3 Starting from a long side, roll up into a spiral; seal edge. Place seam side down on the prepared baking sheet. Bring ends together to form a ring. Moisten ends; pinch together to seal ring. Using kitchen scissors or a sharp knife, make a cut from the outside edge toward center, leaving about 1 inch attached. Repeat around the edge at 1-inch intervals. Gently turn each slice slightly so the same side of all slices faces upward.

4 Cover and let rise in a warm place for 45 to 60 minutes or until nearly double. Bake in a 350°F oven for 30 to 35 minutes or until bread sounds hollow when lightly tapped (the center may be lighter in color). If necessary, cover loosely with foil the last 10 minutes to prevent overbrowning. Remove from baking sheet; cool on a wire rack. Drizzle with Chocolate-Hazelnut Icing.

Chocolate-Hazelnut Icing: In a microwave-safe small bowl microwave ¼ cup chocolate-hazelnut spread on 100-percent power (high) for 30 to 60 seconds or until of drizzling consistency.

*Note: The Test Kitchen recommends 1 egg for either size recipe.

Nutrition Facts per serving: 196 cal., 7 g total fat (1 g sat. fat), 14 mg chol., 144 mg sodium, 28 g carbo., 5 g pro.

Not only does this coffee ring have a luscious cream cheese filling, it also boasts a glistening orange or raspberry glaze.

Sunshine Coffee Cake

1½-POUND	INGREDIENTS
½ cup	milk
2	eggs
¼ cup	butter or margarine, cut up
3 tablespoons	water
3 cups	bread flour
3 tablespoons	sugar
½ teaspoon	salt
2¼ teaspoons	active dry yeast
	or bread machine yeast
½ of an 8-ounce package	cream cheese, softened
2 tablespoons	sugar
1	egg yolk
⅓ cup	orange marmalade
	or raspberry preserves

PREP:
30 minutes

RISE:
30 minutes

BAKE:
20 minutes

MAKES:
1½-pound recipe
(16 servings)

1 Add the first 8 ingredients to the machine according to the manufacturer's directions. Select the dough cycle. When cycle is complete, remove dough. Punch down. Cover and let rest for 10 minutes.

2 Line a large baking sheet with foil and grease foil. Place the dough on the prepared baking sheet and roll into a 12-inch circle. Cut the dough, cutting from the edge of dough to within 1½ inches of the center, into 16 wedges.

3 For filling, in a small mixing bowl beat cream cheese, the 2 tablespoons sugar, and egg yolk with an electric mixer just until combined. Spread the dough with half of the filling. Starting at the wide end of each wedge, roll up to within 2 inches of the center of bread. Gently turn 1 wedge toward the center; turn the next away from the center. Repeat with the remaining wedges.

4 Spoon the remaining filling into the center of the bread. Cover and let rise in a warm place about 30 minutes or until nearly double.

5 Bake in a 375°F oven about 20 minutes or until bread sounds hollow when lightly tapped. Remove from baking sheet; cool slightly on a wire rack. In a small saucepan heat the orange marmalade over medium heat until melted. Drizzle over coffee cake. Serve warm.

Nutrition Facts per serving: 265 cal., 10 g total fat (6 g sat. fat), 65 mg chol., 170 mg sodium, 39 g carbo., 6 g pro.

Whether it is fruity or chocolatey—design a loaf to perfectly satisfy your sweet tooth. Simply mix and match some of your favorite flavors from the options below, and follow these guidelines for the correct methods and ingredient proportions.

Basic Sweet Bread

	1½-POUND	I N G R E D I E N T S
PREP: 15 minutes	1 cup	milk
	3 tablespoons	water
MAKES: 1½-pound recipe (16 slices)	1 tablespoon	margarine, butter, shortening, or cooking oil
	3 cups	bread flour
		or
		2 cups bread flour plus 1 cup whole wheat flour
	4 teaspoons	sugar or honey
	³/₄ teaspoon	salt
	1 teaspoon	active dry yeast or bread machine yeast

1 Select one or more of the Flavoring Options. Add the ingredients to the machine according to the manufacturer's directions. Select the basic white bread cycle, or if using whole wheat flour, select the whole grain cycle, if available. If desired, drizzle the cooled loaf with a Flavored Glaze.

Flavoring Options:
• 1 to 2 teaspoons finely shredded lemon peel or orange peel
• ³/₄ teaspoon ground cinnamon, apple pie spice, or pumpkin pie spice, or ¹/₄ teaspoon ground nutmeg, cloves, or allspice
• ¹/₃ cup semisweet or milk chocolate pieces
• 2 tablespoons unsweetened cocoa powder *(Note:* Increase sugar to ¹/₄ cup.)
• ¹/₃ cup chopped candied orange peel, lemon peel, or cherries
• ¹/₃ cup dried cherries, cranberries, blueberries, or raspberries *(Note:* Do not use dried apricots or other fruit treated with sulfur.)
• ¹/₃ cup chopped pecans, walnuts, macadamia nuts, or almonds

Flavored Glazes:
Basic Glaze In a small bowl stir together ¹/₂ cup sifted powdered sugar and ¹/₄ teaspoon vanilla. Stir in enough milk, fruit juice, rum, or liqueur (1 to 3 teaspoons) to make a glaze of drizzling consistency.
Chocolate Glaze In a small bowl stir together ¹/₂ cup sifted powdered sugar, 1 tablespoon unsweetened cocoa powder, and ¹/₄ teaspoon vanilla. Stir in enough milk (1 to 3 teaspoons) to make a glaze of drizzling consistency.

Flavored BUTTERS and SPREADS

PAIR YOUR FAVORITE bread or roll with one of these easy-to-make flavored butters or spreads. Each recipe makes enough so you can enjoy some now and save some for later. Store leftovers in the refrigerator up to 2 weeks or in the freezer up to 1 month.

Herb Butter

MAKES: about ½ cup (eight 1-tablespoon servings)

❶ In a small bowl stir together ½ cup softened butter or margarine and ½ teaspoon *each* dried thyme and marjoram, crushed, or 1 teaspoon dried basil, crushed. Cover and chill at least 1 hour to blend flavors. To serve, let stand at room temperature about 30 minutes or until soft enough to spread.

Nutrition Facts per serving: 100 cal., 11 g total fat (7 g sat. fat), 31 mg chol., 116 mg sodium, 0 g carbo., 0 g pro.

Lemon-Pepper Butter

MAKES: about ½ cup (eight 1-tablespoon servings)

❶ In a food processor bowl combine ½ cup softened butter or margarine, 2 teaspoons finely shredded lemon peel, 2 teaspoons lemon juice, and 1 teaspoon cracked or coarsely ground black pepper. Cover and process until smooth.

❷ Cover and chill at least 1 hour to blend flavors. To serve, let stand at room temperature about 30 minutes or until soft enough to spread.

Nutrition Facts per serving: 109 cal., 12 g total fat (8 g sat. fat), 33 mg chol., 124 mg sodium, 0 g carbo.,0 g pro.

Parmesan-Garlic Butter

MAKES: about ⅔ cup (ten 1-tablespoon servings)

❶ In a small mixing bowl beat ½ cup softened butter or margarine, ⅓ cup grated Parmesan cheese, and ¼ teaspoon garlic powder with an electric mixer on medium speed until smooth. Stir in 2 tablespoons snipped fresh parsley or 2 teaspoons dried parsley flakes. Cover and chill at least 1 hour to blend flavors. To serve, let stand at room temperature about 30 minutes or until soft enough to spread.

Nutrition Facts per serving: 96 cal., 10 g total fat (6 g sat. fat), 27 mg chol., 155 mg sodium, 0 g carbo., 2 g pro.

Dried Tomato-Pepper Butter

MAKES: about ⅔ cup (ten 1-tablespoon servings)

❶ In a small bowl stir together ½ cup softened butter or margarine; ¼ cup drained and finely snipped, oil-packed dried tomatoes; and ½ teaspoon cracked black pepper. Cover and chill at least 1 hour to blend flavors. To serve, let stand at room temperature about 30 minutes or until soft enough to spread.

Nutrition Facts per serving: 92 cal., 10 g total fat (6 g sat. fat), 26 mg chol., 106 mg sodium, 1 g carbo., 0 g pro.

Green Onion Butter

MAKES: about ½ cup (eight 1-tablespoon servings)

❶ In a small bowl stir together ½ cup softened butter or margarine, 2 tablespoons sliced green onion, 1 tablespoon grated fresh ginger, 1 teaspoon bottled minced garlic, and 1 teaspoon soy sauce. Cover and chill at least 1 hour to blend flavors. To serve, let stand at room temperature about 30 minutes or until soft enough to spread.

Nutrition Facts per serving: 102 cal., 11 g total fat (7 g sat. fat), 31 mg chol., 159 mg sodium, 0 g carbo., 0 g pro.

Roasted Red Pepper Butter

MAKES: about ⅔ cup (ten 1-tablespoon servings)

❶ In a small mixing bowl beat ½ cup softened butter or margarine; ¼ cup drained and chopped, bottled roasted red sweet peppers; and ½ to 1 teaspoon bottled minced garlic with an electric mixer on medium speed until smooth. Cover and chill at least 1 hour to blend flavors. To serve, let stand at room temperature about 30 minutes or until soft enough to spread. Stir before serving.

Nutrition Facts per serving: 87 cal., 10 g total fat (6 g sat. fat), 26 mg chol., 99 mg sodium, 0 g carbo., 0 g pro.

Mustard-Sage Butter

MAKES: about $1/2$ cup (eight 1-tablespoon servings)

❶ In a small bowl stir together $1/2$ cup softened butter or margarine; 2 tablespoons snipped fresh sage or $1/2$ teaspoon dried sage, crushed; and 2 to 4 teaspoons Dijon-style mustard or prepared mustard. Cover and chill at least 1 hour to blend flavors. To serve, let stand at room temperature about 30 minutes or until soft enough to spread.

Nutrition Facts per serving: 110 cal., 12 g total fat (8 g sat. fat), 33 mg chol., 153 mg sodium, 0 g carbo., 0 g pro.

Parmesan Butter

MAKES: about $1/2$ cup (eight 1-tablespoon servings)

❶ In a small mixing bowl beat $1/2$ cup softened butter or margarine, 2 tablespoons grated Parmesan cheese, and 1 tablespoon snipped fresh basil or $1/2$ teaspoon dried basil, crushed, with an electric mixer on medium speed until smooth. Cover and chill at least 1 hour to blend flavors. To serve, let stand at room temperature about 30 minutes or until soft enough to spread.

Nutrition Facts per serving: 113 cal., 13 g total fat (8 g sat. fat), 34 mg chol., 147 mg sodium, 0 g carbo., 1 g pro.

Cream Cheese Butter

MAKES: about 1 cup (sixteen 1-tablespoon servings)

❶ In a small mixing bowl beat two 3-ounce packages softened cream cheese, $1/4$ cup softened butter or margarine, and 1 teaspoon vanilla with an electric mixer on medium to high speed until light and fluffy. Gradually beat in $1 1/4$ cups sifted powdered sugar. Serve immediately. Or cover and chill until ready to serve. Let stand at room temperature for 15 to 30 minutes or until soft enough to spread.

Nutrition Facts per serving: 93 cal., 7 g total fat (4 g sat. fat), 19 mg chol., 61 mg sodium, 8 g carbo., 1 g pro.

Apricot Butter

MAKES: about $3/4$ cup (twelve 1-tablespoon servings)

❶ Place 3 tablespoons snipped dried apricots in a small bowl; add enough boiling water to cover. Let stand for 5 minutes; drain well.

❷ In a small mixing bowl combine drained apricots, $1/2$ cup softened butter or margarine, 2 teaspoons sugar, and $1 1/2$ teaspoons grated fresh ginger or $1/2$ teaspoon ground ginger. Beat with an electric mixer on medium to high speed until light and fluffy. Cover and chill at least 1 hour to blend flavors. To serve, let stand at room temperature about 30 minutes or until soft enough to spread.

Nutrition Facts per serving: 75 cal., 9 g total fat (6 g sat. fat), 21 mg chol., 78 mg sodium, 3 g carbo., 0 g pro.

Nut 'n' Honey Butter

MAKES: about 1 cup (sixteen 1-tablespoon servings)

❶ In a small bowl stir together $1/2$ cup toasted, finely chopped pecans or almonds; $1/2$ cup softened butter or margarine; and 1 teaspoon honey. Cover and chill at least 1 hour to blend flavors. To serve, let stand at room temperature about 30 minutes or until soft enough to spread.

Nutrition Facts per serving: 74 cal., 8 g total fat (4 g sat. fat), 15 mg chol., 58 mg sodium, 1 g carbo., 1 g pro.

Citrus Butter

MAKES: about $1/2$ cup (eight 1-tablespoon servings)

❶ In a small mixing bowl beat $1/2$ cup softened butter or margarine, 1 tablespoon powdered sugar, $1/2$ teaspoon finely shredded lemon peel or orange peel, and 1 teaspoon lemon juice or orange juice with an electric mixer on medium to high speed until light and fluffy. Cover and chill at least 1 hour to blend flavors. To serve, let stand at room temperature about 30 minutes or until soft enough to spread.

Nutrition Facts per serving: 103 cal., 11 g total fat (8 g sat. fat), 31 mg chol., 116 mg sodium, 1 g carbo., 0 g pro.

Orange-Ginger Butter

MAKES: about 1 cup (sixteen 1-tablespoon servings)

❶ In a small saucepan heat and stir ¹/₂ cup orange marmalade just until melted. Remove from heat. In a small mixing bowl beat ¹/₂ cup softened butter or margarine with an electric mixer on medium to high speed until light and fluffy. Beat in melted marmalade, 1 tablespoon finely snipped crystallized ginger, and 1 tablespoon balsamic vinegar or cider vinegar. Cover and chill at least 1 hour to blend flavors.

Nutrition Facts per serving: 78 cal., 5 g total fat (4 g sat. fat), 15 mg chol., 60 mg sodium, 8 g carbo., 0 g pro.

Jalapeño Pepper Butter

MAKES: about 1 cup (sixteen 1-tablespoon servings)

❶ In a small saucepan heat and stir ¹/₂ cup jalapeño pepper jelly just until melted. Remove from heat. In a small mixing bowl beat ¹/₂ cup softened butter or margarine with an electric mixer on medium to high speed until light and fluffy. Beat in melted jelly and 1 tablespoon balsamic vinegar or cider vinegar. Cover and chill at least 1 hour to blend flavors.

Nutrition Facts per serving: 77 cal., 6 g total fat (4 g sat. fat), 15 mg chol., 60 mg sodium, 7 g carbo., 0 g pro.

Peach-Nut Butter

MAKES: about 1¹/₂ cups (twenty-four 1-tablespoon servings)

❶ Place 1 cup pecans or almonds in blender container or food processor bowl. Cover and blend or process until finely chopped. Transfer to a medium bowl.

❷ Place ¹/₂ cup softened butter or margarine and ¹/₂ cup peach preserves in the blender container or food processor bowl. Cover and blend or process until nearly smooth, stopping to scrape down sides as necessary. Add to the nuts in bowl; mix well. Cover and chill at least 1 hour to blend flavors.

Nutrition Facts per serving: 85 cal., 7 g total fat (3 g sat. fat), 10 mg chol., 40 mg sodium, 6 g carbo., 1 g pro.

Chocolate-Nut Spread

MAKES: about 1 cup (sixteen 1-tablespoon servings)

❶ In a small heavy saucepan heat 2 ounces semisweet chocolate over low heat until chocolate begins to melt, stirring constantly. Immediately remove from heat; stir until smooth. Cool slightly.

❷ Place 1 cup unsalted roasted cashews or toasted blanched almonds in a blender container or food processor bowl. Cover and blend or process until nuts are very finely chopped, stopping to scrape down sides as necessary. Add ¹/₄ cup softened butter or margarine. Cover and blend or process until nearly smooth. Transfer to a small bowl. Stir in melted chocolate. Serve at room temperature.

Nutrition Facts per serving: 91 cal., 8 g total fat (3 g sat. fat), 8 mg chol., 30 mg sodium, 5 g carbo., 2 g pro.

Herbed Feta Spread

MAKES: about 1¹/₂ cups (twenty-four 1-tablespoon servings)

❶ In a medium mixing bowl combine one 8-ounce package reduced-fat cream cheese (Neufchâtel), one 4-ounce package crumbled garlic-and-herb feta cheese, 1 tablespoon milk, and several dashes freshly ground black pepper. Beat with an electric mixer on medium speed until smooth. Serve immediately. Or cover and chill until ready to serve. Let stand at room temperature for 15 to 30 minutes or until soft enough to spread.

Nutrition Facts per serving: 37 cal., 3 g total fat (2 g sat. fat), 12 mg chol., 91 mg sodium, 1 g carbo., 2 g pro.

Pesto-Cream Cheese Spread

MAKES: about 1¹/₂ cups (twenty-four 1-tablespoon servings)

❶ In a medium bowl stir together one 8-ounce package softened cream cheese and one 7-ounce container purchased pesto. Serve immediately. Or cover and chill until ready to serve. Stir before using.

Nutrition Facts per serving: 76 cal., 7 g total fat (2 g sat. fat), 11 mg chol., 73 mg sodium, 1 g carbo., 1 g pro.

Mediterranean Walnut Spread

MAKES: about 1¼ cups (twenty 1-tablespoon servings)

❶ Drain 1 cup canned garbanzo beans (about half of a 15-ounce can), reserving liquid. In a blender container or food processor bowl combine beans, 2 tablespoons of the reserved liquid, ½ cup chopped walnuts, ½ cup lightly packed fresh basil leaves, 2 tablespoons olive oil, 2 to 3 teaspoons lemon juice, ⅛ teaspoon salt, and ⅛ teaspoon black pepper. Cover and blend or process until nearly smooth, adding additional reserved liquid if mixture appears stiff.

❷ Serve spread immediately. Or cover and chill until ready to serve.

Nutrition Facts per serving: 34 cal., 3 g total fat (0 g sat. fat), 0 mg chol., 25 mg sodium, 1 g carbo., 1 g pro.

Spiced Berry-Carrot Cheese Spread

MAKES: about 1¼ cups (twenty 1-tablespoon servings)

❶ In a small bowl stir together one 8-ounce tub apple-cinnamon cream cheese, 1 teaspoon finely shredded orange peel, and 1 tablespoon orange juice. Stir in ½ cup dried cranberries, snipped; ⅓ cup finely shredded carrot; and ¼ cup toasted, chopped pecans or walnuts. Serve immediately. Or cover and chill until ready to serve.

Nutrition Facts per serving: 59 cal., 4 g total fat (2 g sat. fat), 9 mg chol., 37 mg sodium, 5 g carbo., 1 g pro.

Veggie Confetti Spread

MAKES: about 1¼ cups (twenty 1-tablespoon servings)

❶ In a small bowl stir together one 3-ounce package softened cream cheese; 1 small zucchini, seeded and very finely chopped; 1 small carrot, very finely chopped; 1 small red sweet pepper, very finely chopped; and 2 tablespoons snipped fresh chives. Serve immediately. Or cover and chill until ready to serve.

Nutrition Facts per serving: 18 cal., 2 g total fat (1 g sat. fat), 5 mg chol., 14 mg sodium, 1 g carbo., 0 g pro.

Basil and Tomato Cream Cheese Spread

MAKES: about 1 cup (sixteen 1-tablespoon servings)

❶ In a small bowl stir together one 8-ounce package softened cream cheese; ¼ cup drained and snipped, oil-packed dried tomatoes; 1 tablespoon snipped fresh basil or ½ teaspoon dried basil, crushed; and ⅛ teaspoon black pepper. Serve immediately. Or cover and chill until ready to serve. Let stand at room temperature for 15 to 30 minutes or until soft enough to spread.

Nutrition Facts per serving: 53 cal., 5 g total fat (3 g sat. fat), 16 mg chol., 47 mg sodium, 1 g carbo., 1 g pro.

Cheese Bread Spread

MAKES: about 1 cup (sixteen 1-tablespoon servings)

❶ In a small mixing bowl beat ½ cup softened butter or margarine with an electric mixer on medium to high speed for 30 seconds. Beat in ¼ teaspoon Worcestershire sauce, ⅛ teaspoon paprika, and dash garlic powder. Stir in 1 cup shredded sharp cheddar cheese (4 ounces) and 1 tablespoon grated Romano or Parmesan cheese.

❷ To serve, spread the cheese mixture on thick slices of bread. Broil about 4 inches from the heat for 2 to 4 minutes or until cheese is melted.

Nutrition Facts per serving: 83 cal., 9 g total fat (6 g sat. fat), 24 mg chol., 110 mg sodium, 0 g carbo., 2 g pro.

Spiced Peach Spread

MAKES: about 1 cup (sixteen 1-tablespoon servings)

❶ In a small saucepan combine 1 cup snipped dried peaches, ½ cup water, ¼ cup sugar, and ½ teaspoon apple pie spice or pumpkin pie space. Bring to boiling over medium heat; reduce heat. Cover and simmer about 20 minutes or until peaches are very soft. Transfer to a food processor bowl or blender container. Cover and process or blend until nearly smooth. Serve immediately. Or cover and chill until ready to serve.

Nutrition Facts per serving: 36 cal., 0 g total fat (0 g sat. fat), 0 mg chol., 1 mg sodium, 9 g carbo., 0 g pro.

HOLIDAY
FARE

If your home boasts a revolving door on Christmas—with the comings and goings of friends and relatives all day—keep plenty of this luscious sweet loaf on the table.

Pecan-Cherry Bread

PREP:
15 minutes

MAKES:
1½-pound recipe
(16 slices)
OR
2-pound recipe
(22 slices)

1½-POUND*	INGREDIENTS	2-POUND*
¾ cup	milk	1 cup
1	egg**	1
2 tablespoons	kirsch or cherry brandy	3 tablespoons
	or orange juice	
2 tablespoons	margarine or butter, cut up	3 tablespoons
3 cups	bread flour	4 cups
¼ cup	sugar	⅓ cup
¾ teaspoon	salt	1 teaspoon
1¼ teaspoons	active dry yeast	1½ teaspoons
	or bread machine yeast	
½ cup	broken pecans, toasted	⅔ cup
⅓ cup	dried tart cherries	½ cup
1 recipe	Kirsch Glaze	1 recipe

1 Select the loaf size. Add the ingredients, except the Kirsch Glaze, to the machine according to the manufacturer's directions. Select the basic white bread cycle. Drizzle the cooled loaf with Kirsch Glaze.

Kirch Glaze: In a small bowl stir together ½ cup sifted powdered sugar and 1 teaspoon kirsch or cherry brandy or orange juice. Stir in enough milk (1 to 2 teaspoons) to make a glaze of drizzling consistency.

*Note: For the 1½-pound loaf, the bread machine pan must have a capacity of 10 cups or more. For the 2-pound loaf, the bread machine pan must have a capacity of 12 cups or more.

**Note: The Test Kitchen recommends 1 egg for either size recipe.

Nutrition Facts per slice: 178 cal., 5 g total fat (1 g sat. fat), 14 mg chol., 137 mg sodium, 28 g carbo., 4 g pro.

This bread is reminiscent of the Welsh bread called Bara Brith. It is speckled with currants and spices and traditionally served on holidays and at harvest festivals.

Currant Bread

1½-POUND*	INGREDIENTS	2-POUND*
³/₄ cup	milk**	³/₄ cup
¹/₄ cup	water	¹/₂ cup
1	egg**	1
1 tablespoon	shortening or cooking oil	4 teaspoons
3 cups	bread flour	4 cups
3 tablespoons	packed brown sugar	¹/₄ cup
³/₄ teaspoon	salt	1 teaspoon
³/₄ teaspoon	ground cinnamon	1 teaspoon
	or pumpkin pie spice	
1 teaspoon	active dry yeast	1¹/₄ teaspoons
	or bread machine yeast	
1 cup	dried currants or dark raisins	1¹/₃ cups

PREP:
10 minutes

MAKES:
1½-pound recipe
(18 slices)
OR
2-pound recipe
(24 slices)

1 Select the loaf size. Add the ingredients to the machine according to the manufacturer's directions. Select the basic white bread cycle.

*Note:: For the 1½-pound loaf, the bread machine pan must have the capacity of 10 cups or more. For the 2-pound loaf, the bread machine pan must have a capacity of 12 cups or more.

**Note:: The Test Kitchen recommends ¾ cup milk and 1 egg for either size recipe.

Nutrition Facts per slice: 128 cal., 2 g total fat (0 g sat. fat), 13 mg chol., 99 mg sodium, 25 g carbo., 4 g pro.

Using Light-Color Dried Fruits

Light-colored dried fruits, such as apricots or apples, treated with sulfur as a preservative may inhibit yeast performance. Therefore, do not substitute these fruits for others called for in our recipes. If you're adapting a recipe to your bread machine and it contains a light-colored dried fruit, substitute another dried fruit. Or use the dough cycle of your machine and lightly knead in the fruit by hand before shaping the bread, then bake it in the oven.

The sensational combination of white chocolate with cranberries produces a taste so sublime it's simply irresistible. Make this bread a sweet beginning—or ending—to your day.

White Chocolate-Cranberry Loaf

PREP: 15 minutes	1½-POUND*	INGREDIENTS	2-POUND*
	¾ cup	milk	1 cup
MAKES:	1	egg**	1
1½-pound recipe (18 slices)	2 tablespoons	water	3 tablespoons
OR	1 tablespoon	margarine or butter	4 teaspoons
2-pound recipe (22 slices)	1 teaspoon	vanilla	1½ teaspoons
	3 cups	bread flour	4 cups
	2 tablespoons	sugar**	2 tablespoons
	¾ teaspoon	salt	1 teaspoon
	1 teaspoon	active dry yeast or bread machine yeast	1¼ teaspoons
	2 ounces	white baking bar, chopped	3 ounces
	⅓ cup	dried cranberries	½ cup

❶ Select the loaf size. Add the ingredients to the machine according to the manufacturer's directions. Select the basic white bread cycle.

*Note: For the 1½-pound loaf, the bread machine pan must have a capacity of 10 cups or more. For the 2-pound loaf, the bread machine must have a capacity of 12 cups or more.

**Note: The Test Kitchen recommends 1 egg and 2 tablespoons sugar for either recipe size.

Nutrition Facts per slice: 129 cal., 3 g total fat (1 g sat. fat), 14 mg chol., 109 mg sodium, 22 g carbo., 4 g pro.

White Baking Bars versus White Chocolate

Are white baking bars and white chocolate the same? Bakers use them interchangeably. Both products contain cocoa butter, sugar, milk, and vanilla or vanillan, but white baking bars are less costly than white chocolate and less temperamental. Neither are true chocolate, because they lack chocolate liquor, a byproduct of processed cocoa beans.

Rich with sour cream and chock-full of dried fruits, this five-spice scented loaf is perfect for gift-giving. Package in tinted cellophane, tie with colorful ribbon, and it's a wrap!

Festive Five-Spice Bread

1½-POUND	INGREDIENTS	2-POUND
½ cup	dairy sour cream	²/₃ cup
½ cup	water	²/₃ cup
1 tablespoon	margarine or butter	4 teaspoons
1 teaspoon	vanilla	1½ teaspoons
3 cups	bread flour	4 cups
3 tablespoons	sugar	¼ cup
¾ teaspoon	salt	1 teaspoon
½ teaspoon	five-spice powder	¾ teaspoon
1¼ teaspoons	active dry yeast or bread machine yeast	1½ teaspoons
¾ cup	snipped mixed dried berries and cherries	1 cup
1 recipe	Powdered Sugar Glaze	1 recipe

PREP:
15 minutes

MAKES:
1½-pound recipe
(16 slices)
OR
2-pound recipe
(22 slices)

1 Select the loaf size. Add the ingredients, except the Powdered Sugar Glaze, to the machine according to the manufacturer's directions. Select the basic white bread cycle. Drizzle the cooled loaf with Powdered Sugar Glaze.

Powdered Sugar Glaze: In a small bowl stir together 1 cup sifted powdered sugar and 1 teaspoon vanilla. Stir in enough milk (4 to 6 teaspoons) to make a glaze of drizzling consistency.

Nutrition Facts per slice: 175 cal., 3 g total fat (1 g sat. fat), 3 mg chol., 116 mg sodium, 34 g carbo., 4 g pro.

Spice Blends

While the number "five" figures prominently in the name of Chinese five-spice powder, some blends have up to six or seven spices, or as few as four. A typical mix includes ground anise seeds, star anise, cloves, cinnamon, and Szechwan peppercorns. Chinese markets stock it, as do most supermarkets.

This spicy, full-flavored bread makes good company for a fragrant cup of tea. Cut into shapes and serve with cream cheese and fruit for an extra-festive high tea.

Gingerbread Loaf

PREP:
10 minutes

MAKES:
1½-pound recipe
(16 slices)
OR
2-pound recipe
(22 slices)

1½-POUND*	INGREDIENTS	2-POUND*
²/₃ cup	milk	³/₄ cup
1	egg(s)	2
¼ cup	mild-flavored molasses	¹/₃ cup
3 tablespoons	margarine or butter, cut up	¼ cup
3 cups	bread flour	4 cups
1 tablespoon	brown sugar	4 teaspoons
³/₄ teaspoon	salt	1 teaspoon
³/₄ teaspoon	ground cinnamon	1 teaspoon
³/₄ teaspoon	ground ginger	1 teaspoon
1 teaspoon	active dry yeast	1½ teaspoons
	or bread machine yeast	
1 recipe	Lemon Icing (optional)	1 recipe

1 Select the loaf size. Add the ingredients, except the Lemon Icing, to the machine according to the manufacturer's directions. Select the basic white bread cycle. If desired, drizzle the cooled loaf with Lemon Icing.

Lemon Icing: In a small bowl stir together ½ cup sifted powdered sugar, 1 teaspoon lemon juice, and ¼ teaspoon vanilla. Stir in enough milk (1 to 3 teaspoons) to make an icing of drizzling consistency.

*Note: For the 1½-pound loaf, the bread machine pan must have a capacity of 10 cups or more. For the 2-pound loaf, the bread machine pan must have a capacity of 12 cups or more.

Nutrition Facts per slice: 138 cal., 3 g total fat (1 g sat. fat), 14 mg chol., 136 mg sodium, 23 g carbo., 4 g pro.

Re-create the loving memories of your mother's kitchen with the smells of this classic loaf. Serve up thick slices spread with our mouthwatering Citrus Butter (page 264).

Raisin-Ginger Bread

1½-POUND*	INGREDIENTS	2-POUND*
¾ cup	milk	1 cup
1	egg**	1
3 tablespoons	margarine or butter, cut up	¼ cup
2 tablespoons	mild-flavored molasses	3 tablespoons
3 cups	bread flour	4 cups
¾ teaspoon	salt	1 teaspoon
¾ teaspoon	ground cinnamon	1 teaspoon
¾ teaspoon	ground ginger	1 teaspoon
¼ teaspoon	ground cloves	½ teaspoon
1 teaspoon	active dry yeast	1¼ teaspoons
	or bread machine yeast	
½ cup	dark raisins	⅔ cup

PREP:
10 minutes

MAKES:
1½-pound recipe
(20 slices)
OR
2-pound recipe
(27 slices)

1 Select the loaf size. Add the ingredients to the machine according to the manufacturer's directions. Select the basic white bread cycle.

*Note: For the 1½-pound loaf, the bread machine pan must have a capacity of 10 cups or more. For the 2-pound loaf, the bread machine pan must have a capacity of 12 cups or more.

**Note: The Test Kitchen recommends 1 egg for either size recipe.

Nutrition Facts per slice: 115 cal., 3 g total fat (1 g sat. fat), 11 mg chol., 109 mg sodium, 20 g carbo., 3 g pro.

Mild or Robust Molasses Flavor?

Light molasses, produced from the first boiling of the juices of sugarcane, has a mild flavor and pale color. Dark molasses, from the second boiling, is less sweet, but more robust. You can use either in a recipe, but substituting one for the other will result in a mild versus robust molasses flavor.

Fill your kitchen with the ultimate of holiday aromas—mincemeat. Traditionally used as a filling for pies, tarts, and cookies, mincemeat jazzes up this spiced oat bread.

Mincemeat Loaf

PREP:
10 minutes

MAKES:
1½-pound recipe
(16 slices)
OR
2-pound recipe
(22 slices)

1½-POUND*	INGREDIENTS	2-POUND*
¾ cup	water	1 cup
½ cup	mincemeat	⅔ cup
1 tablespoon	margarine or butter	4 teaspoons
3 cups	bread flour	4 cups
⅓ cup	regular or quick-cooking rolled oats	½ cup
1 tablespoon	brown sugar	4 teaspoons
¾ teaspoon	salt	1 teaspoon
¼ teaspoon	ground cinnamon**	¼ teaspoon
1¼ teaspoons	active dry yeast or bread machine yeast	1½ teaspoons

① Select the loaf size. Add the ingredients to the machine according to the manufacturer's directions. Select the basic white bread cycle.

*Note: For the 1½-pound loaf, the bread machine pan must have a capacity of 10 cups or more. For the 2-pound loaf, the bread machine pan must have a capacity of 12 cups or more.

**Note: The Test Kitchen recommends ¼ teaspoon cinnamon for either size recipe.

Nutrition Facts per slice: 125 cal., 1 g total fat (0 g sat. fat), 0 mg chol., 136 mg sodium, 24 g carbo., 3 g pro.

Old-Style Mincemeat

Despite its name, mincemeat—that luscious holiday pie filling—is most often meat-free. But this wasn't always true. Originally, beef suet and ground meat were part of the recipe, devised as a way to preserve meat. Now the combination of ingredients is usually chopped apples, raisins, spices, and sometimes rum or brandy.

The golden pumpkin color of this loaf, combined with its mild ginger flavor and dates, makes it a special breakfast or snack. Slice and spread with a little Orange-Ginger Butter (page 265).

Ginger-Pumpkin Bread

1½-POUND*	INGREDIENTS	2-POUND*
½ cup	milk	⅔ cup
½ cup	canned pumpkin	⅔ cup
1	egg**	1
2 tablespoons	margarine or butter, cut up	3 tablespoons
3 cups	bread flour	4 cups
1 tablespoon	brown sugar	2 tablespoons
¾ teaspoon	salt	1 teaspoon
¼ teaspoon	ground nutmeg	½ teaspoon
1 teaspoon	active dry yeast	1¼ teaspoons
	or bread machine yeast	
½ cup	snipped pitted whole dates	⅔ cup
2 tablespoons	finely snipped crystallized	3 tablespoons
	ginger	

PREP:
15 minutes

MAKES:
1½-pound recipe
(16 slices)
OR
2-pound recipe
(22 slices)

1 Select the loaf size. Add the ingredients to the machine according to the manufacturer's directions. Select the basic white bread cycle.

*Note: For the 1½-pound loaf, the bread machine pan must have a capacity of 10 cups or more. For the 2-pound loaf, the bread machine pan must have a capacity of 12 cups of more.

**Note: The Test Kitchen recommends 1 egg for either size recipe.

Nutrition Facts per slice: 139 cal., 2 g total fat (1 g sat. fat), 14 mg chol., 126 mg sodium, 25 g carbo., 4 g pro.

Toast the season with this spirit-laced raisin-orange bread. For extra citrus flavor, serve it with a thin smear of orange or lemon curd.

Holiday Spirit Bread

PREP:
35 minutes

MAKES:
1½-pound recipe
(16 slices)

1½-POUND*	INGREDIENTS
½ cup	dark raisins
3 tablespoons	bourbon, cream sherry, orange liqueur,
	or orange juice
⅔ cup	milk
1	egg
2 tablespoons	margarine or butter, cut up
3 cups	bread flour
3 tablespoons	brown sugar
1½ teaspoons	finely shredded orange peel
¾ teaspoon	salt
½ teaspoon	ground nutmeg
1 teaspoon	active dry yeast
	or bread machine yeast

1 In a small bowl combine the raisins and bourbon. Let stand for 30 minutes. Drain raisins, reserving the bourbon.

2 Add the ingredients to the machine according to the manufacturer's directions, adding the bourbon with the milk and the raisins as directed. Select the basic white bread cycle and, if available, the light color setting.

*Note: The bread machine pan must have a capacity of 10 cups or more.

Nutrition Facts per slice: 147 cal., 2 g total fat (0 g sat. fat), 21 mg chol., 126 mg sodium, 27 g carbo., 5 g pro.

Individual cranberry-filled spirals make up this elegant Yuletide wreath. Placed on a festive platter, it's impressive enough to serve as the center of attraction at a holiday buffet.

Cranberry-Orange Wreath

1½-POUND	INGREDIENTS
⅓ cup	milk
⅓ cup	water
1	egg
3 tablespoons	margarine or butter, cut up
3 cups	bread flour
⅓ cup	packed brown sugar
¾ teaspoon	salt
1 teaspoon	active dry yeast
	or bread machine yeast
¾ cup	cranberries
2 tablespoons	granulated sugar
2 tablespoons	water
1 tablespoon	cornstarch
1 tablespoon	cold water
¼ cup	orange marmalade
1 recipe	Powdered Sugar Glaze (page 271)
	Chopped almonds, toasted

PREP:
35 minutes

RISE:
30 minutes

BAKE:
15 minutes

MAKES:
1½-pound recipe
(16 servings)

① Add the first 8 ingredients to machine according to manufacturer's directions. Select dough cycle. When cycle is complete, remove dough. Punch down. Cover and let rest 10 minutes.

② Meanwhile, for filling, in a small saucepan combine the cranberries, granulated sugar, and the 2 tablespoons water. Bring to boiling; reduce heat. Cook for 2 to 3 minutes or until cranberry skins pop and mixture thickens slightly, stirring frequently. Combine cornstarch and the 1 tablespoon water; stir into mixture. Cook and stir until mixture is very thick and just begins to bubble. Remove from heat. Stir in orange marmalade; transfer to a small bowl. Cover surface with plastic wrap; cool.

③ Grease 2 large baking sheets; set aside. Divide the dough in half. On a lightly floured surface, roll 1 portion into a 12-inch circle; cut into 8 wedges. Spread about 2 teaspoons filling onto each wedge. Starting at the wide end of each wedge, loosely roll toward the point. Arrange wedges, points down, on a prepared baking sheet to form a wreath shape. Repeat with the remaining dough and filling, forming a wreath shape on the remaining baking sheet.

④ Cover and let rise in a warm place for 30 to 45 minutes or until nearly double. Bake in a 350°F oven for 15 to 20 minutes or until golden brown. Remove; cool slightly on wire racks. Drizzle with Powdered Sugar Glaze and sprinkle with nuts. Cool on wire racks.

Nutrition Facts per serving: 185 cal., 3 g total fat (1 g sat. fat), 14 mg chol., 135 mg sodium, 35 g carbo., 4 g pro.

Weave some holiday magic by treating friends and family to this dazzling loaf bursting with cranberries and pecans.

Twisted Cranberry Bread

PREP: 30 minutes	1½-POUND	INGREDIENTS	2-POUND
	½ cup	milk	¾ cup
RISE: 30 minutes	1	egg(s)	2
	¼ cup	water	⅓ cup
BAKE: 25 minutes	2 tablespoons	margarine or butter, cut up	3 tablespoons
	3 cups	bread flour	4 cups
MAKES:	2 tablespoons	sugar	3 tablespoons
1½-pound recipe (18 slices)	¾ teaspoon	salt	1 teaspoon
OR	1¼ teaspoons	active dry yeast	1½ teaspoons
2-pound recipe (24 slices)		or bread machine yeast	
	2 teaspoons	margarine or butter, melted	1 tablespoon
	1 recipe	Cranberry Filling	1 recipe
	1 recipe	Orange Glaze	1 recipe

① Select the recipe size. Add the first 8 ingredients to the machine according to the manufacturer's directions. Select the dough cycle. When cycle is complete, remove dough. Punch down. Cover and let rest for 10 minutes.

② *For the 1½-pound recipe:* Grease a baking sheet; set aside. On a lightly floured surface, roll the dough into a 14×10-inch rectangle. Brush with the melted margarine and sprinkle with Cranberry Filling. Starting from a long side, roll up into a spiral; seal edge. Place on the prepared baking sheet. Cut roll in half lengthwise; turn cut sides up. Loosely twist halves together, keeping cut sides up. Press ends together to seal. Cover and let rise in a warm place about 30 minutes or until nearly double.

③ Bake in a 375°F oven about 25 minutes or until golden brown. If necessary, cover loosely with foil the last 10 minutes to prevent overbrowning. Remove from baking sheet; cool on a wire rack. Drizzle with Orange Glaze.

For the 2-pound recipe: Prepare as above, except divide the dough in half. Roll each portion into a 12×8-inch rectangle. Brush each rectangle with half of the melted margarine and sprinkle each with half of the Cranberry Filling. Form 2 loaves on 2 greased baking sheets. Continue as above.

Cranberry Filling: In a small bowl stir together ½ cup finely chopped cranberries, ¼ cup packed brown sugar, 2 tablespoons finely chopped pecans, 1½ teaspoons finely shredded orange peel, and ½ teaspoon ground allspice.

Orange Glaze: In a small bowl stir together ½ cup sifted powdered sugar and enough orange juice (1 to 3 teaspoons) to make a glaze of drizzling consistency.

Nutrition Facts per slice: 138 cal., 3 g total fat (1 g sat. fat), 12 mg chol., 117 mg sodium, 24 g carbo., 4 g pro.

Savor the hint of nutmeg in this enchanting nut loaf—it's picture-perfect for a Hanukkah celebration or any other festive occasion.

Hanukkah Braid

1½-POUND	INGREDIENTS
¾ cup	water
1	egg
¼ cup	margarine or butter, cut up
3 cups	bread flour
¼ cup	sugar
¾ teaspoon	salt
¼ teaspoon	ground nutmeg
1¼ teaspoons	active dry yeast
	or bread machine yeast
⅓ cup	chopped pecans
1 recipe	Powdered Sugar Icing

PREP:
30 minutes

RISE:
35 minutes

BAKE:
25 minutes

MAKES:
1½-pound recipe
(16 slices)

1 Add the ingredients, except the Powdered Sugar Icing, to the machine according to the manufacturer's directions. Select the dough cycle. When cycle is complete, remove dough. Punch down. Cover and let rest for 10 minutes. Grease a large baking sheet; set aside.

2 Divide the dough into thirds. On a lightly floured surface, roll each portion into an 18-inch rope. To shape, line up the ropes, 1 inch apart, on the prepared baking sheet. Starting in the middle, loosely braid by bringing the left rope under center rope. Bring the right rope under new center rope. Repeat to the end. On the other end, braid by bringing the outside ropes alternately over the center rope to center. Press ends together to seal; tuck under loaf.

3 Cover and let rise in a warm place for 35 to 45 minutes or until nearly double. Bake in a 375°F oven for 25 to 30 minutes or until bread sounds hollow when lightly tapped. Remove from baking sheet; cool on a wire rack. Drizzle with Powdered Sugar Icing.

Powdered Sugar Icing: In a small bowl stir together 1 cup sifted powdered sugar and ¼ teaspoon vanilla. Stir in enough milk (1 to 2 tablespoons) to make an icing of drizzling consistency.

Nutrition Facts per slice: 176 cal., 5 g total fat (1 g sat. fat), 13 mg chol., 148 mg sodium, 28 g carbo., 4 g pro.

Candied fruits and peels aren't just for fruitcake. Here they star in a spectacular bread shaped to resemble everybody's favorite holiday blossom.

Poinsettia Bread

	1½-POUND	I N G R E D I E N T S
PREP: 30 minutes	²/₃ cup	milk
	¼ cup	margarine or butter, cut up
RISE: 30 minutes	1	egg
	2 tablespoons	water
BAKE: 25 minutes	3 cups	bread flour
	¼ cup	sugar
MAKES: 1½-pound recipe (16 servings)	¾ teaspoon	salt
	2 teaspoons	active dry yeast
		or bread machine yeast
	½ cup	diced, mixed candied
		fruits and peels, finely chopped
	3 tablespoons	sugar
	2 tablespoons	margarine or butter, melted
	1	egg yolk
	1 teaspoon	water
	1 recipe	Powdered Sugar Icing

1 Add the first 8 ingredients to the machine according to the manufacturer's directions. Select the dough cycle. When cycle is complete, remove dough. Punch down. Cover and let rest for 10 minutes. Meanwhile, for filling, in a small bowl stir together candied fruits and the 3 tablespoons sugar. Grease a large baking sheet; set aside.

2 On a lightly floured surface, roll the dough into a 16×12-inch rectangle. Brush with the melted margarine and sprinkle with filling. Starting from a short side, roll up into a spiral; seal edge. Using a sharp knife, diagonally cut the roll into 12 slices. Set aside the 2 end slices. On the prepared baking sheet, arrange the remaining slices, cut sides down, in a circle with pointed ends out, overlapping slices slightly and leaving a 4-inch circle in center. Place the 2 end pieces in the center. Cover and let rise in a warm place for 30 to 40 minutes or until nearly double. In a small bowl combine egg yolk and the 1 teaspoon water; brush over dough.

3 Bake in a 350°F oven about 25 minutes or until bread sounds hollow when lightly tapped. If necessary, cover loosely with foil the last 10 minutes to prevent overbrowning. Remove from baking sheet; cool on a wire rack. Drizzle with Powdered Sugar Icing.

Powdered Sugar Icing: Stir together 1 cup sifted powdered sugar and ½ teaspoon vanilla. Stir in enough milk (1 to 2 tablespoons) to make an icing of drizzling consistency.

Nutrition Facts per serving: 209 cal., 6 g total fat (1 g sat. fat), 27 mg chol., 161 mg sodium, 35 g carbo., 4 g pro.

Italians serve panettone (pronounced pahn-EHT-tohn)—a fruit-loaded bread—at Christmas and other special occasions. A sweet wine, such as sauterne, is a nice accompaniment.

Panettone

1¹/₂-POUND	INGREDIENTS	2-POUND
²/₃ cup	milk	³/₄ cup
¹/₄ cup	water	¹/₃ cup
1	egg*	1
2 tablespoons	butter or margarine, cut up	3 tablespoons
1 tablespoon	honey	4 teaspoons
1 teaspoon	vanilla	1¹/₂ teaspoons
3 cups	bread flour	4 cups
1¹/₂ teaspoons	anise seeds, crushed	2 teaspoons
³/₄ teaspoon	salt	1 teaspoon
¹/₄ teaspoon	ground cloves	¹/₂ teaspoon
1¹/₄ teaspoons	active dry yeast	1¹/₂ teaspoons
	or bread machine yeast	
¹/₄ cup	dark raisins	¹/₃ cup
¹/₄ cup	dried currants	¹/₃ cup
¹/₄ cup	diced candied citron	¹/₃ cup
¹/₄ cup	chopped pecans or walnuts	¹/₃ cup

PREP:
20 minutes

RISE:
40 minutes

BAKE:
35 minutes

MAKES:
1¹/₂-pound recipe
(16 slices)
OR
2-pound recipe
(22 slices)

① Select the recipe size. Add the ingredients to the machine according to manufacturer's directions. Select the dough cycle. When cycle is complete, remove dough. Punch down. Cover and let rest for 10 minutes. Grease a 10-inch fluted tube pan; set aside.

② On a lightly floured surface, roll the dough into a 22-inch rope. Place in the prepared tube pan. Moisten ends; press together to seal ring. Cover and let rise in a warm place for 40 to 50 minutes or until nearly double.

③ Bake in a 350°F oven for 35 for 40 minutes or until bread sounds hollow when lightly tapped. Remove from pan; cool on a wire rack.

*Note: The Test Kitchen recommends 1 egg for either size recipe.

Nutrition Facts per slice: 155 cal., 4 g total fat (1 g sat. fat), 14 mg chol., 127 mg sodium, 26 g carbo., 4 g pro.

Pan Options

The tall, cylindrical metal mold for panettone measures about 7¹/₂ inches in diameter by 4 inches high, but you can substitute an extra-deep cake pan. New from Italy are the ovenproof paper panettone molds used by professional bakers that serve as pan and gift box in one. Kitchenware stores and some catalogs carry both types of molds, particularly at Christmas.

This wreath does a typical wreath one better because it not only looks and smells wonderful, it also is fully edible. Pass the Herb Butter (page 263) for a change of taste.

Seeded Challah Wreath

PREP: 30 minutes	1½-POUND	INGREDIENTS	2-POUND
	¾ cup	water	1 cup
RISE: 45 minutes	2	eggs*	2
	2 tablespoons	cooking oil	3 tablespoons
BAKE: 20 minutes	2¼ cups	bread flour	2½ cups
	1 cup	whole wheat flour	1½ cups
MAKES: 1½-pound recipe (16 servings)	2 tablespoons	brown sugar	3 tablespoons
	1 tablespoon	poppy seeds, flax seeds, or dill seeds	4 teaspoons
OR	¾ teaspoon	salt	1 teaspoon
2-pound recipe (22 servings)	1 teaspoon	active dry yeast or bread machine yeast	1¼ teaspoons
	1	egg yolk	1
	1 tablespoon	water	1 tablespoon

1 Select the recipe size. Add the first 9 ingredients to the machine according to the manufacturer's directions. Select the dough cycle. When cycle is complete, remove dough. Punch down. Cover and let rest for 10 minutes.

2 *For the 1½-pound recipe:* Lightly grease a large baking sheet; set aside. Divide the dough in half. On a lightly floured surface, roll each portion into a 25-inch rope. To shape, line up the ropes, 1 inch apart. Loosely twist the ropes together. Bring ends together to form a ring. Moisten ends; pinch together to seal ring. Transfer to the prepared baking sheet. Cover and let rise in a warm place about 45 minutes or until nearly double.

3 In a small bowl combine egg yolk and the 1 tablespoon water; brush over loaf. Bake in a 350°F oven for 20 to 30 minutes or until golden brown. Remove from baking sheet; cool on a wire rack.

For the 2-pound recipe: Prepare as above, except divide the dough into fourths. Roll each portion into a 20-inch rope. Form 2 rings and transfer to 2 lightly greased baking sheets. Continue as above.

*Note: The Test Kitchen recommends 2 eggs for either size recipe.

Nutrition Facts per serving: 132 cal., 3 g total fat (1 g sat. fat), 40 mg chol., 110 mg sodium, 21 g carbo., 4 g pro.

Spiced apple rings, pureed in the blender, make the tantalizing filling for this classy loaf.

Spiced Apple Braid

1½-POUND	INGREDIENTS
⅓ cup	milk
⅓ cup	apple juice
⅓ cup	margarine or butter, cut up
1	egg
3 cups	bread flour
3 tablespoons	sugar
¾ teaspoon	salt
1¼ teaspoons	active dry yeast
	or bread machine yeast
1 (14-ounce) jar	spiced apple rings, drained
1	slightly beaten egg white
1 tablespoon	water
1 recipe	Powdered Sugar Glaze

PREP:
35 minutes

RISE:
45 minutes

BAKE:
30 minutes

MAKES:
1½-pound recipe
(16 slices)

❶ Add the first 8 ingredients to the machine according to the manufacturer's directions. Select the dough cycle. When cycle is complete, remove dough. Punch down. Cover and let rest for 10 minutes. Meanwhile, for filling, place apples in a blender container. Cover and blend until nearly smooth. In a small bowl combine egg white and water. Set aside.

❷ Grease a baking sheet; set aside. On a lightly floured surface, roll the dough into a 16×12-inch rectangle. Cut into three 16×4-inch strips. Spread about ¼ cup filling down the center of each strip. Brush edges of dough with some of the egg white mixture. Fold dough in half lengthwise to enclose filling; pinch edges together to seal.

❸ To shape, line up the filled ropes, seam sides down, 1 inch apart on the prepared baking sheet. Starting in the middle, loosely braid by bringing the left rope under center rope. Bring the right rope under new center rope. Repeat to the end. On the other end, braid by bringing the outside ropes alternately over the center rope to center. Press ends together to seal; tuck under loaf. Brush with more of the egg white mixture. Cover and let rise in a warm place for 45 to 60 minutes or until nearly double. Brush with the remaining egg white mixture.

❹ Bake in a 350°F oven about 30 minutes or until bread sounds hollow when lightly tapped. If necessary, cover loosely with foil the last 10 to 15 minutes to prevent overbrowning. Remove from baking sheet; cool on a wire rack. Drizzle with Powdered Sugar Glaze.

Powdered Sugar Glaze: Stir together 1 cup sifted powdered sugar and ½ teaspoon vanilla. Stir in enough milk (3 to 4 teaspoons) to make a glaze of drizzling consistency.

Nutrition Facts per slice: 194 cal., 5 g total fat (1 g sat. fat), 14 mg chol., 159 mg sodium, 34 g carbo., 4 g pro.

Similar to many sweets sold in the Christmas markets of southern Germany, this fruit-and-nut-studded loaf tastes great with coffee or traditional Glühwein (glew-vighn), a mulled wine.

Bavarian Christmas Bread

PREP:
15 minutes

MAKES:
1½-pound recipe
(16 slices)
OR
2-pound recipe
(22 slices)

1½-POUND	INGREDIENTS	2-POUND
¾ cup	milk	1 cup
¼ cup	water	⅓ cup
2 tablespoons	margarine or butter, cut up	3 tablespoons
1 tablespoon	kirsch or milk	2 tablespoons
3 cups	bread flour	4 cups
2 tablespoons	sugar	3 tablespoons
¾ teaspoon	salt	1 teaspoon
½ teaspoon	ground mace	¾ teaspoon
¼ teaspoon	ground cardamom	½ teaspoon
1 teaspoon	active dry yeast	1¼ teaspoons
	or bread machine yeast	
½ cup	snipped, pitted dried plums (prunes)	⅔ cup
	or dark raisins	
⅓ cup	chopped hazelnuts (filberts)	½ cup
1 recipe	Powdered Sugar Icing (optional)	1 recipe

1 Select the loaf size. Add the ingredients, except the Powdered Sugar Icing, to the machine according to the manufacturer's directions. Select the basic white bread cycle. If desired, drizzle the cooled loaf with Powdered Sugar Icing.

Powdered Sugar Icing: In a small bowl stir together ⅔ cup sifted powdered sugar and ½ teaspoon vanilla. Stir in enough milk (2 to 3 teaspoons) to make an icing of drizzling consistency.

Nutrition Facts per slice: 150 cal., 4 g total fat (1 g sat. fat), 1 mg chol., 123 mg sodium, 25 g carbo., 4 g pro.

Kirsch Background

Kirschwasser (or kirsch) is a crystal-clear brandy infused with the flavor of cherries. The German name means "cherry water." The neighboring regions of France, Germany, and Switzerland have perfected the art of distilling this fine fruit spirit. Enjoy kirschwasser as an after-dinner digestive or in recipes.

Filled with some of the best-loved tastes of Christmas—nutmeg, eggnog, and candied fruits and peels—this loaf brims with holiday cheer.

Holiday Eggnog Bread

$1\frac{1}{2}$-POUND*	INGREDIENTS	2-POUND*
$\frac{1}{2}$ cup	canned or dairy eggnog	$\frac{3}{4}$ cup
$\frac{1}{4}$ cup	water	$\frac{1}{3}$ cup
1	egg**	1
2 tablespoons	margarine or butter, cut up	3 tablespoons
3 cups	bread flour	4 cups
2 tablespoons	sugar	3 tablespoons
$\frac{3}{4}$ teaspoon	salt	1 teaspoon
$\frac{1}{4}$ teaspoon	ground nutmeg	$\frac{1}{2}$ teaspoon
$1\frac{1}{4}$ teaspoons	active dry yeast	$1\frac{1}{2}$ teaspoons
	or bread machine yeast	
$\frac{1}{3}$ cup	diced mixed candied fruits and peels	$\frac{1}{3}$ cup
1 recipe	Eggnog Glaze	1 recipe

PREP:
15 minutes

MAKES:
$1\frac{1}{2}$-pound recipe
(20 slices)
OR
2-pound recipe
(27 slices)

① Select the loaf size. Add the ingredients, except the Eggnog Glaze, to the machine according to the manufacturer's directions. Select the basic white bread cycle. Drizzle the cooled loaf with Eggnog Glaze.

Eggnog Glaze: In a small bowl stir together 1 cup sifted powdered sugar and enough canned or dairy eggnog (1 to 2 tablespoons) to make a glaze of drizzling consistency.

***Note:** For the $1\frac{1}{2}$-pound loaf, the bread machine pan must have a capacity of 10 cups or more. For the 2-pound loaf, the bread machine pan must have a capacity of 12 cups or more.

****Note:** The Test Kitchen recommends 1 egg for either size loaf.

Nutrition Facts per slice: 133 cal., 2 g total fat (0 g sat. fat), 11 mg chol., 102 mg sodium, 25 g carbo., 3 g pro.

Candied Fruit Primer

Candied fruits come in a variety of colors and flavors, which adds a festive note to holiday cooking. Candied fruit favorites include citron; pineapple; red and green cherries; and orange, grapefruit, and lemon peels. Note that candied fruit is not the same as dried fruit—it is cooked in a sugar syrup as its means of preservation. Find it either in the produce aisle (along with the dates and other dried fruits) or alongside baking supplies. Once home, store candied fruit in a tightly sealed container in the freezer up to six months.

Combine fresh apples and creamy eggnog to make this tender, moist holiday loaf.
For a finishing touch, nothing tops an Eggnog Glaze. How sweet it is!

Apple-Eggnog Bread

PREP:
15 minutes

MAKES:
1½-pound recipe
(16 slices)
OR
2-pound recipe
(22 slices)

1½-POUND*	INGREDIENTS	2-POUND*
½ cup	canned or dairy eggnog	¾ cup
¼ cup	water**	¼ cup
½ cup	chopped, peeled apple	¾ cup
1	egg**	1
2 tablespoons	margarine or butter, cut up	3 tablespoons
¼ teaspoon	rum flavoring	½ teaspoon
3 cups	bread flour	4 cups
2 tablespoons	sugar	3 tablespoons
¾ teaspoon	salt	1 teaspoon
¼ teaspoon	ground nutmeg	½ teaspoon
1¼ teaspoons	active dry yeast or bread machine yeast	1½ teaspoons
1 recipe	Eggnog Glaze	1 recipe

1 Select the loaf size. Add the ingredients, except the Eggnog Glaze, to the machine according to the manufacturer's directions, adding the apple with the liquid. Select the basic white bread cycle. Drizzle the cooled loaf with Eggnog Glaze.

Eggnog Glaze: In a small bowl stir together 1 cup sifted powdered sugar and enough canned or dairy eggnog (1 to 2 tablespoons) to make a glaze of drizzling consistency.

*Note: For the 1½-pound loaf, the bread machine pan must have a capacity of 10 cups or more. For the 2-pound loaf, the bread machine pan must have a capacity of 12 cups or more.

**Note: Out Test Kitchen recommends ¼ cup water and 1 egg for either size recipe.

Nutrition Facts per slice: 155 cal., 3 g total fat (0 g sat. fat), 13 mg chol., 127 mg sodium, 28 g carbo., 4 g pro.

Skip the cookie routine—leave Santa a slice or two of this chocolate-and-citrus delight.

Chocolate-Orange Braid

1½-POUND	INGREDIENTS	2-POUND
¾ cup	milk	1 cup
1	egg(s)	2
¼ cup	margarine or butter, cut up	⅓ cup
2 tablespoons	water	3 tablespoons
3 cups	bread flour	4 cups
⅓ cup	sugar	½ cup
⅓ cup	unsweetened cocoa powder	½ cup
1 tablespoon	finely shredded orange peel	4 teaspoons
¾ teaspoon	salt	1 teaspoon
1¼ teaspoons	active dry yeast	1½ teaspoons
	or bread machine yeast	
1 recipe	Chocolate Powdered Sugar Glaze	1 recipe

PREP:
30 minutes

RISE:
1 hour

BAKE:
35 minutes

MAKES:
1½-pound recipe
(24 slices)
OR
2-pound recipe
(30 slices)

1 Select the recipe size. Add the ingredients, except the Chocolate Powdered Sugar Glaze, to the machine according to the manufacturer's directions. Select the dough cycle. When cycle is complete, remove dough. Punch down. Cover and let rest for 10 minutes.

2 *For the 1½-pound recipe:* Lightly grease a baking sheet; set aside. Divide the dough into thirds. On a lightly floured surface, roll each portion into a 16-inch rope. To shape, line up the ropes, 1 inch apart, on the prepared baking sheet. Starting in the middle, loosely braid by bringing the left rope under the center rope. Bring the right rope under the new center rope. Repeat to the end. On the other end, braid by bringing the outside ropes alternately over the center rope to center. Press ends together to seal; tuck under loaf. Cover and let rise in a warm place about 1 hour or until nearly double.

3 Bake in a 325°F oven for 35 to 40 minutes or until bread sounds hollow when lightly tapped. If necessary, cover loosely with foil the last 10 to 15 minutes to prevent overbrowning. Remove from baking sheet; cool on a wire rack. Drizzle with Chocolate Powdered Sugar Glaze.

For the 2-pound recipe: Prepare as above, except divide the dough into 6 portions. Roll each portion into a 16-inch rope. Form 2 braids on 2 lightly greased baking sheets, using 3 ropes for each. Continue as above.

Chocolate Powdered Sugar Glaze: In a small bowl stir together 1 cup sifted powdered sugar, 1 tablespoon unsweetened cocoa powder, and ½ teaspoon vanilla. Stir in enough milk (1 to 2 tablespoons) to make a glaze of drizzling consistency.

Nutrition Facts per slice: 120 cal., 3 g total fat (1 g sat. fat), 9 mg chol., 96 mg sodium, 21 g carbo., 3 g pro.

Enchant that hard-to-buy-for-person on your shopping list with this fruit-and-nut loaf.
If you like, team it with some pretty mugs and packets of cocoa mix or flavored coffee.

Fruited Christmas Wreath

	1½-POUND	INGREDIENTS	2-POUND
PREP: 40 minutes	³/₄ cup	milk*	³/₄ cup
	1	egg(s)	2
RISE: 30 minutes	¹/₄ cup	margarine or butter, cut up	¹/₃ cup
	3 cups	bread flour	4 cups
BAKE: 25 minutes	¹/₄ cup	sugar	¹/₃ cup
	³/₄ teaspoon	salt	1 teaspoon
MAKES: 1½-pound recipe (12 servings)	¹/₄ teaspoon	ground nutmeg	¹/₂ teaspoon
	1¹/₄ teaspoons	active dry yeast	1¹/₂ teaspoons
OR		or bread machine yeast	
2-pound recipe (16 servings)	2 tablespoons	margarine or butter, melted*	2 tablespoons
	1 recipe	Fruit Filling	1 recipe
	1 recipe	Powdered Sugar Icing (page 289)	1 recipe

1 Select the recipe size. Add the first 8 ingredients to the machine according to the manufacturer's directions. Select the dough cycle. When cycle is complete, remove dough. Punch down. Cover and let rest for 10 minutes. Grease a 12-inch pizza pan; set aside.

2 Divide the 1½-pound dough in half. On a lightly floured surface, roll each portion into a 10-inch circle. (Divide the 2-pound dough in half; roll each portion into a 12-inch circle.) Place a circle of dough on the prepared pizza pan. Brush with some of the melted margarine and spread with the Fruit Filling. Top with the second circle of dough. Place a 2-inch-diameter glass, upright, in the center of the dough to use as a guide (the center remains intact). Cut the 1½-pound dough, cutting from the edge of dough just to the bottom of the glass, into 12 wedges (cut the 2-pound dough into 16 wedges). Remove glass. Twist each wedge 2 times. Brush with the remaining melted margarine. Cover and let rise in a warm place for 30 to 40 minutes or until nearly double.

3 Bake in a 350°F oven for 25 to 30 minutes or until bread sounds hollow when lightly tapped. If necessary, cover loosely with foil the last 10 minutes to prevent overbrowning. Remove from pan; cool slightly on a wire rack. Drizzle with Powdered Sugar Icing.

Fruit Filling: In a small saucepan combine one 6-ounce package mixed dried fruit bits and ½ cup orange juice. Bring to boiling; remove from heat. Cover and let stand for 10 minutes; drain. Stir in ³/₄ cup chopped pecans, ¹/₄ cup sugar, and ¹/₂ teaspoon ground cinnamon. Transfer to a small bowl; cover and chill until needed.

*Note: The Test Kitchen recommends ³/₄ cup milk and 2 tablespoons melted margarine or butter for either size recipe.

Nutrition Facts per serving: 343 cal., 12 g total fat (2 g sat. fat), 19 mg chol., 225 mg sodium, 55 g carbo., 6 g pro.

A high-rising bread filled with a spiral of nutty-sweet filling, potica (paw-TEE-tzah) is a beloved holiday tradition that hails from Slovenia, where secret family recipes for the treat are lovingly passed from one generation to the next.

Hazelnut Potica

1½-POUND	INGREDIENTS	
½ cup	milk	
3	egg yolks	
¼ cup	water	
¼ cup	margarine or butter, cut up	
3 cups	bread flour	
¼ cup	sugar	
¾ teaspoon	salt	
1½ teaspoons	active dry yeast	
	or bread machine yeast	
3 cups	hazelnuts (filberts), toasted and ground	
1 cup	sugar	
1 teaspoon	ground cinnamon	
3	egg whites	
¼ cup	milk	
¼ cup	margarine or butter, softened	
½ teaspoon	vanilla	
1 recipe	Powdered Sugar Icing	

PREP:
35 minutes

RISE:
1 hour

BAKE:
50 minutes

MAKES:
1½-pound recipe
(16 slices)

1 Add first 8 ingredients to machine according to manufacturer's directions. Select dough cycle. When cycle is complete, remove dough. Punch down. Cover and let rest for 10 minutes.

2 Meanwhile, for filling, in a medium bowl stir together hazelnuts, the 1 cup sugar, and cinnamon. Stir in egg whites, the ¼ cup milk, the softened margarine, and vanilla. Generously grease a 10-inch fluted tube pan; set aside.

3 Divide the dough in half. On a lightly floured surface, roll each portion into an 18×12-inch rectangle. Spread each rectangle with half of the filling. Starting from a long side, loosely roll up into a spiral; seal edge. Place 1 roll seam side up in the prepared tube pan. Moisten ends; press together to seal ring. Place the second roll on top of the first roll in pan, sealing as above. Cover and let rise in a warm place about 1 hour or until nearly double.

4 Bake in a 350°F oven for 50 to 60 minutes or until bread sounds hollow when lightly tapped. If necessary, cover loosely with foil the last 15 minutes to prevent overbrowning. Remove from pan; cool on a wire rack. Drizzle with Powdered Sugar Icing.

Powdered Sugar Icing: Stir together 1 cup sifted powdered sugar and ¼ teaspoon vanilla. Stir in enough milk (1 to 2 tablespoons) to make an icing of drizzling consistency.

Nutrition Facts per slice: 408 cal., 23 g total fat (3 g sat. fat), 41 mg chol., 195 mg sodium, 45 g carbo., 9 g pro.

This updated version of the Italian holiday favorite adds a few dried cherries to the traditional flavors of raisins, citron, pine nuts, and anise. Rich and wonderful, the bread can be served for breakfast or dessert.

Festive Fruit-and-Nut Panettone

PREP:
20 minutes

RISE:
45 minutes

BAKE:
55 minutes

MAKES:
2-pound recipe
(12 slices)

INGREDIENTS	2-POUND
milk	1 cup
eggs	2
butter, cut up	½ cup
bread flour	3¾ cups
granulated sugar	½ cup
finely shredded lemon peel	1 tablespoon
anise seeds	1 teaspoon
salt	½ teaspoon
active dry yeast	4½ teaspoons
or bread machine yeast	
dried tart cherries	1 cup
pine nuts	¾ cup
Nonstick cooking spray	
golden raisins	½ cup
slightly beaten egg	1
water	1 tablespoon
pine nuts	1 tablespoon
Sifted powdered sugar (optional)	

1 Add the first 11 ingredients to the machine according to the manufacturer's directions. Select the dough cycle.

2 Meanwhile, coat an 8×3-inch springform pan or soufflé dish with cooking spray. For collar, cut a piece of clean brown wrapping paper into a 25×6-inch strip. Fit the collar around the inside of the prepared pan, overlapping slightly. Coat inside of collar with cooking spray.

3 When cycle is complete, remove dough. Punch down. On a lightly floured surface, gently knead the raisins into dough. Shape the dough into a ball. Place in the prepared pan and flatten slightly to cover bottom of pan. Cover and let rise in a warm place for 45 to 60 minutes or until nearly double. In a small bowl combine the beaten egg and water; brush over top of loaf. Sprinkle with the 1 tablespoon pine nuts.

4 Bake in a 350°F oven for 55 to 60 minutes or until a wooden skewer inserted into center of bread comes out clean. If necessary, cover loosely with foil the last 10 to 15 minutes to prevent overbrowning. Cool in pan on a wire rack for 10 minutes. Remove from pan; cool on wire rack. If desired, sprinkle with powdered sugar.

Nutrition Facts per slice: 386 cal., 15 g total fat (6 g sat. fat), 57 mg chol., 189 mg sodium, 56 g carbo., 10 g pro.

Full of homemade goodness, this handsome loaf topped with decorative twisted ropes is a magnificent addition to any holiday menu.

Holiday Loaf

1½-POUND	INGREDIENTS	2-POUND
⅔ cup	water	¾ cup
1	egg(s)	2
¼ cup	margarine or butter, cut up	⅓ cup
3 cups	bread flour	4 cups
3 tablespoons	sugar	¼ cup
¾ teaspoon	salt	1 teaspoon
1 teaspoon	active dry yeast	1¼ teaspoons
	or bread machine yeast	
1	egg yolk	1
1 tablespoon	water	1 tablespoon

PREP:
30 minutes

RISE:
30 minutes

BAKE:
40 minutes

MAKES:
1½-pound recipe
(16 slices)
OR
2-pound recipe
(22 slices)

1 Select the recipe size. Add the first 7 ingredients to the machine according to the manufacturer's directions. Select the dough cycle. When cycle is complete, remove dough. Punch down. Cover and let rest for 10 minutes.

2 *For the 1½-pound recipe:* Grease a 2-quart casserole; set aside. Set aside one-fourth of the dough. Shape remaining dough into a ball; place in prepared casserole. In a small bowl combine egg yolk and the 1 tablespoon water; brush some of the mixture over top of loaf.

3 Divide the reserved dough into fourths; roll each portion into a 10-inch rope. Twist 2 ropes together; place slightly off center across top of loaf, tucking ends under ropes. Repeat with the remaining 2 ropes, placing parallel to first twist on top of loaf. Cover and let rise in a warm place about 30 minutes or until nearly double. Brush with remaining egg yolk mixture.

4 Bake in a 325°F oven for 40 to 45 minutes or until bread sounds hollow when lightly tapped. If necessary, cover loosely with foil the last 10 to 15 minutes to prevent overbrowning. Remove from casserole; cool on a wire rack.

For the 2-pound recipe: Prepare as above, except divide the dough into thirds. Shape 2 portions into balls; place each portion in a greased 1-quart casserole. Brush with some of the egg yolk mixture. Divide the remaining dough into 8 portions; roll into 8-inch ropes. Form 4 twisted ropes; place 2 on top of each loaf. Continue as above.

Nutrition Facts per slice: 136 cal., 4 g total fat (1 g sat. fat), 27 mg chol., 139 mg sodium, 21 g carbo., 4 g pro.

Nestling inside this ring of tender bread is an irresistible, tropically inspired cream cheese filling. As if that's not enough, a spirited rum glaze and a sprinkling of toasted coconut tops it all off.

Papaya-Coconut Wreath

	1½-POUND	INGREDIENTS
PREP: 30 minutes	½ cup	milk
	¼ cup	water
RISE: 40 minutes	1	egg
	2 tablespoons	margarine or butter, cut up
BAKE: 25 minutes	3 cups	bread flour
	2 tablespoons	sugar
MAKES: 1½-pound recipe (16 servings)	¾ teaspoon	salt
	1¼ teaspoons	active dry yeast or bread machine yeast
	1 (8-ounce) package	cream cheese, softened
	½ cup	finely snipped dried papaya, mango, or pineapple
	⅓ cup	flaked coconut
	2 tablespoons	peach or apricot spreadable fruit or preserves
	1 recipe	Rum Glaze

❶ Add the first 8 ingredients to machine according to manufacturer's directions. Select dough cycle. When cycle is complete, remove dough. Punch down. Cover and let rest for 10 minutes.

❷ Meanwhile, for filling, in a medium bowl stir together cream cheese, dried fruit, the ⅓ cup coconut, and spreadable fruit. Grease a large baking sheet; set aside.

❸ On a lightly floured surface, roll dough into a 15x10-inch rectangle. Spread with filling. Starting from a long side, roll up into a spiral; seal edge. Place seam side down on prepared baking sheet. Bring ends together to form a ring. Moisten ends; seal ring. Make a cut from the outside edge toward center, leaving about ¾ inch attached. Repeat around edge at 1-inch intervals. Gently turn each slice slightly so the same side of all slices faces upward.

❹ Cover and let rise in a warm place for 40 to 50 minutes or until nearly double. Bake in a 350°F oven for 25 to 30 minutes or until bread sounds hollow when lightly tapped. If necessary, cover loosely with foil the last 10 minutes to prevent overbrowning. Remove from baking sheet; cool on a wire rack. Drizzle with Rum Glaze; sprinkle with additional coconut.

Rum Glaze: Stir together 1 cup sifted powdered sugar and 2 teaspoons rum or a few drops rum flavoring. Stir in enough milk (1 to 2 tablespoons) to make a glaze of drizzling consistency.

Nutrition Facts per serving: 226 cal., 8 g total fat (4 g sat. fat), 29 mg chol., 179 mg sodium, 33 g carbo., 5 g pro.

Packed with red and green cherries, this festive coffee cake makes a colorful centerpiece for a holiday brunch buffet.

Candied Fruit Ring

1½-POUND	INGREDIENTS	2-POUND
⅓ cup	orange juice	½ cup
¼ cup	water	⅓ cup
1	egg*	1
3 tablespoons	margarine or butter, cut up	¼ cup
3 cups	bread flour	4 cups
⅓ cup	packed brown sugar	½ cup
¾ teaspoon	salt	1 teaspoon
1¾ teaspoons	active dry yeast	2¼ teaspoons
	or bread machine yeast	
1	slightly beaten egg white*	1
⅓ cup	granulated sugar	½ cup
½ teaspoon	ground cardamom	¾ teaspoon
¾ cup	finely chopped pecans	1 cup
½ cup	finely chopped candied cherries	¾ cup
1 recipe	Powdered Sugar Icing (page 289)	1 recipe

PREP:
30 minutes

RISE:
45 minutes

BAKE:
30 minutes

MAKES:
1½-pound recipe
(16 slices)
OR
2-pound recipe
(20 slices)

1 Select the recipe size. Add the first 8 ingredients to machine according to manufacturer's directions. Select the dough cycle. When cycle is complete, remove dough. Punch down. Cover and let rest for 10 minutes. Meanwhile, for filling, in a small bowl combine egg white, granulated sugar, and cardamom. Stir in pecans and candied cherries. Set aside.

2 *For the 1½-pound recipe:* Grease a baking sheet; set aside. On a lightly floured surface, roll dough into an 18×12-inch rectangle. Spread with the filling. Starting from a long side, roll up into a spiral; seal edge. Place, seam side down, on the prepared baking sheet. Bring ends together to form a ring. Moisten ends; seal ring. Make decorative cuts about 1 inch apart on top of ring. Cover and let rise in a warm place for 45 to 60 minutes or until nearly double.

3 Bake in a 350°F oven for 30 to 35 minutes or until golden brown. Remove from baking sheet; cool on a wire rack. Drizzle with Powdered Sugar Icing.

For the 2-pound recipe: Prepare as above, except divide the dough in half. Roll each portion into a 16×8-inch rectangle. Spread each rectangle with half of the filling. Form 2 rings on 2 greased baking sheets. Continue as above.

*Note: Out Test Kitchen recommends 1 egg for either size dough and 1 egg white for either size filling.

Nutrition Facts per slice: 227 cal., 6 g total fat (1 g sat. fat), 13 mg chol., 135 mg sodium, 39 g carbo., 4 g pro.

White and semisweet chocolate dough, a holiday shape, a pink-and-white glaze, and sugar-dusted sparkle—these magical ingredients make for memorable holiday mornings.

Peppermint Candy Cane Loaf

	1½-POUND	I N G R E D I E N T S
PREP: 35 minutes	½ cup	milk
	¼ cup	water
RISE: 45 minutes	1	egg
	2 tablespoons	margarine or butter, cut up
BAKE: 25 minutes	3 cups	bread flour
	2 tablespoons	granulated sugar
MAKES: 1½-pound recipe (18 slices)	¾ teaspoon	salt
	1¼ teaspoons	active dry yeast
		or bread machine yeast
	½ cup	white baking pieces
	½ cup	semisweet chocolate pieces
	1 recipe	Peppermint Glaze
		Coarse sugar

1 Add the first 8 ingredients to the machine according to the manufacturer's directions. Select the dough cycle. When cycle is complete, remove dough. Punch down. Cover and let rest for 10 minutes. Grease a large baking sheet; set aside.

2 On a lightly floured surface, roll the dough into a 20×10-inch rectangle. Cut rectangle in half lengthwise to make two 20×5-inch rectangles. Sprinkle the white baking pieces down the center of one of the rectangles. Sprinkle the semisweet chocolate pieces down the center of the other rectangle. Moisten edges of dough. Fold dough in half lengthwise to enclose filling; pinch edges together to seal. Gently roll the dough into ropes.

3 Place the filled ropes, seam sides down, 1 inch apart on the prepared baking sheet. Twist the ropes together; press ends together to seal. Curve one end to form a candy cane shape. Cover and let rise in a warm place for 45 to 60 minutes or until nearly double.

4 Bake in a 350°F oven about 25 minutes or until bread sounds hollow when lightly tapped. Remove from baking sheet; cool slightly on a wire rack. Drizzle with white and pink Peppermint Glaze. Sprinkle with coarse sugar. Serve warm.

Peppermint Glaze: In a small bowl stir together ¾ cup sifted powdered sugar and a few drops peppermint extract. Stir in enough milk (2 to 4 teaspoons) to make a glaze of drizzling consistency. For white glaze, set aside half of the mixture. For pink glaze, stir 1 drop red liquid food coloring into the remaining mixture.

Nutrition Facts per slice: 165 cal., 4 g total fat (2 g sat. fat), 13 mg chol., 124 mg sodium, 28 g carbo., 4 g pro.

Decorated Christmas trees may be fascinating to look at, but with this distinctive recipe they're also fabulous to eat. Twisted ropes of dough dotted with dried cherries and filled with cinnamon make up the branches of this delectable pine.

Cherry Christmas Coffee Bread

1½-POUND	INGREDIENTS
¾ cup	milk
¼ cup	water
¼ cup	butter or margarine, cut up
1	egg
3½ cups	bread flour
¼ cup	sugar
¾ teaspoon	salt
1 teaspoon	active dry yeast
	or bread machine yeast
1 cup	dried tart cherries
½ cup	sugar
1 tablespoon	all-purpose flour or bread flour
1 teaspoon	ground cinnamon
3 tablespoons	butter
1 recipe	Powdered Sugar Icing (page 289)
	Halved candied cherries

PREP:
40 minutes

RISE:
30 minutes

BAKE:
12 minutes

MAKES:
1½-pound recipe
(16 servings)

1 Add the first 9 ingredients to the machine according to the manufacturer's directions. Select the dough cycle. When cycle is complete, remove dough. Punch down. Cover and let rest for 10 minutes.

2 Meanwhile, for filling, in a small bowl combine the ½ cup sugar, all-purpose flour, and cinnamon. Using a pastry blender, cut in the 3 tablespoons butter until mixture resembles coarse crumbs. Set aside.

3 Grease 2 large baking sheets; set aside. Divide the dough in half. On a lightly floured surface, roll 1 portion into a 12×6-inch rectangle. Sprinkle with half of the filling. Fold in half lengthwise to make a 12×3-inch rectangle; cut into twelve 3×1-inch strips.

4 Twist the strips. Arrange the twisted strips on a prepared baking sheet to form a tree shape. Use 10 strips for the lower branches, placing cut ends toward the center, and 1 strip for the base. Cut the remaining strip in half; use for top branches. Repeat with the remaining dough and filling, forming a second tree shape on the remaining baking sheet.

5 Cover and let rise in a warm place about 30 minutes or until nearly double. Bake in a 375°F oven for 12 to 15 minutes or until golden brown. Remove from baking sheets; cool on wire racks. Drizzle with Powdered Sugar Icing and garnish with candied cherries.

Nutrition Facts per serving: 257 cal., 6 g total fat (3 g sat. fat), 27 mg chol., 170 mg sodium, 46 g carbo., 5 g pro.

Reminiscent of native loaves from the Alsace region of France, this version uses smoked meats instead of dried fruits. Flecked with ham and black pepper, it can serve as a savory hors d'oeuvre.

Savory Kugelhopf

1½-POUND*	INGREDIENTS	2-POUND*
³/₄ cup	half-and-half, light cream, or milk**	³/₄ cup
²/₃ cup	finely chopped cooked ham	³/₄ cup
	or	
8 slices	bacon, crisp-cooked, drained, and crumbled	10 slices
¹/₄ cup	water	¹/₃ cup
1	egg**	1
2 tablespoons	margarine or butter, cut up	3 tablespoons
3 cups	bread flour	4 cups
1 tablespoon	sugar	4 teaspoons
³/₄ teaspoon	salt	1 teaspoon
¹/₄ teaspoon	coarsely ground black pepper**	¹/₄ teaspoon
1 teaspoon	active dry yeast or bread machine yeast	1¹/₄ teaspoons

PREP:
15 minutes

MAKES:
1½-pound recipe
(16 slices)
OR
2-pound recipe
(22 slices)

1 Select the loaf size. Add the ingredients to the machine according to the manufacturer's directions. Select the basic white bread cycle.

*Note: For the 1½-pound loaf, the bread machine pan must have a capacity of 10 cups or more. For the 2-pound loaf, the bread machine pan must have a capacity of 12 cups or more.

**Note: The Test Kitchen recommends ¾ cup half-and-half, cream, or milk; 1 egg; and ¼ teaspoon pepper for either size recipe.

Nutrition Facts per slice: 137 cal., 4 g total fat (1 g sat. fat), 21 mg chol., 196 mg sodium, 20 g carbo., 5 g pro.

Kugelhopf Variations

Although generally thought of as Austrian, kugelhopf is also claimed by bakers from Alsace, Germany, and Poland. You may know it by one of its many spellings—kugelhopf, gugelhupf, sugelhupf, and its many versions—and types—sweet, savory, with eggs and without. Enjoyed by many, kugelhopf's origination and variations really don't matter once you've taken a delicious bite.

In December the Swedes honor the Italian Saint Lucia in a celebration. The elaborate festivities always include these saffron and raisin buns.

St. Lucia Buns

1½-POUND	INGREDIENTS	2-POUND
¾ cup	milk	1 cup
1	egg(s)	2
¼ cup	margarine or butter, cut up	⅓ cup
3 cups	bread flour	4 cups
3 tablespoons	packed brown sugar	¼ cup
1½ teaspoons	finely shredded orange peel	2 teaspoons
¾ teaspoon	salt	1 teaspoon
⅛ teaspoon	thread saffron, crushed	¼ teaspoon
1 teaspoon	active dry yeast	1½ teaspoons
	or bread machine yeast	
1	slightly beaten egg	1
1 tablespoon	water	1 tablespoon
12	raisins	16
	Granulated sugar	

PREP:
40 minutes

RISE:
30 minutes

BAKE:
10 minutes

MAKES:
1½-pound recipe
(12 buns)
OR
2-pound recipe
(16 buns)

1 Select the recipe size. Add the first 9 ingredients to the machine according to the manufacturer's directions. Select the dough cycle. When cycle is complete, remove dough. Punch down. Cover and let rest for 10 minutes. Grease a large baking sheet; set aside.

2 Divide the 1½-pound dough into 24 portions (divide the 2-pound dough into 32 portions). On a lightly floured surface, roll each portion into a smooth 10-inch rope. Form each rope into an "S" shape and curve each end into a coil. Cross 2 of these "S"-shape ropes to form an X. Repeat with the remaining "S"-shape ropes. Place buns on the prepared baking sheet. Cover and let rise in a warm place about 30 minutes or until nearly double.

3 In a small bowl combine the beaten egg and water; brush over buns. Place a raisin in the center of each bun. Sprinkle the buns with granulated sugar. Bake in a 375°F oven about 10 minutes or until golden brown. Remove from baking sheet; cool on wire racks.

Nutrition Facts per bun: 196 cal., 6 g total fat (1 g sat. fat), 37 mg chol., 198 mg sodium, 30 g carbo., 6 g pro.

Offer these pretty cardamom-flavored rosettes as dessert or a breakfast treat on special occasions. For a pretty touch, use a decorator's bag fitted with a large star tip to fill the rosettes with lemon curd.

Lemon Curd Rosettes

PREP: 55 minutes	1½-POUND	INGREDIENTS	2-POUND
	¾ cup	water	1 cup
RISE: 30 minutes	2	egg yolks	3
	3 tablespoons	margarine or butter, cut up	¼ cup
BAKE: 10 minutes	3 cups	bread flour	4 cups
	¼ cup	sugar	⅓ cup
MAKES: 1½-pound recipe (24 rolls) OR 2-pound recipe (32 rolls)	1 teaspoon	salt	1¼ teaspoons
	¾ teaspoon	ground cardamom	1 teaspoon
	1½ teaspoons	active dry yeast	2 teaspoons
		or bread machine yeast	
	1	egg yolk	1
	1 tablespoon	water	1 tablespoon
	⅓ cup	lemon curd	½ cup

1 Select the recipe size. Add the first 8 ingredients to the machine according to the manufacturer's directions. Select the dough cycle. When cycle is complete, remove dough. Punch down. Cover and let rest for 10 minutes. Grease baking sheets; set aside.

2 Divide the 1½-pound dough into 24 portions (divide the 2-pound dough into 32 portions). On a lightly floured surface, roll each portion into a 12-inch rope. Tie each rope into a loose knot, leaving 2 long ends. Tuck the top end under the knot; bring the bottom end up and tuck into the top center of the knot.

3 Place rolls, 2 to 3 inches apart, on the prepared baking sheets. Cover and let rise in a warm place about 30 minutes or until nearly double. In a small bowl combine the 1 egg yolk and the 1 tablespoon water; brush over rolls.

4 Bake in a 375°F oven for 10 to 12 minutes or until golden brown. Remove from baking sheets; cool on wire racks. Spoon about ½ teaspoon lemon curd into the center of each roll.

Nutrition Facts per roll: 97 cal., 2 g total fat (1 g sat. fat), 28 mg chol., 109 mg sodium, 16 g carbo., 3 g pro.

Consider these rich, golden buns a work in progress to complete at the table. Serve them split and ready to fill with a cloud of sweetened whipped cream or your best homemade preserves.

Holiday Cream-Filled Buns

1½-POUND	INGREDIENTS	2-POUND
²/₃ cup	milk	¾ cup
¼ cup	water	⅓ cup
¼ cup	margarine or butter, cut up	⅓ cup
3 cups	bread flour	4 cups
⅓ cup	granulated sugar	½ cup
¾ teaspoon	salt	1 teaspoon
1¼ teaspoons	active dry yeast	1½ teaspoons
	or bread machine yeast	
	Sifted powdered sugar	
1 recipe	Cream Filling	1 recipe
	or seedless red raspberry or strawberry jam	

PREP:
30 minutes

RISE:
20 minutes

BAKE:
15 minutes

MAKES:
1½-pound recipe
(12 buns)
OR
2-pound recipe
(16 buns)

1 Select the recipe size. Add the first 7 ingredients to the machine according to the manufacturer's directions. Select the dough cycle. When cycle is complete, remove dough. Punch down. Cover and let rest for 10 minutes. Grease a large baking sheet; set aside.

2 Divide the 1½-pound dough into 12 portions (divide the 2-pound dough into 16 portions). Using lightly floured hands, shape each portion into a ball, tucking edges under to make a smooth top. Place buns, about 2 inches apart, on the prepared baking sheet. Cover and let rise in a warm place for 20 to 30 minutes or until nearly double.

3 Bake in a 375°F oven about 15 minutes or until golden brown. Immediately sprinkle tops lightly with powdered sugar. Remove from baking sheet; cool on wire racks.

4 To serve, cut a slit in each bun. Fill each with about 1 teaspoon Cream Filling.

Cream Filling: In a chilled small mixing bowl combine ⅓ cup whipping cream and 1 tablespoon sugar. Beat with the chilled beaters of an electric mixer on medium speed or with a rotary beater until soft peaks form. By hand, fold in ⅓ cup dairy sour cream.

Nutrition Facts per bun: 229 cal., 8 g total fat (3 g sat. fat), 13 mg chol., 192 mg sodium, 33 g carbo., 5 g pro.

These yummy, golden brown sweet rolls are like doughnuts but are filled with either chocolate or fruit preserves. During Hanukkah, Israeli vendors sell sufganyot by the basketfuls.

Sufganyot

	1½-POUND	INGREDIENTS	2-POUND
PREP: 45 minutes	³/₄ cup	water	1 cup
	1	egg*	1
COOK: 2 minutes per batch	4 teaspoons	cooking oil	2 tablespoons
	¹/₂ teaspoon	vanilla*	¹/₂ teaspoon
MAKES:	3 cups	bread flour	4 cups
1½-pound recipe (16 doughnuts)	¹/₄ cup	granulated sugar	¹/₃ cup
OR	¹/₂ teaspoon	salt	³/₄ teaspoon
2-pound recipe (22 doughnuts)	¹/₄ teaspoon	ground cinnamon	¹/₂ teaspoon
	1¹/₄ teaspoons	active dry yeast	1¹/₂ teaspoons
		or bread machine yeast	
	¹/₄ cup	chocolate-hazelnut spread	¹/₃ cup
		or fruit preserves (such as seedless red raspberry	
		or blackberry)	
		Cooking oil for deep-fat frying	
		Sifted powdered sugar	

1 Select the recipe size. Add the first 9 ingredients to the machine according to the manufacturer's directions. Select the dough cycle. When cycle is complete, remove dough. Punch down. Cover and let rest for 10 minutes.

2 Divide the 1½-pound dough in half (divide the 2-pound dough into thirds). On a lightly floured surface, roll each portion to ¼-inch thickness. Cut the dough with a floured 2½-inch biscuit cutter, dipping cutter into flour between cuts. Reroll as necessary. Place about ½ teaspoon chocolate-hazelnut spread onto centers of half of the circles. Lightly moisten edges of circles; top with remaining circles. Press edges together with fingers or a fork to seal.

3 Fry the doughnuts, 2 or 3 at a time, in deep, hot oil (365°F) about 2 minutes or until golden brown, turning once. Using a slotted spoon, remove doughnuts from oil and drain on paper towels. Sprinkle with powdered sugar. Cool on wire racks.

*Note: The Test Kitchen recommends 1 egg and ½ teaspoon vanilla for either size recipe.

Nutrition Facts per doughnut: 164 cal., 5 g total fat (1 g sat. fat), 13 mg chol., 72 mg sodium, 26 g carbo., 4 g pro.

In some countries, the feast of Epiphany—the day the three kings visited the Christ child— is the focus of holiday celebrations. This fruity almond loaf is similar to ones traditionally served on that day.

Three Kings' Ring

1½-POUND	INGREDIENTS
½ cup	milk
1	egg
¼ cup	water
2 tablespoons	margarine or butter, cut up
3 cups	bread flour
⅓ cup	sugar
¾ teaspoon	salt
1½ teaspoons	active dry yeast
	or bread machine yeast
¼ cup	sugar
2 teaspoons	ground cinnamon
¾ cup	diced mixed candied fruits and peels
½ cup	chopped almonds, toasted
3 tablespoons	margarine or butter, softened
1 recipe	Orange Icing

PREP: 30 minutes

RISE: 40 minutes

BAKE: 25 minutes

MAKES: 1½-pound recipe (12 servings)

1 Add the first 8 ingredients to the machine according to the manufacturer's directions. Select the dough cycle. When cycle is complete, remove dough. Punch down. Cover and let rest for 10 minutes.

2 Meanwhile, for filling, in a small bowl combine the ¼ cup sugar and cinnamon. Add the candied fruits and almonds; toss gently to coat. Set aside.

3 Line a baking sheet with foil and grease foil; set aside. On a lightly floured surface, roll the dough into a 20×12-inch rectangle. Spread with the softened margarine and sprinkle with the filling. Starting from a long side, roll up into a spiral; seal edge. Place seam side down on the prepared baking sheet. Bring ends together to form a ring. Moisten ends; pinch together to seal ring. Flatten slightly. Using kitchen scissors or a sharp knife, make 12 cuts from the outside edge toward center, cutting about two-thirds of the way toward center. Cover and let rise in a warm place for 40 to 50 minutes or until nearly double.

4 Bake in a 350°F oven for 25 to 30 minutes or until bread sounds hollow when lightly tapped. If necessary, cover loosely with foil the last 15 minutes to prevent overbrowning. Remove from baking sheet; cool on a wire rack. Drizzle with Orange Icing.

Orange Icing: In a small bowl stir together 1 cup sifted powdered sugar and ¼ teaspoon vanilla. Stir in enough orange juice (3 to 4 teaspoons) to make an icing of drizzling consistency.

Nutrition Facts per serving: 316 cal., 9 g total fat (1 g sat. fat), 19 mg chol., 201 mg sodium, 54 g carbo., 6 g pro.

Ask Cupid what's the best treat for Valentine's Day and the sprite will recommend these rich, nutty hearts.

Almond-Filled Hearts

	1½-POUND	INGREDIENTS	2-POUND
PREP: 50 minutes	⅔ cup	milk	1 cup
RISE: 30 minutes	1	egg*	1
	2 tablespoons	margarine or butter, cut up	3 tablespoons
BAKE: 12 minutes	3 cups	bread flour	4 cups
	2 tablespoons	granulated sugar	3 tablespoons
MAKES: 1½-pound recipe (10 rolls)	¾ teaspoon	salt	1 teaspoon
	1¼ teaspoons	active dry yeast or bread machine yeast	1½ teaspoons
OR 2-pound recipe (12 rolls)	1 recipe	Almond Filling	1 recipe
		Red-colored or plain coarse sugar (optional)	

1 Select the recipe size. Add the first 7 ingredients to the machine according to the manufacturer's directions. Select the dough cycle. When cycle is complete, remove dough. Punch down. Cover and let rest for 10 minutes. Grease large baking sheets; set aside.

2 *For the 1½-pound recipe:* On a lightly floured surface, roll dough into a 22½×10-inch rectangle. Cut into ten 10×2¼-inch strips. Divide the Almond Filling into 10 portions; roll each portion into a 9½-inch rope. Place a rope lengthwise down the center of each strip of dough. Moisten edges of dough. Fold dough in half lengthwise to enclose filling; pinch edges together to seal. Place seam sides down on the prepared baking sheets. Form each filled strip into a heart shape; moisten ends and pinch together at base of heart to seal.

3 Cover and let rise in a warm place for 30 to 40 minutes or until nearly double. If desired, brush with a little additional milk and sprinkle with coarse sugar. Bake in a 350°F oven for 12 to 15 minutes or until golden brown. Remove from baking sheets; cool on wire racks.

For the 2-pound recipe: Prepare as above, except roll the dough into a 27×10-inch rectangle. Cut into twelve 10×2¼-inch strips. Divide the Almond Filling into 12 portions. Continue as above.

Almond Filling: In a medium mixing bowl beat one 8-ounce can almond paste, crumbled; ¼ cup granulated sugar; 1 tablespoon all-purpose flour; and 1 egg yolk with an electric mixer until smooth. (Or combine the ingredients in a food processor bowl. Cover and process until mixture clings together.)

*Note: The Test Kitchen recommends 1 egg for either size recipe.

Nutrition Facts per roll: 324 cal., 10 g total fat (2 g sat. fat), 44 mg chol., 206 mg sodium, 49 g carbo., 10 g pro.

Serve this cherry-filled cinnamon roll with steaming mugs of hot chocolate for a surefire way to steal someone's heart on Valentine's Day.

Sweetheart Cinnamon Roll

1½-POUND	INGREDIENTS
¾ cup	milk
1	egg
¼ cup	margarine or butter, cut up
3 cups	bread flour
¼ cup	sugar
¾ teaspoon	salt
1¼ teaspoons	active dry yeast
	or bread machine yeast
2 tablespoons	margarine or butter, softened
¼ cup	sugar
1 teaspoon	ground cinnamon
⅔ cup	dried tart cherries, snipped
1 recipe	Powdered Sugar Icing

PREP:
35 minutes

RISE:
30 minutes

BAKE:
20 minutes

MAKES:
1½-pound recipe
(16 servings)

① Add the first 7 ingredients to the machine according to the manufacturer's directions. Select the dough cycle. When cycle is complete, remove dough. Punch down. Cover and let rest for 10 minutes. Grease a large baking sheet; set aside.

② On a lightly floured surface, roll the dough into an 18×12-inch rectangle. Spread with the softened margarine. In a small bowl stir together ¼ cup sugar and cinnamon; sprinkle evenly over dough. Sprinkle with dried cherries.

③ Starting from a long side, roll up into a spiral; seal edge. Place seam side up on the prepared baking sheet. Fold half of the roll over the top of other half; press ends together to seal. Starting ¾ inch from the sealed end, cut down the center all the way through the dough layers, cutting through the folded end. Turn cut sides out so they face up and touch each other, forming a heart shape. Cover and let rise in a warm place about 30 minutes or until nearly double.

④ Bake in a 350°F oven for 20 to 25 minutes or until bread sounds hollow when lightly tapped. Remove from baking sheet; cool slightly on a wire rack. Drizzle with Powdered Sugar Icing. Serve warm.

Powdered Sugar Icing: In a small bowl stir together 1 cup sifted powdered sugar and ¼ teaspoon vanilla. Stir in enough milk (1 to 2 tablespoons) to make an icing of drizzling consistency.

Nutrition Facts per serving: 208 cal., 5 g total fat (1 g sat. fat), 14 mg chol., 170 mg sodium, 36 g carbo., 4 g pro.

Sample this cream cheese-filled loaf and you'll know you've been blessed with the luck of the Irish.

St. Patrick's Shamrock

	1½-POUND	INGREDIENTS
PREP: 35 minutes	³/₄ cup	milk
	¹/₄ cup	margarine or butter, cut up
RISE: 30 minutes	1	egg
	2 tablespoons	water
BAKE: 25 minutes	3 cups	bread flour
	¹/₄ cup	granulated sugar
MAKES: 1½-pound recipe (16 servings)	³/₄ teaspoon	salt
	1¹/₄ teaspoons	active dry yeast
		or bread machine yeast
	2 (3-ounce) packages	cream cheese, softened
	¹/₄ cup	granulated sugar
	1	egg yolk
	¹/₂ teaspoon	vanilla
	1	slightly beaten egg white
	1 tablespoon	water
	1 tablespoon	green-colored coarse sugar

1 Add the first 8 ingredients to machine according to manufacturer's directions. Select dough cycle. When cycle is complete, remove dough. Punch down. Cover and let rest for 10 minutes.

2 Meanwhile, for filling, in a medium mixing bowl beat cream cheese, ¹/₄ cup granulated sugar, egg yolk, and vanilla with an electric mixer on medium speed until smooth. Generously grease a baking sheet; set aside.

3 On a lightly floured surface, roll the dough into a 15×10-inch rectangle. Cut into three 10×5-inch strips. Spread one-third of the filling down center of each strip. Moisten edges of dough. Fold dough in half lengthwise to enclose filling; seal. Gently roll dough into ropes.

4 On the prepared baking sheet, shape a rope into a loop, attaching 1 end about 2 inches above the other end to form 1 leaf and stem of shamrock. Shape the remaining ropes into loops; attach 1 on either side of first loop near the stem. Cover and let rise in a warm place about 30 minutes or until nearly double. In a small bowl combine egg white and the 1 tablespoon water; brush over shamrock. Sprinkle with green sugar.

5 Bake in a 350°F oven for 25 to 30 minutes or until bread sounds hollow when lightly tapped. Remove from baking sheet; cool on a wire rack. Store any leftover bread in refrigerator.

Nutrition Facts per serving: 199 cal., 8 g total fat (3 g sat. fat), 39 mg chol., 180 mg sodium, 27 g carbo., 5 g pro.

A golden sweet yeast loaf is an Old-World tradition that can't be improved upon—unless you use a bread machine to make it! This one reveals a lovely swirl of raisins and nuts when sliced.

Rumanian Easter Bread

1½-POUND	INGREDIENTS	2-POUND
½ cup	milk	⅔ cup
¼ cup	water	⅓ cup
¼ cup	margarine or butter, cut up	⅓ cup
1	egg*	1
3 cups	bread flour	4 cups
⅓ cup	sugar	½ cup
¾ teaspoon	salt	1 teaspoon
1 teaspoon	active dry yeast	1¼ teaspoons
	or bread machine yeast	
¾ cup	sugar	1 cup
½ cup	water	⅔ cup
2 cups	ground pecans	2½ cups
1 cup	golden raisins	1⅓ cups
1 teaspoon	finely shredded lemon peel	1¼ teaspoons
¾ teaspoon	ground cinnamon	1 teaspoon
1	slightly beaten egg	1
1 tablespoon	milk	1 tablespoon

PREP:
30 minutes

RISE:
30 minutes

BAKE:
30 minutes

MAKES:
1½-pound recipe
(24 slices)
OR
2-pound recipe
(32 slices)

1 Select the recipe size. Add the first 8 ingredients to the machine according to the manufacturer's directions. Select the dough cycle. When cycle is complete, remove dough. Punch down. Cover and let rest for 10 minutes.

2 Meanwhile, for filling, combine the ¾ or 1 cup sugar and the ½ or ⅔ cup water. Bring to boiling; reduce heat. Boil gently, uncovered, for 5 minutes. Remove from heat; stir in pecans, raisins, lemon peel, and cinnamon. Cool slightly. Grease a large baking sheet; set aside.

3 Divide the 1½-pound dough in half. On a lightly floured surface, roll each portion into a 10×8-inch rectangle. (Divide the 2-pound dough in half; roll each portion into a 12×10-inch rectangle.) Spread each rectangle with half of the filling. Starting from a short side, roll up into a spiral; seal edge and ends. Place loaves, seam sides down, on the prepared baking sheet. Cover and let rise in a warm place about 30 minutes or until nearly double. In a small bowl combine the beaten egg and the 1 tablespoon milk; brush over loaves.

4 Bake in a 350°F oven for 30 to 35 minutes or until bread sounds hollow when lightly tapped. If necessary, cover loosely with foil the last 10 minutes to prevent overbrowning. Remove from baking sheet; cool on wire racks.

*Note: The Test Kitchen recommends 1 egg for either size recipe.

Nutrition Facts per slice: 204 cal., 9 g total fat (1 g sat. fat), 18 mg chol., 99 mg sodium, 29 g carbo., 4 g pro.

Give the Easter baskets a grown-up twist. Tuck a loaf of this eye-catching date-and-walnut spiral into a decorative bread basket and delight someone special.

Easter Date Bread

PREP: 30 minutes	1½-POUND	INGREDIENTS	2-POUND
	½ cup	milk	⅔ cup
RISE: 45 minutes	1	egg(s)	2
	¼ cup	water	⅓ cup
BAKE: 25 minutes	¼ cup	butter or margarine, cut up	⅓ cup
	3 cups	bread flour	4 cups
MAKES: 1½-pound recipe (24 slices)	¼ cup	granulated sugar	⅓ cup
	¾ teaspoon	salt	1 teaspoon
	¾ teaspoon	finely shredded lemon peel	1 teaspoon
OR	1½ teaspoons	active dry yeast	1¾ teaspoons
2-pound recipe (36 slices)		or bread machine yeast	
	1 cup	ground walnuts	1⅓ cups
	¾ cup	snipped, pitted whole dates	1 cup
	¼ cup	granulated sugar	⅓ cup
	¼ cup	currant jelly	6 tablespoons
		Sifted powdered sugar	

1 Select the recipe size. Add the first 9 ingredients to the machine according to the manufacturer's directions. Select the dough cycle. When cycle is complete, remove dough. Punch down. Cover and let rest for 10 minutes. Meanwhile, for filling, in a medium bowl combine walnuts, dates, and ¼ or ⅓ cup sugar. Set aside.

2 *For the 1½-pound recipe:* Grease a large baking sheet; set aside. Divide the dough in half. On a lightly floured surface, roll each portion into a 16×10-inch rectangle. Spread each rectangle with 2 tablespoons jelly to within ½ inch of the edges. Sprinkle each with half of the filling. Starting from a long side, loosely roll up into a spiral. (If rolled too tightly, the filling may cause the dough to crack during baking.) Moisten edge; pinch firmly to seal. Place seam sides down on the prepared baking sheet, tucking ends under loaves.

3 Cover and let rise in a warm place for 45 to 60 minutes or until nearly double. If desired, brush with a little additional milk. Bake in a 350°F oven for 25 to 30 minutes or until bread sounds hollow when lightly tapped. If necessary, cover loosely with foil the last 10 to 15 minutes to prevent overbrowning. Remove from baking sheet; cool on wire racks. Sprinkle with powdered sugar.

For the 2-pound recipe: Prepare as above, except divide dough into thirds. Roll each portion into a 14×10-inch rectangle. Spread each rectangle with 2 tablespoons jelly and sprinkle each with one-third of the filling. Continue as above, using 2 greased large baking sheets.

Nutrition Facts per slice: 158 cal., 6 g total fat (2 g sat. fat), 14 mg chol., 93 mg sodium, 24 g carbo., 3 g pro.

This bread machine adaptation of Russian Easter bread isn't the traditional cylindrical shape, but everything else about it is as authentic as can be. It's brimming with the traditional ingredients: raisins, saffron, and candied fruits and peels.

Russian Kulich

1½-POUND*	INGREDIENTS	2-POUND*
⅓ cup	dark raisins	½ cup
2 tablespoons	orange juice	3 tablespoons
Dash	ground saffron	Few dashes
⅓ cup	water	½ cup
¼ cup	milk	⅓ cup
1	egg**	1
2 tablespoons	margarine or butter, cut up	3 tablespoons
1 teaspoon	vanilla	1½ teaspoons
¼ teaspoon	almond extract**	¼ teaspoon
3 cups	bread flour	4 cups
2 tablespoons	granulated sugar	3 tablespoons
¾ teaspoon	salt	1 teaspoon
1½ teaspoons	active dry yeast or bread machine yeast	2 teaspoons
⅓ cup	diced mixed candied fruits and peels	½ cup
1 recipe	Almond Glaze	1 recipe

PREP:
20 minutes

MAKES:
1½-pound recipe
(16 slices)
OR
2-pound recipe
(22 slices)

❶ Select the loaf size. In a small bowl combine the raisins, orange juice, and saffron. Let stand for 10 minutes. Drain, reserving the juice mixture.

❷ Add the ingredients, except the Almond Glaze, to the machine according to the manufacturer's directions, adding the juice mixture with the liquid and the raisins as directed. Select the basic white bread cycle. Drizzle the cooled loaf with Almond Glaze. If desired, garnish with additional candied fruits and peels.

Almond Glaze: In a small bowl stir together 1¼ cups sifted powdered sugar, 1 teaspoon light-colored corn syrup, ½ teaspoon vanilla, and ¼ teaspoon almond extract. Stir in enough milk (1 to 2 tablespoons) to make a glaze of drizzling consistency.

*Note: For the 1½-pound loaf, the bread machine pan must have a capacity of 10 cups or more. For the 2-pound loaf, the bread machine pan must have a capacity of 12 cups or more.

**Note: The Test Kitchen recommends 1 egg and ¼ teaspoon almond extract for either size recipe.

Nutrition Facts per slice: 166 cal., 2 g total fat (0 g sat. fat), 14 mg chol., 124 mg sodium, 32 g carbo., 4 g pro.

Hip hop into spring with these whimsical bunnies. They're made from a rich egg dough that's kissed with a touch of nutmeg.

Easter Rabbits

PREP: 40 minutes	1½-POUND	INGREDIENTS	2-POUND
	¾ cup	milk	1 cup
RISE: 35 minutes	1	egg*	1
	3 tablespoons	margarine or butter, cut up	¼ cup
BAKE: 10 minutes	3 cups	bread flour	4 cups
	¼ cup	sugar	⅓ cup
MAKES: 1½-pound recipe (14 rolls)	¾ teaspoon	salt	1 teaspoon
	¼ teaspoon	ground nutmeg*	¼ teaspoon
OR	1¼ teaspoons	active dry yeast	1½ teaspoons
2-pound recipe (21 rolls)		or bread machine yeast	
	1	slightly beaten egg white	1
	1 tablespoon	water	1 tablespoon

1 Select the recipe size. Add the first 8 ingredients to the machine according to the manufacturer's directions. Select the dough cycle. When cycle is complete, remove dough. Punch down. Cover and let rest for 10 minutes. Lightly grease baking sheets; set aside.

2 On a lightly floured surface, roll the 1½-pound dough into a 14×8-inch rectangle. Cut lengthwise into fifteen 14-inch strips, each about ½ inch wide. Reserve 1 strip to form tails. (Roll the 2-pound dough into a 14×12-inch rectangle; cut lengthwise into twenty-three 14-inch strips, each about ½ inch wide. Reserve 2 strips to form tails.) Gently roll the dough strips into ropes.

3 On the prepared baking sheets, shape each rabbit by crossing 1 end of a rope over the other to form a loop, overlapping about 2 inches from each end. Twist the ends of rope once at the point where the dough overlaps. Shape the ends into points to resemble ears. Shape small portions from reserved strip(s) into smooth balls for tails. Place a ball on top of dough at bottom of each loop, moistening if necessary to get tail to stick.

4 Cover and let rise in a warm place for 35 to 45 minutes or until nearly double. In a small bowl combine egg white and water; brush over rabbits. Bake in a 375°F oven about 10 minutes or until golden brown. Remove from baking sheets; cool on wire racks.

*Note: The Test Kitchen recommends 1 egg and ¼ teaspoon nutmeg for either size recipe.

Nutrition Facts per roll: 156 cal., 4 g total fat (1 g sat. fat), 16 mg chol., 159 mg sodium, 26 g carbo., 5 g pro.

It's hard to say what kids will love more—the bunny shape or the chocolatey taste. Make it once, and it's sure to become a highly anticipated Easter event each year after.

Chocolate Bunny Bread

PREP:
30 minutes

RISE:
40 minutes

BAKE:
30 minutes

MAKES:
1½-pound recipe
(20 servings)

1½-POUND	I N G R E D I E N T S
²/₃ cup	milk
¼ cup	water
1	egg
2 tablespoons	margarine or butter, cut up
2 teaspoons	vanilla
3 cups	bread flour
¹/₃ cup	sugar
¼ cup	unsweetened cocoa powder
³/₄ teaspoon	salt
1½ teaspoons	active dry yeast
	or bread machine yeast
¹/₃ cup	miniature semisweet chocolate
	pieces
1 recipe	Powdered Sugar Glaze

1 Add the first 10 ingredients to the machine according to the manufacturer's directions. Select the dough cycle. When cycle is complete, remove dough. Punch down. On a lightly floured surface, gently knead the chocolate pieces into dough. Cover and let rest for 10 minutes. Grease 2 large baking sheets; set aside.

2 Pinch off two 1½-inch balls of dough; set aside. On a lightly floured surface, divide the remaining dough in half. Roll each portion into a 20-inch rope.

3 On a prepared baking sheet, shape each bunny by crossing 1 end of a rope over the other to form a loop, overlapping 4 to 5 inches from each end. Twist the ends of rope once at the point where the dough overlaps. Shape the ends into points to resemble ears. Shape the reserved dough into smooth balls for tails. Place a ball on top of dough at bottom of each loop, moistening if necessary to get tail to stick.

4 Cover and let rise in a warm place for 40 to 50 minutes or until nearly double. Bake in a 350°F oven about 30 minutes or until bread sounds hollow when lightly tapped. If necessary, cover loosely with foil the last 10 minutes to prevent overbrowning. Remove from baking sheets; cool on wire racks. Drizzle with Powdered Sugar Glaze.

Powdered Sugar Glaze: In a small bowl combine 1 cup sifted powdered sugar and 1 teaspoon vanilla. Stir in enough milk (1 to 2 tablespoons) to make a glaze of drizzling consistency.

Nutrition Facts per serving: 146 cal., 3 g total fat (1 g sat. fat), 11 mg chol., 109 mg sodium, 25 g carbo., 3 g pro.

Bringing warmth and symbolism to the holiday table, twisted ropes encircle the bread, forming a cross shape on the rich, nutty loaf.

Walnut Easter Bread

PREP:			

	1½-POUND	INGREDIENTS
	¾ cup	milk
	⅓ cup	margarine or butter, cut up
	1	egg
	3 cups	bread flour
	¼ cup	sugar
	¾ teaspoon	salt
	½ teaspoon	ground nutmeg
	1 teaspoon	active dry yeast
		or bread machine yeast
	⅓ cup	finely chopped walnuts
	5	walnut halves
	1	egg yolk
	1 tablespoon	water

PREP:
35 minutes

RISE:
45 minutes

BAKE:
45 minutes

MAKES:
1½-pound recipe
(16 slices)

1. Add the first 9 ingredients to the machine according to the manufacturer's directions. Select the dough cycle. When cycle is complete, remove dough. Punch down. Cover and let rest for 10 minutes. Grease a baking sheet; set aside.

2. Set aside one-third of the dough. On a lightly floured surface, shape the remaining dough into a ball. Place on the prepared baking sheet. Flatten slightly to a 5½-inch round loaf.

3. Divide the reserved dough into 8 portions. Roll each portion into a 10-inch rope. Loosely twist 2 ropes together. Repeat with the remaining ropes, making 4 twisted ropes total.

4. Place 2 of the twisted ropes in a cross shape on top of loaf; tuck rope ends under loaf. Place the remaining twisted ropes around the base of loaf, stretching the ropes if necessary so ends will meet. Moisten ends; press together to seal. Brush center and ends of crossed ropes with water. Press a walnut half in the center and at the ends of the crossed ropes. Cover and let rise in a warm place for 45 to 60 minutes or until nearly double.

5. In a small bowl combine egg yolk and water; brush over loaf. Bake in a 350°F oven for 45 to 50 minutes or until bread sounds hollow when lightly tapped. If necessary, cover loosely with foil the last 20 minutes to prevent overbrowning. Remove from baking sheet; cool on a wire rack.

Nutrition Facts per slice: 173 cal., 7 g total fat (1 g sat. fat), 27 mg chol., 164 mg sodium, 23 g carbo., 5 g pro.

ROLLs, pizza, and BREADSTICKS

Arbiters of good taste at dinner tables everywhere agree: Classic crescent rolls reign supreme. And these are especially irresistible—light, flaky, and oh-so-buttery. What's not to like?

Crescent Rolls

PREP: 25 minutes	1½-POUND	INGREDIENTS	2-POUND
	½ cup	milk	⅔ cup
RISE: 30 minutes	2	eggs*	2
	¼ cup	butter or margarine, cut up	⅓ cup
BAKE: 8 minutes	3 cups	bread flour	3¾ cups
	3 tablespoons	sugar	¼ cup
MAKES: 1½-pound recipe (16 rolls)	¾ teaspoon	salt	1 teaspoon
	1¼ teaspoons	active dry yeast	1½ teaspoons
OR 2-pound recipe (24 rolls)		or bread machine yeast	
	2 tablespoons	butter or margarine, melted	3 tablespoons

1 Select the recipe size. Add the first 7 ingredients to the machine according to the manufacturer's directions. Select the dough cycle. When cycle is complete, remove dough. Punch down. Cover and let rest for 10 minutes. Grease baking sheets; set aside.

2 *For the 1½-pound recipe:* Divide the dough in half. On a lightly floured surface, roll each portion into a 12-inch circle. Brush each circle with half of the melted butter. Cut each circle into 8 wedges. Starting at the wide end of each wedge, loosely roll toward the point. Place rolls, points down, 2 to 3 inches apart on the prepared baking sheets. Curve the end of each roll to form a crescent shape. Cover and let rise in a warm place for 30 to 40 minutes or until nearly double.

3 Bake in a 375°F oven for 8 to 10 minutes or until golden brown. Remove from baking sheets; cool slightly on wire racks. Serve warm or cool.

For the 2-pound recipe: Prepare as above, except divide the dough into thirds. After rolling, brush each circle with one-third of the melted butter. Continue as above.

*Note: The Test Kitchen recommends 2 eggs for either size recipe.

Nutrition Facts per roll: 153 cal., 5 g total fat (3 g sat. fat), 39 mg chol., 156 mg sodium, 22 g carbo., 4 g pro.

Here's a whole wheat take on one of the all-time-great American dinner rolls. Hearty, handsome, and wholesome, they'll bring unmistakable warmth to your table.

Wheat Cloverleaf Rolls

1½-POUND	INGREDIENTS	2-POUND
³/₄ cup	buttermilk or sour milk*	1 cup
1	egg(s)	2
¹/₄ cup	margarine or butter, cut up	¹/₃ cup
1¹/₂ cups	bread flour	2¹/₄ cups
1¹/₂ cups	whole wheat flour	2 cups
2 tablespoons	sugar	3 tablespoons
³/₄ teaspoon	salt	1 teaspoon
1 teaspoon	active dry yeast	1¹/₄ teaspoons
	or bread machine yeast	
1	slightly beaten egg white	1
1 tablespoon	water	1 tablespoon
	Sesame seeds, poppy seeds,	
	and/or caraway seeds	

PREP:
35 minutes

RISE:
20 minutes

BAKE:
12 minutes

MAKES:
1½-pound recipe
(16 rolls)
OR
2-pound recipe
(24 rolls)

1 Select the recipe size. Add the first 8 ingredients to the machine according to the manufacturer's directions. Select the dough cycle. When cycle is complete, remove dough. Punch down. Cover and let rest for 10 minutes.

2 *For the 1¹/₂-pound recipe:* Lightly grease sixteen 2¹/₂-inch muffin cups. Divide the dough in half. Divide each portion into 24 pieces (48 pieces total). Shape each piece into a ball, tucking edges under to make a smooth top. Place 3 balls in each muffin cup.

3 In a small bowl combine egg white and water; brush over rolls. Sprinkle lightly with sesame seeds. Cover and let rise in a warm place for 20 to 25 minutes or until nearly double.

4 Bake in a 375°F oven for 12 to 15 minutes or until golden brown. Remove from muffin cups; cool slightly on wire racks. Serve warm or cool.

For the 2-pound recipe: Prepare as above, except divide the dough in half; divide each portion into 36 pieces (72 pieces total). Shape into balls; place 3 balls in each of 24 lightly greased 2¹/₂-inch muffin cups. Continue as above.

*Note: To make ³/₄ cup sour milk, place 2¹/₄ teaspoons lemon juice or vinegar in a 1-cup liquid measuring cup. Add enough milk to measure ³/₄ cup liquid; stir. To make 1 cup sour milk, place 1 tablespoon lemon juice or vinegar in a 1-cup liquid measuring cup. Add enough milk to measure 1 cup liquid; stir. Let stand for 5 minutes before using.

Nutrition Facts per roll: 129 cal., 4 g total fat (1 g sat. fat), 14 mg chol., 154 mg sodium, 20 g carbo., 4 g pro.

As their name suggests, pine nuts come from pine trees. They're usually found in supermarkets next to other nuts—though sometimes they're tucked away in the produce section.

Pine Nut Rolls

PREP:	1½-POUND	INGREDIENTS	2-POUND
35 minutes			
	⅔ cup	milk	¾ cup
RISE:	1	egg(s)	2
30 minutes	3 tablespoons	margarine or butter, cut up	¼ cup
	1 tablespoon	honey	4 teaspoons
BAKE:	3 cups	bread flour	4 cups
15 minutes	¾ teaspoon	salt	1 teaspoon
MAKES:	1 teaspoon	active dry yeast	1¼ teaspoons
1½-pound recipe (18 rolls)		or bread machine yeast	
OR	⅔ cup	finely chopped pine nuts	¾ cup
2-pound recipe (24 rolls)		or almonds	
	½ cup	grated Parmesan cheese	⅔ cup
	⅓ cup	snipped fresh parsley	½ cup
	3 tablespoons	margarine or butter, melted	¼ cup
	1	slightly beaten egg white	1
	1 tablespoon	water	1 tablespoon

❶ Select the recipe size. Add the first 7 ingredients to the machine according to the manufacturer's directions. Select the dough cycle. When cycle is complete, remove dough. Punch down. Cover and let rest for 10 minutes.

❷ Meanwhile, for filling, in a small bowl stir together pine nuts, Parmesan cheese, and parsley. Grease baking sheets; set aside.

❸ *For the 1½-pound recipe:* Divide the dough in half. On a lightly floured surface, roll 1 portion into a 13½×12-inch rectangle. Brush with half of the melted margarine and sprinkle with half of the filling. Starting from a long side, roll up into a spiral; seal edge. Cut into nine 1½-inch slices. Place rolls seam sides down on prepared baking sheets. Let rest for 5 minutes.

❹ Using a wooden spoon handle, press the center of each roll lengthwise to make a deep crease. Repeat with the remaining dough, remaining melted margarine, and remaining filling. In a small bowl combine egg white and water; brush over rolls. Cover and let rise in a warm place about 30 minutes or until nearly double.

❺ Bake in a 375°F oven about 15 minutes or until golden brown. Remove from baking sheets; cool slightly on wire racks. Serve warm or cool.

For the 2-pound recipe: Prepare as above, except roll each portion of dough into an 18×12-inch rectangle. Fill and roll up; cut into twelve 1½-inch slices. Continue as above.

Nutrition Facts per roll: 174 cal., 9 g total fat (2 g sat. fat), 15 mg chol., 197 mg sodium, 19 g carbo., 6 g pro.

For a deep, rich flavor, use sharp cheddar cheese in these party-special rolls.

Cheddar Cheese Bows

1½-POUND	INGREDIENTS
1 cup	milk
1²/₃ cups	shredded cheddar, Swiss, or Monterey Jack cheese
1	egg
3 cups	bread flour
3 tablespoons	sugar
³/₄ teaspoon	salt
1 teaspoon	active dry yeast or bread machine yeast
¹/₃ cup	finely shredded Parmesan cheese

PREP:
35 minutes

RISE:
20 minutes

BAKE:
12 minutes

MAKES:
1½-pound recipe
(24 rolls)

1 Add the first 7 ingredients to the machine according to the manufacturer's directions, adding the cheddar cheese with the milk. Select the dough cycle. When cycle is complete, remove dough. Punch down. Cover and let rest for 10 minutes. Line baking sheets with foil and grease foil; set aside.

2 Divide the dough in half. On a lightly floured surface, roll each portion into a 12-inch square. Cut into twelve 12×1-inch strips.

3 On the prepared baking sheets, shape each strip into a bow by forming 2 loops, overlapping in the center about 1½ inches from each end. Take 1 end of dough in each hand and twist once at the point where the dough overlaps. Press dough together in center to seal. Cover and let rise in a warm place for 20 to 30 minutes or until nearly double.

4 Brush rolls with a little additional milk; sprinkle with Parmesan cheese. Bake in a 375°F oven about 12 minutes or until golden brown. Remove from baking sheets; cool slightly on wire racks. Serve warm or cool.

Nutrition Facts per roll: 156 cal., 5 g total fat (3 g sat. fat), 32 mg chol., 207 mg sodium, 21 g carbo., 8 g pro.

Moist and tender, with the nutty taste of wheat germ, these flavorful rolls are sure to be a hit at your Thanksgiving table. Serve warm with Orange-Ginger Butter (page 265).

Sweet Potato Pull-Apart Rolls

	1½-POUND	I N G R E D I E N T S	2-POUND
PREP: 40 minutes	³/₄ cup	drained and mashed, canned sweet potatoes	1 cup
RISE: 30 minutes	¹/₂ cup	milk	³/₄ cup
BAKE: 18 minutes	1	egg*	1
	2 tablespoons	margarine or butter, cut up	3 tablespoons
MAKES: 1½-pound recipe (16 rolls) OR 2-pound recipe (24 rolls)	2¹/₂ cups	bread flour	3¹/₃ cups
	¹/₂ cup	whole wheat flour	²/₃ cup
	¹/₂ cup	toasted wheat germ	²/₃ cup
	1 tablespoon	brown sugar	4 teaspoons
	³/₄ teaspoon	salt	1 teaspoon
	1¹/₄ teaspoons	active dry yeast or bread machine yeast	1¹/₂ teaspoons
	1	slightly beaten egg white	1
	1 tablespoon	water	1 tablespoon

❶ Select the recipe size. Add the first 10 ingredients to the machine according to the manufacturer's directions. Select the dough cycle. When cycle is complete, remove dough. Punch down. Cover and let rest for 10 minutes.

❷ *For the 1½-pound recipe:* Lightly grease two 8×1½-inch round baking pans; set aside. Divide the dough into 16 portions. Shape each portion into a ball, tucking edges under to make a smooth top. Divide the rolls between the prepared baking pans. Cover and let rise in a warm place about 30 minutes or until nearly double.

❸ In a small bowl combine egg white and water; brush over rolls. Sprinkle with additional wheat germ. Bake in a 375°F oven about 18 minutes or until light brown. Cool in pans on wire racks for 10 minutes. Remove from pans; cool slightly on wire racks. Serve warm or cool.

For the 2-pound recipe: Prepare as above, except divide dough into 24 portions. Shape into balls; divide between 2 lightly greased 9×1½-inch round baking pans. Continue as above.

*Note: The Test Kitchen recommends 1 egg for either size recipe.

Nutrition Facts per roll: 144 cal., 3 g total fat (1 g sat. fat), 14 mg chol., 138 mg sodium, 24 g carbo., 6 g pro.

Wheat bran, oats, and dried cherries make these wholesome nuggets the perfect crossover bread. You can serve them as sweet rolls with coffee or tea or as a savory partner for soups or salads.

Oatmeal-Cherry Rolls

1½-POUND	INGREDIENTS
1¼ cups	milk
2 tablespoons	margarine or butter, cut up
3 cups	bread flour
⅓ cup	regular or quick-cooking
	rolled oats
⅓ cup	unprocessed wheat bran
1 tablespoon	brown sugar
¾ teaspoon	salt
1 teaspoon	active dry yeast
	or bread machine yeast
½ cup	snipped dried tart cherries
	or dark raisins

PREP:
25 minutes

RISE:
30 minutes

BAKE:
25 minutes

MAKES:
1½-pound recipe
(24 rolls)

1 Add the ingredients to the machine according to the manufacturer's directions. Select the dough cycle. When cycle is complete, remove dough. Punch down. Cover and let rest for 10 minutes. Lightly grease 2 baking sheets or two 9×1½-inch round baking pans; set aside.

2 Divide the dough into 24 portions. Shape each portion into a ball, tucking edges under to make a smooth top. Place the rolls on the prepared baking sheets. Cover and let rise in a warm place about 30 minutes or until nearly double.

3 Bake in a 350°F oven about 25 minutes or until golden brown. Brush rolls with additional melted margarine. Remove from baking sheets; cool slightly on wire racks. Serve warm or cool.

Nutrition Facts per roll: 96 cal., 2 g total fat (0 g sat. fat), 2 mg chol., 87 mg sodium, 17 g carbo., 3 g pro.

Once you've tried these sensational home-baked hamburger buns, supermarket buns won't have the same appeal.

Hamburger Wheat Buns

PREP:
25 minutes

RISE:
1 hour

BAKE:
12 minutes

MAKES:
1½-pound recipe
(6 buns)

1½-POUND	INGREDIENTS
1 cup	milk
4 teaspoons	honey
4 teaspoons	margarine or butter
2 cups	whole wheat flour
1 cup	bread flour
³⁄₄ teaspoon	salt
1 teaspoon	active dry yeast
	or bread machine yeast
1	slightly beaten egg
	Sesame seeds or poppy seeds

1 Add the first 7 ingredients to the machine according to the manufacturer's directions. Select the dough cycle. When cycle is complete, remove dough. Punch down. Cover and let rest for 10 minutes. Grease baking sheets; set aside.

2 Divide the dough into 6 portions. Shape each portion into a ball, tucking edges under to make a smooth top. Place buns 4 inches apart on the prepared baking sheets. Flatten slightly to 3½-inch rounds.

3 Cover and let rise in a warm place about 1 hour or until nearly double. Brush the buns with beaten egg; sprinkle with sesame seeds. Bake in a 375°F oven for 12 to 15 minutes or until buns sound hollow when lightly tapped. Remove from baking sheets; cool on a wire rack.

Nutrition Facts per bun: 107 cal., 2 g total fat (0 g sat. fat), 2 mg chol., 122 mg sodium, 20 g carbo., 3 g pro.

Seasoned Hamburger Wheat Buns: Prepare as above, except add 2 teaspoons sesame seeds, poppy seeds, snipped fresh chives, or dried minced onion to the machine with flours.

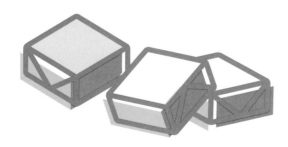

Just bite into these rolls flavored three times with chocolate and you'll understand why the botanical name of the cacao tree, Theobroma cacao, translates as "food of the gods."

Triple Chocolate Crescents

1½-POUND	INGREDIENTS	2-POUND
²/₃ cup	milk	³/₄ cup
¼ cup	water	¹/₃ cup
¼ cup	margarine or butter, cut up	¹/₃ cup
1	egg*	1
3 cups	bread flour	4 cups
¼ cup	sugar	¹/₃ cup
¼ cup	unsweetened cocoa powder	¹/₃ cup
³/₄ teaspoon	salt	1 teaspoon
1½ teaspoons	active dry yeast	2 teaspoons
	or bread machine yeast	
2 (1½-ounce) bars	milk chocolate	3 (1½-ounce) bars
1 recipe	Chocolate Glaze	1 recipe

PREP:
30 minutes

RISE:
20 minutes

BAKE:
12 minutes

MAKES:
1½-pound recipe
(20 rolls)
OR
2-pound recipe
(30 rolls)

1 Select the recipe size. Add the first 9 ingredients to the machine according to the manufacturer's directions. Select the dough cycle. When cycle is complete, remove dough. Punch down. Cover and let rest for 10 minutes. Grease baking sheets; set aside.

2 Divide the 1½-pound dough in half (divide the 2-pound dough into thirds). On a lightly floured surface, roll each portion into a 10-inch circle. Cut each circle into 10 wedges. Break each chocolate bar into 10 pieces; place 1 piece onto the wide end of each wedge. Starting at the wide end of each wedge, loosely roll toward the point.

3 Place rolls, points down, on the prepared baking sheets. Curve the end of each roll to form a crescent shape. Cover and let rise in a warm place for 20 to 30 minutes or until nearly double. Bake in a 375°F oven for 12 to 15 minutes or until rolls sound hollow when lightly tapped. Remove from baking sheets; cool slightly on wire racks. Drizzle with Chocolate Glaze. Serve warm or cool.

Chocolate Glaze: In a small bowl stir together 1 cup sifted powdered sugar, 2 tablespoons unsweetened cocoa powder, and ½ teaspoon vanilla. Stir in enough milk (1 to 2 tablespoons) to make a glaze of drizzling consistency.

*Note: The Test Kitchen recommends 1 egg for either size recipe.

Nutrition Facts per roll: 161 cal., 5 g total fat (1 g sat. fat), 11 mg chol., 119 mg sodium, 26 g carbo., 4 g pro.

If you can't resist a good doughnut, you'll love these buttery morsels. Their appealing flavor comes from the balance of tangy lemon peel with the sweetness of two types of sugar.

Buttery Sugar Rolls

	1¹/₂-POUND	INGREDIENTS	2-POUND
PREP: 30 minutes	³/₄ cup	milk	1 cup
RISE: 30 minutes	¹/₄ cup	butter or margarine, cut up	¹/₃ cup
	1	egg*	1
BAKE: 15 minutes	3 cups	bread flour	4 cups
	¹/₄ cup	granulated sugar	¹/₃ cup
MAKES: 1¹/₂-pound recipe (12 rolls)	1 teaspoon	finely shredded lemon peel	1¹/₄ teaspoons
	¹/₄ teaspoon	salt*	¹/₄ teaspoon
OR	1¹/₂ teaspoons	active dry yeast	2 teaspoons
2-pound recipe (20 rolls)		or bread machine yeast	
	3 tablespoons	butter or margarine, softened	¹/₄ cup
	1	slightly beaten egg	1
	1 tablespoon	water	1 tablespoon
	1 tablespoon	coarse sugar	4 teaspoons

1 Select the recipe size. Add the first 8 ingredients to machine according to manufacturer's directions. Select the dough cycle. When cycle is complete, remove dough. Punch down. Cover and let rest for 10 minutes. Grease a 15×10×1-inch baking pan; set aside.

2 *For the 1¹/₂-pound recipe:* On a lightly floured surface, roll the dough into a 12×8-inch rectangle. Spread with the softened butter. Starting from a long side, fold one-third of the dough over the center third. Fold the remaining third of dough over the center third, forming 3 equal layers. Moisten and seal edges. Cut crosswise into twelve 1-inch strips.

3 Place rolls, cut sides down, in the prepared baking pan. Cover and let rise in a warm place about 30 minutes or until nearly double. In a small bowl combine the beaten egg and water; brush over rolls. Sprinkle with coarse sugar.

4 Bake in a 375°F oven for 15 to 18 minutes or until golden brown. Remove from pan; cool slightly on wire racks. Serve warm or cool.

For the 2-pound recipe: Prepare as above, except divide the dough in half. Roll each half into a 10×8-inch rectangle. Spread each rectangle with half of the softened butter. Fold each rectangle as above; cut each into ten 1-inch strips. Continue as above.

*Note: The Test Kitchen recommends 1 egg and ¹/₄ teaspoon salt for either size recipe.

Nutrition Facts per roll: 225 cal., 8 g total fat (5 g sat. fat), 54 mg chol., 137 mg sodium, 31 g carbo., 6 g pro.

Rich and buttery, brioche traditionally are shaped with elegant topknots.

Brioche

1½-POUND	INGREDIENTS
3	eggs
⅓ cup	milk
¼ cup	margarine or butter, cut up
3⅓ cups	bread flour
3 tablespoons	sugar
¾ teaspoon	salt
1 teaspoon	active dry yeast
	or bread machine yeast
1	slightly beaten egg
1 tablespoon	sugar

PREP:
35 minutes

RISE:
40 minutes

BAKE:
12 minutes

MAKES:
1½-pound recipe
(18 rolls)

1 Add the first 7 ingredients to the machine according to the manufacturer's directions. Select the dough cycle. When cycle is complete, remove dough. Punch down. Cover and let rest for 10 minutes. Grease eighteen 2½-inch muffin pans or 3-inch fluted individual brioche pans; set aside.

2 Divide the dough into 4 portions; set 1 portion aside. Divide each of the remaining 3 portions into 6 pieces (18 pieces total). Shape each piece into a ball, tucking edges under to make a smooth top. Place in the prepared pans.

3 Divide the reserved portion of dough into 18 pieces; shape into balls. Using a floured finger, make an indentation in each large ball. Press a small bowl into each indentation. Cover and let rise in a warm place about 40 minutes or until nearly double.

4 In a small bowl combine the beaten egg and the 1 tablespoon sugar. Brush some of the egg mixture over rolls. Bake in a 375°F oven for 12 to 15 minutes or until golden brown, brushing again with egg mixture after 7 minutes. Remove from pans; cool slightly on wire racks. Serve warm or cool.

Nutrition Facts per roll: 227 cal., 8 g total fat (2 g sat. fat), 81 mg chol., 212 mg sodium, 33 g carbo., 8 g pro.

Sour cream lends extra richness to these twice-twisted golden strips that have luscious lemon flavor both in the dough and in the glaze.

Lemon Twists

PREP: 35 minutes	1½-POUND	INGREDIENTS	2-POUND
	²/₃ cup	milk	³/₄ cup
RISE: 20 minutes	¼ cup	dairy sour cream	½ cup
	1	egg*	1
BAKE: 12 minutes	2 tablespoons	margarine or butter, cut up	3 tablespoons
	3 cups	bread flour	4 cups
MAKES: 1½-pound recipe (24 rolls) OR 2-pound recipe (32 rolls)	1 tablespoon	sugar	4 teaspoons
	³/₄ teaspoon	salt	1 teaspoon
	1¼ teaspoons	active dry yeast	1½ teaspoons
		or bread machine yeast	
	½ cup	finely chopped walnuts	²/₃ cup
	¹/₃ cup	sugar	½ cup
	3 tablespoons	margarine or butter, melted	¼ cup
	2 teaspoons	finely shredded lemon peel	1 tablespoon
	1 recipe	Lemon Glaze	1 recipe

① Select the recipe size. Add the first 8 ingredients to the machine according to the manufacturer's directions. Select the dough cycle. When cycle is complete, remove dough. Punch down. Cover and let rest for 10 minutes. Meanwhile, for filling, in a small bowl combine walnuts, the ⅓ or ½ cup sugar, melted margarine, and lemon peel. Line baking sheets with parchment paper or foil and grease paper or foil; set aside.

② *For the 1½-pound recipe:* On a lightly floured surface, roll the dough into a 16×12-inch rectangle. Spread with filling. Cut in half crosswise to make two 12×8-inch rectangles. Brush edges with water. Fold each rectangle in half lengthwise; seal edges. Cut each crosswise into twelve 4×1-inch strips. Twist each strip twice. Place on prepared baking sheets, pressing ends down. Cover and let rise in a warm place for 20 to 30 minutes or until nearly double.

③ Bake in a 375°F oven for 12 to 15 minutes or until golden brown. Remove from baking sheets; cool slightly on wire racks. Drizzle with Lemon Glaze. Serve warm or cool.

For the 2-pound recipe: Prepare as above, except roll the dough into a 16-inch square. Fill and cut into two 16×8-inch rectangles. Fold each rectangle in half lengthwise; cut each crosswise into sixteen 4×1-inch strips. Continue as above.

Lemon Glaze: In a small bowl stir together 1 cup sifted powdered sugar and 1 teaspoon lemon juice. Stir in enough milk (2 to 4 teaspoons) to make a glaze of drizzling consistency.

***Note:** The Test Kitchen recommends 1 egg for either size recipe.

Nutrition Facts per roll: 141 cal., 5 g total fat (1 g sat. fat), 10 mg chol., 103 mg sodium, 21 g carbo., 3 g pro.

The secret to the awesome flavor and texture of these pecan-filled spirals is the whipping cream that's poured over the rolls before they're baked.

Creamy Caramel Rolls

1½-POUND	INGREDIENTS
1 cup	milk
1	egg
2 tablespoons	margarine or butter, cut up
3¾ cups	bread flour
⅓ cup	granulated sugar
1½ teaspoons	finely shredded orange peel
	(optional)
¾ teaspoon	salt
1 teaspoon	active dry yeast
	or bread machine yeast
⅔ cup	packed brown sugar
⅓ cup	finely chopped pecans
⅓ cup	margarine or butter, softened
3 tablespoons	light-colored corn syrup
¾ cup	whipping cream

PREP:
35 minutes

RISE:
30 minutes

BAKE:
35 minutes

MAKES:
1½-pound recipe
(24 rolls)

1 Add the first 8 ingredients to the machine according to the manufacturer's directions. Select the dough cycle. When cycle is complete, remove dough. Punch down. Cover and let rest for 10 minutes.

2 Meanwhile, for filling, in a small bowl stir together brown sugar, pecans, softened margarine, and corn syrup. Grease a 13×9×2-inch baking pan; set aside.

3 Divide the dough in half. On a lightly floured surface, roll each portion into a 12-inch square. Spread each square with half of the filling to within ½ inch of the edges. Roll up into a spiral; seal edge. Cut each into twelve 1-inch slices. Place rolls, cut sides down, in the prepared baking pan.

4 Cover and let rise in a warm place about 30 minutes or until nearly double. Pour the whipping cream over rolls. Bake in a 350°F oven about 35 minutes or until golden brown. Cool in pan on a wire rack for 5 minutes. Invert onto a serving plate. Serve warm.

Nutrition Facts per roll: 294 cal., 12 g total fat (3 g sat. fat), 35 mg chol., 186 mg sodium, 42 g carbo., 6 g pro.

If there are coconut lovers in your crowd, surprise them with these buttery crescents. Toasting the coconut helps enrich its tropical nutty flavor.

Coconut-Filled Sweet Rolls

PREP:	1½-POUND	INGREDIENTS	2-POUND
25 minutes	¾ cup	milk	1 cup
RISE:	1	egg*	1
30 minutes	3 tablespoons	margarine or butter, cut up	¼ cup
BAKE:	1 tablespoon	water*	1 tablespoon
20 minutes	3 cups	bread flour	4 cups
	¼ cup	sugar	⅓ cup
MAKES:	¾ teaspoon	salt	1 teaspoon
1½-pound recipe (12 rolls)	1¼ teaspoons	active dry yeast	1½ teaspoons
OR		or bread machine yeast	
2-pound recipe (16 rolls)	¼ cup	sugar	⅓ cup
	2 tablespoons	margarine or butter, melted	3 tablespoons
	⅔ cup	coconut, toasted	¾ cup
	1 recipe	Powdered Sugar Glaze	1 recipe

1 Select the recipe size. Add the first 8 ingredients to the machine according to the manufacturer's directions. Select the dough cycle. When cycle is complete, remove dough. Punch down. Cover and let rest for 10 minutes. Meanwhile, for filling, in a small bowl stir together ¼ or ⅓ cup sugar and the melted margarine.

2 *For the 1½-pound recipe:* Grease a 13×9×2-inch baking pan; set aside. On a lightly floured surface, roll the dough into a 12-inch circle. Spread with the filling and sprinkle with coconut. Cut the circle into 12 wedges. Starting at the wide end of each wedge, loosely roll toward the point. Place rolls points down in the prepared baking pan.

3 Cover and let rise in a warm place about 30 minutes or until nearly double. Bake in a 350°F oven for 20 to 25 minutes or until golden brown. Cool in pan on a wire rack for 2 minutes. Invert onto wire rack; cool slightly. Invert again onto a serving plate. Drizzle with Powdered Sugar Glaze. Sprinkle with additional coconut. Serve warm.

For the 2-pound recipe: Prepare as above, except divide the dough in half and roll each portion into a 10-inch circle. Spread each circle with half of the filling and sprinkle each with half of the coconut. Cut each circle into 8 wedges. Roll up wedges; place in a greased 15×10×1-inch baking pan. Continue as above.

Powdered Sugar Glaze: Stir together 1 cup sifted powdered sugar and 1 teaspoon vanilla. Stir in enough milk (3 to 4 teaspoons) to make a glaze of drizzling consistency.

Note: The Test Kitchen recommends 1 egg and 1 tablespoon water for either size recipe.

Nutrition Facts per roll: 268 cal., 8 g total fat (3 g sat. fat), 19 mg chol., 204 mg sodium, 45 g carbo., 6 g pro.

Bake a batch of these incredible sticky buns and you'll have everyone flocking to the kitchen. But shoo them away until you've had time to add the maple icing. It's worth the wait.

Mini Maple Buns

1½-POUND	INGREDIENTS
⅔ cup	milk
⅓ cup	maple-flavored syrup
⅓ cup	margarine or butter, cut up
1	egg
3 cups	bread flour
¾ teaspoon	salt
1¼ teaspoons	active dry yeast
	or bread machine yeast
½ cup	finely chopped pecans
¼ cup	packed brown sugar
3 tablespoons	margarine or butter, softened
1 tablespoon	all-purpose flour or bread flour
2 teaspoons	ground cinnamon
3 tablespoons	butter
1½ cups	sifted powdered sugar
3 tablespoons	maple-flavored syrup
2 to 3 teaspoons	milk

PREP:
30 minutes

RISE:
25 minutes

BAKE:
12 minutes

MAKES:
1½-pound recipe
(32 buns)

1 Add the first 8 ingredients to the machine according to the manufacturer's directions. Select the dough cycle. When cycle is complete, remove dough. Punch down. Cover and let rest for 10 minutes. Meanwhile, for filling, in a small bowl stir together brown sugar, softened margarine, all-purpose flour, and cinnamon. Grease large baking sheets; set aside.

2 On a lightly floured surface, roll the dough into a 14×12-inch rectangle. Spread with the filling to within ¼ inch of the edges. Cut in half crosswise to make two 12×7-inch rectangles. Starting from a long side, roll up each rectangle into a spiral; seal edge. Cut each into 16 slices. Place rolls cut sides down 1 inch apart on the prepared baking sheets. Cover and let rise in a warm place about 25 minutes or until nearly double. Brush rolls with a little additional milk. Bake in a 375°F oven for 12 to 15 minutes or until golden brown.

3 For icing, in a small saucepan heat the 3 tablespoons butter over medium-low heat for 7 to 10 minutes or until light brown. Remove from heat. Stir in powdered sugar and the 3 tablespoons maple syrup. Stir in enough of the 2 to 3 teaspoons milk to make an icing of drizzling consistency.

4 Remove buns from baking sheets; cool slightly on wire racks. Drizzle with icing. Serve warm.

Nutrition Facts per bun: 137 cal., 6 g total fat (1 g sat. fat), 10 mg chol., 102 mg sodium, 20 g carbo., 2 g pro.

These rolls are a little bit sweet, a little bit savory—and a hundred percent delicious.
Try them with main-dish salads for the perfect ladies' luncheon treat.

Spiral Cheese Rolls

PREP:	1½-POUND	I N G R E D I E N T S
30 minutes	⅔ cup	milk
RISE:	1 (8-ounce) tub	honey-nut cream cheese
30 minutes	1	egg
BAKE:	2 tablespoons	water
12 minutes	3 cups	bread flour
	¾ teaspoon	salt
MAKES:	½ teaspoon	dried thyme, crushed
1½-pound recipe	1¼ teaspoons	active dry yeast
(24 rolls)		or bread machine yeast
	1 recipe	Powdered Sugar Icing

1 Add the milk, ¼ cup of the cream cheese, and the remaining ingredients, except the Powdered Sugar Icing, to the machine according to the manufacturer's directions. Select the dough cycle. When cycle is complete, remove dough. Punch down. Cover and let rest for 10 minutes. Grease twenty-four 2½-inch muffin cups; set aside.

2 Divide the dough in half. On a lightly floured surface, roll each portion into a 12×8-inch rectangle. Spread each rectangle with half of the remaining cream cheese. Starting from a long side, roll up into a spiral; seal edge. Cut each into twelve 1-inch slices. Place rolls, cut sides down, in the prepared muffin cups. Cover and let rise in a warm place about 30 minutes or until nearly double.

3 Bake in a 375°F oven for 12 to 15 minutes or until golden brown. Remove from muffin pans; cool slightly on wire racks. Drizzle with Powdered Sugar Icing. Serve warm.

Powdered Sugar Icing: In a small bowl stir together 1 cup sifted powdered sugar and ¼ teaspoon vanilla. Stir in enough milk (1 to 2 tablespoons) to make an icing of drizzling consistency.

Nutrition Facts per roll: 116 cal., 3 g total fat (2 g sat. fat), 18 mg chol., 109 mg sodium, 18 g carbo., 3 g pro.

In Eastern Europe, these tender "pillows" filled with poppy seeds and raisins symbolize good luck and prosperity.

Poppy Seed Kolacky

1½-POUND	INGREDIENTS	2-POUND
½ cup	milk	¾ cup
2	eggs*	2
¼ cup	margarine or butter, cut up	⅓ cup
3 cups	bread flour	4 cups
⅓ cup	sugar	½ cup
¾ teaspoon	salt	1 teaspoon
¾ teaspoon	finely shredded lemon peel	1 teaspoon
1 teaspoon	active dry yeast	1¼ teaspoons
	or bread machine yeast	
1 recipe	Poppy Seed Filling	1 recipe

PREP:
30 minutes

RISE:
45 minutes

BAKE:
10 minutes

MAKES:
1½-pound recipe
(12 rolls)
OR
2-pound recipe
(18 rolls)

1 Select the recipe size. Add the ingredients, except the Poppy Seed Filling, to the machine according to the manufacturer's directions. Select the dough cycle. When cycle is complete, remove dough. Punch down. Cover and let rest for 10 minutes. Grease baking sheets; set aside.

2 Divide the 1½-pound dough into 12 portions (divide the 2-pound dough into 18 portions). Shape each portion into a ball, tucking edges under to make a smooth top. On a lightly floured surface, roll each ball of dough into a 3½-inch circle. Place circles 3 inches apart on the prepared baking sheets. Cover and let rise in a warm place for 45 to 60 minutes or until nearly double.

3 Using a floured thumb, make a large indentation in the center of each circle. Spoon the Poppy Seed Filling into indentations. Bake in a 375°F oven for 10 to 12 minutes or until golden brown. Remove from baking sheets; cool slightly on wire racks. Serve warm or cool.

Poppy Seed Filling: In a small bowl combine ¾ cup golden or dark raisins and enough boiling water to cover. Let stand for 10 minutes; drain well. In a blender container or food processor bowl combine raisins, ¼ cup poppy seeds, ¼ cup honey, 1 tablespoon margarine or butter, and ⅛ teaspoon ground allspice. Cover and blend or process until nearly smooth. Transfer to a small saucepan. Bring to boiling; reduce heat. Simmer, uncovered, for 2 to 3 minutes or until slightly thickened, stirring frequently. Cool.

*Note: The Test Kitchen recommends 2 eggs for either size recipe.

Nutrition Facts per roll: 274 cal., 8 g total fat (2 g sat. fat), 36 mg chol., 207 mg sodium, 46 g carbo., 7 g pro.

Marzipan is a confection made from almond paste, sugar, and, often egg whites. In this can't-miss recipe, it's combined with cocoa powder and used to fill these mouthwatering pinwheels.

Chocolate Marzipan Swirls

PREP:	1½-POUND	INGREDIENTS	2-POUND
30 minutes	2	eggs	3
RISE:	⅓ cup	milk	½ cup
45 minutes	¼ cup	water	⅓ cup
BAKE:	¼ cup	margarine or butter, cut up	⅓ cup
20 minutes	3 cups	bread flour	4 cups
MAKES:	3 tablespoons	sugar	¼ cup
1½-pound recipe (16 rolls)	¾ teaspoon	salt	1 teaspoon
OR	1½ teaspoons	active dry yeast or bread machine yeast	2 teaspoons
2-pound recipe (24 rolls)	1 recipe	Chocolate-Almond Filling	1 recipe
	1 recipe	Powdered Sugar Glaze	1 recipe
	¼ cup	sliced almonds, toasted*	¼ cup

❶ Select the recipe size. Add the first 8 ingredients to the machine according to the manufacturer's directions. Select the dough cycle. When cycle is complete, remove dough. Punch down. Cover and let rest for 10 minutes.

❷ *For the 1½-pound recipe:* Grease a 13×9×2-inch baking pan; set aside. On a lightly floured surface, roll the dough into a 16×12-inch rectangle. Spread with the Chocolate-Almond Filling. Starting from a long side, roll up into a spiral; seal edge. Cut into sixteen 1-inch slices. Place rolls, cut sides down, in the prepared baking pan. Cover and let rise in a warm place about 45 minutes or until nearly double.

❸ Bake in a 375°F oven about 20 minutes or until golden brown. Cool in pan on a wire rack for 5 minutes. Invert onto wire rack. Drizzle with Powdered Sugar Glaze and sprinkle with almonds. Serve warm.

For the 2-pound recipe: Prepare as above, except divide dough in half. Roll each portion into a 12×8-inch rectangle. Spread each rectangle with half of the filling; roll up. Cut each into twelve 1-inch slices; place in a greased 15×10×1-inch baking pan. Continue as above.

Chocolate-Almond Filling: In a medium mixing bowl beat one 8-ounce can almond paste, crumbled; ¼ cup sugar; 1 egg white; 2 tablespoons unsweetened cocoa powder; and 2 tablespoons milk with an electric mixer until nearly smooth.

Powdered Sugar Glaze: Stir together 1½ cups sifted powdered sugar and 1 teaspoon vanilla. Stir in enough milk (1 to 2 tablespoons) to make a glaze of drizzling consistency.

*Note: The Test Kitchen recommends ¼ cup almonds for either size recipe.

Nutrition Facts per roll: 270 cal., 9 g total fat (1 g sat. fat), 27 mg chol., 151 mg sodium, 41 g carbo., 7 g pro.

A small amount of honey mustard is added to the dough of these attractive spirals. Their flavor makes them ideal for serving with a baked ham dinner.

Honey Mustard Spirals

1½-POUND	INGREDIENTS	2-POUND
¾ cup	milk	1 cup
¼ cup	honey mustard	⅓ cup
2 tablespoons	margarine or butter, cut up	3 tablespoons
1 tablespoon	water	2 tablespoons
3 cups	bread flour	4 cups
1 tablespoon	brown sugar	4 teaspoons
½ teaspoon	salt	¾ teaspoon
⅛ teaspoon	black pepper	¼ teaspoon
1 teaspoon	active dry yeast	1¼ teaspoons
	or bread machine yeast	
1	slightly beaten egg white	1
1 tablespoon	honey mustard	1 tablespoon

PREP:
30 minutes

RISE:
30 minutes

BAKE:
10 minutes

MAKES:
1½-pound recipe
(24 rolls)
OR
2-pound recipe
(32 rolls)

1 Select the recipe size. Add the first 9 ingredients to the machine according to the manufacturer's directions. Select the dough cycle. When cycle is complete, remove dough. Punch down. Cover and let rest for 10 minutes. Grease baking sheets; set aside.

2 Divide the 1½-pound dough in half. On a lightly floured surface, roll each portion into a 12×6-inch rectangle. Cut each rectangle into twelve 12×½-inch strips. (Divide the 2-pound dough in half. Roll each portion into a 12×8-inch rectangle; cut each into sixteen 12×½-inch strips.) Coil each strip into a spiral.

3 Place rolls 2 inches apart on the prepared baking sheets. Cover and let rise in a warm place about 30 minutes or until nearly double. In a small bowl combine egg white and the 1 tablespoon honey mustard; brush over rolls.

4 Bake in a 375°F oven for 10 to 12 minutes or until golden brown. Remove from baking sheets; cool slightly on wire racks. Serve warm or cool.

Nutrition Facts per roll: 83 cal., 1 g total fat (0 g sat. fat), 1 mg chol., 65 mg sodium, 15 g carbo., 3 g pro.

Kids will enjoy helping make these twists. The combination of peanut butter, honey, and semisweet chocolate pieces makes for a special morning or afternoon treat.

Chocolate-Peanut Butter Twists

PREP:	$1^1/_2$-POUND	INGREDIENTS	2-POUND
30 minutes	$^1/_2$ cup	milk	$^2/_3$ cup
RISE:	$^1/_4$ cup	water	$^1/_3$ cup
30 minutes	1	egg*	1
BAKE:	3 tablespoons	margarine or butter, cut up	$^1/_4$ cup
10 minutes	3 cups	bread flour	4 cups
MAKES:	2 tablespoons	sugar	3 tablespoons
$1^1/_2$-pound recipe	$^3/_4$ teaspoon	salt	1 teaspoon
(18 rolls)	$1^1/_4$ teaspoons	active dry yeast	$1^1/_2$ teaspoons
OR		or bread machine yeast	
2-pound recipe	$^1/_3$ cup	creamy peanut butter	$^1/_2$ cup
(24 rolls)	1 tablespoon	honey	2 tablespoons
	$^1/_3$ cup	miniature semisweet chocolate pieces	$^1/_2$ cup

1 Select the recipe size. Add the first 8 ingredients to the machine according to the manufacturer's directions. Select the dough cycle. When cycle is complete, remove dough. Punch down. Cover and let rest for 10 minutes.

2 Meanwhile, for filling, in a small bowl combine the peanut butter and honey. Grease baking sheets; set aside.

3 *For the 1½-pound recipe:* On a lightly floured surface, roll the dough into an 18×12-inch rectangle. Spread with the filling to within ½ inch of the edges. Sprinkle with chocolate pieces, pressing lightly into dough. Starting from a long side, fold one-third of the dough over center third. Fold the remaining third of dough over center third, forming 3 equal layers. Moisten and seal edges. Cut crosswise into eighteen 4×1-inch strips. Twist each strip twice.

4 Place strips, 2 inches apart, on the prepared baking sheets, pressing ends down. Cover and let rise in a warm place about 30 minutes or until nearly double.

5 Bake in a 350°F oven for 10 to 12 minutes or until golden brown. Remove from baking sheets; cool slightly on wire racks. Serve warm or cool.

For the 2-pound recipe: Prepare as above, except roll dough into a 24×12-inch rectangle; fill, fold, and cut dough crosswise into twenty-four 4×1-inch strips. Continue as above.

*Note: The Test Kitchen recommends 1 egg for either size recipe.

Nutrition Facts per roll: 159 cal., 6 g total fat (1 g sat. fat), 12 mg chol., 141 mg sodium, 22 g carbo., 5 g pro.

Express the bounty of the season with petite bread cornucopias. One at each place setting, filled with a flavored butter (pages 263–265), and your guests will be charmed.

Cornucopia Rolls

1½-POUND	INGREDIENTS	2-POUND
1 cup	water	1⅓ cups
2 tablespoons	milk	3 tablespoons
2 tablespoons	olive oil or cooking oil	3 tablespoons
2½ cups	bread flour	3⅓ cups
½ cup	cornmeal	⅔ cup
½ cup	grated Parmesan cheese	⅔ cup
½ teaspoon	salt	¾ teaspoon
1 teaspoon	active dry yeast	1¼ teaspoons
	or bread machine yeast	
1	slightly beaten egg white	1
1 tablespoon	water	1 tablespoon

PREP:
35 minutes

RISE:
20 minutes

BAKE:
15 minutes

MAKES:
1½-pound recipe
(18 rolls)
OR
2-pound recipe
(24 rolls)

1 Select the recipe size. Add the first 8 ingredients to the machine according to the manufacturer's directions. Select the dough cycle. When cycle is complete, remove dough. Punch down. Cover and let rest for 10 minutes. Grease large baking sheets; set aside.

2 Meanwhile, cut 18 (or 24 for 2-pound) 9-inch squares from heavy foil. Fold each square in half diagonally to form a triangle. Hold triangle with long side at bottom. Roll a lower corner over to meet top point, forming a cone. Bring other lower corner around front of cone.

3 Divide the 1½-pound dough into 18 portions (divide the 2-pound dough into 24 portions). On a lightly floured surface, roll each portion into a 16-inch rope. Wrap each rope around a foil cone, starting at the point and coiling dough around the cone to completely cover foil. Place on the prepared baking sheets.

4 In a small bowl combine egg white and the 1 tablespoon water; brush over rolls. Cover and let rise in a warm place about 20 minutes or until nearly double.

5 Bake in a 350°F oven for 15 to 20 minutes or until golden brown. Remove foil cones; cool rolls slightly on wire racks. Serve warm or cool.

Nutrition Facts per roll: 111 cal., 3 g total fat (1 g sat. fat), 2 mg chol., 116 mg sodium, 17 g carbo., 4 g pro.

For pizza to rival that of the best pizzeria, pile this freshly made crust with your favorite sauce and toppings.

Pizza Dough

PREP:
15 minutes

MAKES:
1½-pound recipe
(6 servings)
OR
2-pound recipe
(9 servings)

1½-POUND	INGREDIENTS	2-POUND
1 cup	water	1⅓ cups
4 teaspoons	olive oil or cooking oil	2 tablespoons
3 cups	bread flour	4 cups
¾ teaspoon	salt	1 teaspoon
1 teaspoon	active dry yeast	1¼ teaspoons
	or bread machine yeast	

1 Select the recipe size. Add the ingredients to the machine according to the manufacturer's directions. Select the dough cycle. When cycle is complete, remove dough. Punch down. Cover and let rest for 10 minutes. Use to make thin-crust or thick-crust pizzas.

For thin-crust pizzas using the 1½-pound dough: Grease two 11- or 12-inch pizza pans or large baking sheets and, if desired, sprinkle with yellow cornmeal; set aside. Divide the dough in half. On a lightly floured surface, roll each portion into a 12- to 13-inch circle. Transfer to the prepared pans, building up edges slightly. Prick crusts with a fork. *Do not let rise.* Bake in a 425°F oven for 10 to 12 minutes or until light brown. Add desired toppings. Bake for 10 to 15 minutes more or until edges of crust are golden brown and toppings are bubbly. Makes two 11- or 12-inch pizzas.

For thin-crust pizzas using the 2-pound dough: Prepare as above for thin-crust pizzas, except use 2 greased 13- or 14-inch pizza pans or large baking sheets. Roll each portion of dough into a 14- to 15-inch circle. Continue as above. Makes two 13- or 14-inch pizzas.

For thick-crust pizza using the 1½-pound dough: Grease a 13- or 14-inch pizza pan and, if desired, sprinkle with yellow cornmeal. Using greased fingers, press dough into the prepared pan, building up the edges. Cover and let rise in a warm place for 30 to 45 minutes or until nearly double. Bake in a 375°F oven for 20 to 25 minutes or until light brown. Add desired toppings. Bake for 15 to 20 minutes more or until toppings are bubbly. Makes one 13- or 14-inch pizza.

For thick-crust pizzas using the 2-pound dough: Prepare as above for thick-crust pizza, except use 2 greased 13×9×2-inch baking pans. Divide the dough in half. Press each portion into a prepared pan, building up the edges. Continue as above. Makes two 13×9-inch pizzas.

Nutrition Facts per serving (without toppings): 276 cal., 4 g total fat (1 g sat. fat), 0 mg chol., 269 mg sodium, 50 g carbo., 8 g pro.

While traditional Italian flavors taste great on this robust crust, it's also terrific topped with Mexican toppings. Try it with refried beans, salsa, sweet pepper, and co-jack or Colby cheese.

Cornmeal-Parmesan Pizza Dough

1½-POUND	INGREDIENTS	2-POUND
1 cup	water	1⅓ cups
2 tablespoons	olive oil or cooking oil	3 tablespoons
2½ cups	bread flour	3⅓ cups
½ cup	cornmeal	⅔ cup
½ cup	grated Parmesan cheese	⅔ cup
¾ teaspoon	salt	1 teaspoon
1 teaspoon	active dry yeast	1¼ teaspoons
	or bread machine yeast	

PREP:
20 minutes

MAKES:
1½-pound recipe
(6 servings)
OR
2-pound recipe
(9 servings)

1 Select the recipe size. Add the ingredients to the machine according to the manufacturer's directions. Select the dough cycle. When cycle is complete, remove dough. Punch down. Cover and let rest for 10 minutes. Use to make thin-crust or thick-crust pizzas.

For thin-crust pizzas using the 1½-pound dough: Grease two 11- or 12-inch pizza pans or large baking sheets and, if desired, sprinkle with yellow cornmeal; set aside. Divide the dough in half. On a lightly floured surface, roll each portion into a 12- to 13-inch circle. Transfer to the prepared pans, building up edges slightly. Prick crusts with a fork. *Do not let rise.* Bake in a 425°F oven for 10 to 12 minutes or until light brown. Add desired toppings. Bake for 10 to 15 minutes more or until edges of crust are golden brown and toppings are bubbly. Makes two 11- or 12-inch pizzas.

For thin-crust pizzas using the 2-pound dough: Prepare as above for thin-crust pizzas, except use 2 greased 13- or 14-inch pizza pans or large baking sheets. Roll each portion of dough into a 14- to 15-inch circle. Continue as above. Makes two 13- or 14-inch pizzas.

For thick-crust pizza using the 1½-pound dough: Grease a 13- or 14-inch pizza pan and, if desired, sprinkle with yellow cornmeal. Using greased fingers, press dough into the prepared pan, building up the edges. Cover and let rise in a warm place for 30 to 45 minutes or until nearly double. Bake in a 375°F oven for 20 to 25 minutes or until light brown. Add desired toppings. Bake for 15 to 20 minutes more or until toppings are bubbly. Makes one 13- or 14-inch pizza.

For thick-crust pizzas using the 2-pound dough: Prepare as above for thick-crust pizza, except use 2 greased 13×9×2-inch baking pans. Divide the dough in half. Press each portion into a prepared pan, building up the edges. Continue as above. Makes two 13×9-inch pizzas.

Nutrition Facts per serving (without toppings): 328 cal., 8 g total fat (2 g sat. fat), 7 mg chol., 424 mg sodium, 51 g carbo., 12 g pro.

For a bistro-style change of pace, top this herb-seasoned crust with refrigerated Alfredo sauce instead of traditional pizza sauce and layer on cooked chicken, oil-packed dried tomatoes, and Monterey Jack cheese.

Herbed Whole Wheat Pizza Dough

PREP:
20 minutes

MAKES:
1½-pound recipe
(6 servings)
OR
2-pound recipe
(9 servings)

1½-POUND	INGREDIENTS	2-POUND
1 cup	water	1⅓ cups
2 tablespoons	olive oil or cooking oil	3 tablespoons
2 cups	bread flour	2⅔ cups
1 cup	whole wheat flour	1⅓ cups
2 teaspoons	dried basil, oregano, or Italian seasoning, crushed	1 tablespoon
¾ teaspoon	salt	1 teaspoon
¼ teaspoon	garlic powder	½ teaspoon
1 teaspoon	active dry yeast or bread machine yeast	1¼ teaspoons

1 Select the recipe size. Add the ingredients to the machine according to the manufacturer's directions. Select the dough cycle. When cycle is complete, remove dough. Punch down. Cover and let rest for 10 minutes. Use to make thin-crust or thick-crust pizzas.

For thin-crust pizzas using the 1½-pound dough: Grease two 11- or 12-inch pizza pans or large baking sheets and, if desired, sprinkle with yellow cornmeal; set aside. Divide the dough in half. On a lightly floured surface, roll each portion into a 12- to 13-inch circle. Transfer to the prepared pans, building up edges slightly. Prick crusts with a fork. *Do not let rise.* Bake in a 425°F oven for 10 to 12 minutes or until light brown. Add desired toppings. Bake for 10 to 15 minutes more or until edges of crust are golden brown and toppings are bubbly. Makes two 11- or 12-inch pizzas.

For thin-crust pizzas using the 2-pound dough: Prepare as above for thin-crust pizzas, except use 2 greased 13- or 14-inch pizza pans or large baking sheets. Roll each portion of dough into a 14- to 15-inch circle. Continue as above. Makes two 13- or 14-inch pizzas.

For thick-crust pizza using the 1½-pound dough: Grease a 13- or 14-inch pizza pan and, if desired, sprinkle with yellow cornmeal. Using greased fingers, press dough into the prepared pan, building up the edges. Cover and let rise in a warm place for 30 to 45 minutes or until nearly double. Bake in a 375°F oven for 20 to 25 minutes or until light brown. Add desired toppings. Bake for 15 to 20 minutes more or until toppings are bubbly. Makes one 13- or 14-inch pizza.

For thick-crust pizzas using the 2-pound dough: Prepare as above for thick-crust pizza, except use 2 greased 13×9×2-inch baking pans. Divide the dough in half. Press each portion into a prepared pan, building up the edges. Continue as above. Makes two 13×9-inch pizzas.

Nutrition Facts per serving (without toppings): 276 cal., 6 g total fat (1 g sat. fat), 0 mg chol., 269 mg sodium, 48 g carbo., 9 g pro.

A sausage, mushroom, and roasted pepper filling plus plenty of cheese make this family-pleasing recipe the ultimate in stuffed pizza.

Pizza Rustica

1½-POUND	INGREDIENTS
1 cup	water
4 teaspoons	olive oil or cooking oil
3 cups	bread flour
¾ teaspoon	salt
1½ teaspoons	active dry yeast
	or bread machine yeast
1 pound	bulk hot or mild Italian sausage
2 cups	sliced fresh mushrooms
1 cup	chopped onion
1 cup	pizza sauce
½ of a (7-ounce) jar	roasted red sweet peppers,
	drained and chopped
1 cup	shredded mozzarella cheese
1	slightly beaten egg
1 tablespoon	water
2 teaspoons	sesame seeds

PREP:
35 minutes

BAKE:
45 minutes

COOL:
20 minutes

MAKES:
1½-pound recipe
(8 servings)

1 Add the first 5 ingredients to the machine according to the manufacturer's directions. Select the dough cycle. When cycle is complete, remove dough. Punch down. Cover and let rest for 10 minutes. Meanwhile, for filling, in a large skillet cook sausage, mushrooms, and onion until sausage is brown and onion is tender. Drain off fat. Pat meat mixture with paper towels. Stir in pizza sauce and roasted peppers. Set aside.

2 Grease the bottom and sides of a 9×3-inch springform pan. Shape one-fourth of the dough into a small ball. Shape the remaining dough into a large ball. On a lightly floured surface, roll the large ball into a 16-inch circle. Fit dough into the bottom and up the sides of the prepared pan, allowing dough to extend slightly over edges. Sprinkle with half of the cheese; top with the filling. Sprinkle with the remaining cheese; press lightly into filling.

3 Roll the small ball of dough into a 9-inch circle; place on top of filling. In a small bowl combine egg and the 1 tablespoon water; brush some of the mixture over dough. Fold edges of bottom dough over top dough; press lightly to seal. Brush with the remaining egg mixture. Cut slits in dough for steam to escape. Sprinkle with sesame seeds.

4 Bake in a 350°F oven for 45 to 50 minutes or until golden brown. Cool in pan on a wire rack for 20 minutes. To serve, use a metal spatula to loosen the pizza from edges of pan; remove side of pan. Cut the pizza into wedges.

Nutrition Facts per serving: 420 cal., 18 g total fat (6 g sat. fat), 67 mg chol., 824 mg sodium, 44 g carbo., 20 g pro.

Stuffed with a colorful array of roasted vegetables, this pretty pizza makes an eye-catching—
and hearty—main course. Simply serve it with a tossed green salad, and you're set for supper.

Roasted Vegetable-Stuffed Pizza

	1½-POUND	INGREDIENTS
PREP: 40 minutes	1 cup	water
	4 teaspoons	olive oil
BAKE: 50 minutes	1½ cups	bread flour
	1½ cups	whole wheat flour
COOL: 20 minutes	1 teaspoon	salt
	1½ teaspoons	active dry yeast
MAKES: 1½-pound recipe (8 servings)		or bread machine yeast
	3 cups	fresh mushrooms, quartered
	2 medium	zucchini, halved lengthwise
		and sliced ½ inch thick
	2 medium	red sweet peppers, cut into 1-inch strips
	2 medium	yellow and/or green sweet peppers,
		cut into 1-inch strips
	4 cloves	garlic, quartered
	1 tablespoon	olive oil
	1 cup	pasta sauce
	1½ cups	shredded pizza cheese
	1 tablespoon	milk

1 Add first 6 ingredients to machine according to manufacturer's directions. Select dough cycle. When complete, remove dough. Punch down. Cover; let rest 10 minutes. Meanwhile, for filling, in a shallow roasting pan combine mushrooms, zucchini, sweet peppers, and garlic. Add the 1 tablespoon oil; toss. Bake in a 450°F oven about 20 minutes or until tender and brown on edges, stirring occasionally. Transfer to a large bowl. Stir in pasta sauce; set aside.

2 Grease bottom and sides of a 9-inch springform pan. Shape one-fourth of the dough into a small ball. Shape remaining dough into a large ball. On a lightly floured surface, roll large ball into a 16-inch circle. Fit into bottom and up sides of prepared pan, allowing dough to extend slightly over edges. Sprinkle with half of the cheese; top with filling. Sprinkle with remaining cheese; press lightly into filling. Roll small ball of dough into a 9-inch circle; place on filling. Brush dough with some of the milk. Fold edges of bottom dough over top dough; press lightly to seal. Brush with remaining milk. Cut slits in dough for steam to escape.

3 Bake in a 350°F oven for 50 to 60 minutes or until golden brown and edges sound hollow when lightly tapped. Cool in pan on a wire rack for 20 minutes. To serve, use a metal spatula to loosen pizza from edges of pan; remove side of pan. Cut pizza into wedges.

Nutrition Facts per serving: 326 cal., 12 g total fat (4 g sat. fat), 19 mg chol., 595 mg sodium, 44 g carbo., 14 g pro.

With its irresistible caramelized onions and subtle sprinkling of nuts, this sophisticated bread will offer that perfect "something extra" you're looking for to serve as part of an appetizer spread.

Onion and Walnut Focaccia

1½-POUND	INGREDIENTS
³/₄ cup	water
¹/₄ cup	cooking oil
3 cups	bread flour
³/₄ teaspoon	salt
1 teaspoon	active dry yeast
	or bread machine yeast
2 tablespoons	margarine or butter
4 medium	onions, halved lengthwise
	and thinly sliced (4 cups)
1½ teaspoons	sugar
¹/₃ cup	coarsely chopped walnuts
	or pine nuts

PREP:
25 minutes

RISE:
30 minutes

BAKE:
17 minutes

MAKES:
1½-pound recipe
(12 servings)

❶ Add the first 5 ingredients to the machine according to the manufacturer's directions. Select the dough cycle. When cycle is complete, remove dough. Punch down. Cover and let rest for 10 minutes.

❷ Grease an 11- or 12-inch pizza pan. Place the dough on the prepared pan. Using the palms of your hands, press the dough into an even round, just slightly smaller than the pan. Using your fingertips, poke the dough all over to dimple the surface. Cover and let rise in a warm place about 30 minutes or until nearly double.

❸ Meanwhile, for topping, in a large saucepan melt the margarine. Add onions. Cover and cook over medium-low heat about 15 minutes or until onions are tender and golden brown, stirring occasionally. Sprinkle with sugar. Cook, uncovered, for 10 to 15 minutes more or until browned, stirring occasionally.

❹ Bake the dough in a 425°F oven for 7 to 10 minutes or until light brown. Spoon the topping over dough; sprinkle with nuts. Bake for 10 minutes more. Remove from pan; cool slightly on a wire rack. Serve warm.

Nutrition Facts per serving: 223 cal., 9 g total fat (1 g sat. fat), 0 mg chol., 158 mg sodium, 30 g carbo., 5 g pro.

Though focaccia originally hails from Italy, the flatbread is fast becoming a stateside favorite. This version, topped with almonds and figs, pairs deliciously with Alfredo-style pasta dishes.

Rosemary-Fig Focaccia

PREP:
25 minutes

RISE:
30 minutes

BAKE:
20 minutes

MAKES:
1½-pound recipe
(12 servings)

1½-POUND	INGREDIENTS
³/₄ cup	water
¹/₄ cup	cooking oil
3 cups	bread flour
2 teaspoons	snipped fresh rosemary
	or
³/₄ teaspoon	dried rosemary, crushed
³/₄ teaspoon	salt
1 teaspoon	active dry yeast
	or bread machine yeast
¹/₃ cup	coarsely chopped almonds
¹/₄ cup	coarsely snipped dried figs
	Margarine or butter, melted
	(optional)

1 Add the first 8 ingredients to the machine according to the manufacturer's directions. Select the dough cycle. When cycle is complete, remove dough. Punch down. Cover and let rest for 10 minutes.

2 Grease an 11- or 12-inch pizza pan. Place the dough on the prepared pan. Using the palms of your hands, press the dough into an even round, just slightly smaller than the pan. Using your fingertips, poke the dough all over to dimple the surface.

3 Cover and let rise in a warm place about 30 minutes or until nearly double. Bake in a 400°F oven about 20 minutes or until edges are golden brown. Remove from pan; cool slightly on a wire rack. If desired, brush with melted margarine. Serve warm or cool.

Nutrition Facts per serving: 194 cal., 7 g total fat (1 g sat. fat), 0 mg chol., 137 mg sodium, 28 g carbo., 5 g pro.

Do the Dough Now—Bake it Later

If you choose, you can tailor recipes that use the dough cycle to fit your schedule. Simply prepare the dough as directed and store the dough in an airtight container in the refrigerator up to 24 hours. (The container must be at least twice the size of the dough. The dough could rise enough to burst out of a small container.) When you're ready to bake the bread, bring the dough to room temperature, then shape and bake as directed in the recipe.

Slightly sweet cooked onion and tangy goat cheese strike a perfect flavor balance on this delectable focaccia. It's great served with soups or salads or as a bread for sandwiches.

Goat Cheese and Onion Focaccia

1½-POUND	INGREDIENTS	2-POUND
1 cup	water	1¼ cups
2 tablespoons	olive oil or cooking oil	3 tablespoons
3 cups	bread flour	4 cups
1 tablespoon	snipped fresh basil	4 teaspoons
	or	
½ teaspoon	dried basil, crushed	¾ teaspoon
1 teaspoon	sugar	1½ teaspoons
¾ teaspoon	salt	1 teaspoon
1 teaspoon	active dry yeast	1¼ teaspoons
	or bread machine yeast	
2 medium	onions, sliced	2 large
1 tablespoon	snipped fresh rosemary	2 tablespoons
	or	
½ teaspoon	dried rosemary, crushed	1 teaspoon
1 tablespoon	olive oil or cooking oil*	1 tablespoon
4 ounces	goat cheese (chèvre), crumbled	6 ounces

PREP:
25 minutes

RISE:
30 minutes

BAKE:
18 minutes

MAKES:
1½-pound recipe
(12 servings)
OR
2-pound recipe
(16 servings)

1 Select the recipe size. Add the first 7 ingredients to the machine according to the manufacturer's directions. Select the dough cycle. When cycle is complete, remove dough. Punch down. Cover and let rest for 10 minutes.

2 Meanwhile, for filling, in a large skillet cook the onions and rosemary in the 1 tablespoon hot oil about 2 minutes or just until onions are tender. Cool slightly.

3 For the 1½-pound dough, grease two 11- or 12-inch pizza pans. (For the 2-pound dough, grease two 13- or 14-inch pizza pans.) Divide the dough in half. Place the dough on the prepared pans. Using the palms of your hands, press the dough into even rounds, just slightly smaller than the pans. Using your fingertips, poke the dough all over to dimple the surface. Spread with the filling.

4 Cover and let rise in a warm place about 30 minutes or until nearly double. Sprinkle with the goat cheese. Bake in a 400°F oven for 18 to 20 minutes or until edges are golden brown. Remove from pans; cool slightly on wire racks. Serve warm.

*Note: The Test Kitchen recommends 1 tablespoon oil for either size filling.

Nutrition Facts per serving: 191 cal., 7 g total fat (2 g sat. fat), 8 mg chol., 190 mg sodium, 26 g carbo., 6 g pro.

Not all olives are created equal. You can change the flavor of this pesto-accented flatbread by varying the type of olive you use. Black mission olives have a smooth, mellow flavor while Greek kalamata olives are rich and fruity, and French niçoise olives are more nutty.

Olive Focaccia

PREP:	1¹/₂-POUND	INGREDIENTS	2-POUND
25 minutes			
	³/₄ cup	water	1 cup
RISE:	¹/₄ cup	coarsely chopped, pitted	¹/₃ cup
30 minutes		ripe olives	
BAKE:	¹/₄ cup	olive oil or cooking oil	¹/₃ cup
25 minutes	3 cups	bread flour	4 cups
MAKES:	2 tablespoons	snipped fresh savory	3 tablespoons
1¹/₂-pound recipe (12 servings)		or	
OR	1¹/₂ teaspoons	dried savory, crushed	2 teaspoons
2-pound recipe (18 servings)	1 teaspoon	sugar	1¹/₂ teaspoons
	³/₄ teaspoon	salt	1 teaspoon
	1 teaspoon	active dry yeast	1¹/₄ teaspoons
		or bread machine yeast	
	¹/₄ to ¹/₃ cup	purchased pesto	¹/₃ to ¹/₂ cup

1 Select the recipe size. Add the first 8 ingredients to the machine according to the manufacturer's directions. Select the dough cycle. When cycle is complete, remove dough. Punch down. Cover and let rest for 10 minutes.

2 For the 1¹/₂-pound dough, grease an 11- or 12-inch pizza pan. (For the 2-pound dough, grease a 13- or 14-inch pizza pan.) Place the dough on the prepared pan. Using the palms of your hands, press the dough into an even round, just slightly smaller than the pan. Using your fingertips, poke the dough all over to dimple the surface. Spread with the pesto. Cover and let rise in a warm place about 30 minutes or until nearly double.

3 Bake in a 400°F oven for 25 to 30 minutes or until edges are golden brown. Remove from pan; cool slightly on a wire rack. Serve warm or cool.

Nutrition Facts per serving: 206 cal., 9 g total fat (1 g sat. fat), 1 mg chol., 186 mg sodium, 26 g carbo., 5 g pro.

If you're a fan of the fiery chile, this reved-up bread will suit you just fine. For the best combinations, team this robust loaf with plain roasted, broiled, or grilled meats, poultry, or fish.

Jalapeño-Cheddar Focaccia

1½-POUND	INGREDIENTS	2-POUND
¾ cup	milk	1 cup
2 tablespoons	olive oil or cooking oil	3 tablespoons
1 small	fresh jalapeño chile pepper, seeded and finely chopped	1 medium
3 cups	bread flour	4 cups
2 teaspoons	sugar	1 tablespoon
¾ teaspoon	salt	1 teaspoon
1 teaspoon	active dry yeast or bread machine yeast	1¼ teaspoons
½ cup	finely shredded cheddar cheese	⅔ cup

PREP:
25 minutes

RISE:
30 minutes

BAKE:
20 minutes

MAKES:
1½-pound recipe
(12 servings)
OR
2-pound recipe
(16 servings)

1 Select the recipe size. Add the first 7 ingredients to the machine according to the manufacturer's directions. Select the dough cycle. When cycle is complete, remove dough. Punch down. Cover and let rest for 10 minutes. Grease large baking sheets; set aside.

2 Divide the 1½-pound dough into thirds (divide the 2-pound dough into fourths). Place the dough on the prepared baking sheets. Using the palms of your hands, press each portion into an even round, about 7 inches in diameter. Using your fingertips, poke the dough all over to dimple the surface. Cover and let rise in a warm place about 30 minutes or until nearly double. Sprinkle with the cheddar cheese.

3 Bake in a 400°F oven about 20 minutes or until edges are golden brown. Remove from baking sheets; cool slightly on wire racks. Serve warm or cool.

Nutrition Facts per serving: 174 cal., 5 g total fat (2 g sat. fat), 6 mg chol., 171 mg sodium, 27 g carbo., 6 g pro.

Too Hot to Handle?

Because hot chile peppers, such as jalapeños, contain volatile oils that can burn your skin and eyes, avoid direct contact with chiles as much as possible. When working with chile peppers, wear plastic or rubber gloves. No gloves? Work with plastic bags over your hands. If your bare hands do touch the chile peppers, wash your hands well with soap and water.

Sweet and spicy, these tender rounds make tasty after-school snacks. Look for coarse or decorator's sugar where cake and cookie decorating supplies are sold.

Cinnamon-Sugar Rounds

	1½-POUND	I N G R E D I E N T S	2-POUND
PREP: 25 minutes	¾ cup	milk	1 cup
RISE: 30 minutes	¼ cup	margarine or butter, cut up	⅓ cup
	1	egg*	1
BAKE: 15 minutes	3 cups	bread flour	4 cups
	1 tablespoon	granulated sugar	4 teaspoons
	¾ teaspoon	salt	1 teaspoon
MAKES: 1½-pound recipe (12 servings) OR 2-pound recipe (16 servings)	1 teaspoon	active dry yeast	1¼ teaspoons
		or bread machine yeast	
	3 tablespoons	coarse sugar	¼ cup
	1 teaspoon	ground cinnamon	1¼ teaspoons
	1 tablespoon	margarine or butter, melted	4 teaspoons

1 Select the recipe size. Add the first 7 ingredients to the machine according to the manufacturer's directions. Select the dough cycle. When cycle is complete, remove dough. Punch down. Cover and let rest for 10 minutes. Grease large baking sheets; set aside.

2 Divide the 1½-pound dough into thirds (divide the 2-pound dough into fourths). Place the dough on the prepared baking sheets. Using the palms of your hands, press each portion into an even round, about 7 inches in diameter. Using your fingertips, poke the dough all over to dimple the surface. Cover and let rise in a warm place about 30 minutes or until nearly double.

3 In a small bowl stir together the coarse sugar and cinnamon. Brush the dough with melted margarine; sprinkle with sugar-cinnamon mixture. Bake in a 350°F oven for 15 to 20 minutes or until edges are golden brown. Remove from baking sheets; cool slightly on wire racks. Serve warm or cool.

*Note: The Test Kitchen recommends 1 egg for either size recipe.

Nutrition Facts per serving: 198 cal., 6 g total fat (1 g sat. fat), 19 mg chol., 203 mg sodium, 30 g carbo., 5 g pro.

Types of White Sugar

When a recipe calls for sugar, use white granulated sugar, sold in fine granulation. Coarse sugar, also called pearl or decorator's sugar, is a coarse granulation that adds glitter and sweetness to the tops of breads, cookies, and cakes. Superfine (also labeled ultrafine or caster sugar) is a finer grind that dissolves readily, which makes it the best choice for frostings, meringues, and beverages.

Here's one of the best ways we know of to take advantage of the bounty of summer's fresh herbs. Serve these crusty wedges alongside a caprese salad (that's slices of fresh mozzarella and tomatoes and basil leaves drizzled with olive oil) for a fresh and light summer lunch.

Garden Herb Flatbread

1½-POUND	INGREDIENTS
1 cup	milk
½ cup	sliced green onions
3 tablespoons	olive oil or cooking oil
¼ teaspoon	bottled minced garlic
3 cups	bread flour
1 tablespoon	sugar
2 teaspoons	snipped fresh oregano
	or
½ teaspoon	dried oregano, crushed
2 teaspoons	snipped fresh thyme
	or
½ teaspoon	dried thyme, crushed
2 teaspoons	snipped fresh sage
	or
½ teaspoon	dried sage, crushed
¾ teaspoon	salt
1 teaspoon	active dry yeast
	or bread machine yeast
2 tablespoons	olive oil or cooking oil
2 teaspoons	snipped fresh thyme
	or
½ teaspoon	dried thyme, crushed

PREP:
35 minutes

BAKE:
11 minutes

MAKES:
1½-pound recipe
(12 servings)

1 Add the first 11 ingredients to the machine according to the manufacturer's directions. Select the dough cycle. When cycle is complete, remove dough. Punch down. Cover and let rest for 10 minutes. Grease 2 baking sheets or 12-inch pizza pans; set aside.

2 Divide the dough in half. On a lightly floured surface, roll each portion into a 12-inch circle. Transfer to the prepared baking sheets. Brush the dough with the 2 tablespoons olive oil. Using a fork, prick the entire surface of each circle several times. Sprinkle with 2 teaspoons fresh or ½ teaspoon dried thyme. *Do not let rise.*

3 Bake in a 400°F oven for 11 to 13 minutes or until crisp and golden brown. Remove from baking sheets; cool slightly on wire racks. Serve warm or cool.

Nutrition Facts per serving: 191 cal., 7 g total fat (1 g sat. fat), 2 mg chol., 157 mg sodium, 27 g carbo., 5 g pro.

Delightfully different, this crisp and savory flatbread is wonderful for your appetizer platter.
Serve with thin slices of prosciutto, a selection of cheeses, and cut-up fresh fruit.

Onion-Mustard Flatbread

	1½-POUND	INGREDIENTS	2-POUND
PREP: 35 minutes	2 cups	finely chopped onions	2⅔ cups
	1 tablespoon	bottled minced garlic	4 teaspoons
BAKE: 11 minutes	2 tablespoons	olive oil or cooking oil*	2 tablespoons
	4 teaspoons	mustard seeds	2 tablespoons
MAKES: 1½-pound recipe (16 servings)	4 teaspoons	Dijon-style mustard	2 tablespoons
	1 teaspoon	dried thyme, crushed	1½ teaspoons
OR	1 cup	milk	1⅓ cups
2-pound recipe (24 servings)	3 tablespoons	olive oil or cooking oil	¼ cup
	3 cups	bread flour	4 cups
	1 tablespoon	sugar	4 teaspoons
	¾ teaspoon	salt	1 teaspoon
	1 teaspoon	active dry yeast	1¼ teaspoons
		or bread machine yeast	

1 Select the recipe size. In a large skillet cook the onions and garlic in the 2 tablespoons hot oil until tender. Stir in mustard seeds, Dijon mustard, and thyme. Cook and stir for 1 minute. Cool slightly.

2 Add ⅓ cup (or ½ cup for 2-pound) of the onion mixture and the remaining ingredients to the machine according to the manufacturer's directions. Select the dough cycle. When cycle is complete, remove dough. Punch down. Cover and let rest for 10 minutes. Grease 2 baking sheets or 12-inch pizza pans; set aside.

3 Divide the 1½-pound dough in half (divide the 2-pound dough into thirds). On a lightly floured surface, roll each portion into a 12-inch circle. Transfer to the prepared baking sheets. Using a fork, prick the entire surface of each circle several times. Spread with the remaining onion mixture. *Do not let rise.*

4 Bake in a 400°F oven for 11 to 13 minutes or until crisp and golden brown. Remove from baking sheets; cool slightly on wire racks. Serve warm or cool.

*Note: The Test Kitchen recommends 2 tablespoons oil for either size recipe when cooking onions and garlic.

Nutrition Facts per serving: 155 cal., 5 g total fat (1 g sat. fat), 1 mg chol., 140 mg sodium, 23 g carbo., 4 g pro.

Three types of flour plus a dynamite mix of caraway and anise seeds make this great-tasting bread stand out from the competition.

Multigrain Flatbread

1½-POUND	INGREDIENTS
1 cup	**buttermilk or sour milk***
¼ cup	water
2 tablespoons	**dark-colored corn syrup**
1½ cups	bread flour
¾ cup	**whole wheat flour**
¾ cup	rye flour
¾ teaspoon	**salt**
½ teaspoon	caraway seeds
¼ teaspoon	**anise seeds (optional)**
1 teaspoon	active dry yeast
	or bread machine yeast
	Milk or buttermilk

PREP:
25 minutes

BAKE:
11 minutes

MAKES:
1½-pound recipe
(16 servings)

1 Add the first 10 ingredients to the machine according to the manufacturer's directions. Select the dough cycle. When cycle is complete, remove dough. Punch down. Cover and let rest for 10 minutes. Grease 2 baking sheets or 12-inch pizza pans; set aside.

2 Divide the dough into fourths. Cover and refrigerate 2 of the portions. On a lightly floured surface, roll each of the remaining 2 portions into a 12-inch circle. Transfer to the prepared baking sheets. Using a fork, prick the entire surface of each circle several times. Brush with a little milk. *Do not let rise.*

3 Bake in a 400°F oven for 11 to 13 minutes or until crisp and golden brown. Remove from baking sheets; cool slightly on wire racks. Repeat with remaining dough. Serve warm or cool.

*Note: To make 1 cup sour milk, place 1 tablespoon lemon juice or vinegar in a 1-cup liquid measuring cup. Add enough milk to measure 1 cup liquid; stir. Let stand for 5 minutes before using.

Nutrition Facts per serving: 98 cal., 1 g total fat (0 g sat. fat), 1 mg chol., 119 mg sodium, 20 g carbo., 3 g pro.

This Middle Eastern bread bakes up flat and crispy with a pleasing golden color, making it the perfect choice to serve with any leafy salad.

Armenian Flatbread

PREP:
25 minutes

BAKE:
16 minutes

MAKES:
1½-pound recipe
(24 servings)

1½-POUND	INGREDIENTS
1 cup	milk
4 teaspoons	water
4 teaspoons	olive oil
3 cups	bread flour
1 tablespoon	sugar
¾ teaspoon	salt
1 teaspoon	active dry yeast
	or bread machine yeast
2 tablespoons	milk
1 tablespoon	sesame seeds

1 Add the first 7 ingredients to the machine according to the manufacturer's directions. Select the dough cycle. When cycle is complete, remove dough. Punch down. Cover and let rest for 10 minutes. Grease 3 baking sheets; set aside.

2 Divide the dough into thirds. On a lightly floured surface, roll each portion into a 12-inch circle. Transfer to the prepared baking sheets. Brush the dough with the 2 tablespoons milk. Using a fork, prick the entire surface of each circle several times. Sprinkle with the sesame seeds. *Do not let rise.*

3 Bake in a 350°F oven for 16 to 18 minutes or until crisp and golden brown. Remove from baking sheets; cool slightly on wire racks. Serve warm or cool.

Nutrition Facts per serving: 79 cal., 1 g total fat (0 g sat. fat), 1 mg chol., 80 mg sodium, 14 g carbo., 3 g pro.

This recipe captures that pleasingly tuggy texture aficionados seek in a breadstick. Vary the toppings as desired, and you can have a variety of breadsticks to please many tastes.

As-You-Wish Breadsticks

1½-POUND	INGREDIENTS
1 cup	milk
2 tablespoons	cooking oil
3 cups	bread flour
2 tablespoons	sugar
¾ teaspoon	salt
1 teaspoon	active dry yeast
	or bread machine yeast
1	slightly beaten egg white
1 tablespoon	water
	Sesame seeds, caraway seeds,
	coarse salt, or grated Romano cheese

PREP:
35 minutes

BAKE:
15 minutes

MAKES:
1½-pound recipe
(32 breadsticks)

1 Add the first 6 ingredients to the machine according to the manufacturer's directions. Select the dough cycle. When cycle is complete, remove dough. Punch down. Cover and let rest for 10 minutes. Grease baking sheets; set aside.

2 Divide the dough into 32 portions. On a lightly floured surface, roll each portion into an 8-inch rope. Place breadsticks on the prepared baking sheets. In a small bowl combine egg white and water; brush over breadsticks. Sprinkle with sesame seeds.

3 Bake in a 350°F oven for 15 to 20 minutes or until golden brown. Remove from baking sheets; cool slightly on wire racks. Serve warm or cool.

Nutrition Facts per breadstick: 66 cal., 2 g total fat (0 g sat. fat), 1 mg chol., 61 mg sodium, 11 g carbo., 2 g pro.

Warming Liquids

Should you bring liquids to room temperature before you add them to the bread machine? That depends on your machine. Some brands have a long standing time, which means that milk and other liquids can be used directly from the refrigerator. Other machines have a built-in sensor that will preheat the ingredients as needed. However, many machines specify bringing the liquids to room temperature before adding. Therefore, to decide whether to bring liquids to room temperature before using, follow the directions in your owner's manual. To bring refrigerated milk to room temperature quickly, pour 1 cup milk into a microwave-safe liquid measuring cup. Microwave on 100-percent power (high) for 30 to 45 seconds.

Here's a breadstick with a kick! Serve it with a steaming bowl of chili for a dynamite dinnertime duo.

Pepper-Cheese Breadsticks

PREP:
40 minutes

BAKE:
10 minutes

MAKES:
1½-pound recipe
(30 breadsticks)

1½-POUND	INGREDIENTS
1 cup	water
½ cup	shredded Monterey Jack cheese
	with jalapeño peppers
	or shredded Monterey Jack cheese
2 tablespoons	cooking oil
3 cups	bread flour
¼ cup	grated Parmesan cheese
1 teaspoon	dried Italian seasoning, crushed
¾ teaspoon	salt
½ teaspoon	cracked black pepper
1 teaspoon	active dry yeast
	or bread machine yeast
1	slightly beaten egg white
1 tablespoon	water
	Cracked black pepper, coarse salt,
	or grated Parmesan cheese

❶ Add the first 9 ingredients to the machine according to the manufacturer's directions. Select the dough cycle. When cycle is complete, remove dough. Punch down. Cover and let rest for 10 minutes. Grease baking sheets; set aside.

❷ Divide the dough into thirds. On a lightly floured surface, roll each portion into a 14×10-inch rectangle. Using a pizza cutter or sharp knife, cut the dough lengthwise into twenty 14×½-inch strips.

❸ For each breadstick, pick up 2 strips together and twist several times; press ends together. Place breadsticks, ½ inch apart, on the prepared baking sheets. In a small bowl combine egg white and the 1 tablespoon water; brush over breadsticks. Sprinkle with pepper.

❹ Bake in a 400°F oven for 10 to 12 minutes or until golden brown. Remove from baking sheets; cool slightly on wire racks. Serve warm or cool.

Nutrition Facts per breadstick: 69 cal., 2 g total fat (1 g sat. fat), 3 mg chol., 87 mg sodium, 10 g carbo., 3 g pro.

Italian seasoning lends a pleasant herb flavor to these breadsticks. Add a sprinkling of Parmesan cheese to each breadstick just before baking.

Parmesan-Herb Breadsticks

1½-POUND	INGREDIENTS	2-POUND
1 cup	water	1¼ cups
2 tablespoons	cooking oil or olive oil	3 tablespoons
2⅓ cups	bread flour	3 cups
⅔ cup	whole wheat flour	1 cup
⅓ cup	grated Parmesan cheese	½ cup
1 teaspoon	dried Italian seasoning, crushed	1¼ teaspoons
¾ teaspoon	salt	1 teaspoon
1 teaspoon	active dry yeast or bread machine yeast	1¼ teaspoons
1	slightly beaten egg white	1
1 tablespoon	water	1 tablespoon
1 tablespoon	grated Parmesan cheese	2 tablespoons

PREP:
30 minutes

RISE:
30 minutes

BAKE:
15 minutes

MAKES:
1½-pound recipe
(24 breadsticks)
OR
2-pound recipe
(32 breadsticks)

1 Select the recipe size. Add the first 8 ingredients to the machine according to the manufacturer's directions. Select the dough cycle. When cycle is complete, remove dough. Punch down. Cover and let rest for 10 minutes. Grease baking sheets; set aside.

2 Divide the 1½-pound dough into 24 portions (divide the 2-pound dough into 32 portions). On a lightly floured surface, roll each portion into an 8-inch rope. Place breadsticks, 2 inches apart, on the prepared baking sheets. Cover and let rise in a warm place about 30 minutes or until nearly double.

3 In a small bowl combine egg white and the 1 tablespoon water; brush over breadsticks. Sprinkle with the 1 or 2 tablespoons Parmesan cheese. Bake in a 350°F oven for 15 to 20 minutes or until golden brown. Remove from baking sheets; cool slightly on wire racks. Serve warm or cool.

Nutrition Facts per breadstick: 78 cal., 2 g total fat (1 g sat. fat), 1 mg chol., 100 mg sodium, 12 g carbo., 3 g pro.

Bagels originated from an Eastern European-Jewish baking tradition. Do you want to know the secret to their chewy texture and sheen? Boiling them in water before baking them.

Bagels

PREP: 25 minutes	1½-POUND	INGREDIENTS	2-POUND
	1 cup	water	1⅓ cups
RISE: 20 minutes	2 teaspoons	cooking oil	1 tablespoon
	3 cups	bread flour	4 cups
BROIL: 3 minutes	1 tablespoon	sugar	4 teaspoons
	¾ teaspoon	salt	1 teaspoon
COOK: 7 minutes per batch	1 teaspoon	active dry yeast	1¼ teaspoons
		or bread machine yeast	
BAKE: 25 minutes	6 cups	water	6 cups
	1 tablespoon	sugar	1 tablespoon
MAKES: 1½-pound recipe (9 bagels) OR 2-pound recipe (12 bagels)	1	slightly beaten egg white	1
	1 tablespoon	water	1 tablespoon
		Poppy seeds or sesame seeds	
		(optional)	

1 Select the recipe size. Add the first 6 ingredients to the machine according to the manufacturer's directions. Select the dough cycle. When cycle is complete, remove dough. Punch down. Cover and let rest for 10 minutes. Grease a large baking sheet; set aside.

2 Divide the 1½-pound dough into 9 portions (divide the 2-pound dough into 12 portions). Working quickly, shape each portion into a ball, tucking edges under to make a smooth top. Punch a hole in the center; pull gently to make a 2-inch hole. Place on the prepared baking sheet. Cover and let rise in a warm place for 20 minutes (start timing after the first bagel is shaped). Broil about 5 inches from the heat for 3 to 4 minutes or until set, turning once halfway through broiling (tops should not brown).

3 Meanwhile, generously grease another large baking sheet; set aside. In a Dutch oven bring the 6 cups water and 1 tablespoon sugar to boiling; reduce heat. Add bagels, 4 or 5 at a time, and simmer for 7 minutes, turning once. Using a slotted spoon, remove bagels from water and drain on paper towels. (If some bagels fall slightly, they may rise when baked.) Place bagels on the prepared baking sheet. In a small bowl combine egg white and the 1 tablespoon water; brush over bagels. If desired, sprinkle with poppy seeds.

4 Bake in a 375°F oven for 25 to 30 minutes or until tops are golden brown. Remove from baking sheet; cool on wire racks.

Nutrition Facts per bagel: 183 cal., 2 g total fat (0 g sat. fat), 0 mg chol., 186 mg sodium, 35 g carbo., 6 g pro.

Pita bread rounds create their own pockets as they bake. Slice open an end and tuck in your favorite sandwich filling.

Pita Bread

1½-POUND	INGREDIENTS
1 cup	water
3 tablespoons	olive oil
3 cups	bread flour
1½ teaspoons	salt
1 teaspoon	sugar
1 tablespoon	active dry yeast
	or bread machine yeast

PREP:
25 minutes

BAKE:
4 minutes per batch

MAKES:
1½-pound recipe
(12 pitas)

1 Add the ingredients to the machine according to the manufacturer's directions. Select the dough cycle. When cycle is complete, remove dough. Punch down.

2 Divide the dough into 12 portions. Shape each portion into a ball. Cover with a damp towel and let rest for 10 minutes. Grease a baking sheet; set aside.

3 On a lightly floured surface, roll 2 balls of dough into 6- to 7-inch circles. Place the circles on the prepared baking sheet. Bake in a 450°F oven for 2 minutes. (If dough puffs, lightly press down with the back of a pancake turner.) Turn with a pancake turner; bake for 2 minutes more.

4 Remove from baking sheet; cool on a wire rack. Repeat with the remaining balls of dough, 2 at a time.

Nutrition Facts per pita: 158 cal., 4 g total fat (1 g sat. fat), 0 mg chol., 292 mg sodium, 26 g carbo., 4 g pro.

English muffin aficionados say cutting the muffins in half with a knife is a sin—it ruins their texture. The best way to split the crunchy rounds is with a fork—so there are lots of peaks and valleys to hold butter, honey, or preserves.

Whole Wheat English Muffins

PREP:
25 minutes

RISE:
30 minutes

COOK:
25 minutes per batch

MAKES:
1½-pound recipe
(9 muffins)

1½-POUND	INGREDIENTS
1¼ cups	milk
2 tablespoons	shortening
2 cups	whole wheat flour
1 cup	bread flour
⅓ cup	cracked wheat
1 tablespoon	brown sugar
¾ teaspoon	salt
1 teaspoon	active dry yeast
	or bread machine yeast
	Yellow cornmeal

1 Add the first 8 ingredients to the machine according to the manufacturer's directions. Select the dough cycle. When cycle is complete, remove dough. Punch down. Cover and let rest for 10 minutes.

2 On a lightly floured surface, roll the dough to slightly less than ½-inch thickness. Cut the dough with a floured 4-inch round cutter, dipping cutter into flour between cuts. Reroll as necessary. Dip both sides of each round into cornmeal to coat. (If necessary, to make cornmeal adhere, lightly brush rounds with water.) Cover and let rise in a warm place about 30 minutes or until nearly double. (If desired, do not let rise. Cover and refrigerate for 2 to 24 hours.)

3 In an ungreased electric skillet set at 325°F cook muffins, 4 or 5 at a time, for 25 to 30 minutes or until muffins sound hollow when lightly tapped, turning every 5 minutes. (Or on an ungreased large griddle or in an ungreased large skillet cook muffins, 4 or 5 at a time, over low heat for 25 to 30 minutes, turning frequently.) Cool on wire racks. To serve, split muffins horizontally and toast or broil.

Nutrition Facts per muffin: 321 cal., 5 g total fat (2 g sat. fat), 5 mg chol., 297 mg sodium, 62 g carbo., 12 g pro.

Enjoy these soft, tuggy knots plain—or dip them in your favorite flavored mustard or melted cheese spread.

Pretzels

1½-POUND	INGREDIENTS	2-POUND
1 cup	milk	**1⅓ cups**
2 tablespoons	water	3 tablespoons
1 tablespoon	cooking oil	**4 teaspoons**
3 cups	bread flour	4 cups
2 tablespoons	sugar	**3 tablespoons**
¾ teaspoon	salt	1 teaspoon
1¼ teaspoons	active dry yeast	**1½ teaspoons**
	or bread machine yeast	
8 cups	water	8 cups
2 tablespoons	salt	**2 tablespoons**
1	slightly beaten egg white	1
1 tablespoon	water	**1 tablespoon**
	Sesame seeds or coarse salt	

PREP:
40 minutes

BAKE:
24 minutes

COOK:
2 minutes per batch

MAKES:
1½-pound recipe
(16 pretzels)
OR
2-pound recipe
(22 pretzels)

1 Select the recipe size. Add the first 7 ingredients to the machine according to the manufacturer's directions. Select the dough cycle. When cycle is complete, remove dough. Punch down. Cover and let rest for 10 minutes. Grease 2 large baking sheets; set aside.

2 On a lightly floured surface, roll the 1½-pound dough into a 12×8-inch rectangle. Cut lengthwise into sixteen 12×½-inch strips. (Roll 2-pound dough into a 12×11-inch rectangle; cut lengthwise into twenty-two 12×½-inch strips.) Gently roll the strips into 16-inch ropes.

3 Shape each pretzel by crossing 1 end of a rope over the other to form a circle, overlapping about 4 inches from each end. Take 1 end of dough in each hand and twist once at the point where the dough overlaps. Carefully lift each end across to the edge of the circle opposite it. Tuck ends under edges to make a pretzel shape; moisten ends and press to seal. Place on the prepared baking sheets. *Do not let rise.*

4 Bake in a 475°F oven for 4 minutes. Remove from oven. Reduce oven temperature to 350°F. Meanwhile, generously grease another 2 large baking sheets; set aside. In a Dutch oven bring the 8 cups water and the 2 tablespoons salt to boiling. Add pretzels, 3 or 4 at a time, and boil gently for 2 minutes, turning once. Using a slotted spoon, remove pretzels from water and drain on paper towels. Let stand for a few seconds. Place pretzels, about ½ inch apart, on the prepared baking sheets.

5 In a small bowl combine egg white and the 1 tablespoon water; brush over pretzels. Sprinkle with sesame seeds. Bake in the 350°F oven for 20 to 25 minutes or until golden brown. Remove from baking sheets; cool on wire racks.

Nutrition Facts per pretzel: 119 cal., 2 g total fat (0 g sat. fat), 1 mg chol., 245 mg sodium, 21 g carbo., 4 g pro.

Pretzels don't always have to be salty or savory. Here's a citrusy, sweet take on the old-fashioned favorite.

Cinnamon-Orange Pretzels

PREP:
40 minutes

BAKE:
24 minutes

COOK:
2 minutes per batch

MAKES:
1½-pound recipe
(20 pretzels)
OR
2-pound recipe
(28 pretzels)

1½-POUND	INGREDIENTS	2-POUND
1 cup	milk	1⅓ cups
1	egg*	1
3 tablespoons	margarine or butter, cut up	¼ cup
3 cups	bread flour	4 cups
3 tablespoons	granulated sugar	¼ cup
2 teaspoons	finely shredded orange peel	2½ teaspoons
¾ teaspoon	salt	1 teaspoon
¾ teaspoon	ground cinnamon	1 teaspoon
1 teaspoon	active dry yeast	1½ teaspoons
	or bread machine yeast	
12 cups	water	12 cups
1	slightly beaten egg white	1
1 tablespoon	water	1 tablespoon
	Coarse sugar	

1 Select the recipe size. Add the first 9 ingredients to the machine according to the manufacturer's directions. Select the dough cycle. When cycle is complete, remove dough. Punch down. Cover and let rest for 10 minutes. Grease 2 or 3 large baking sheets; set aside.

2 On a lightly floured surface, roll the 1½-pound dough into a 12×10-inch rectangle. Cut lengthwise into twenty 12×½-inch strips. (Roll 2-pound dough into a 16×14-inch rectangle; cut lengthwise into twenty-eight 16×½-inch strips.) Gently roll the strips into 16-inch ropes.

3 Shape each pretzel by crossing 1 end of a rope over the other to form a circle, overlapping about 4 inches from each end. Take 1 end of dough in each hand and twist once at the point where the dough overlaps. Carefully lift each end across to the edge of the circle opposite it. Tuck ends under edges to make a pretzel shape; moisten ends and press to seal. Place on the prepared baking sheets. *Do not let rise.*

4 Bake in a 475°F oven for 4 minutes. Remove from oven. Reduce oven temperature to 350°F. Meanwhile, generously grease another 2 or 3 large baking sheets; set aside. In a Dutch oven bring the 12 cups water to boiling. Add pretzels, 3 or 4 at a time, and boil gently for 2 minutes, turning once. Using a slotted spoon, remove pretzels and drain on paper towels. Let stand for a few seconds. Place, about ½ inch apart, on prepared baking sheets.

5 Combine egg white and the 1 tablespoon water; brush over pretzels. Sprinkle with coarse sugar. Bake in the 350°F oven about 20 minutes or until golden brown. Remove and cool.

*Note: The Test Kitchen recommends 1 egg for either size recipe.

Nutrition Facts per pretzel: 111 cal., 3 g total fat (1 g sat. fat), 12 mg chol., 113 mg sodium, 18 g carbo., 3 g pro.

Make your own doughnuts? You bet! You'll think these glazed doughnuts are worth every minute it takes to make them after you take one warm and wonderful bite.

Doughnuts

1½-POUND	INGREDIENTS	2-POUND
¾ cup	milk	1 cup
1	egg(s)	2
3 tablespoons	margarine or butter, cut up	¼ cup
2 tablespoons	water*	2 tablespoons
3 cups	bread flour	4 cups
¼ cup	sugar	⅓ cup
½ teaspoon	salt	¾ teaspoon
1½ teaspoons	active dry yeast	2 teaspoons
	or bread machine yeast	
	Cooking oil for deep-fat frying	
1 recipe	Powdered Sugar Glaze	1 recipe

PREP:
35 minutes

RISE:
45 minutes

COOK:
2 minutes per batch

MAKES:
1½-pound recipe
(16 doughnuts)
OR
2-pound recipe
(22 doughnuts)

1 Select the recipe size. Add the first 8 ingredients to the machine according to the manufacturer's directions. Select the dough cycle. When cycle is complete, remove dough. Punch down. Cover and let rest for 10 minutes.

2 Divide the dough in half. On a lightly floured surface, roll each portion to ½-inch thickness. Cut dough with a floured doughnut cutter, dipping cutter into flour between cuts. Reroll as necessary. Cover and let rise in a warm place for 45 to 60 minutes or until light.

3 Fry doughnuts 2 or 3 at a time in deep, hot oil (365°F) about 2 minutes or until golden brown, turning once. Using a slotted spoon, remove doughnuts from oil and drain on paper towels. Spread with Powdered Sugar Glaze. Cool slightly on wire racks. Serve warm or cool.

Powdered Sugar Glaze: In a medium bowl combine 1½ cups sifted powdered sugar and ½ teaspoon vanilla. Stir in enough milk (2 to 3 tablespoons) to make a glaze of spreading consistency.

*Note: The Test Kitchen recommends 2 tablespoons water for either size recipe.

Nutrition Facts per doughnut: 166 cal., 7 g total fat (1 g sat. fat), 14 mg chol., 102 mg sodium, 23 g carbo., 4 g pro.

The traditional French fritter or beignet is a puffy, deep-fried doughnutlike pastry. Try them topped—as they typically are in New Orleans—with powdered sugar.

New Orleans Beignets

PREP: 30 minutes	1½-POUND	INGREDIENTS	2-POUND
	²/₃ cup	buttermilk or sour milk**	³/₄ cup
COOK: 1 minute per batch	¼ cup	water	⅓ cup
	1	egg*	1
MAKES: 1½-pound recipe (32 beignets) OR 2-pound recipe (48 beignets)	1 tablespoon	margarine or butter	4 teaspoons
	1 teaspoon	vanilla	1½ teaspoons
	3 cups	bread flour	4 cups
	¼ cup	granulated sugar	⅓ cup
	³/₄ teaspoon	salt	1 teaspoon
	1¼ teaspoons	active dry yeast	1½ teaspoons
		or bread machine yeast	
		Cooking oil for deep-fat frying	
		Sifted powdered sugar	

1 Select the recipe size. Add the first 9 ingredients to the machine according to the manufacturer's directions. Select the dough cycle. When cycle is complete, remove dough. Punch down. Cover and let rest for 10 minutes.

2 Divide the 1½-pound dough in half (divide 2-pound dough into thirds). On a lightly floured surface, roll each portion into a 9-inch square. Cut each square into sixteen 2¼-inch squares.

3 Fry the beignets, 2 or 3 at a time, in deep, hot oil (375°F) for 1 to 2 minutes or until golden brown, turning once. Using a slotted spoon, remove beignets from oil and drain on paper towels. Sprinkle with powdered sugar. Cool slightly on wire racks. Serve warm or cool.

*Note: The Test Kitchen recommends 1 egg for either size recipe.

**Note: To make ²/₃ cup sour milk, place 2 teaspoons lemon juice or vinegar in a 1-cup liquid measuring cup. Add enough milk to measure ²/₃ cup liquid; stir. To make ³/₄ cup sour milk, place 2¼ teaspoons lemon juice or vinegar in a 1-cup liquid measuring cup. Add enough milk to measure ³/₄ cup liquid; stir. Let stand for 5 minutes before using.

Nutrition Facts per beignet: 77 cal., 2 g total fat (1 g sat. fat), 7 mg chol., 62 mg sodium, 12 g carbo., 2 g pro.

These impressive little bundles, tied with a jaunty chive ribbon, look very black tie but toss together as easily as a T-shirt and jeans. They suit every occasion from brunch to cocktails.

Beggar's Packages

1½-POUND	INGREDIENTS	2-POUND
1 cup	water	1¼ cups
1 tablespoon	olive oil or cooking oil	4 teaspoons
3 cups	bread flour	4 cups
1 teaspoon	sugar	1½ teaspoons
¾ teaspoon	garlic salt	1 teaspoon
½ teaspoon	dried Italian seasoning, crushed	¾ teaspoon
1 teaspoon	active dry yeast	1¼ teaspoons
	or bread machine yeast	
1 (3-ounce) package	cream cheese	½ of an (8-ounce) package
2 tablespoons	chopped walnuts, toasted	¼ cup
1 tablespoon	all-purpose flour or bread flour	4 teaspoons
1 tablespoon	snipped fresh chives	4 teaspoons
1	egg yolk	1
1 teaspoon	water	1 teaspoon

PREP:
35 minutes

RISE:
30 minutes

BAKE:
20 minutes

MAKES:
1½-pound recipe
(16 packages)
OR
2-pound recipe
(24 packages)

1 Select the recipe size. Add the first 7 ingredients to the machine according to the manufacturer's directions. Select the dough cycle. When cycle is complete, remove dough. Punch down. Cover and let rest for 10 minutes.

2 Meanwhile, for filling, in a small bowl stir together the cream cheese, walnuts, all-purpose flour, and chives. Grease baking sheets; set aside.

3 Divide the 1½-pound dough in half (divide the 2-pound dough into thirds). On a lightly floured surface, roll each portion into a 10-inch square. Cut each square into sixteen 2½-inch squares. Place about 1½ teaspoons filling in the centers of half of the squares. Moisten edges; place the remaining squares on top. Seal edges by pressing with a fork. Place on the prepared baking sheets.

4 Cover and let rise in a warm place about 30 minutes or until nearly double. In a small bowl combine egg yolk and the 1 teaspoon water; brush over dough.

5 Bake in a 350°F oven about 20 minutes or until golden brown. Remove from baking sheets; cool slightly on wire racks. If desired, use an additional chive to tie a "string" around each package. Serve warm.

Nutrition Facts per package: 132 cal., 4 g total fat (2 g sat. fat), 19 mg chol., 114 mg sodium, 20 g carbo., 4 g pro.

Ground beef, vegetables, and pizza sauce fill these turnoverlike Italian favorites.

Calzones

PREP:	1½-POUND	INGREDIENTS	2-POUND
35 minutes	1 cup	water	1⅓ cups
BAKE:	2 tablespoons	olive oil or cooking oil	3 tablespoons
12 minutes	1 teaspoon	bottled minced garlic	1½ teaspoons
MAKES:	3 cups	bread flour	4 cups
1½-pound recipe	2 teaspoons	dried basil, crushed	1 tablespoon
(8 calzones)	¾ teaspoon	salt	1 teaspoon
OR	1¼ teaspoons	active dry yeast	1½ teaspoons
2-pound recipe		or bread machine yeast	
(12 calzones)	12 ounces	lean ground beef	1 pound
	¾ cup	sliced fresh mushrooms	1 cup
	⅓ cup	chopped green sweet pepper	½ cup
	¾ cup	shredded mozzarella cheese	1 cup
	¾ cup	pizza sauce	1 cup
	1 tablespoon	milk	4 teaspoons

1 Select the recipe size. Add the first 7 ingredients to the machine according to the manufacturer's directions. Select the dough cycle. When cycle is complete, remove dough. Punch down. Cover and let rest for 10 minutes.

2 Meanwhile, for filling, in a large skillet cook the ground beef, mushrooms, and sweet pepper until meat is brown. Drain off fat. Stir in mozzarella cheese and pizza sauce. Grease baking sheets; set aside.

3 Divide the 1½-pound dough in half. On a lightly floured surface, roll each portion into a 10-inch square. Cut each square into four 5-inch squares. (Divide the 2-pound dough in half. Roll each portion into a 15×10-inch rectangle; cut each rectangle into six 5-inch squares.)

4 Divide the filling among the squares; moisten edges. Lift a corner of each square and stretch to the opposite corner over filling. Seal edges by pressing with a fork. Transfer calzones to the prepared baking sheets. Prick tops with fork; brush with milk. *Do not let rise.*

5 Bake in a 425°F oven for 12 to 15 minutes or until golden brown. Remove from baking sheets; cool slightly on wire racks. Serve warm. If desired, serve the calzones with additional warmed pizza sauce.

Nutrition Facts per calzone: 329 cal., 10 g total fat (3 g sat. fat), 33 mg chol., 392 mg sodium, 41 g carbo., 17 g pro.

Discover the joys of these spicy, savory pies. Filled with a zesty mushroom and sausage mixture, they're hearty enough to satisfy a crowd of hungry football fans gathered 'round the TV.

Sausage-Mushroom Stromboli

1½-POUND	INGREDIENTS	2-POUND
1 cup	water	1⅓ cups
2 tablespoons	olive oil or cooking oil	3 tablespoons
2 cloves	garlic, minced	3 cloves
3 cups	bread flour	4 cups
2 teaspoons	dried Italian seasoning, crushed	1 tablespoon
¾ teaspoon	salt	1 teaspoon
1 teaspoon	active dry yeast or bread machine yeast	1¼ teaspoons
12 ounces	bulk hot or mild Italian sausage	1 pound
2 cups	sliced fresh mushrooms	3 cups
1 cup	chopped onion	1⅓ cups
1 (8-ounce) can	pizza sauce	1 (15-ounce) can
1 cup	shredded mozzarella cheese (optional)	1½ cups
	Milk	

PREP:
25 minutes

BAKE:
30 minutes

MAKES:
1½-pound recipe
(6 servings)
OR
2-pound recipe
(8 servings)

1 Select the recipe size. Add the first 7 ingredients to the machine according to the manufacturer's directions. Select the dough cycle. When cycle is complete, remove dough. Punch down. Cover and let rest for 10 minutes.

2 Meanwhile, for filling, in a large skillet cook sausage, mushrooms, and onion until sausage is brown and onion is tender. Drain off fat. Pat meat mixture with paper towels. Stir in pizza sauce. Grease 2 large baking sheets; set aside.

3 Divide the 1½-pound dough in half. On a lightly floured surface, roll each portion into an 11-inch circle. (Divide the 2-pound dough in half; roll each portion into a 13-inch circle.) Transfer the dough to the prepared baking sheets. Spread half of each circle with half of the filling to within 1 inch of the edges. If desired, sprinkle with cheese. Moisten edges; fold the dough in half over filling. Seal edges by pressing with a fork. Cut slits in the tops so steam can escape; brush with a little milk. *Do not let rise.*

4 Bake in a 425°F oven for 30 to 35 minutes or until light brown. Remove from baking sheets; cool slightly on wire racks. Serve warm.

Nutrition Facts per serving: 463 cal., 17 g total fat (5 g sat. fat), 32 mg chol., 873 mg sodium, 58 g carbo., 18 g pro.

Sharp feta cheese and lamb combine for the filling of these hearty sandwiches. Add a Greek salad and you'll have the perfect casual dinner.

Lamb and Feta Stuffed Bundles

PREP:	1½-POUND	INGREDIENTS	2-POUND
25 minutes	¾ cup	buttermilk or sour milk (page 184)	1 cup
BAKE:	¼ cup	margarine or butter, cut up	⅓ cup
20 minutes	1	egg*	1
	1 tablespoon	water	4 teaspoons
MAKES:	2 cups	bread flour	2⅔ cups
1½-pound recipe	1 cup	whole wheat flour	1⅓ cups
(8 bundles)	2 tablespoons	sugar	3 tablespoons
OR	¾ teaspoon	salt	1 teaspoon
2-pound recipe	1¼ teaspoons	active dry yeast	1½ teaspoons
(10 bundles)		or bread machine yeast	
	12 ounces	ground lamb or ground beef	1 pound
	½ cup	crumbled feta cheese	¾ cup
	¼ cup	sliced green onions	⅓ cup
	2 tablespoons	chopped pitted ripe olives	¼ cup
	⅛ teaspoon	garlic salt	¼ teaspoon
	2 teaspoons	margarine or butter, melted	1 tablespoon
	1 (8-ounce) carton	plain yogurt	1½ cups
	1 teaspoon	snipped fresh mint	1½ teaspoons

❶ Select the recipe size. Add the first 9 ingredients to the machine according to the manufacturer's directions. Select the dough cycle. When cycle is complete, remove dough. Punch down. Cover and let rest for 10 minutes.

❷ Meanwhile, for filling, in a large skillet cook the ground lamb until brown. Drain off fat. Stir in the feta cheese, green onions, olives, and garlic salt. Cool slightly. Grease a large baking sheet; set aside.

❸ Divide the 1½-pound dough into 8 portions (divide the 2-pound dough into 10 portions). On a lightly floured surface, roll each portion into a 6-inch circle. Place about ¼ cup filling in center of each circle. Bring dough up around filling, pleating and pinching dough firmly to seal. Place, sealed sides down, 2 inches apart on prepared baking sheet. *Do not let rise.*

❹ Bake in a 350°F oven for 20 to 25 minutes or until golden brown. Remove from baking sheet; cool slightly on wire racks. Brush with the melted margarine. For sauce, in a small bowl stir together the yogurt and mint. Serve the warm bundles with sauce.

*Note: The Test Kitchen recommends 1 egg for either size recipe.

Nutrition Facts per bundle: 389 cal., 16 g total fat (5 g sat. fat), 64 mg chol., 476 mg sodium, 43 g carbo., 18 g pro.

SOUPS
AND STEWS

BONUS
CHAPTER

Herbes de Provence, niçoise olives, and capers give this dish its country French accent. Long, slow simmering tenderizes the meat.

French Beef Stew

PREP:
25 minutes

COOK:
1¾ hours

MAKES:
4 servings

AMOUNT	INGREDIENTS
1 pound	boneless beef round
1 tablespoon	olive oil
1 small	onion, chopped
1 cup	dry white wine
2 cups	water
1 teaspoon	dried herbes de Provence, crushed
¼ teaspoon	salt
¼ teaspoon	black pepper
8 tiny	new potatoes (about 6 ounces)
8	pearl onions, peeled
1 large	tomato, peeled, cored, seeded, and chopped
¼ cup	niçoise olives, pitted, or pitted kalamata olives
2 tablespoons	drained capers
8 ounces	haricots verts or small green beans, trimmed and cut into 3-inch lengths
1 tablespoon	snipped fresh flat-leaf parsley

1 Trim fat from meat. Cut meat into 1-inch pieces. In a Dutch oven brown meat, half at a time, in hot oil; drain off fat. Return all meat to Dutch oven. Add chopped onion. Cook and stir until onion is tender.

2 Add wine to Dutch oven, stirring to scrape up the browned bits from bottom of pan. Stir in water, herbes de Provence, salt, and pepper. Bring to boiling; reduce heat. Cover and simmer about 1¼ hours or until meat is nearly tender.

3 Stir in new potatoes and pearl onions. Return to boiling; reduce heat. Cover and simmer about 30 minutes or until meat and vegetables are tender. Stir in chopped tomato, olives, and capers; heat through.

4 Meanwhile, in a covered medium saucepan cook haricots verts in a small amount of boiling water for 5 to 7 minutes or until crisp-tender; drain.

5 Serve the stew with haricots verts and sprinkle with parsley.

Nutrition Facts per serving: 289 cal., 8 g total fat (2 g sat. fat), 65 mg chol., 438 mg sodium, 17 g carbo., 28 g pro.

This stick-to-the-ribs sensation is an adaptation of an old recipe from Switzerland where it's traditional to use polenta in a variety of ways, including as a topper for soups and stews.

Polenta Beef Stew

AMOUNT	INGREDIENTS
2 pounds	boneless beef chuck
1/4 cup	all-purpose flour
1 teaspoon	garlic powder
1 teaspoon	dried thyme, crushed
1 teaspoon	dried basil, crushed
1/2 teaspoon	salt
1/2 teaspoon	black pepper
2 tablespoons	olive oil
1 medium	onion, chopped
1/4 teaspoon	dried rosemary, crushed
6 cloves	garlic, minced
1 (14-ounce) can	beef broth
1 1/2 cups	dry red wine or beef broth
8 ounces	boiling onions
5 medium	carrots, cut into 1-inch chunks
1 recipe	Polenta
1/2 cup	snipped fresh flat-leaf parsley
1/4 cup	tomato paste

PREP:
25 minutes

COOK:
2 hours

MAKES:
8 servings

1 Trim fat from meat. Cut meat into 1-inch pieces. In a plastic bag combine flour, garlic powder, thyme, basil, salt, and pepper. Add meat pieces, a few at a time, shaking to coat. In a Dutch oven brown meat, half at a time, in hot oil; drain off fat. Return all meat to Dutch oven. Add chopped onion, rosemary, and garlic. Cook and stir until onion is tender.

2 Add beef broth and wine. Bring to boiling; reduce heat. Cover and simmer for 1 1/2 hours. Stir in boiling onions and carrots. Return to boiling; reduce heat. Cover and simmer about 30 minutes more or until meat and vegetables are tender. Meanwhile, prepare the Polenta. Just before serving, stir the parsley and tomato paste into stew. Serve the stew with Polenta. If desired, garnish with additional parsley.

Polenta: In a large saucepan bring 3 cups milk just to a simmer over medium heat. In a medium bowl combine 1 cup cornmeal, 1 cup water, and 1 teaspoon salt. Stir cornmeal mixture slowly into hot milk. Cook and stir until mixture comes to a boil. Reduce heat to low. Cook, uncovered, for 10 to 15 minutes or until thick, stirring occasionally. (If mixture is too thick, stir in additional milk.) Stir in 2 tablespoons margarine or butter until melted.

Nutrition Facts per serving: 508 cal., 26 g total fat (10 g sat. fat), 88 mg chol., 736 mg sodium, 32 g carbo., 29 g pro.

A hint of unsweetened cocoa brings new flavor to traditional Hungarian goulash.

Beef Goulash Soup

PREP:
25 minutes

COOK:
20 minutes

MAKES:
4 servings

AMOUNT	INGREDIENTS
6 ounces	boneless beef sirloin
1 teaspoon	olive oil
1 medium	onion, cut into thin wedges
2 cups	water
1 (14$\frac{1}{2}$-ounce) can	low-sodium tomatoes, cut up
1 (14-ounce) can	beef broth
$\frac{1}{2}$ cup	thinly sliced carrot
1 teaspoon	unsweetened cocoa powder
1 clove	garlic, minced
1 cup	thinly sliced cabbage
1 ounce	dried wide noodles (about $\frac{3}{4}$ cup)
2 teaspoons	paprika
$\frac{1}{4}$ cup	fat-free dairy sour cream

1 Trim fat from meat. Cut meat into $\frac{1}{2}$-inch pieces. In a large saucepan cook meat in hot oil over medium-high heat until meat is brown. Add onion wedges; cook and stir about 3 minutes or until onion is tender.

2 Stir in water, undrained tomatoes, beef broth, carrot, cocoa powder, and garlic. Bring to boiling; reduce heat. Simmer, uncovered, about 15 minutes or until meat is tender.

3 Stir in cabbage, noodles, and paprika. Simmer, uncovered, for 5 to 7 minutes more or until noodles are tender but still firm. Remove from heat. Stir in sour cream.

Nutrition Facts per serving: 178 cal., 6 g total fat (2 g sat. fat), 34 mg chol., 400 mg sodium, 17 g carbo., 15 g pro.

One serving of this Asian-inspired soup provides more than half of your daily vitamin C and vitamin A requirements—thanks to the dynamic duo, broccoli and carrots.

Teriyaki Beef Soup

AMOUNT	INGREDIENTS
8 ounces	boneless beef sirloin
1 large	shallot, thinly sliced
2 teaspoons	olive oil
4 cups	water
1 cup	apple juice or apple cider
2	carrots, cut into
	thin bite-size strips
⅓ cup	uncooked long grain rice
1 tablespoon	grated fresh ginger
1 teaspoon	instant beef bouillon granules
3 cloves	garlic, minced
2 cups	coarsely chopped broccoli
1 to 2 tablespoons	light teriyaki sauce
1 tablespoon	dry sherry (optional)

START TO FINISH:
40 minutes

MAKES:
5 servings

❶ Trim fat from meat. Cut meat into thin bite-size strips. In a large saucepan cook meat and shallot in hot oil over medium-high heat for 2 to 3 minutes or until meat is brown. Remove meat mixture; set aside.

❷ In the same saucepan combine water, apple juice, carrot strips, rice, ginger, bouillon granules, and garlic. Bring to boiling; reduce heat. Cover and simmer about 15 minutes or until carrots are tender.

❸ Stir in meat mixture and broccoli. Cover and simmer about 3 minutes more or until broccoli is crisp-tender. Stir in teriyaki sauce and, if desired, sherry.

Nutrition Facts per serving: 197 cal., 6 g total fat (2 g sat. fat), 30 mg chol., 382 mg sodium, 22 g carbo., 13 g pro.

Looking for a new way to serve always easy, always satisfying ground beef? Try this family favorite—it's quick, stuffed with colorful vegetables, and low fat, to boot.

Hamburger-Vegetable Soup

PREP:
20 minutes

COOK:
15 minutes

MAKES:
6 servings

AMOUNT	INGREDIENTS
1 pound	lean ground beef or pork
$1/2$ cup	chopped onion
$1/2$ cup	chopped green sweet pepper
4 cups	beef broth
1 cup	frozen whole kernel corn
1 ($7^1/2$-ounce) can	tomatoes, cut up
$1/2$ of a 10-ounce package	frozen lima beans
$1/2$ cup	chopped peeled potato or loose-pack frozen hash brown potatoes
1 medium	carrot, cut into thin bite-size strips
1 tablespoon	snipped fresh basil or
1 teaspoon	dried basil, crushed
1 teaspoon	Worcestershire sauce
1	bay leaf
$1/8$ teaspoon	black pepper

1 In a large saucepan cook ground beef, onion, and sweet pepper until meat is brown and onion is tender. Drain off fat. Stir in beef broth, corn, undrained tomatoes, lima beans, potato, carrot, basil, Worcestershire sauce, bay leaf, and black pepper.

2 Bring to boiling; reduce heat. Cover and simmer for 15 to 20 minutes or until vegetables are tender. Discard bay leaf.

Nutrition Facts per serving: 243 cal., 10 g total fat (4 g sat. fat), 48 mg chol., 652 mg sodium, 19 g carbo., 20 g pro.

This robust pork stew takes on an autumn orange from the russet-colored sweet potatoes. It celebrates the season with assorted root vegetables, apples, and tomatoes simmered with melt-in-your-mouth pork sirloin.

Hearty Pork and Ale Stew

AMOUNT	INGREDIENTS
1 pound	boneless pork sirloin
2 tablespoons	all-purpose flour
1/2 teaspoon	crushed red pepper
2 cloves	garlic, minced
1 tablespoon	cooking oil
3 cups	vegetable broth
1 (12-ounce) can	beer
	or
1 1/2 cups	vegetable broth
2 large	sweet potatoes, peeled and cut into 1-inch cubes
3 medium	parsnips, peeled and sliced 3/4 inch thick
1 medium	onion, cut into thin wedges
2 tablespoons	snipped fresh thyme
	or
1 1/2 teaspoons	dried thyme, crushed
1 tablespoon	brown sugar
1 tablespoon	Dijon-style mustard
4 large	plum tomatoes, coarsely chopped
2 small	green apples, cored and cut into wedges

PREP: 25 minutes

COOK: 35 minutes

MAKES: 6 servings

1 Trim fat from meat. Cut meat into 3/4-inch pieces. In a plastic bag combine flour and red pepper. Add meat pieces, a few at a time, shaking to coat.

2 In a Dutch oven cook meat and garlic in hot oil over medium-high heat until meat is brown. Stir in the 3 cups vegetable broth, beer, sweet potatoes, parsnips, onion, thyme, brown sugar, and Dijon mustard.

3 Bring to boiling; reduce heat. Cover and simmer for 30 minutes. Stir in tomatoes and apples. Return to boiling; reduce heat. Cover and simmer about 5 minutes more or until meat, vegetables, and apples are tender.

Nutrition Facts per serving: 288 cal., 7 g total fat (2 g sat. fat), 48 mg chol., 571 mg sodium, 36 g carbo., 20 g pro.

This quick-to-fix pork stew gets a jump-start from the robust flavors of chipotle chile peppers, cumin, and picante sauce.

Chunky Pork Chili

START TO FINISH:
30 minutes

MAKES:
4 servings

AMOUNT	INGREDIENTS
12 ounces	pork tenderloin
2 teaspoons	chili powder
2 teaspoons	ground cumin
1 small	onion, chopped
4 cloves	garlic, minced
2 teaspoons	cooking oil
1 cup	beer or beef broth
1 medium	yellow or red sweet pepper, cut into $1/2$-inch pieces
$1/2$ cup	bottled picante sauce or salsa
1 to 2 tablespoons	finely chopped chipotle chile peppers in adobo sauce
1 (15-ounce) can	red beans or pinto beans, rinsed and drained
$1/2$ cup	fat-free or light dairy sour cream
$1/4$ cup	snipped fresh cilantro

1 Trim any fat from meat. Cut meat into $3/4$-inch pieces. In a medium bowl combine meat, chili powder, and cumin; toss to coat. Set aside.

2 In a large saucepan cook onion and garlic in hot oil over medium-high heat about 3 minutes or until onion is tender. Add seasoned meat. Cook and stir about 3 minutes or until meat is brown. Stir in beer, sweet pepper, picante sauce, and chipotle peppers.

3 Bring to boiling; reduce heat. Simmer, uncovered, about 5 minutes or just until meat is tender. Stir in beans; heat through. Top each serving with sour cream and cilantro.

Nutrition Facts per serving: 286 cal., 5 g total fat (1 g sat. fat), 60 mg chol., 778 mg sodium, 31 g carbo., 27 g pro.

Asian cooks have long known that the peppery, slightly sweet taste of ginger perfectly matches mild-flavored pork. Here, the combination is even better joined with a bit of fresh mint.

Gingered Pork and Cabbage Soup

AMOUNT	INGREDIENTS
6 cups	vegetable broth
	or chicken broth
8 ounces	boneless pork sirloin
1 large	onion, chopped
2 teaspoons	grated fresh ginger
4 cloves	garlic, minced
1 tablespoon	cooking oil
3 small	tomatoes, chopped
2 medium	carrots, finely chopped
½ cup	dried anelli pasta
4 cups	thinly sliced Chinese cabbage
¼ cup	snipped fresh mint
	Chinese cabbage leaves (optional)

START TO FINISH:
40 minutes

MAKES:
6 servings

1 In a medium saucepan bring vegetable broth to boiling. Meanwhile, trim fat from meat. Cut meat into ½-inch pieces. In a large saucepan cook meat, onion, ginger, and garlic in hot oil over medium-high heat until meat is brown and onion is tender.

2 Add hot vegetable broth to meat mixture. Bring to boiling. Stir in tomatoes and carrots. Return to boiling; reduce heat. Cover and simmer for 15 minutes.

3 Stir in pasta and cook, uncovered, for 6 to 8 minutes or until pasta is tender but still firm. Stir in the sliced Chinese cabbage and mint. If desired, garnish each serving with Chinese cabbage leaves.

Nutrition Facts per serving: 141 cal., 6 g total fat (1 g sat. fat), 16 mg chol., 961 mg sodium, 21 g carbo., 8 g pro.

Easy Vegetable Broth

When a recipe calls for vegetable broth, you can use canned broth or bouillon cubes, or prepare a homemade broth. An easy way to make your own vegetable broth is to save the water in which vegetables are boiled and freeze it in a covered container. Keep saving the liquid from the vegetables you prepare, and soon you will have a basic broth ready to use.

Southern cooks are renowned for pairing ham with vegetables. In this creamy chowder, smoky bits of cooked ham simmer with yellow squash, red sweet pepper, potato, and green onion.

Southern Ham Chowder

START TO FINISH:	AMOUNT	INGREDIENTS
35 minutes	1½ cups	thinly sliced yellow summer squash or zucchini
MAKES:	½ cup	chopped red or green sweet pepper
3 or 4 servings	½ teaspoon	dried thyme, crushed
	1 tablespoon	margarine or butter
	2 cups	water
	1½ cups	chopped potato
	Dash	black pepper
	6 ounces	thinly sliced cooked ham or turkey ham, chopped
	¾ cup	finely chopped green onions
	½ cup	half-and-half or light cream

1 In a large saucepan cook the squash, sweet pepper, and thyme in hot margarine over medium heat about 3 minutes or until squash is tender. Stir in water, potato, and black pepper.

2 Bring to boiling; reduce heat. Cover and simmer for 12 to 15 minutes or until potato is tender. Remove from heat. Mash mixture slightly with a potato masher. Stir in ham, green onions, and half-and-half; heat through.

Nutrition Facts per serving: 261 cal., 12 g total fat (5 g sat. fat), 45 mg chol., 755 mg sodium, 23 g carbo., 16 g pro.

Chowder or Bisque?

Do you know the difference between a chowder and a bisque? A chowder typically is a thick, milk- or cream-based soup that contains a variety of seafood and vegetables. It also describes a thick, rich chunky soup. Chowders often are thickened with potatoes or a roux, a flour and fat mixture. A bisque is a thick, rich, and creamy soup made of puréed shellfish or fish, and, sometimes, meat or vegetables. Traditionally, it is thickened with rice.

Aromatic cumin, paprika, cinnamon, and saffron give this chicken and vegetable stew a full-bodied taste in a short cooking time.

Moroccan Chicken Stew

AMOUNT	INGREDIENTS
1 cup	quick-cooking couscous
12 ounces	skinless, boneless chicken thighs
	or breast halves, cut into 1-inch pieces
1/3 cup	sliced shallots
3 cloves	garlic, minced
1 tablespoon	olive oil
1/2 teaspoon	salt
1/2 teaspoon	paprika
1/2 teaspoon	ground cumin
1/4 teaspoon	ground cinnamon
1/4 teaspoon	ground saffron or turmeric
1/8 teaspoon	ground red pepper
6 ounces	baby pattypan squash
	or
1 1/2 cups	sliced zucchini
1 cup	slender baby carrots, tops trimmed,
	or packaged peeled baby carrots
1 cup	reduced-sodium chicken broth
1/4 cup	golden or dark raisins
	Fresh mint (optional)

START TO FINISH:
30 minutes

MAKES:
4 servings

❶ Cook couscous according to package directions, except omit the oil and salt; keep warm. Meanwhile, in a large nonstick skillet cook chicken, shallots, and garlic in hot oil over medium-high heat for 2 minutes, stirring occasionally.

❷ In a small bowl stir together salt, paprika, cumin, cinnamon, saffron, and ground red pepper; sprinkle evenly over chicken mixture. Cook and stir about 2 minutes more or until chicken is no longer pink.

❸ Cut any large pieces of squash and carrots in half; add to chicken mixture. Stir in chicken broth and raisins. Bring to boiling; reduce heat. Cover and simmer for 6 to 8 minutes or until vegetables are crisp-tender.

❹ Serve the stew over couscous. If desired, garnish with fresh mint.

Nutrition Facts per serving: 363 cal., 7 g total fat (1 g sat. fat), 45 mg chol., 496 mg sodium, 51 g carbo., 24 g pro.

This tangy, out-of-the-ordinary soup contains a generous amount of tender chicken, which contrasts well with the crisp tortilla strips.

Chicken and Lime Soup

START TO FINISH:	AMOUNT	INGREDIENTS
1 hour	6 cups	chicken broth
	1 pound	skinless, boneless chicken
MAKES:		breast halves
6 servings	1/2 cup	chopped onion
	1/2 cup	chopped green sweet pepper
	1 clove	garlic, minced
	1 tablespoon	cooking oil
	1 cup	chopped tomato
		or
	1 (7 1/2-ounce) can	tomatoes, undrained and cut up
	3/4 teaspoon	dried oregano, crushed
	1 teaspoon	finely shredded lime peel
	3 tablespoons	lime juice
	6 (6- to 7-inch)	corn or flour tortillas
		Nonstick cooking spray
		Fresh habanero or jalapeño chile peppers,
		seeded and chopped (optional)
		Thin lime slices (optional)

❶ In a large Dutch oven bring chicken broth to boiling. Add chicken; reduce heat. Cover and simmer about 15 minutes or until chicken is no longer pink (170°F). Remove chicken from broth; set aside to cool. Shred the chicken; set aside. Strain the broth through a large sieve or colander lined with two layers of 100-percent-cotton cheesecloth; set aside.

❷ In the same Dutch oven cook onion, sweet pepper, and garlic in hot oil until tender. Stir in the strained broth, tomato, and oregano. Bring to boiling. Stir in lime peel and lime juice; reduce heat. Cover and simmer for 20 minutes. Stir in the shredded chicken; heat through.

❸ Meanwhile, cut the tortillas in half. Cut crosswise into 1/2-inch strips. Lightly coat the strips with cooking spray. Arrange the strips in a single layer on a baking sheet. Bake in a 350°F oven about 10 minutes or until light brown and crisp.

❹ Serve the soup with tortilla strips. If desired, garnish with chile peppers and lime slices.

Nutrition Facts per serving: 220 cal., 7 g total fat (1 g sat. fat), 41 mg chol., 856 mg sodium, 18 g carbo., 22 g pro.

Garlic and a splash of Madeira give this chicken and rice soup a high intensity flavor. It's a sunny twist on old-fashioned chicken and rice soup.

Wild Rice-Chicken Soup

AMOUNT	INGREDIENTS
1 (6.2-ounce) package	quick-cooking long grain and wild rice mix
2 (14-ounce) cans	reduced-sodium chicken broth
1 tablespoon	snipped fresh thyme
	or
1 teaspoon	dried thyme, crushed
4 cloves	garlic, minced
4 cups	chopped tomatoes
1 (9-ounce) package	frozen, chopped cooked chicken breast
1 cup	finely chopped zucchini
¼ teaspoon	freshly ground black pepper
1 tablespoon	Madeira or dry sherry (optional)

START TO FINISH:
25 minutes

MAKES:
6 servings

❶ Prepare the long grain and wild rice mix according to package directions, except omit the seasoning packet and margarine.

❷ Meanwhile, in a Dutch oven combine chicken broth, dried thyme (if using), and garlic. Bring to boiling. Stir in fresh thyme (if using), tomatoes, chicken, zucchini, and pepper.

❸ Return to boiling; reduce heat. Cover and simmer for 5 minutes. Stir in cooked rice and, if desired, Madeira; heat through.

Nutrition Facts per serving: 236 cal., 5 g total fat (1 g sat. fat), 38 mg chol., 440 mg sodium, 31 g carbo., 18 g pro.

Just a pinch of saffron goes a long way in adding flavor and more intense color to food. The aromatic spice is a tad expensive, so feel free to leave it out. This soup is terrific with or without it.

Ravioli-Chicken Soup

START TO FINISH:
25 minutes

MAKES:
4 servings

AMOUNT	INGREDIENTS
	Nonstick cooking spray
12 ounces	**skinless, boneless chicken breast halves, cut into $^1/_2$-inch pieces**
6 cups	**reduced-sodium chicken broth**
$^1/_2$ cup	**sliced leek or chopped onion**
1 tablespoon	**finely chopped fresh ginger**
$^1/_4$ teaspoon	**thread saffron, slightly crushed (optional)**
1 (9-ounce) package	**refrigerated vegetable ravioli or herb-chicken tortellini**
$^1/_2$ cup	**baby spinach leaves or shredded spinach**

1 Lightly coat a large saucepan with cooking spray. Heat skillet over medium-high heat. Add chicken; cook and stir for 3 minutes. Carefully add chicken broth, leek, ginger, and, if desired, saffron.

2 Bring to boiling. Stir in ravioli. Return to boiling; reduce heat. Simmer, uncovered, for 5 to 9 minutes or until ravioli is tender but still firm, stirring occasionally. Top each serving with spinach.

Nutrition Facts per serving: 222 cal., 3 g total fat (0 g sat. fat), 59 mg chol., 1221 mg sodium, 21 g carbo., 29 g pro.

Decide how zesty you want this Tex-Mex soup to be, then choose from mild, medium, or hot salsa.

Chicken and Salsa Soup

AMOUNT	INGREDIENTS
1³/₄ cups	water
1 (14-ounce) can	reduced-sodium chicken broth
8 ounces	skinless, boneless chicken breast halves or thighs, cut into bite-size pieces
1 to 2 teaspoons	chili powder
1 (11-ounce) can	whole kernel corn with sweet peppers, drained
1 cup	bottled chunky garden-style salsa
2 ounces	Monterey Jack cheese with jalapeño peppers, shredded
3 cups	broken tortilla chips

START TO FINISH:
25 minutes

MAKES:
4 servings

1 In a large saucepan combine water, chicken broth, chicken, and chili powder. Bring to boiling; reduce heat. Cover and simmer for 8 minutes. Stir in corn. Simmer, uncovered, for 5 minutes more. Stir in salsa; heat through.

2 Sprinkle each serving with cheese. Serve with tortilla chips.

Nutrition Facts per serving: 319 cal., 9 g total fat (3 g sat. fat), 42 mg chol., 989 mg sodium, 32 g carbo., 20 g pro.

Good Bets for Broth

When you don't have time to make broth from scratch, choose from one of these:
• Canned broths: Some brands of canned chicken or beef broth can be used straight from the can. However, others are condensed and need diluting.
• Instant bouillon granules or cubes make an easy, instant broth: For 1 cup, dissolve 1 teaspoon of granules or 1 cube in 1 cup of hot water. These products can be purchased in beef, chicken, fish, or vegetable flavors.
• Remember that these substitutions are generally saltier than homemade broths. Hold off on adding extra salt until you've tasted the dish at the end of cooking. (Recipes were tested using canned broth; if using homemade, you may need more salt.)

Some creamy soups start with a white saucelike base. As easy as that is, we've made this recipe even easier by eliminating that step and using a refrigerated light Alfredo sauce instead.

Creamy Chicken-Vegetable Soup

START TO FINISH:
30 minutes

MAKES:
4 servings

AMOUNT	INGREDIENTS
3 cups	chicken broth
2 medium	carrots, thinly sliced
2 stalks	celery, thinly sliced
1 cup	chopped cooked chicken or turkey
1 small	zucchini, thinly sliced (about 1 cup)
$^1/_2$ cup	uncooked instant rice
1 (10-ounce) container	refrigerated light Alfredo sauce
$^1/_4$ cup	chopped, bottled roasted red sweet peppers
	or
1 (4-ounce) jar	diced pimiento, drained
1 tablespoon	snipped fresh thyme

❶ In a Dutch oven combine chicken broth, carrots, and celery. Bring to boiling; reduce heat. Cover and simmer for 10 minutes.

❷ Stir in chicken, zucchini, and rice. Remove from heat. Cover and let stand about 5 minutes or until rice is tender. Stir in Alfredo sauce, roasted sweet peppers, and thyme; heat through.

Nutrition Facts per serving: 349 cal., 14 g total fat (7 g sat. fat), 65 mg chol., 1,286 mg sodium, 34 g carbo., 22 g pro.

Small pasta such as tiny shell macaroni or broken linguine lets the pasta cook quickly so the vegetables retain their flavor and nutrition.

Turkey and Pasta Soup

AMOUNT	INGREDIENTS
3 (14-ounce) cans	reduced-sodium chicken broth
1 medium	onion, chopped
1 medium	carrot, sliced
1 small	red and/or yellow sweet pepper, chopped
3 cloves	garlic, minced
	Nonstick cooking spray
6 ounces	turkey breast tenderloin, cut into thin bite-size strips
3 ounces	dried small pasta (such as tiny bow ties)
1 teaspoon	snipped fresh thyme
	or
1/4 teaspoon	dried thyme, crushed
1/4 teaspoon	black pepper
3 cups	torn spinach leaves
2 tablespoons	finely shredded Parmesan cheese

START TO FINISH: 35 minutes

MAKES: 8 servings

❶ In a large saucepan bring chicken broth to boiling. Add onion, carrot, sweet pepper, and garlic. Return to boiling; reduce heat. Simmer, uncovered, for 10 minutes.

❷ Meanwhile, coat a medium skillet with cooking spray. Heat over medium-high heat. Add turkey; cook and stir for 2 to 3 minutes or until turkey is no longer pink. Remove from heat.

❸ Stir pasta, dried thyme (if using), and black pepper into broth mixture. Return to boiling; reduce heat. Simmer, uncovered, for 5 to 6 minutes or until pasta is tender but still firm, stirring occasionally. Stir in turkey and spinach. Cook, uncovered, for 1 to 2 minutes more or just until spinach is wilted. If using, stir in fresh thyme. Sprinkle each serving with Parmesan.

Nutrition Facts per serving: 212 cal., 4 g total fat (1 g sat. fat), 21 mg chol., 990 mg sodium, 27 g carbo., 17 g pro.

There are about as many versions of chili as there are cooks. This one combines turkey with black beans, chili powder, cumin, cocoa, red pepper, and a splash of coffee for an unusually good meal in a bowl.

Tantalizing Turkey Chili

PREP:
25 minutes

COOK:
30 minutes

MAKES:
6 servings

AMOUNT	INGREDIENTS
1 large	**onion, chopped**
1 medium	green sweet pepper, chopped
1 medium	**red sweet pepper, chopped**
3 cloves	garlic, minced
2 teaspoons	**olive oil or cooking oil**
1 pound	uncooked ground turkey
	or uncooked turkey, chopped
1 (28-ounce) can	**crushed tomatoes**
1 (15-ounce) can	black beans, rinsed and drained
1 cup	**water**
$^{1}/_{4}$ cup	cider vinegar
2 to 3 tablespoons	**strong coffee**
2 to 3 teaspoons	chili powder
2 teaspoons	**unsweetened cocoa powder**
1 teaspoon	ground cumin
$^{1}/_{4}$ to $^{1}/_{2}$ teaspoon	**ground red pepper**
	Shredded cheddar cheese
	(optional)

1 In a Dutch oven cook onion, sweet peppers, and garlic in hot oil over medium-high heat for 3 minutes. Add turkey. Cook about 3 minutes or until turkey is brown. Drain off fat.

2 Stir in tomatoes, black beans, water, vinegar, coffee, chili powder, cocoa powder, cumin, and ground red pepper. Bring to boiling; reduce heat. Cover and simmer for 30 minutes, stirring occasionally.

3 If desired, sprinkle each serving with cheddar cheese and additional chopped onion.

Nutrition Facts per serving: 246 cal., 8 g total fat (2 g sat. fat), 60 mg chol., 566 mg sodium, 25 g carbo., 20 g pro.

Refrigerated tortellini and Italian-seasoned tomatoes eliminate the work and fuss of this hearty soup that's loaded with old-world flavor.

Sausage-Tortellini Soup

AMOUNT	INGREDIENTS
	Nonstick cooking spray
1 pound	smoked chicken sausage, halved lengthwise and cut into 1-inch slices
1 large	onion, cut into thin wedges
2 cloves	garlic, minced
2 (14-ounce) cans	chicken broth
1 (14$\frac{1}{2}$-ounce) can	diced tomatoes with basil, oregano, and garlic
1 cup	water
2 (9-ounce) packages	refrigerated mushroom or cheese tortellini
1 (10-ounce) package	frozen baby lima beans
$\frac{1}{4}$ cup	slivered fresh basil
2 tablespoons	finely shredded Parmesan cheese

PREP:
20 minutes

COOK:
15 minutes

MAKES:
6 to 8 servings

1 Lightly coat a Dutch oven with cooking spray. Heat over medium heat. Add sausage, onion, and garlic; cook until sausage is brown and onion is tender. Drain off fat. Stir in chicken broth, undrained tomatoes, and water.

2 Bring to boiling; reduce heat. Cover and simmer for 10 minutes. Stir in tortellini and lima beans. Return to boiling; reduce heat. Simmer, uncovered, for 5 to 6 minutes or until tortellini and beans are tender, stirring occasionally. Stir in basil. Sprinkle each serving with Parmesan cheese.

Nutrition Facts per serving: 527 cal., 18 g total fat (6 g sat. fat), 62 mg chol., 1636 mg sodium, 60 g carbo., 32 g pro.

When you need a no-fail main dish, rely on this rich-tasting, easy-to-assemble fish soup. If red snapper or orange roughy isn't available, try it with cod or sole.

Red Pepper and Snapper Soup

START TO FINISH:	AMOUNT	I N G R E D I E N T S
50 minutes	1¼ pounds	fresh or frozen skinless red snapper, orange roughy, or other firm-fleshed fish fillets
MAKES:	3 medium	red sweet peppers, coarsely chopped
5 servings	1 cup	chopped shallots or onions
	2 tablespoons	olive oil
	3 (14-ounce) cans	reduced-sodium chicken broth
	¼ teaspoon	salt
	¼ teaspoon	black pepper
	⅛ teaspoon	ground red pepper
	½ cup	snipped fresh flat-leaf parsley

1 Thaw fish, if frozen. Rinse fish; pat dry with paper towels. Cut fish into 1-inch pieces; set aside.

2 In a large saucepan or Dutch oven cook sweet peppers and shallots in hot oil over medium heat for 5 minutes. Carefully add 1 can chicken broth. Bring to boiling; reduce heat. Cover and simmer about 20 minutes or until peppers are very tender. Cool slightly.

3 Pour half of the pepper mixture into a blender container. Cover and blend until nearly smooth. Pour into a medium bowl. Repeat with remaining pepper mixture. Return all mixture to saucepan. Stir in remaining chicken broth, salt, black pepper, and ground red pepper.

4 Bring to boiling; reduce heat. Stir in fish. Cover and simmer about 5 minutes or until fish flakes easily when tested with a fork, stirring once or twice. Stir in parsley.

Nutrition Facts per serving: 223 cal., 8 g total fat (1 g sat. fat), 42 mg chol., 859 mg sodium, 10 g carbo., 27 g pro.

The sweet essence of fresh fennel blends nicely with fish, tomatoes, garlic, and onion. This orange-scented soup tastes as good as it smells.

Fish Provençale

AMOUNT	INGREDIENTS
8 ounces	fresh or frozen skinless haddock, grouper, or halibut fillets
1 small	fennel bulb
3 cups	vegetable broth or chicken broth
1 large	onion, finely chopped
1 cup	cut-up yellow summer squash and/or zucchini
1 cup	dry white wine, vegetable broth, or chicken broth
1 teaspoon	finely shredded orange peel or lemon peel
3 cloves	garlic, minced
2 cups	chopped tomatoes
	or
1 (14½-ounce) can	diced tomatoes, undrained
2 tablespoons	snipped fresh thyme

START TO FINISH:
30 minutes

MAKES:
4 servings

① Thaw fish, if frozen. Rinse fish; pat dry with paper towels. Cut fish into 1-inch pieces; set aside.

② Cut off and discard the upper stalks of fennel. Remove any wilted outer layers; cut a thin slice from base. Cut fennel in half lengthwise and thinly slice.

③ In a large saucepan combine fennel, vegetable broth, onion, squash, wine, orange peel, and garlic. Bring to boiling; reduce heat. Cover and simmer for 10 minutes. Stir in fish, tomatoes, and thyme. Cook, uncovered, for 2 to 3 minutes or until fish flakes easily when tested with a fork. If desired, garnish with additional thyme.

Nutrition Facts per serving: 156 cal., 3 g total fat (0 g sat. fat), 18 mg chol., 752 mg sodium, 15 g carbo., 14 g pro.

Soup Making with Wine

Adding wine to soup often enhances its flavor. Sherry or Madeira blends well with chicken or veal soup. A strongly flavored soup with beef benefits from a tablespoon of dry red table wine. And dry white table wine adds zest to fish soup, crab or lobster bisque, or creamy chowder. Be thrifty with salt in soup to which wine is added, as the wine intensifies saltiness.

As eye-catching as party streamers and confetti, this full-flavored fish stew gets it's appeal from a rainbow of sweet peppers, jalapeño chile pepper, potatoes, and watercress.

Salmon Confetti Chowder

	AMOUNT	I N G R E D I E N T S
START TO FINISH: 25 minutes	2 cups	frozen pepper stir-fry vegetables (yellow, green, and red sweet peppers and onion)
	2 tablespoons	chopped, seeded fresh jalapeño chile pepper
MAKES: 4 servings	1 tablespoon	butter or margarine
	2 tablespoons	all-purpose flour
	2 cups	fat-free milk
	1 cup	fat-free half-and-half
	2 cups	refrigerated diced potatoes with onions
	1 (14³/₄-ounce) can	salmon, drained, flaked, and skin and bones removed
	¹/₄ cup	snipped watercress
	¹/₂ teaspoon	salt
	¹/₂ teaspoon	black pepper
	¹/₂ teaspoon	finely shredded lemon peel

1 In a large saucepan cook stir-fry vegetables and jalapeño pepper in hot butter for 3 to 5 minutes or until tender. Stir in flour. Add milk and half-and-half. Cook and stir over medium heat until mixture is slightly thickened. Cook and stir for 2 minutes more.

2 Stir in potatoes, salmon, watercress, salt, black pepper, and lemon peel; heat through.

Nutrition Facts per serving: 349 cal., 10 g total fat (2 g sat. fat), 61 mg chol., 1,174 mg sodium, 33 g carbo., 29 g pro.

Pink shrimp, emerald peas, red peppers, and tender pork—all part of classic Spanish paella—
make up this rice-based soup.

Spanish-Style Soup

AMOUNT	INGREDIENTS
8 ounces	lean boneless pork
1 teaspoon	cooking oil
1/2 cup	thinly sliced green onions
1/3 cup	chopped red sweet pepper
1 clove	garlic, minced
2 (14-ounce) cans	reduced-sodium chicken broth
1/2 cup	uncooked long grain rice
1	bay leaf
1/2 teaspoon	dried oregano, crushed
1/4 teaspoon	salt
1/8 teaspoon	ground red pepper
1/8 teaspoon	ground turmeric
8 ounces	peeled and deveined fresh shrimp
1 cup	frozen peas
1 tablespoon	snipped fresh parsley (optional)

START TO FINISH:
35 minutes

MAKES:
4 servings

1 Trim fat from meat. Cut meat into ¾-inch pieces. In a large saucepan cook meat in hot oil until meat is slightly pink in center. Remove meat, reserving drippings in saucepan. Cook green onions, sweet pepper, and garlic in the reserved drippings for 2 minutes.

2 Stir in chicken broth, rice, bay leaf, oregano, salt, ground red pepper, and turmeric. Bring to boiling; reduce heat. Cover and simmer for 15 minutes. Stir in meat, shrimp, and peas.

3 Cover and simmer for 3 to 5 minutes more or until shrimp turn opaque. Remove bay leaf. If desired, sprinkle each serving with parsley.

Nutrition Facts per serving: 256 cal., 7 g total fat (2 g sat. fat), 113 mg chol., 860 mg sodium, 25 g carbo., 23 g pro.

With clams, onion, celery, tomatoes, and thyme, this version has its roots in the time-honored Eastern seaboard tradition. But we've also added sweet potatoes, chile peppers, and lime juice for extra interest.

Caribbean Clam Chowder

START TO FINISH:
35 minutes

MAKES:
4 servings

AMOUNT	INGREDIENTS
¹/₂ pint	shucked clams
	or
1 (6¹/₂-ounce) can	minced clams
2 cups	peeled and cubed
	sweet potatoes (1 to 2 medium)
¹/₂ cup	chopped onion
1 stalk	celery, chopped
¹/₄ cup	chopped red sweet pepper
1¹/₂ teaspoons	snipped fresh thyme
	or
¹/₂ teaspoon	dried thyme, crushed
2 cloves	garlic, minced
1 (10-ounce) can	chopped tomatoes and
	green chile peppers
1 tablespoon	lime juice
1 tablespoon	dark rum (optional)

1 Drain clams, reserving juice. Add enough water to clam juice to make 2¹/₂ cups liquid. If using fresh clams, chop clams; set aside.

2 In a large saucepan bring clam liquid to boiling. Stir in sweet potatoes, onion, celery, sweet pepper, dried thyme (if using), and garlic. Return to boiling; reduce heat. Cover and simmer about 10 minutes or until sweet potatoes are tender. Remove from heat.

3 Mash mixture slightly with a potato masher. Stir in fresh thyme (if using), clams, undrained tomatoes, lime juice, and, if desired, rum; heat through.

Nutrition Facts per serving: 128 cal., 1 g total fat (0 g sat. fat), 19 mg chol., 337 mg sodium, 22 g carbo., 9 g pro.

Aromatic cumin and anise seeds complement this duo of black beans and white kidney beans.

Black and White Bean Soup

AMOUNT	INGREDIENTS
2 large	fresh poblano chile peppers
3 cloves	garlic, unpeeled
	Olive oil-flavor nonstick
	cooking spray
1 cup	finely chopped onion
2 (14-ounce) cans	vegetable broth
2 (15-ounce) cans	black beans, rinsed and drained
1 (15-ounce) can	white kidney (cannellini)
	or Great Northern beans, rinsed and drained
1 (6-ounce) can	tomato paste
1 tablespoon	balsamic vinegar
1¹/₂ teaspoons	dried marjoram, crushed
1¹/₂ teaspoons	cumin seeds, toasted and crushed
1¹/₂ teaspoons	anise seeds, crushed

PREP:
35 minutes

COOK:
5 minutes

STAND:
15 minutes

MAKES:
4 servings

1 To roast peppers, line a baking sheet with foil; set aside. Halve peppers lengthwise and remove stems, seeds, and membranes. Place peppers, cut sides down, on the prepared baking sheet. Bake in a 425°F oven about 20 minutes or until skins are bubbly and brown. Wrap peppers in the foil; let stand for 15 to 20 minutes or until cool enough to handle. Using a paring knife, pull skin off gently and slowly; finely chop peppers.

2 Meanwhile, in a small skillet cook garlic for 6 to 8 minutes or until slightly softened and light brown, stirring frequently. Cool slightly; peel and mince garlic.

3 Lightly coat a large saucepan with cooking spray. Heat over medium heat. Add roasted peppers, garlic, and onion; cook about 3 minutes or until onion is tender. Stir in ¹/₂ cup of the vegetable broth, stirring to scrape up any browned bits from bottom of saucepan.

4 Stir in the remaining vegetable broth, black beans, white kidney beans, tomato paste, vinegar, marjoram, cumin seeds, and anise seeds. Bring to boiling; reduce heat. Cover and simmer for 5 minutes.

Nutrition Facts per serving: 265 cal., 2 g total fat (0 g sat. fat), 0 mg chol., 1145 mg sodium, 59 g carbo., 22 g pro.

Perfume your kitchen with the exotic aroma of this beguiling chili spiced with cinnamon.

Tunisian Vegetable Chili

START TO FINISH:	AMOUNT	INGREDIENTS
30 minutes		Nonstick cooking spray
	1 medium	onion, chopped
MAKES:	**1 medium**	**carrot, sliced**
4 servings	1 small	yellow or green sweet pepper,
		cut into $^1/_2$-inch pieces
	1 (15-ounce) can	**Great Northern, white kidney (cannellini),**
		or pinto beans, rinsed and drained
	1 (14$^1/_2$-ounce) can	diced tomatoes
	$^1/_2$ cup	**apple juice or apple cider**
	$^1/_3$ cup	raisins
	2 teaspoons	**chili powder**
	$^3/_4$ teaspoon	ground cinnamon
	$^1/_4$ teaspoon	**salt**
	Several dashes	bottled hot pepper sauce
	2 cups	**hot cooked couscous**
	$^1/_4$ cup	finely chopped peanuts (optional)

1 Lightly coat a medium saucepan with cooking spray. Heat over medium heat. Add onion, carrot, and sweet pepper; reduce heat to medium-low. Cover and cook for 8 to 10 minutes or just until carrot is tender, stirring occasionally.

2 Stir in beans, undrained tomatoes, apple juice, raisins, chili powder, cinnamon, salt, and hot pepper sauce. Bring to boiling; reduce heat. Cover and cook for 5 minutes, stirring occasionally.

3 Serve the chili over couscous. If desired, sprinkle with peanuts.

Nutrition Facts per serving: 261 cal., 1 g total fat (0 g sat. fat), 0 mg chol., 581 mg sodium, 59 g carbo., 12 g pro.

No-Fat Cooking Tip

Using nonstick cooking spray instead of oil or butter for cooking vegetables keeps the fat and calories low in your recipes. But if you prefer, try cooking vegetables in a small amount of broth, water, or juice. Nonstick pans make cooking with either the nonstick cooking spray or liquid even easier.

Winter favorites, turnip and rutabaga, join forces with barley and white kidney beans for a meatless main dish that's as substantial as it is tasty.

Turnip and Barley Stew

AMOUNT	INGREDIENTS
1 large	onion, cut into wedges
4 cloves	garlic, minced
1 tablespoon	olive oil or cooking oil
2 medium	turnips, peeled and cut into ½-inch cubes
1 small	rutabaga, peeled and cut into ½-inch cubes
2 teaspoons	dried sage, crushed
1 teaspoon	ground cumin
3 (14-ounce) cans	vegetable broth
¾ cup	quick-cooking barley
1 (15-ounce) can	white kidney (cannellini) beans, rinsed and drained
⅓ cup	snipped fresh flat-leaf parsley
½ teaspoon	black pepper

PREP:
25 minutes

COOK:
15 minutes

MAKES:
6 servings

① In a Dutch oven cook onion and garlic in hot oil over medium heat until onion is tender. Stir in turnips, rutabaga, sage, and cumin; cook and stir for 1 minute more.

② Stir in vegetable broth and barley. Bring to boiling; reduce heat. Cover and simmer about 15 minutes or until vegetables and barley are tender. Stir in beans, parsley, and pepper; heat through.

Nutrition Facts per serving: 157 cal., 4 g total fat (0 g sat. fat), 0 mg chol., 955 mg sodium, 34 g carbo., 7 g pro.

The cheesy cornmeal topping is a hearty addition to this fiber-rich, meatless, lentil-and-veggie soup.

Tamale-Topped Lentil Soup

	AMOUNT	INGREDIENTS
PREP: 20 minutes	3$\frac{1}{2}$ cups	water
	2 medium	stalks celery, sliced
COOK: 40 minutes	1 medium	onion, chopped
	$\frac{1}{2}$ cup	brown lentils, rinsed and drained
MAKES: 6 servings	1 (14$\frac{1}{2}$-ounce) can	stewed tomatoes
	2 medium	carrots, sliced
	1 cup	frozen whole kernel corn
	1 cup	frozen cut green beans
	1 cup	sliced zucchini
		and/or yellow summer squash
	1 small	green sweet pepper, chopped
	$\frac{3}{4}$ teaspoon	salt
	$\frac{3}{4}$ teaspoon	chili powder
	$\frac{1}{4}$ teaspoon	ground cumin
	$\frac{1}{8}$ teaspoon	black pepper
	1 clove	garlic, minced
	1 recipe	Tamale Topper
	$\frac{1}{4}$ cup	shredded cheddar cheese (1 ounce)

1 In a Dutch oven combine 1$\frac{1}{2}$ cups of the water, the celery, onion, and lentils. Bring to boiling; reduce heat. Cover and simmer about 25 minutes or until lentils are tender; drain.

2 Stir in the remaining 2 cups water, the undrained tomatoes, carrots, corn, green beans, zucchini, sweet pepper, salt, chili powder, cumin, black pepper, and garlic. Return to boiling; reduce heat.

3 Meanwhile, prepare Tamale Topper. Drop the topper in 6 portions on top of hot stew. Cover (do not lift cover while cooking) and simmer about 15 minutes or until a wooden toothpick inserted in topper comes out clean. Just before serving, sprinkle with cheddar cheese.

Tamale Topper: In a medium saucepan combine $\frac{2}{3}$ cup cornmeal and $\frac{1}{4}$ teaspoon salt. Gradually stir in 1 cup milk. Cook and stir until thickened and bubbly. Gradually stir cornmeal mixture into 1 beaten egg. Stir in $\frac{1}{2}$ cup shredded cheddar cheese (2 ounces).

Nutrition Facts per serving: 286 cal., 8 g total fat (4 g sat. fat), 53 mg chol., 666 mg sodium, 43 g carbo., 13 g pro.

SANDWICHES

BONUS
CHAPTER

Old-fashioned steak sandwiches seem ho-hum when you compare them to this sirloin, onion, and roasted pepper combo that's served on sourdough bread.

Beef and Sweet Onion Sandwiches

START TO FINISH:
25 minutes

MAKES:
4 sandwiches

AMOUNT	INGREDIENTS
12 ounces	boneless beef sirloin
	or top round steak, cut 1 inch thick
$1/2$ teaspoon	coarsely ground black pepper
2 teaspoons	cooking oil
1 medium	sweet onion (such as
	Vidalia or Walla Walla), sliced
2 tablespoons	Dijon-style mustard
$1^1/2$ cups	packaged prewashed spinach
	or mixed salad greens, shredded
8 (1-inch) slices	sourdough or rye bread, toasted
$1/2$ of a (7-ounce)	roasted red sweet peppers,
jar	drained and cut into $1/2$-inch strips

❶ Trim fat from meat. Sprinkle both sides of meat with pepper; press in lightly. In a large heavy skillet heat oil over medium-high heat. Add meat; reduce heat to medium. Cook for 9 to 12 minutes for medium-rare (145°F) to medium (160°F), turning once. Remove meat, reserving drippings in skillet. Cover meat and keep warm.

❷ Cook onion in the reserved drippings about 5 minutes or until onion is crisp-tender. (If necessary, add more oil during cooking.) Stir in Dijon mustard; remove from heat.

❸ Just before serving, cut meat into thin bite-size strips. To assemble, arrange spinach on 4 of the bread slices. Top with meat strips, onion mixture, and roasted pepper strips; add the remaining bread slices.

Nutrition Facts per sandwich: 335 cal., 12 g total fat (4 g sat. fat), 57 mg chol., 553 mg sodium, 30 g carbo., 25 g pro.

Sweet and Juicy Onions

All onions are not created equal—some are sweeter than others. The onions called for in Beef and Sweet Onion Sandwiches are milder, sweeter, and less pungent than common yellow and white onions. Sweet onions generally have thin, light outer skins, a high water content, and a high sugar content. They bruise easily and are fragile, so they have a fairly short storage life.

Rémoulade is a sharp, sweet-salty sauce that's a super complement to cold meats and fish. Flavored with a medley of mayonnaise, mustard, anchovies, capers, pickles, and herbs, rémoulade will keep for several days in the refrigerator—if it's not eaten first.

Roast Beef and Turkey with Rémoulade

AMOUNT	INGREDIENTS
¹/₂ cup	mayonnaise or salad dressing
1 tablespoon	snipped fresh parsley
2 teaspoons	drained capers
2 teaspoons	finely chopped sweet or dill pickle
2 teaspoons	anchovy paste (optional)
¹/₂ teaspoon	Dijon-style mustard
¹/₈ teaspoon	dried tarragon, crushed
¹/₈ teaspoon	black pepper
1 small clove	garlic, minced
1 (12-inch)	plain or seasoned, round focaccia bread
2 large or 4 small	romaine lettuce leaves
1 medium	tomato, thinly sliced
6 to 8 ounces	sliced roast beef
6 to 8 ounces	sliced smoked turkey

START TO FINISH:
20 minutes

MAKES:
6 servings

① For rémoulade, in a small bowl stir together mayonnaise, parsley, capers, pickle, anchovy paste (if desired), Dijon mustard, tarragon, pepper, and garlic. Set aside.

② Using a long serrated knife, slice the focaccia bread in half horizontally. Spread cut surfaces of bread halves with rémoulade. Layer ingredients on bottom half of bread in the following order: lettuce, tomato, roast beef, and turkey. Replace the top half of bread. Cut into wedges.

Nutrition Facts per serving: 431 cal., 22 g total fat (5 g sat. fat), 51 mg chol., 462 mg sodium, 39 g carbo., 22 g pro.

Surprise your palate with the flavor of curry and mustard in every bite of these tasty burgers.

Grilled Burgers with Curry Mustard

	AMOUNT	INGREDIENTS
PREP: 15 minutes	½ cup	finely shredded carrot
	¼ cup	thinly sliced green onions
GRILL: 10 minutes	¼ cup	soft whole wheat bread crumbs
	2 tablespoons	milk
MAKES: 4 sandwiches	¼ teaspoon	dried Italian seasoning, crushed
	¼ teaspoon	garlic salt
	Dash	black pepper
	12 ounces	lean ground beef or uncooked ground turkey or chicken
	4	whole wheat hamburger buns, split and toasted
		Shredded zucchini (optional)
		Sliced tomato (optional)
	1 recipe	Curry Mustard (optional)

1 In a medium bowl stir together carrot, green onions, bread crumbs, milk, Italian seasoning, garlic salt, and pepper. Add ground meat; mix well. Shape meat mixture into four ½-inch-thick patties.

2 Place patties on the rack of an uncovered grill directly over medium coals. Grill for 10 to 13 minutes or until meat is done (160°F for beef; 165°F for turkey or chicken), turning once halfway through grilling. (Or place patties on the unheated rack of a broiler pan. Broil 3 to 4 inches from the heat for 10 to 12 minutes, turning once halfway through broiling.)

3 Serve the burgers in buns. If desired, top with zucchini, tomato, and Curry Mustard.

Curry Mustard: In a small bowl stir together ¼ cup Dijon-style mustard and ½ teaspoon curry powder. Makes ¼ cup.

Nutrition Facts per sandwich: 257 cal., 9 g total fat (4 g sat. fat), 54 mg chol., 409 mg sodium, 24 g carbo., 20 g pro.

These are definitely not your mother's sloppy joes. We've added fresh vegetables and herbs to the spicy tomato-meat combination.

Spicy Sloppy Joes

AMOUNT	INGREDIENTS
1 pound	lean ground beef
1 medium	onion, chopped
2 cloves	garlic, minced
1 cup	chopped zucchini
1 cup	chopped yellow summer squash
1 cup	sliced fresh mushrooms
³⁄₄ cup	chopped green sweet pepper
1 (16-ounce) jar	salsa
1 teaspoon	dried basil, crushed
¹⁄₂ teaspoon	dried parsley flakes
¹⁄₂ teaspoon	dried rosemary, crushed
6 to 8	hamburger buns
	or kaiser rolls, split and toasted

START TO FINISH:
30 minutes

MAKES:
6 to 8 sandwiches

1 In a large skillet cook ground beef, onion, and garlic until meat is brown. Drain off fat. Stir in zucchini, yellow squash, mushrooms, and sweet pepper. Cover and cook over low heat for 5 to 7 minutes or until vegetables are tender.

2 Stir in salsa, basil, parsley, and rosemary. Simmer, uncovered, about 10 minutes or until most of the liquid is evaporated. Serve the meat mixture in buns.

Nutrition Facts per sandwich: 358 cal., 14 g total fat (4 g sat. fat), 47 mg chol., 648 mg sodium, 40 g carbo., 22 g pro.

With fresh-tasting Jicama Coleslaw topping the ever-popular pork tenderloin, this hearty sandwich is the sort of twist-on-the-classic that you'd expect to find at contemporary brew pubs across the country.

Pork Tenderloin Sandwiches

PREP:	AMOUNT	INGREDIENTS
35 minutes	1 recipe	Jicama Coleslaw
CHILL:	1 (12-ounce)	pork tenderloin
2 hours	3 tablespoons	all-purpose flour
COOK:	1/4 teaspoon	onion powder or garlic powder
4 minutes	1/4 teaspoon	ground red pepper
	1/4 teaspoon	black pepper
MAKES:	2 tablespoons	cooking oil
4 sandwiches	4 slices	Muenster cheese
	4	hamburger buns, kaiser rolls,
		or sourdough rolls, split and toasted
		Red onion slices (optional)

1 Prepare Jicama Coleslaw. Cover and chill for 2 to 24 hours.

2 Trim any fat from meat. Cut meat crosswise into 4 slices. Place each slice between 2 pieces of plastic wrap. Using the heel of your hand, press lightly to 1/4-inch thickness. Remove plastic wrap.

3 In a shallow dish combine flour, onion powder, ground red pepper, and black pepper. Dip the meat into flour mixture, turning to coat. In a large skillet heat oil over medium-high heat. Add meat; reduce heat to medium. Cook for 4 to 6 minutes or until meat is slightly pink in center, turning once. (If necessary, cook in 2 batches, adding more oil during cooking.)

4 To assemble, place the meat and Muenster cheese on bottom halves of buns. Top each with a few red onion slices (if desired) and about 1/4 cup of the Jicama Coleslaw; replace the top halves of buns. Serve additional Jicama Coleslaw as a side dish.

Jicama Coleslaw: For dressing, in a screw-top jar combine 3 tablespoons vinegar, 3 tablespoons salad oil, 1 tablespoon honey, 1/4 teaspoon salt, 1/8 to 1/4 teaspoon black pepper, and, if desired, several dashes bottled hot pepper sauce. Cover and shake well. In a salad bowl combine 4 cups peeled jicama cut into thin bite-size strips, 1 cup shredded red or green cabbage, 1 cup shredded carrots, and 1/4 cup thinly sliced green onions. Pour dressing over vegetable mixture; toss gently to coat.

Nutrition Facts per sandwich: 500 cal., 22 g total fat (8 g sat. fat), 77 mg chol., 559 mg sodium, 40 g carbo., 34 g pro.

Serve in-season fruits—grapes or watermelon in the summer, apples or pears in the fall—as a fresh side to this hearty hot sandwich. Year-round, it will be a hit with your family. (Don't forget the chips and pickles too.)

Grilled Ham-on-Rye Special

AMOUNT	INGREDIENTS
¼ cup	bottled Thousand Island salad dressing
1 teaspoon	prepared mustard
1 cup	packaged shredded cabbage with carrot (coleslaw mix)
1 tablespoon	margarine or butter
8 slices	rye or whole wheat bread
4 ounces	thinly sliced cooked ham
4 ounces	thinly sliced Swiss or Colby cheese

START TO FINISH:
20 minutes

MAKES:
4 sandwiches

1 In a medium bowl stir together Thousand Island salad dressing and mustard. Add shredded cabbage; toss to coat.

2 Spread a thin layer of margarine on one side of each bread slice. Turn 4 of the bread slices spread sides down; add half of the ham. Spoon on the cabbage mixture; top with cheese slices and the remaining ham. Add the remaining bread slices spread sides up.

3 Heat a large skillet or griddle over medium heat. Add sandwiches; reduce heat to medium-low. Cook for 4 to 6 minutes or until bread is golden brown and cheese starts to melt, turning once.

Nutrition Facts per sandwich: 409 cal., 20 g total fat (8 g sat. fat), 47 mg chol., 976 mg sodium, 40 g carbo., 19 g pro.

You won't find this sandwich at your local greasy spoon. It boasts a sophisticated blend of chèvre-topped chicken, roasted sweet peppers, and fresh basil.

Chicken and Pepper Sandwiches

	AMOUNT	INGREDIENTS
PREP: 15 minutes	¼ cup	olive oil
	4 teaspoons	red wine vinegar
MARINATE: 15 minutes	1 tablespoon	snipped fresh thyme
	½ teaspoon	salt
COOK: 8 minutes	¼ teaspoon	crushed red pepper
	4	skinless, boneless chicken breast halves (about 1¼ pounds total)
MAKES: 4 sandwiches		Nonstick cooking spray
	4 (1-inch) bias-cut slices	French bread, toasted
	¼ cup	semisoft cheese with herbs or semisoft goat cheese (chèvre)
	1 (7-ounce) jar	roasted red sweet peppers, drained and cut into strips
	½ cup	fresh basil, watercress, or baby spinach leaves

1 For marinade, in a small bowl whisk together oil, vinegar, thyme, salt, and crushed red pepper. Set aside 2 tablespoons of the marinade for brushing bread.

2 Place each chicken piece between 2 pieces of plastic wrap. Using the flat side of a meat mallet, pound lightly to about ½-inch thickness. Remove plastic wrap. Place chicken in a resealable plastic bag. Add the remaining marinade; seal bag. Marinate at room temperature about 15 minutes or in the refrigerator about 1 hour, turning bag once. Drain chicken, discarding marinade.

3 Coat a large skillet with cooking spray. Heat over medium heat. Brush both sides of bread slices with the reserved marinade. Add bread to skillet and cook for 2 to 4 minutes or until lightly toasted, turning once. Remove bread from skillet. Increase heat to medium-high.

4 Add chicken to skillet and cook for 8 to 10 minutes or until chicken is no longer pink (170°F), turning once. If chicken browns too quickly, reduce heat to medium. Remove from heat. Spread or sprinkle chicken with cheese.

5 To assemble, place the chicken on toasted bread slices. Top with roasted sweet pepper strips and basil leaves.

Nutrition Facts per sandwich: 418 cal., 20 g total fat (5 g sat. fat), 82 mg chol., 629 mg sodium, 21 g carbo., 37 g pro.

Like any Monte Cristo deserving of its opulent name, this batter-dipped, golden brown sandwich oozes with melted cheese. But in our version, fresh pears add a particularly regal touch. A light salad with a coleslaw dressing would provide a terrific contrast.

Chicken and Pear Monte Cristo

AMOUNT	INGREDIENTS
4 to 6 teaspoons	prepared horseradish
8 thick slices	firm-textured white bread
8 thin slices	mozzarella cheese
8 thin slices	cooked chicken or turkey breast
	(12 ounces total)
1 to 2 medium	pears, peeled, cored, and thinly sliced
2	slightly beaten eggs
$^2/_3$ cup	half-and-half, light cream,
	or whipping cream

PREP:
15 minutes

BAKE:
25 minutes

MAKES:
8 servings

1 Spread the horseradish on 1 side of 4 of the bread slices. Top each with a slice of cheese, a slice of chicken, and several pear slices. Add another slice of cheese and a slice of chicken. Top with a slice of bread.

2 Meanwhile, grease a 15×10×1-inch baking pan; set aside. In a shallow dish combine eggs and half-and-half. Dip the sandwiches into egg mixture, turning and allowing each side to stand about 10 seconds to absorb egg mixture. Place sandwiches in the prepared baking pan.

3 Bake in a 350°F oven for 15 minutes. Carefully turn sandwiches; bake about 10 minutes more or just until bread is golden brown and cheese melts. Cut each sandwich into 4 triangles.

Nutrition Facts per serving: 321 cal., 16 g total fat (8 g sat. fat), 116 mg chol., 428 mg sodium, 19 g carbo., 26 g pro.

Perfect Pears

Juicy, ripe pears are great not only for snacking out of hand, but they add a honey-sweet flavor and, if left unpeeled, a lovely color to recipes. While often thought of as a fall and winter fruit, numerous varieties and extended growing seasons mean pears of all sizes and colors can be plucked practically year-round from supermarket shelves. Some tips:

• Look for pears that are free from bruises and cuts. Select firm pears if you plan to bake them.

• To ripen pears, place them in a paper bag at room temperature for 2 to 3 days. Or store them in a fruit bowl in a cool, dark place. You'll know they're ripe when the stem end yields to pressure when touched.

• Ripe pears can be kept in the refrigerator for several days.

Southern barbecue goes gourmet! These substantial sandwiches feature spicy grilled turkey tucked into buns with grilled tomatillos and fresh spinach. Try them with sweet potato chips, a tasty alternative to regular chips.

Barbecued Turkey Tenderloins

PREP:
15 minutes

GRILL:
20 minutes

MAKES:
4 sandwiches

AMOUNT	INGREDIENTS
½ cup	bottled onion-hickory barbecue sauce
1 tablespoon	tahini (sesame seed paste)*
1 small	fresh jalapeño chile pepper, seeded and finely chopped
4	tomatillos, husked and halved lengthwise, or
½ cup	bottled salsa verde
2	turkey breast tenderloins (about 1 pound total)
	Spinach leaves
4	hamburger buns or French-style rolls, split and toasted

1 For sauce, in a small bowl combine barbecue sauce, tahini, and jalapeño pepper. Transfer half of the sauce to another bowl for basting turkey. Reserve the remaining sauce until ready to serve. If using, thread tomatillos onto two 8- to 10-inch metal skewers; set aside.

2 Brush both sides of turkey with some of the basting sauce. Place turkey on the rack of an uncovered grill directly over medium coals. Grill about 20 minutes or until turkey is no longer pink (170°F), turning and brushing once with the remaining basting sauce halfway through grilling. Place tomatillos on the grill rack next to turkey the last 8 minutes of grilling or until tender, turning once halfway through grilling. Thinly slice turkey; chop tomatillos.

3 To assemble, place spinach, turkey, and tomatillos or salsa verde on bottom halves of buns. Top with the reserved sauce; replace the top halves of buns.

*Note: Tahini is a thick paste that is made by crushing sesame seeds. It is most often used in Middle Eastern dishes and can be found in the ethnic foods section of most supermarkets.

Nutrition Facts per sandwich: 378 cal., 8 g total fat (2 g sat. fat), 50 mg chol., 776 mg sodium, 45 g carbo., 30 g pro.

A spicy cilantro spread elevates these submarine sandwiches from ordinary to exceptional.

Smoked Turkey Dagwood

AMOUNT	INGREDIENTS
½ cup	mayonnaise or salad dressing
2 tablespoons	snipped fresh cilantro
1	fresh jalapeño chile pepper,
	seeded and finely chopped
½ teaspoon	ground cumin
1	avocado, seeded, peeled,
	and thinly sliced
1 tablespoon	lime juice
8 (½-inch) slices	sourdough bread, toasted
16 thin slices	smoked turkey
	(about 8 ounces total)
8 slices	tomato
8 slices	peppered bacon,
	crisp-cooked and drained

START TO FINISH:
25 minutes

MAKES:
4 sandwiches

1 For chile mayonnaise, in a small bowl combine mayonnaise, cilantro, jalapeño pepper, and cumin. If desired, cover and chill up to 2 days.

2 In a small bowl combine avocado slices and lime juice; toss gently to coat. Set aside.

3 To assemble, spread the chile mayonnaise on one side of the bread slices. Top 4 of the bread slices with turkey, tomato, bacon, and avocado; add the remaining bread slices.

Nutrition Facts per sandwich: 560 cal., 40 g total fat (8 g sat. fat), 56 mg chol., 1245 mg sodium, 33 g carbo., 21 g pro.

The Right Avocado

If you're after neat little cubes or slices of avocado, choose firm fruits—not rock-hard ones—that give a little under gentle pressure. If you plan to mash the avocado to make guacamole, choose fruits that feel soft to your fingers. If you want to shop ahead, buy firm avocados. Stored at room temperature, they'll ripen in 3 to 4 days. Speed ripening by placing avocados in a brown paper bag or in a fruit ripening bowl. When they're ripe, put them in the refrigerator and use within a few days.

A skinny version of the New Orleans specialty, this muffuletta won't disappoint you. Smoked lean turkey breast, piquant pepperoncini, and mouthwatering artichoke hearts are tucked between focaccia. An added bonus—it's a great totable lunch.

Muffuletta

START TO FINISH:
20 minutes

MAKES:
6 servings

AMOUNT	INGREDIENTS
1 (12-inch)	plain or seasoned, round focaccia bread
	Lettuce leaves
6 ounces	thinly sliced mesquite-smoked turkey breast
4 ounces	thinly sliced reduced-fat salami or thinly sliced turkey salami
5 ounces	thinly sliced reduced-fat provolone or mozzarella cheese
⅓ cup	pepperoncini salad peppers or giardiniera (pickled mixed vegetables), drained and chopped
¼ cup	chopped pitted green olives
¼ cup	thinly sliced canned artichoke hearts
¼ cup	bottled fat-free Italian salad dressing

1 Using a long serrated knife, slice the focaccia bread in half horizontally. Layer ingredients on bottom half of bread in the following order: lettuce, turkey, salami, and cheese.

2 In a small bowl combine pepperoncini, olives, artichoke hearts, and salad dressing; spoon evenly over cheese. Replace the top half of bread. Cut into wedges.

Nutrition Facts per serving: 275 cal., 9 g total fat (3 g sat. fat), 45 mg chol., 1262 mg sodium, 27 g carbo., 21 g pro.

Slicing Flatbreads

Large, irregularly shaped focaccia and other flatbreads are a refreshing change of pace from perfectly shaped sandwich breads. To slice them horizontally for sandwiches, use a long, thin serrated knife. Holding your hand flat, gently press on the top of the bread to hold it in place while you carefully slice the bread in half.

Honey not only seasons the grilled tuna for this imaginative sandwich, it also adds a sweet note to the shallot mayonnaise.

Updated Tuna Melt

AMOUNT	INGREDIENTS
12 ounces	fresh or frozen tuna steaks, cut ³/₄ to 1 inch thick
¹/₄ cup	balsamic vinegar
2 tablespoons	honey
¹/₄ cup	mayonnaise or salad dressing
2 tablespoons	finely chopped shallots or red onion
4 slices	provolone cheese (3 ounces)
8 (¹/₂-inch) slices	sourdough or Italian bread, toasted

START TO FINISH:
30 minutes

MAKES:
4 sandwiches

❶ Thaw fish, if frozen. Rinse fish; pat dry with paper towels. Cut fish into 4 serving-size pieces; set aside. In a small saucepan bring balsamic vinegar to boiling; reduce heat. Simmer, uncovered, for 3 to 4 minutes or until vinegar is reduced by half (about 2 tablespoons).

❷ For sauce, in a small bowl stir together 1 tablespoon of the reduced vinegar and 1 tablespoon of the honey; set aside for basting fish. In another small bowl combine the remaining vinegar, the remaining honey, mayonnaise, and shallots. Cover and chill until ready to serve.

❸ In a grill with a cover arrange medium-hot coals around a drip pan. Test for medium heat above the pan. Place fish on the grill rack over drip pan. Cover and grill for 7 to 9 minutes per ¹/₂-inch thickness of fish or until fish flakes easily when tested with a fork, turning and brushing once with basting sauce halfway through grilling. Top the fish with cheese slices. Cover and grill about 1 minute more or just until cheese melts.

❹ To assemble, spread the mayonnaise mixture on one side of the bread slices. Top 4 of the bread slices with fish; add the remaining bread slices, spread sides down.

Nutrition Facts per sandwich: 489 cal., 22 g total fat (6 g sat. fat), 51 mg chol., 601 mg sodium, 40 g carbo., 30 g pro.

Keep prep time to a minimum by using deli coleslaw to top these hearty sandwiches. But if you happen to have a few minutes to spare, stir together your favorite coleslaw recipe, use some of it as a sandwich topper, and refrigerate the rest for tomorrow night's supper.

Sole-Slaw Sandwiches

	AMOUNT	INGREDIENTS
PREP: 15 minutes	1 to 1¼ pounds	fresh or frozen sole or flounder fillets
		Nonstick cooking spray
BAKE: 8 minutes	⅓ cup	seasoned fine dry bread crumbs
	⅓ cup	grated Parmesan cheese
MAKES: 4 sandwiches	¼ teaspoon	black pepper
	¼ cup	milk
	3 tablespoons	all-purpose flour
	1 cup	deli coleslaw
	4	whole wheat hamburger buns, split and toasted

1 Thaw fish, if frozen. Rinse fish; pat dry with paper towels. Cut fish into 4 serving-size pieces. Lightly coat a baking sheet with cooking spray; set aside.

2 In a shallow dish combine bread crumbs, Parmesan cheese, and pepper. Place milk and flour in two separate shallow dishes.

3 Fold under ends of fish so each piece is slightly larger than bun. Dip the fish into the flour; dip into milk. Dip into crumb mixture, turning to coat. Arrange fish pieces on the prepared baking sheet so they don't touch each other.

4 Bake in a 400°F oven for 8 to 10 minutes or until fish flakes easily when tested with a fork. Meanwhile, drain excess liquid from coleslaw. Serve the fish in buns with coleslaw.

Nutrition Facts per sandwich: 308 cal., 6 g total fat (3 g sat. fat), 70 mg chol., 700 mg sodium, 32 g carbo., 31 g pro.

Why say sandwich when you can say panini? The Italian word sounds so much more enticing, with a promise of unexpected delights—even if it does simply mean bread roll in Italian!

Eggplant Panini

AMOUNT	INGREDIENTS
1 cup	torn arugula
2 teaspoons	red wine vinegar
1 teaspoon	olive oil
1/3 cup	seasoned fine dry bread crumbs
2 tablespoons	grated pecorino Romano or Parmesan cheese
1	slightly beaten egg
1 tablespoon	milk
2 tablespoons	all-purpose flour
1/2 teaspoon	salt
1 medium	eggplant, cut crosswise into 1/2-inch slices
1 tablespoon	olive oil
3 ounces	fresh mozzarella cheese, thinly sliced
1 (12-inch)	plain or seasoned, round focaccia bread
1 large	tomato, thinly sliced

START TO FINISH:
25 minutes

MAKES:
6 servings

1 In a small bowl toss together arugula, vinegar, and the 1 teaspoon oil; set aside. In a shallow dish combine bread crumbs and Romano cheese. In another shallow dish combine egg and milk. In a third shallow dish combine flour and salt. Dip the eggplant slices into flour mixture; dip into egg mixture. Dip into crumb mixture, turning to coat.

2 In a large nonstick skillet heat the 1 tablespoon oil over medium heat. Add eggplant slices; cook for 6 to 8 minutes or until light brown, turning once. (If necessary, add more oil during cooking.) Top the eggplant with mozzarella cheese; reduce heat to low. Cover and cook just until cheese starts to melt.

3 Using a long serrated knife, slice the focaccia bread in half horizontally. Place the eggplant slices, cheese sides up, on bottom half of bread. Top with the arugula mixture and tomato slices. Replace top half of bread. Cut into wedges.

Nutrition Facts per serving: 318 cal., 10 g total fat (4 g sat. fat), 48 mg chol., 447 mg sodium, 45 g carbo., 13 g pro.

If you've never considered using Brie in a sandwich, here's a delicious way to try it. The cooked onions and garden-fresh tomatoes and basil serve as exquisite accents to the creamy cheese.

Sautéed Onion and Tomato Sandwiches

START TO FINISH:
20 minutes

MAKES:
4 sandwiches

AMOUNT	INGREDIENTS
2 medium	onions, sliced
1 teaspoon	olive oil
	Honey mustard
8 slices	hearty whole grain bread (toasted, if desired)
3 small	red and/or yellow tomatoes, thinly sliced
4	lettuce leaves, shredded
	Small basil leaves
4 ounces	soft, spreadable Brie or cream cheese

1 In a large skillet cook onions in hot oil over medium-high heat for 5 to 7 minutes or until tender and just starting to brown. Cool slightly.

2 To assemble, lightly spread honey mustard on 1 side of 4 of the bread slices. Top with cooked onions, tomato slices, and lettuce. Sprinkle with basil leaves. Spread the Brie cheese on 1 side of the remaining bread slices; place on sandwiches, spread sides down.

Nutrition Facts per sandwich: 287 cal., 12 g total fat (6 g sat. fat), 28 mg chol., 490 mg sodium, 35 g carbo., 12 g pro.

Jazz Up Sandwich Spreads

Give spreads a creative twist and your sandwiches will rise from lunch standbys to special fare.
• The next time you reach for the mayonnaise or salad dressing, mix in pickle relish, chopped olives, chopped roasted red sweet peppers, capers, or a sprinkling of curry powder or celery salt.
• Take mustard to the next level by adding a little dry white wine or honey to Dijon, brown, or yellow mustard. Or splash in some balsamic, fruit-flavored, or nut-flavored vinegar for a flavor boost.
• Create new spreads by mixing Dijon mustard or your favorite bottled salad dressing into sour cream, mayonnaise, or plain yogurt.

When the weather turns hot, stay cool with this hearty sandwich featuring the flavors of the cold soup, gazpacho. Tomatoes and cucumbers are mixed with black beans, then scooped into grilled French bread "bowls."

Grilled Gazpacho Sandwiches

AMOUNT	INGREDIENTS
1 medium	cucumber, seeded and chopped
1 cup	cooked or canned black beans, rinsed and drained
1/4 cup	snipped fresh cilantro
2 tablespoons	cider vinegar
1 tablespoon	olive oil
1	pickled jalapeño chile pepper, finely chopped
1/2 to 1 teaspoon	chili powder
1 clove	garlic, minced
3 large	tomatoes, halved
1 large	sweet onion (such as Vidalia or Walla Walla), cut into 1/2-inch slices
1 loaf	French bread
1 cup	shredded white cheddar or cheddar cheese (4 ounces)

PREP:
20 minutes

GRILL:
14 minutes

MAKES:
6 sandwiches

1 In a medium bowl combine cucumber, black beans, cilantro, vinegar, oil, jalapeño pepper, chili powder, and garlic. Season to taste with salt and black pepper. Set aside.

2 In a grill with a cover arrange medium coals in bottom of grill. Place tomatoes and onion on the lightly greased grill rack directly over coals. Grill, uncovered, for 12 to 15 minutes or until vegetables are lightly charred, turning onion once halfway through grilling. Transfer vegetables to a cutting board; cool slightly. Coarsely chop vegetables; stir into bean mixture.

3 Meanwhile, slice French bread in half lengthwise. Cut each bread half crosswise into 3 pieces. Using a fork, hollow out the bread pieces slightly. Place bread pieces, cut sides down, on grill rack. Grill, uncovered, about 1 minute or until toasted. Remove from grill.

4 Spoon the bean mixture into the bread pieces; sprinkle with cheddar cheese. Return to grill, cheese side up. Cover and grill for 1 to 2 minutes or just until cheese melts.

Nutrition Facts per sandwich: 329 cal., 11 g total fat (5 g sat. fat), 20 mg chol., 634 mg sodium, 46 g carbo., 14 g pro.

Index

METRIC
INFORMATION

The charts on this page provide a guide for converting measurements from the U.S. customary system, which is used throughout this book, to the metric system.

Product Differences

Most of the ingredients called for in the recipes in this book are available in most countries. However, some are known by different names. Here are some common American ingredients and their possible counterparts:

- Sugar (white) is granulated, fine granulated, or castor sugar.
- Powdered sugar is icing sugar.
- All-purpose flour is enriched, bleached or unbleached white household flour. When self-rising flour is used in place of all-purpose flour in a recipe that calls for leavening, omit the leavening agent (baking soda or baking powder) and salt.
- Light-color corn syrup is golden syrup.
- Cornstarch is cornflour.
- Baking soda is bicarbonate of soda.
- Vanilla or vanilla extract is vanilla essence.
- Green, red, or yellow sweet peppers are capsicums or bell peppers.
- Golden raisins are sultanas.

Volume and Weight

The United States traditionally uses cup measures for liquid and solid ingredients. The chart below shows the approximate imperial and metric equivalents. If you are accustomed to weighing solid ingredients, the following approximate equivalents will be helpful.

- 1 cup butter, castor sugar, or rice = 8 ounces = ¹/₂ pound = 250 grams
- 1 cup flour = 4 ounces = ¹/₄ pound = 125 grams
- 1 cup icing sugar = 5 ounces = 150 grams

Canadian and U.S. volume for a cup measure is 8 fluid ounces (237 ml), but the standard metric equivalent is 250 ml.

1 British imperial cup is 10 fluid ounces.

In Australia, 1 tablespoon equals 20 ml, and there are 4 teaspoons in the Australian tablespoon.

Spoon measures are used for smaller amounts of ingredients. Although the size of the tablespoon varies slightly in different countries, for practical purposes and for recipes in this book, a straight substitution is all that's necessary. Measurements made using cups or spoons always should be level unless stated otherwise.

Common Weight Range Replacements

Imperial / U.S.	Metric
¹/₂ ounce	15 g
1 ounce	25 g or 30 g
4 ounces (¹/₄ pound)	115 g or 125 g
8 ounces (¹/₂ pound)	225 g or 250 g
16 ounces (1 pound)	450 g or 500 g
1¹/₄ pounds	625 g
1¹/₂ pounds	750 g
2 pounds or 2¹/₄ pounds	1,000 g or 1 Kg

Oven Temperature Equivalents

Fahrenheit Setting	Celsius Setting*	Gas Setting
300°F	150°C	Gas Mark 2 (very low)
325°F	160°C	Gas Mark 3 (low)
350°F	180°C	Gas Mark 4 (moderate)
375°F	190°C	Gas Mark 5 (moderate)
400°F	200°C	Gas Mark 6 (hot)
425°F	220°C	Gas Mark 7 (hot)
450°F	230°C	Gas Mark 8 (very hot)
475°F	240°C	Gas Mark 9 (very hot)
500°F	260°C	Gas Mark 10 (extremely hot)
Broil	Broil	Grill

*Electric and gas ovens may be calibrated using celsius. However, for an electric oven, increase celsius setting 10 to 20 degrees when cooking above 160°C. For convection or forced air ovens (gas or electric) lower the temperature setting 25°F/10°C when cooking at all heat levels.

Baking Pan Sizes

Imperial / U.S.	Metric
9×1¹/₂-inch round cake pan	22- or 23×4-cm (1.5 L)
9×1¹/₂-inch pie plate	22- or 23×4-cm (1 L)
8×8×2-inch square cake pan	20×5-cm (2 L)
9×9×2-inch square cake pan	22- or 23×4.5-cm (2.5 L)
11×7×1¹/₂-inch baking pan	28×17×4-cm (2 L)
2-quart rectangular baking pan	30×19×4.5-cm (3 L)
13×9×2-inch baking pan	34×22×4.5-cm (3.5 L)
15×10×1-inch jelly roll pan	40×25×2-cm
9×5×3-inch loaf pan	23×13×8-cm (2 L)
2-quart casserole	2 L

U.S. / Standard Metric Equivalents

¹/₈ teaspoon = 0.5 ml	
¹/₄ teaspoon = 1 ml	
¹/₂ teaspoon = 2 ml	
1 teaspoon = 5 ml	
1 tablespoon = 15 ml	
2 tablespoons = 25 ml	
¹/₄ cup = 2 fluid ounces = 50 ml	
¹/₃ cup = 3 fluid ounces = 75 ml	
¹/₂ cup = 4 fluid ounces = 125 ml	
²/₃ cup = 5 fluid ounces = 150 ml	
³/₄ cup = 6 fluid ounces = 175 ml	
1 cup = 8 fluid ounces = 250 ml	
2 cups = 1 pint = 500 ml	
1 quart = 1 litre	